PYRAMID OF SECRETS

About the Author

Alan F. Alford, B Com., FCA, MBA, was born in 1961, and made his first visit to the Pyramids of Egypt as a fourteen-year-old. Following a string of academic successes, he embarked upon a career in finance and accountancy, but after ten years gave it up to write and self-publish a book on ancient mythology, which subsequently became a number eleven bestseller.

Since becoming a full-time author and independent researcher in 1996, Alan Alford has published innovative solutions to the mysteries of Judaeo-Christianity, the Greek myths, Platonic philosophy, and the 'lost continent' of Atlantis.

Pyramid of Secrets is his fifth book, and he is currently working on a sixth – a companion volume on the subject of ancient Egyptian religion and mythology – for publication in 2004.

Alford's aim, in publishing these books, is to lay the groundwork for an eventual unification of all the world's religions.

For further information on this bold venture, visit the official Alan F. Alford website at www.eridu.co.uk, or contact the author directly at alford@eridu.co.uk.

Also by Alan F. Alford

GODS OF THE NEW MILLENNIUM (1996)

THE PHOENIX SOLUTION (1998)

WHEN THE GODS CAME DOWN (2000)

THE ATLANTIS SECRET (2001)

THE MIDNIGHT SUN (2004)

PYRAMID OF SECRETS

The Architecture of the Great Pyramid
Reconsidered in the Light of
Creational Mythology

Alan F. Alford

Eridu Books
http://www.eridu.co.uk

British Library Cataloguing in Publication Data: a CIP catalogue
record of this title is available from the British Library

ISBN 0 9527994 2 1

Printed and bound in Great Britain by Bookcraft Limited.

Eridu Books
P.O. Box 107
Walsall
WS9 9YR
England
http://www.eridu.co.uk

To Sumu, my wife
– my pillar of love and support

CONTENTS

PREFACE

On an isolated limestone plateau, a few miles west of Cairo, there stands a group of monuments that counts collectively as the sole survivor of the Seven Wonders of the Ancient World: the three pyramids of Giza. Here, among this elegant triple arrangement, we find one structure in particular that has befuddled the minds of scholars and laymen alike for hundreds of years. It is known as the Great Pyramid.

Foremost among the Egyptian pyramids in its size, and unique in its precision of build and complex interior design, the Great Pyramid has generated endless speculation on three central issues: Who built it? How was it built? Why was it built? It is the "why" question – arguably the most controversial of all – that is the exclusive focus of this book.

Why did the architect of the Great Pyramid require such phenomenal size and exceptional precision? *Why* did he require such an extraordinary array of passages and chambers? There are few clues in ancient Egyptian writings, and still fewer in the Pyramid itself, whose uninscribed stones stand in mute testimony to the monument's essential mystery.

In search of an answer, the logical first step is to study the civilisation of ancient Egypt, which left behind a legacy of more than one hundred pyramids in all. Such has been the task of modern Egyptology, which has justifiably made the connection between the pyramids and the kings who each, in their personage, encapsulated the mystery of ancient Egyptian religion. Since the death of the king was indisputably a defining moment in ancient Egypt, it is logical to suppose that the pyramid was a tomb for his mummified body. Moreover, since the rebirth, or resurrection, of the king's soul, or spirit, was an integral part of the same defining moment, it is logical also to suppose that the pyramid effected the translation of the king's soul to the sky and 'other world'. Indeed, this second supposition is confirmed absolutely in the names of the pyramids and the inscriptions (the Pyramid Texts) which were included in certain pyramids some two centuries after the Great Pyramid was built (according to the official chronology). Thus Egyptology arrived at the same conclusion that had been reached by the ancient Greeks: that the pyramids were the tombs of the kings, and that the Great Pyramid was the tomb of Khufu (Cheops). But, going one stage further, it declared, in the immortal words of E.A. Wallis Budge, that the Pyramid was 'a tomb *and nothing but a tomb*'.

And yet, doubts have persisted. For, in the case of the Great Pyramid in particular, it is not readily apparent why a tomb needed to be built so big; nor why a tomb needed to be built to such an unprecedented degree of precision; nor why a tomb needed to be given such a complex array of passages and chambers. It is because of these doubts – these unexplained anomalies, as it were – that alternative Pyramid theorists have queued up to suggest that the Pyramid is something *more* than a tomb, or something *other* than a tomb. The problem, in a nutshell, is that whilst the Pyramid is a pyramid, it is a very exceptional and unusual pyramid.

Over the centuries, dozens of different theories have been suggested. For nearly two thousand years, it was claimed that the Pyramid was the Granary of Joseph.[1] In the 19th century, the Pyramid was regarded as a biblical prophecy in stone, or a repository of divinely-inspired weights and measures.[2] Then, in the 20th century, came a deluge of theories: the Pyramid was interpreted as a giant water pump or power plant,[3] a sundial or almanac,[4] an astronomical observatory,[5] a repository of wisdom from a lost civilisation,[6] a temple of initiation,[7] a navigation beacon for alien spacecraft,[8] or an air raid shelter against meteorite impacts.[9]

Whilst history has yet to judge all of these alternative theories, it does reveal a common pattern in that the theorist tends to see in the Pyramid a reflection of his own contemporary culture and the prevailing technology of his day. The monument thus acts as a mirror to modern opinions and beliefs, and, being bare and devoid of inscriptions, is wholly incapable of contradicting the prejudices and preconceptions that are projected onto it in man's over-keen and eager attempts to solve the enigma. In short, the Pyramid tells us more about ourselves than it does about itself.

In consequence, alternative Pyramid theories, lacking for the most part an authentic ancient perspective, are destined to collapse like waves upon the firm shore of common sense (although, to be fair, some useful ideas have occasionally emerged).

This leaves us with the orthodox theory, which, having its roots in the religion of ancient Egypt, has uniquely withstood the test of time, and has even gained strength from the diversity of the speculation that has been arrayed against it. Indeed, such has been the durability of the 'tomb and tomb only' theory that it is nowadays often presented as a fact rather than a theory.

Figure 1.
THE GREAT PYRAMID, VERTICAL SECTION, LOOKING WEST.

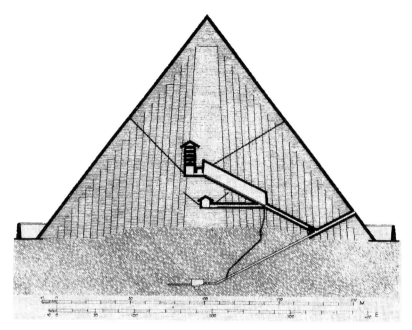

But although Egyptology has made great strides in understanding the civilisation of ancient Egypt, it too has been compromised inevitably by modern-day prejudices and preconceptions, which have coloured its view of Egyptian religion, with a knock-on effect for its interpretation of the pyramids. Here, the main problem has been the Judaeo-Christian bias of Egyptology's founding fathers, who tried to explain Egyptian religion by reference to modern concepts such as monotheism and polytheism. But there have been other biases at work too, such as uniformitarianism, or anti-catastrophism. Together, these biases have left an indelible mark on the modern interpretation of ancient Egypt – an interpretation which has been used unquestioningly by pyramid experts such as I.E.S. Edwards, J.P. Lepre, Mark Lehner, and Miroslav Verner.

How serious is this problem? In 1993, the Egyptologist Dimitri Meeks penned a devastating indictment of his predecessors and colleagues for the bias they had shown in their interpretations of ancient Egypt. In his acclaimed book *La Vie Quotidienne des Dieux Egyptiens* (*Daily Life of the Egyptian Gods*), he wrote:

> From the beginnings of Egyptology, the specialists have always been inclined to make qualitative judgements – this is a symptom of their often well-disguised concern to show us an Egypt that conforms, on

the one hand, to notions of moral and aesthetic decorum palatable to a majority, and, on the other, to our mode of logical thinking. Whether in the domain of beliefs, artistic expression, lifestyle or writing, Egypt is glorified, in the scholarly works or the proliferating exhibitions devoted to it, only for those aspects of its civilisation that command an approving consensus based on the most widely shared contemporary values. Egypt becomes acceptable only when fitted out with the identity we, applying our modes of thinking and being, foist upon it – at the cost of seeing what is alien to us in Egyptian culture as no more than a mask behind which a higher reality is concealed. Indeed, this reality is considered the 'higher' the more it can be made to seem like the ultimate source of *our* contemporary world. We are less interested in acquiring knowledge *of* Egypt than in recognising ourselves *in* Egypt... Appeals to the latest philosophical theories and speculations, or to modern scientific research on multivalued logic and the founding principles of rationality, show to what extent all the questions asked have to do, first and foremost, with the researcher's own way of thinking... What would Egypt become if it were finally taken for what it was – neither morally acceptable nor morally shocking, and still less the mother of our own conceptions – what if not something completely *other*? The time is ripe for posing the question... The moment has come, then, to read or reread the texts, not to bring them into line with our own fantasies, as in the past, but to try to understand what they really mean.[10] (original emphasis)

Is it possible that Egyptology, saturated by 19th and 20th century modes of thinking, has missed the full significance of ancient Egyptian religion, and thus misinterpreted the architecture of the Great Pyramid?

In a companion volume to this book, to be published shortly, I argue that ancient Egyptian religion was not a solar monotheism, or Sun cult, as Egyptologists believe, but rather a 'cult of creation', i.e. a cult whose primary aim was to celebrate and re-enact perpetually the myth of the creation of the Universe. Furthermore, I argue, the king did not personify the Sun-god, or the son of the Sun-god, as Egyptologists maintain, but rather the creator-god, in that his personage embodied the soul, or spirit, of the creator. The pyramid, therefore, was not a symbol of the Sun and a Sun-king, as Egyptologists suggest, but rather a symbol of the creation and a creator-king – a simulacrum of the creator-god in his act of rising from the abyss into the nascent sky. The ancient Egyptian name of the Great Pyramid, *Akhet Khufu*, proves that it was no exception to this rule.

This reinterpretation of Egyptian religion has a major bearing on our understanding of the Great Pyramid in that it indicates unequivocally that it was not just a tomb, but something more than a tomb. Under the solar interpretation of Egyptian religion, the position of the tomb vis-a-vis the pyramid is a moveable feast. Egyptologists thus argue that, despite the general rule to place the tomb beneath the pyramid, the architect of the Great Pyramid raised the tomb into the monument's superstructure, in a bold attempt to keep robbers at bay. Accordingly, the complex interior design of the Pyramid is interpreted as 'a tomb and nothing but a tomb'. Under the creational interpretation of Egyptian religion, however, this argument becomes wholly untenable, since it was a fundamental rule that the body of the king be placed in the earth, beneath the pyramid, in order that his soul, or spirit, would become one with the pyramid; this in accordance with the religious axiom 'the body to earth, the spirit to the sky'.[11] That the architect of the Pyramid would have broken this cardinal rule is inconceivable, for it would have destroyed the vital magic of the pyramid building ritual.

In this book, I use the creational framework to reinterpret the Great Pyramid on three significant levels.

Firstly, I argue that the outstanding scale and precision of the Pyramid was required for religious reasons, in line with the creational symbolism of the monument. In other words, the creational interpretation provides the profound motive for the building of the Pyramid which is lacking in the orthodox, solar interpretation. This idea, if it be accepted, resolves at a stroke two of the three crucial anomalies that form the raison d'etre for alternative Pyramid theories.

Secondly, I argue that the king was buried underneath the Pyramid, at ground level, in a cave-like room called the Grotto, where his mummy may remain hidden to this day.

And thirdly, I suggest that the Pyramid's upper system of passages and chambers – unique to this pyramid – had nothing to do with the tomb of the king, but served an altogether different purpose, namely that of a repository and time capsule.

It is this third level of reinterpretation – the most controversial without a doubt – that accounts for the bulk of this book, and indeed its title *Pyramid of Secrets*.

Today, the Pyramid stands bare and empty, having been plundered in antiquity. But what did its upper chambers originally contain? And might there be additional chambers, yet undiscovered, whose contents remain intact? In attempting to answer these questions, it is all too easy to fall prey to one's preconceptions. What would *we* deposit in a time capsule? What would *we* like to find if a secret chamber is opened? What is in it for *us*? But such an approach would serve only to bring the Pyramid into line with our own fantasies (to borrow Meeks' phrase). Instead, we must ask: what would *they* have deposited in the Pyramid?

On this question, I have taken my lead firstly from the architecture of the Pyramid's chambers, and secondly from the creational theory of the pyramid. For each chamber, I ask: "how might its features make sense if the pyramid is a symbol of the creation of the Universe, and the religion a cult of creation?" By taking this approach, I arrive at the view that the Pyramid was not simply a repository of artefacts, but rather a repository of *a religious idea*, which was expressed in a variety of ways. And, if the reader finds my specific suggestions – which I will leave him to discover – passing strange, then it may be that his surprise is proportionate to my success in eluding the bias of the modern point of view.

I offer this book to the reader not as a complete solution to the mystery of the Great Pyramid, but rather as a penultimate solution that might conceivably act as a platform for future investigations and theories – and, with a fair wind, some dramatic discoveries.

Reading Note 1

It is not my intention in this volume to question the accepted chronology of the pyramids, nor the ownership of pyramids by particular kings. I will therefore present the evidence in accordance with the official time-scale. The reader should bear in mind, however, that for some pyramids the question of ownership has not been definitively settled, whilst their dates of construction may be subject to revision, even by as much as several centuries. Egyptology is far from being an exact science, and it probably never will be.

Reading Note 2

I have used male pronouns throughout this book, and I apologise to anyone who finds this practice offensive; I have done so purely to avoid the constant clumsiness of 'he or she', 'himself or herself', 'his or her', et cetera. In addition, I have used the words 'man', 'men' and 'mankind' to refer, on occasions, to the entire human race. Absolutely no offence is intended towards women, and I certainly do not wish to suggest any inequality between the sexes. Ask my wife if you don't believe me.

Reading Note 3

A Pythagorean dictum: "He who will know, is he who already knows, that there is something here worthy to be known."

CHAPTER ONE

THE PYRAMID DECODED

The field of Egyptology is so very complicated and so all encompassing that it is often difficult to tune into something which is in essence so utterly simple and easy to understand.
(J.P. Lepre, *The Egyptian Pyramids*, 1990)

It is the central premise of this book that the Great Pyramid is a religious monument, whose full significance may be apprehended only through a true understanding of ancient Egyptian religion. Crucially, however, it is argued that Egyptian religion was not simply a Sun cult, as Egyptologists believe, but rather a 'cult of creation', i.e. a cult whose primary aim was to celebrate and re-enact perpetually the myth of the creation of the Universe. Accordingly, the Pyramid's architecture is reconsidered in the light of creational mythology, this being a radically different perspective from that which has been adopted by Egyptologists during the past two hundred years. In this chapter, I present a summary justification for this position by, on the one hand, exposing the limitations and flaws of the orthodox point of view, and, on the other hand, demonstrating the great explanatory power of the creational interpretation. The bottom line is a definitive pronouncement on Egyptian burial practices, with fundamental implications for our understanding of the Pyramid.

For a full justification of the cult of creation hypothesis, the reader is directed to the companion volume, which is to be published shortly.

The Solar Pyramid Theory

To define ancient Egyptian religion is not easy for, as Egyptologists have been at pains to point out, the religion incorporated a bewildering range of practices, from the worship of the Sun, the Moon and the stars, to Nile worship, animism, fetishism and magic. Nevertheless, modern scholars, yielding to the natural urge to impose order on chaos, have identified the religion as basically a Sun cult, framed against a hotchpotch of coarse, superstitious and primitive beliefs, which represented 'the products of the imaginations of their savage, or semi-savage, ancestors'.[1] And this Sun cult, in the eyes of many, was nothing less than a monotheism in which the Sun-god anticipated the One God of the Judaeo-Christian and Islamic religions. In the words of E.A. Wallis Budge, one of the founding fathers of Egyptology:

> The Egyptian in his hymns called many gods 'One', but these gods were all forms of the Sun-god, and, as I understand it, he was a monotheist pure and simple as a Sun-worshipper.[2]

Today, Egyptologists tend to avoid the term 'monotheism' in cognisance of the view, held by many, that the Egyptians practised polytheism. To use the m-word is to stoke up a passionate and ultimately non-productive debate.[3] Nevertheless, the impression is given in Egyptological literature that the Sun cult was the only religion of consequence in ancient Egypt, and that the Sun-god (Atum or Re) was the creator of all things. Whether or not the m-word is used, Egyptian religion is regarded substantially as a Sun cult for the latter two thirds of its four-thousand-year history, and it is this view which has informed modern opinion on the significance of the pyramids, the temples, and the tombs.

What, then, is the religious meaning of the pyramidal form? In seeking to answer this crucial question, Egyptology has uncovered an abundance of clues, and yet failed to find a single inscription that explains why the pyramid was built in clear, prosaic and unambiguous terms. Accordingly, it has had to interpret the evidence, as scanty and fragmentary as it is, in line with its overarching conception of Egyptian religion; in other words, in the context of a Sun cult.

Two lines of evidence have been used thus: the first chronological and circumstantial, the second having a direct bearing on the architecture of the true pyramid (i.e. the smooth-sided variety).

Firstly, it is a fact that the true pyramid replaced the step pyramid in Egypt coterminous with the ascendancy of Re, the Sun-god, during the 4th dynasty of kings, c. 2600 to 2500 BC. During this period, the kings added to their titulary the term *Sa Re*, testifying to the idea that each was the 'son of Re',[4] whilst several adopted Re's name as a suffix to their throne names – hence Djedef-Re, Khaf-Re, Menkau-Re – as if to imply that they were incarnations or images of that god. Moreover, from the time of Sneferu, the kings wrote their throne names inside a cartouche, which is widely regarded as a solar symbol.[5] On this basis, Egyptologists have suspected a shift from a stellar to a solar religion at the time of the

Figure 2.
THE EVOLUTION FROM STEP PYRAMID TO TRUE PYRAMID.

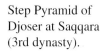

Step Pyramid of
Djoser at Saqqara
(3rd dynasty).

Red Pyramid of
Sneferu at Dahshur
(4th dynasty).

true pyramid; accordingly, the step pyramid is seen as a stellar symbol and a vehicle to an afterlife in the stars, whilst the true pyramid is seen as a solar symbol and a vehicle to an afterlife with the Sun.[6]

The second line of evidence comes from the true pyramid's capstone, or pyramidion, which was known to the Egyptians as *benbenet*, 'the little *benben*', in reference to the sacred stone, the Benben, that stood upon a pillar in the Temple of the Benben in Heliopolis. Now, the Benben Stone upon its pillar is widely regarded as a solar symbol, as is its derivative form the obelisk, whose apex was also called *benbenet*, in like fashion to the capstone of the pyramid. Accordingly, scholars have pronounced that the true pyramid, too, was a symbol of the Sun. J.H. Breasted, one of the Titans of early Egyptology, explains:

> An obelisk is simply a pyramid upon a lofty base which has indeed become the shaft... This pyramidal top is the essential part of the monument and the significant symbol which it bore. The Egyptians

Figure 3.
THE BENBEN PILLAR, THE TRUE PYRAMID, AND THE OBELISK.
All three architectural forms shared a common symbolism.

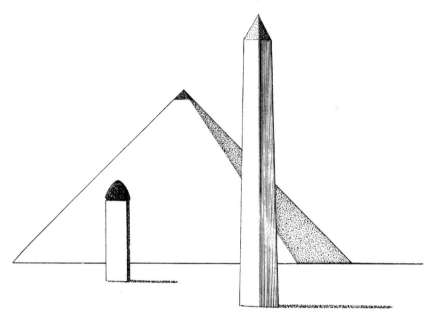

called it a *benben* (or *benbenet*), which we translate 'pyramidion'...
Now the long recognised fact that the obelisk is sacred to the Sun
carries with it the demonstration that it is the *pyramid* surmounting the
obelisk which is sacred to the Sun-god... The pyramidal form of the
king's tomb therefore was of the most sacred significance. The king
was buried under the very symbol of the Sun-god [the Benben Stone]
which stood in the holy of holies in the Sun-temple of Heliopolis.[7]
(original emphasis)

In support of this solar interpretation of the pyramid's capstone, Breasted
cited the pyramidion of Amenemhet III's pyramid at Dahshur (see figure
4), the central motif of which may be translated 'Amenemhet beholds the
perfection of Re', the inscription below adding: 'The face of Amenemhet
is open; he sees the Lord of the Horizon as he sails in the sky.'[8] Both of
these references, claim scholars, are to the Sun-god, thus attesting to the
solar destiny of the king and the solar significance of his pyramid.

Such is the evidence, as tenuous as it is, which has led Egyptologists
to the conclusion that the true pyramid is a solar symbol. But, before we
question the interpretation of this evidence, we must first allow scholars
to round off their theory. How exactly did the true pyramid symbolise the
Sun?

Figure 4.
THE CAPSTONE OF THE AMENEMHET III PYRAMID AT DAHSHUR.

Here, the idea is simple in the extreme. The ancient Egyptians, it is claimed, saw the Sun's rays breaking through the clouds and shining down upon the earth in a pyramidal shape, and were so awe-struck by this phenomenon that they used it as an inspiration and a model for the design of the true pyramid.[9]

One of the first Egyptologists to verbalise this idea was Alexandre Moret, who in 1926 wrote:

> These great triangles forming the sides of the pyramids seem to fall from the sky like the beams of the Sun when its disc, though veiled by storm, pierces the clouds and lets down to earth a ladder of rays.[10]

Later, this same idea was adopted by the renowned pyramid expert I.E.S. Edwards. In his authoritative book *The Pyramids of Egypt* (first edition 1947), Edwards asked: "What did the true pyramid form represent?", and then furnished his readers with the answer in his own words:

> Only one answer suggests itself: the rays of the Sun shining down on earth. A remarkable spectacle may sometimes be seen in the late afternoon of a cloudy winter day at Giza. When standing on the road to Saqqara and gazing westwards at the pyramid plateau, it is possible to see the Sun's rays striking downwards through a gap in the clouds at about the same angle as the slope of the Great Pyramid. The impression made on the mind by the scene is that the immaterial prototype and the material replica are here ranged side by side.[11]

In support of this theory, Edwards cited the Pyramid Texts in which the king was urged to ascend to the heavens upon the rays of the Sun, and concluded that: 'The temptation to regard the true pyramid as a material representation of the Sun's rays and consequently as a means whereby the dead king could ascend to heaven seems irresistible.'[12]

With Edwards' backing, the solar interpretation achieved widespread currency during the 20th century. In 1997, the Italian writer Alberto Siliotti called the true pyramid 'a materialisation of the rays of the Sun in the stone' and 'an expression in rock of the rays of the Sun',[13] whilst, in the same year, the American pyramid expert Mark Lehner described the true pyramid as 'a stone simulacrum of sunlight', and highlighted the fact that, with its original facing intact, the pyramid would have reflected the sunlight to an almost blinding degree.[14] 'Only in this light', wrote Lehner, 'can we appreciate the intensity with which the pyramids symbolised the Sun-god.'[15]

Is the case thus clinched that the true pyramid was a solar symbol? If weight of authoritative opinion were the deciding factor, then the answer would probably be "yes". However, not all Egyptologists would agree. In his recent book, *The Cult of Ra*, Stephen Quirke writes:

> Although it has become a commonplace in Egyptological writing, we ought not to take the solar character of the pyramids for granted. These are complex achievements in world architecture, and there are no explicit ancient Egyptian inscriptions to describe either the way they were created or the motivation behind their dramatic scale and shape... These monuments are not easily reduced to a single theme.[16]

Quirke is indeed right to be cautious, for, as we shall now see, there are some fundamental weaknesses in the arguments that have been made.

Firstly, the idea that solar religion, under the auspices of Re, coincided with the building of the first true pyramids rests on the assumption that Re was primarily the Sun-god. But what of the fact that Re was also the creator-god? To Egyptologists, this point is inconsequential on the basis that the Sun *is* the creator, making the creation secondary;[17] and besides, as J.H. Breasted famously said, the creation myths are just 'simple folk tales of the origins of the world'.[18] However, as I argue at length in the companion volume to this book, this is an unsound and perverted point of view. The creation myths were no folk tales; they represented a single profound and consistent view of the origins of the Universe. Nor was the Sun the creator of this Universe; rather, it was a created object, the most glorious manifestation of the creator-god. Re was therefore the creator-god primarily and the Sun-god secondarily. That this was so at the time when the pyramids were built is proven unequivocally by the fact that the 4th dynasty kings were both Re and 'son of Re' simultaneously, this idea making sense only if Re were the creator-god.[19] The upshot of this is that Re's rise to power during the 4th dynasty would not have signified any change in the fundamental nature of Egyptian religion (which remained a cult of creation), and the evolution of the pyramid form, from stepped to smooth-sided, would not have marked a change in the king's afterlife destination. Rather, the pyramid in both its forms would have symbolised the creation of the Universe, and would have despatched the king's soul to all parts of the created heavens, simultaneously to the Sun, the Moon, and the stars.

Secondly, is the pyramid's capstone, *benbenet*, really a solar symbol as Egyptologists would like to think?

As regards the connection between *benbenet* and the Benben Stone of Heliopolis, this author believes that whilst the Benben does have a solar aspect, its primary symbolism is phallic and creational. In support of this interpretation, the only mention of the Benben in the Pyramid Texts (the earliest set of religious writings in ancient Egypt) places it unequivocally at the scene of creation, the god Atum rising up on high as the Benben Stone at Heliopolis as a curtain-raiser to his creation of the Universe.[20] Furthermore, in a related myth, Atum creates the Universe by erecting and masturbating his phallus, as if to suggest that the Benben pillar was a phallic symbol.[21] In further support of this idea, the name Benben Stone meant literally 'the stone that flowed out', its origins lying in a root word with strong sexual connotations (compare *bnbn* to: *bnn* 'phallus/copulate/ fertilise/beget'; and *bnnt*: 'seed/semen').[22] Scholars have thus described the Benben Stone as the 'solidified seed' or 'petrified semen' of Atum.[23] In addition, it is to be noted that Heliopolis originally bore the Egyptian name Iunu, 'Pillar city', suggesting a phallic, and not a solar, symbolism.

All things considered, the argument seems unassailable that both the Benben Stone upon its pillar and its derivative form the obelisk had a phallic symbolism, as was indeed noted by the eminent scholar Henri Frankfort in 1948:

> The pyramidion on top of the obelisk is called *bnbnt*, and the *bnbn* stone had originated as a drop of seed of Atum or a bull; hence it is likely that the obelisk did not serve merely as an impressive support for the stylized Benben Stone which formed its tip but that it was originally a phallic symbol at Heliopolis, the 'pillar city'.[24]

The full meaning of this phallic symbolism will become apparent in due course, once the creation myth has been explained. But suffice to say for now that if the Benben Stone and the obelisk are creational symbols, then so too is the capstone of the pyramid (*benbenet*).

This brings us to the pyramid capstone of Amenemhet III, which in its references to Re and the Lord of the Horizon (see earlier) provides the only direct evidence for the solar pyramid theory. Or does it? Might it rather be the case that the inscription refers to Re in his guise as creator-god? And might Lord of the Horizon rather refer to the creator-god who was the first to rise from the horizon (*akhet*), prior to the creation of the Sun? In support of this hypothesis, the Re-symbol on the pyramidion is surmounted by a pair of eyes, which was a cipher in Egyptian religion for the Sun and the Moon;[25] the arrangement indeed follows the pattern in the creation myth, where the creator-god rose up and manifested himself in these two orbs. Furthermore, the inscriptions on the pyramidion lend a decided emphasis to the stars. On the reverse face, for example, part of the inscription reads: 'the soul of Amenemhet is higher than the heights of Orion',[26] whilst on the front face, beneath the Re-symbol, the text that supposedly refers to the Sun continues in the following vein:

> The face of Amenemhet is open, he sees the Lord of the Horizon as he sails in the sky. May he [the Lord of the Horizon] cause that he [the king] rise as the Great God, Lord of Time, an indestructible star. May he be stellar among the stars.[27]

Clearly, then, the pyramid capstone of Amenemhet III has an important stellar aspect, in addition to its solar and lunar aspects, and to argue that it is purely a solar symbol, as Egyptologists do, is to be selective with the evidence.

Finally, is it plausible that the pyramidal shape was inspired by the Sun's rays shining down through the clouds? Would this phenomenon, or indeed any other solar phenomenon, have had a sufficient psychological impact on the ancient Egyptians? If the answers are "no", as this author would maintain, then we must look elsewhere for the stimulus, or model, for the smooth-sided pyramid.

In summary, the solar pyramid theory relies heavily on the assumption that ancient Egyptian religion was a Sun cult, fails to take account of the pyramid's non-solar symbolism, and provides no profound motive for the building of the pyramids. If the mystery is to be solved, we must look beyond the Sun to a wider symbolism involving the Sun, the Moon, and the stars.

The Stellar Pyramid Theory

An alternative point of view that has gained momentum in recent years is that the true pyramid was a stellar symbol and a vehicle for the king's afterlife among the stars. Here, several lines of evidence combine to form a compelling case for stellar symbolism, which is not to be gainsaid, nor overlooked, in reaching a view on the monument's overall significance.

Firstly, two pyramids bore names that referred explicitly to the king becoming a star. The first, admittedly a step pyramid, was called 'Horus is the Star at the Head of the Sky', whilst the second, a true pyramid, was called 'Djedefre is a *Sehed*-Star'.[28] In comparison, none of the pyramid names refers explicitly to the Sun.

Secondly, the Pyramid Texts (which were inscribed inside pyramids of the late-5th and 6th dynasties *c.* 2350-2100 BC) place a decided emphasis on the king's afterlife among the stars. Numerous magic spells envisage the king being spiritualised as a star, thereupon to stand in the northern sky as an 'imperishable' star or to traverse from horizon to horizon as a 'dying-and-rising' star. *Pace* E.A. Wallis Budge and J.H. Breasted, it is this author's view that the Pyramid Texts lend greater importance to the stars than to the Sun.[29]

Thirdly, there is evidence of stellar symbolism in the architecture of the pyramids. Whilst I am not entirely convinced that the 'airshafts' of the Great Pyramid were targeted at certain stars, as many Egyptologists believe,[30] it is certainly true that the pyramid's entrance passage, which

Figure 5.
PYRAMID TOMB CHAMBER, 6TH DYNASTY.
On the wall (left), the Pyramid Texts; on the ceiling (right) the stars. Both attest to the stellar significance of the true pyramid.

was generally located in its northern face, was oriented towards the northern circumpolar stars, among which the king intended to dwell for eternity.[31] It almost goes without saying that north was *not* the direction of the Sun.

Finally, again on the subject of architecture, it is pertinent to note that the builders of the 5th and 6th dynasty pyramids chose to decorate the ceilings of the tomb chambers with a panoply of stars, but not with the Sun.[32]

All of this makes a mockery of the solar pyramid theory, and suggests instead that the stars played the more dominant role at the time when the pyramids were built. However, whilst a few Egyptologists have awoken to this fact (Kate Spence, for example),[33] it yet remains unclear how the pyramid's stellar attributes might translate into a theory of its shape and symbolism.

One suggestion, made by Robert Bauval, and more recently by Toby Wilkinson, is that the smooth-sided, flowing design of the true pyramid may have been modelled on an 'oriented' iron meteorite, i.e. a meteorite that retains its orientation as it falls to the earth, thus acquiring a conical shape.[34] Both Bauval and Wilkinson have argued that the Benben Stone of Heliopolis was such a meteorite, and that the apex of the obelisk and the capstone of the pyramid, both named after the Benben Stone, were therefore modelled on the meteorite, which was known metaphorically as a 'fallen star'.[35] From here, it is but one small, logical step to identify the pyramid in its entirety as a simulacrum of a fallen star, which has been inverted, apparently, in an attempt to rescale the heights of the heavens.[36]

Is it plausible that a meteorite inspired the building of the pyramids? Would this phenomenon have had a sufficient psychological impact on the ancient Egyptians? On a cataclysmic scale, the answer must surely be "yes". However, it does not necessarily follow that the meteorite should be equated with a star. Indeed, if we allow Egyptian mythology to be our guide, then the meteorite, in the form of the Benben Stone, had a wider, creational significance. It was not a star per se; rather it was the semen of Atum – the seed of creation; and that creation involved not just the stars, but also the Sun and the Moon.

In summary, whilst there is much to be said for a stellar interpretation of the true pyramid, the fact is that the pyramid also had a solar and lunar symbolism, as evidenced by the inscription on the pyramid capstone of Amenemhet III. And furthermore, we should not overlook the fact that the pyramid had a fundamental connection with the underworld in that the deceased king buried beneath the pyramid was identified with Osiris, the god of the earth and the subterranean regions. If we are serious about determining the pyramid's overall purpose and meaning, then all of the following symbolisms must be weighed in the balance:

• The stars.

• The Sun and the Moon.

• The underworld.

The Myth of Creation

Is there a better way to interpret the true pyramid in accordance with the diversity of its symbolism? Might it be possible to reconcile and unify its stellar, solar, lunar and chthonian aspects?

In a companion volume to this book, to be published shortly, I identify a singular theme behind Egyptian religion – a potential unifying principle no less – that has been overlooked by Egyptology. This singular theme is the myth of creation, i.e. the story of the origin of the Universe, which by definition provides an all-embracing framework for the stars, the Sun, the Moon, and the underworld. If anything is to explain the massive effort that went into the building of the pyramids, then surely it is the creative act, which, despite its mythical status in modern times, was infused five thousand years ago with a unique quality and a degree of profundity that is found wanting in the cycles of the Sun, Moon and stars (exoterically speaking). The creation was indeed the one great mystery of Egypt from the beginning to the end of its mighty civilisation.

What do we know of the creation myth? What exactly does it mean to speak of the act of creation?

To ask this question is to embark on a most difficult investigation, for there is no one Egyptian myth that sets out a clear, logical and connected account of the creation, at least not in a language that the modern mind can comprehend. Instead, what we find, for the most part, is a plurality of creation myths from different religious centres, each rendering the key events in its own idiosyncratic way, using brief and obscure terminology, as if the story was too potent for outright telling. Furthermore, to make matters worse, the sparse and fragmentary information that we possess is scattered across the texts of some three thousand years. As the eminent scholar Henri Frankfort explains:

> The Egyptians were so little prepared to dwell on any change that they did not even describe in any orderly and continuous fashion the supreme change which took place at what they called 'the first time'. We are obliged to reconstruct the creation story from allusions which are frequent and from certain learned commentaries...[37]

The creation story has indeed been reconstructed by Egyptology, but not in a satisfactory way. It may be useful, at this juncture, to summarise the orthodox interpretation, as deficient as it is, in order to understand why scholars have dismissed the creation myth as an inconsequential product of primitive minds.

The starting point, in all Egyptian creation myths, is an abyss of water called Nun, which seemingly stretched in all directions to form a kind of mini-Universe or proto-Universe from which the created Universe would emerge. The exact significance of this primeval ocean remains a mystery to Egyptologists, who cannot understand how, on the one hand, it could be attached physically to the earth (it was the source of the Nile), whilst, on the other hand, it formed the celestial ocean of the sky. In any event, all sources agree that the Nun had given birth to all things – the earth, the sky, the stars, the Sun, and the Moon.

But how exactly did this happen?

Here, the creation myths are reasonably consistent. In the darkness of the Nun, the creator-god (regarded in some cases as the personification of the waters but in other cases as an independent entity) had stirred from his 'sleep of death', conquered the forces of darkness, and emerged as a soul, or spirit, from the primeval ocean. According to this monodramatic version of the myth, the creator-god had *created himself*, no other being having been present at the time. As the god emerged from the waters, so too did the first land, providing him a place on which to stand. This risen earth is known to scholars as the 'primeval hill' or 'primeval mound'.

The primeval mound was the focal point of creation. It was here that the creator-god defeated the forces of chaos, and ordained the birth of the stars, the Sun and the Moon. But how did he bring these celestial bodies into being? Here, the myths are at their most opaque. There is talk of the stars ascending to the sky; of the Sun and Moon rising up from the earth, or being conceived and born in the sky; and there is mention of a time when the sky was separated from the earth. None of these allusions are understood by Egyptology, which assumes that the stars, the Sun and the Moon were simply magicked into existence by the creator-god as he stood triumphantly upon the primeval mound.

Such is the creation myth, as conceived by modern scholars. What is to be made of it?

According to Egyptologists, not a lot. In their view, the story of Nun and the rising primeval mound was inspired by the flooding and receding of the Nile.[38] In other words, there is nothing to this part of the story but a mundane agrarian phenomenon. Meanwhile, the rest of the creation myth is dismissed as a ragbag of imaginative and contradictory ideas on the origins of the Universe, which, far from containing any profound wisdom or esoteric insight, reflect the idle speculations of a simple and primitive people.[39]

Unable to see any merit in the creation myth, Egyptologists have made it subordinate to the Sun cult on the grounds that the functions and titles of the Sun-god included that of creator-god. As they see it, it was the Sun-god who stirred in the watery abyss; the Sun-god who raised himself onto the primeval mound; and the Sun-god who created himself, the Sun, and the other celestial bodies. The Sun was thus the self-created creator of the Universe, and no other creator existed beside him. Granted, this is a preposterous story, but scholars are troubled not a jot, since the myth of creation is, after all, the product of crude and primitive minds.

To be fair, the second half of the 20th century saw Egyptology display a more positive attitude to the creation myth, particularly in the books of Henri Frankfort and R.T. Rundle Clark.[40] Many scholars now accept that the discrepancies in the various creation myths represent, as Frankfort put it, 'a multiplicity of approaches' and 'a meaningful inconsistency';[41] in other words, the Egyptian philosophers used a diverse range of images and allegories to describe a single ineffable mystery. Furthermore, in his 'static universe' theory of the Egyptian culture, Frankfort put forward a theoretical framework for the importance of the creative act:

> In a static world, creation is the only event that really matters
> supremely, since it alone can be said to have made a change. It makes
> the difference between the nothingness of chaos and the fullness of the
> present which has emerged as a result of that unique act.[42]

Unfortunately, this bold insight did nothing to dislodge the idea that the Sun was the creator. With the sole exception of Clark (*Myth and Symbol in Ancient Egypt*, 1959), no Egyptologist has rendered the creation myth in anything but a solar context. Clark, it should be noted, did present the creator-god as a mystical and metaphysical phenomenon, but he stopped short of advocating his primacy over the Sun (or even his independence from the Sun). In short, neither Frankfort, Clark, nor any other scholar, has questioned the assumption that Egyptian religion was primarily a Sun cult.

But what if it could be shown that the creation myth had a cogent and logical basis, hitherto not apprehended by Egyptology? What if, in fact, it had a truly profound basis? Would it not then follow that the true God of ancient Egypt was the creator-god? And would it not also follow that the creator-god had manifested himself in the Sun, and that the Sun-god Re was a creator-god first and foremost? If so, the modern interpretation of ancient Egyptian religion would have to be fundamentally re-evaluated, and the pyramids reinterpreted accordingly.

The Cult of Creation

In due course, the myth of creation will be demystified. But first, it is necessary to behold just how deeply it permeated the fabric of Egyptian society. To keep things brief, I would like to focus on three phenomena that were absolutely pivotal to the civilisation: the city, the temple, and the institution of kingship.

Firstly, it is a revealing fact that all major cities in Egypt claimed to be microcosms of the primeval mound. Memphis was 'the divine emerging primeval island'; Hermopolis was 'the first plot of land on which Re first stood'; Abydos was 'the most ancient land'; Thebes was 'the island emerging from Nun which first came into being when all other places were in obscurity'; Hermonthis was 'the high ground which grew out of Nun'; Esna was 'the divine hill, the top of which emerged from Nun'; Elephantine was 'the city of the beginning... the joining of the land, the primeval hillock of earth, the throne of Re'; and Philae was 'the island in the time of Re'.[43] (Note the references here to Re in his guise as creator-god.) Each major city thus paid tribute to the fundamental importance of the creation myth.

Secondly, it is a well-established fact that the Egyptian temple was a simulacrum of creation. The *British Museum Dictionary of Ancient Egypt* states:

> The temple was considered to be an architectural metaphor for the Universe and for the process of the creation itself. The floor gradually rose, passing through forests of plant-form columns and roofed by images of the constellations or the body of the sky-goddess Nut, allowing the priests to ascend gradually from the outermost edge of the Universe towards the sanctuary, which was a symbol of the inner core of creation, the primeval mound on which the creator-god first brought the world into being.[44]

The importance of the creation myth is thus vouchsafed once again – the temple being the veritable hub of ancient Egyptian religion.

Thirdly, it is well known in Egyptology that the kingship of Egypt was modelled on a kingship that dated to the beginning of the world, and that the pharaoh was tasked with re-enacting the events of creation in a series of rituals that was performed throughout the land, in every year from his coronation to his death. Scholars call this process *creatio continua* – the ongoing renewal of creation. To this end, the king used the knowledge of

Figure 6.
THE TEMPLE OF EDFU.
The Egyptian temple was a simulacrum of the creation of the Universe.

the Universe into which he had been initiated, and the magical power of creative utterance (*hu*) which was automatically at his disposal, to re-perform the founding acts of the First Time (*Zep Tepi*). Every city he established was 'the first' city; every temple he commissioned was 'the first' temple; every obelisk he raised was 'the first' obelisk, or Benben; and if he built a pyramid, it was 'the first' pyramid. He built temples in the image of the Universe; appointed priests and initiated them into his divine knowledge; propagated the cults of the creator-god (in his many and various names); performed rituals and spells that would sustain the forces of order whilst repelling the forces of chaos; appeared gloriously in festivals throughout the land; and last, but not least, made preparations for his own death and his succession by a new king, so that the entire process might continue ad infinitum. From coronation to funeral, then, the king's every act was aimed at repeating the events of creation, in order to rejuvenate the cosmic order (*maat*) which had been laid down by the creator at the beginning of time.

Furthermore – and this is a fact that will prove extremely important in due course – the king was said to embody the creator-god's soul, or spirit (he was held to be the living image of the god, in a spiritual sense); hence his possession of magical powers. In the Egyptian texts, we find the king credited with the appropriate attributes of the creator-god; he was ruler of the sky and the earth, pillar of the sky, and Lord of the Universe.[45] Here, Egyptology imagines the king to be a Sun-king, the incarnation of Re, who was the Sun-god, creator-god, and first king of Egypt (mythically speaking). However, this author is convinced that the king's identity was primarily creational, and that it was always thus, from the very beginning

The King Re-enacts the Creation

[Pharaoh's] authority was founded not in the social, but in the cosmic order. Kingship, in Egypt, was as old as the world. It dated from the day of creation... All theological schools agreed that kingship, the pivot of society, belonged to the basic order of existence and had been introduced at the time of the creation... Thus the whole universe was a monarchy, and the king of the world had been the first king of Egypt. This function had devolved upon his son and successor, Pharaoh. But it had lost nothing of its nature in the transmission... Hence the texts abound in expressions which exalt Pharaoh by describing his acts as reflections, equivalents and repetitions of those of Re.
(Henri Frankfort, *Ancient Egyptian Religion*, 1948)

(Creation) is repeated every day at dawn and every month with the coming of the new moon, perhaps at every recurrent festival. Creation was also repeated in the rebirth of the soul after death and it provided the basic theme in the installation ceremonies of the kings. In fact, most solemn religious rites derived their power or authority from the pretence that they were in some way a return to the original events of creation.
(R.T. Rundle Clark, *Myth and Symbol in Ancient Egypt*, 1959)

The basic principles of life, nature and society were determined by the gods long ago, before the establishment of the kingship. This epoch – *Zep Tepi* – 'the First Time' – stretched from the first stirring of the High God in the primeval waters to the settling of Horus upon the throne and the redemption of Osiris. All proper myths relate events or manifestations of this epoch. Anything whose existence or authority had to be justified or explained must be referred to 'the First Time'. This was true for natural phenomena, rituals, royal insignia, the plans of temples, magical or medical formulae, the hieroglyphic system of writing, the calendar – the whole paraphernalia of the civilisation.
(R.T. Rundle Clark, *Myth and Symbol in Ancient Egypt*, 1959)

In myth, every occurrence, every gesture, every work had the value of a founding act. The rites celebrated in the temple... were reiterations of these founding acts, performed by or for the king. The daily activities of the gods which laid down the foundation of things never ceased to be repeated in the world.
(Dimitri Meeks, *Daily Life of the Egyptian Gods*, 1993)

of Egyptian history.[46]

In summary, the city, the temple, and the kingship each testify to the fundamental importance of the creation myth in ancient Egypt, and lend plausibility to my proposal that the religion was not a Sun cult but a cult of creation. Nevertheless, for this idea to be accepted – for the Sun-god to yield primacy to the creator-god – it is a minimum condition that the myth of creation be viewed not as a 'simple folk tale', as Egyptologists maintain, but as a logical, consistent and profound account of the origins of the Universe. Might it be the case that modern biases, prejudices and preconceptions have prevented us from apprehending the significance of the myth?

The Myth of Creation Reconsidered

In the companion volume to this book, I argue that the Egyptian creation myth represents a coherent theory of the origins of the Universe, albeit conceived in a way that is the veritable antithesis of modern science and religion. Whilst the full argumentation is too complex and detailed to be reproduced here, I set out below the resultant interpretation, structured around four key principles which illustrate all too clearly the gulf that exists between ancient and modern lines of thought. These key principles are: geocentrism; the earth in crisis; body-soul separation; and cataclysm.

The first key principle is geocentrism, literally 'earth at the centre', i.e. earth at the centre of the Universe. The Egyptians believed, in common with other ancient peoples, that the stars (including the planets), the Sun, and the Moon orbited around the earth. But, more to the point, they held that the creation had been geocentric, and that the earth had given birth to the entire Universe. This idea, which is admittedly not as explicit in the Egyptian myths as in the Greek myths say, is absolutely pivotal to our understanding of Egyptian cosmogony, for it implies that the Nun, the primeval ocean from which all things sprung, was originally a kind of water world, or, otherwise said, the earth in a state of flood, the primeval ocean containing, and perhaps permeating, the proto-land which would, in due time, emerge from it. An obvious interpretation, the reader might think. And yet Egyptology, rather strangely, has failed to articulate this interpretation, partly because of its discomfort with the principle of geocentrism (which it rarely, if ever, mentions), and partly because of its inability to rationalise the manifestation of the Nun in the ocean of the sky. This latter point will be explained when we come to our third key principle of the creation myth.

The second key principle is the earth in crisis. This refers to the idea, prevalent in the Egyptian myths, that the proto-earth suffered a traumatic crisis as a curtain-raiser to the act of creation. As a general rule, this story is told by way of allegory, the primeval earth being personified as the creator-god, who has been laid low by old age or else by the attack of a hostile god, serpent, or scorpion, representing the forces of chaos. In one myth, the creator feels sickness and pain, and his members grow weak; in another, his body burns like fire, trembles and shakes; and in yet another myth, his body is dismembered, whereupon his limbs begin to rot and putrefy.[47] More rarely, the earth crisis idea is referred to explicitly, as in a hymn to Ptah-Ta-tanen from the end of the 2nd millennium BC:

> You [Ptah] have stood on the land during its lassitude, from which it recovered only afterwards, when you were in your shape of Ta-tanen ['the risen land'], in your manifestation as the Unifier of the Two Lands.[48]

As we might expect, a recovery of the earth is a precondition to the act of creation, the principal motif here being the reunification of the creator-god's body, and indeed his soul. To this end, the floodwaters on the earth are repatriated to their source; the gods – the issue of the Great God – are brought together in assembly; and the divided limbs of the god are joined back together. That this latter myth allegorises the reconstitution of the primeval earth is made perfectly clear in another hymn to Ptah-Ta-tanen, which informs us that the god reassembled the members of his own body in order to knit together the risen land:

> [O Ptah-Ta-tanen] You built up your own members and fashioned your body when the heavens and the earth were yet unmade, and when the waters [of Nun] had not come forth.

> You knitted together the earth, you assembled your own members, you embraced your own body, and you found yourself in the condition of the One who made his seat, who moulded the Two Lands.[49]

Of course, this idea of *the body of God* undergoing crisis and recovery is an anathema to devotees of modern religion, which may go a long way toward explaining why Egyptology has singularly failed to comprehend this particular aspect of the creation myth.

The third key principle is body-soul separation, this in the context of the primeval earth, which was conceived as a living being of body and soul. In the beginning, this earth had been broken apart, both physically and metaphysically, but upon reassembly the earth-soul had separated from its body and instigated the creation of the Universe. Or, otherwise said, the creator-soul had freed itself from the earth, its body, and risen up into the nascent sky. This separation was known idiomatically as the creator-god going to his *ka*, the word *ka* signifying the 'spiritual double' or 'vital energy' that had been released from the earth.

At this juncture, one must introduce the Great Goddess, the consort of the creator-god, who is often depicted as the power that reassembled and revivified him. She, it would seem, personified the primeval ocean, whilst he personified the primeval earth. (The exception to this rule was the god Nun – a creator in his own right – whose masculinity reflected a monodramatisation of the myth.)[50] Together, the Goddess and the God personified the original mystical fusion that had transformed the watery proto-earth into life. In line with this duality, the creation proceeded in two stages. In the first act, the Great Goddess, the primeval ocean, went to her *ka*, the sky-ocean thus coming into being (hence the below-and-above nature of the Nun, as mentioned earlier), whilst in the second act the Great God, the primeval earth, went to his *ka*, thereupon joining the Goddess for a second mystical union which would spark a further stage of creation, this time in the sky-ocean. (In the monodramatic version of the creation myth, these two events are merged confusingly into one.)

All of this may seem a little weird to the reader, unfamiliar as he may be with concepts such as body-soul duality and the primacy of the spirit, which are the very antithesis of modern materialism. But it should begin to make sense when we consider the fourth principle.

The fourth key principle is cataclysm. In Egyptian myths and rituals, it is suggested that the proto-earth, having recovered from its initial crisis, had swollen, trembled and quaked, and eventually split open, whereupon it had erupted like a volcano, spewing the materials of creation into the sky. Here, the emphasis is on the physical side of things: the swelling of the earth (and the subsidence of the flood) caused the first land to rise up from the Nun; the pressure released by the splitting earth forced part of the primeval ocean upwards to form the sky-ocean; and, in like fashion, part of the material of the proto-earth was blasted into the sky to provide the building blocks for the stars, the Sun, and the Moon (this material was termed *bja*, signifying molten iron). Thus the Universe was created amidst a geocentric 'big bang', the heavens being separated from the earth – just as the ancient myth-makers always insisted.[51]

This story was told by way of allegory, the Great God personifying the primeval earth and the Great Goddess the primeval ocean. The rising of the first land was thus known idiomatically as the creator-god 'raising his head'; the splitting open of the earth was described as the creator-god 'opening his mouth'; and the ejection of the sky-ocean was referred to as the Great Goddess 'going forth in her flood'. But, beyond that, the poets turned to sexual idioms. The eruption of the proto-earth into the sky was portrayed as the creator-god erecting his phallus, masturbating, and ejaculating, or, in the uncut version, the God inseminating the womb of the sky-goddess; some texts even declared unashamedly that the creator-god had raped his own mother.[52] Here, in this genre of allegory, is the archetype of the Benben Stone on its pillar, the pillar representing the phallus of the creator-god, and the stone – probably an iron meteorite – signifying the molten seed with which he had impregnated the sky. Thus the Benben was clearly a phallic symbol, as was the apex of the obelisk and the capstone of the true pyramid, both of which were named after it (benbenet). Each represented the Benben, literally 'the stone that flowed out', which scholars have described accurately as the 'solidified seed' or 'petrified semen' of Atum.

Cataclysm, then, was fundamental to the myth of creation – an irony indeed given that scholars of history and myth have regarded cataclysm as a taboo idea for the past two hundred years. But this is not to suggest that the creation was a mere physical phenomenon, for primacy lay with the soul, or spirit, as per our third principle. Rather, the idea was that the spirit was released from the earth at the same time as the materials of creation were ejected from it, and that the spirit was immanent in those materials. Which is basically to say that the proto-earth sent forth a blast wave of spiritualised seed. That this was the idea is evident from one of the names given to this transformative, procreative earth: akhet, which may be translated 'land (or mountain) of light'.[53] To the Egyptians, light (akhu) was essentially a spiritual phenomenon, which had originated in the abyss with the creator and been made manifest, miraculously, in the iron-dense orbs of the stars, the Sun, and the Moon.

Such then is the myth of creation, as I have decoded it, although I have not yet mentioned the final act which saw the creator-god, now manifest in the Universe, turn back to embrace his body, the newly-risen earth, thus infusing it with his ka, the vital spirit of life. A further commentary on this subject will appear in chapter five.

In summary, the Egyptian creation myth is a relatively straightforward attempt to explain the origins of the Universe, albeit using concepts that seem passing strange to the modern mind. It takes as its starting point a pre-existent proto-earth that has 'died' following an earlier, ill-defined, violent event, and envisages a turnabout that is sparked by the magical power of the soul, or spirit. The proto-earth then gathers itself together, swells, splits and ejects the primeval matter from which the sky-ocean, the stars, the Sun, and the Moon will be born. Everything in the Universe was thus created from the body and soul of the proto-earth – a geocentric myth *par excellence*. In short, the myth describes the 'death' and rebirth of the Universe, which was transformed from an original mini-Universe, the proto-earth, into the present Universe (to the extent that it was known by the Egyptians), this entire process being personified by the death and rebirth of the creator-god.

The creation myth thus provides the religious archetype for the death and rebirth cults that held the inhabitants of ancient Egypt in thrall – the death and rebirth of the Sun (daily, at the winter solstice, and at eclipses); the death and rebirth of the Moon (monthly, and at eclipses), the death and rebirth of the stars (daily, and at longer intervals, for example the reappearance of Sirius after seventy days spent below the horizon);[54] the death and rebirth of the Nile and agriculture; and, of course, the death and rebirth of the king. All of these natural, recurring events were to the Egyptians a perpetual reminder of the one death and rebirth that really mattered – the original one without which none of the other deaths and rebirths could happen – the death and rebirth of the Universe, personified by the death and rebirth of the creator-god.[55]

The true object of worship in ancient Egyptian religion was therefore the creator-god, who personified the great mystery of beginning and who manifested himself in the entire created Universe. Many religious texts indeed proclaim this fact, although they have unfortunately been ignored by Sun-struck Egyptologists. For example, in the 'Hymn to Amun as the Sole God', the creator-god Amun is described as follows:

> Amun, he who came into existence at the beginning. No god came into being before him. There was no other god with him that he might tell his form. He had no mother for whom his name was made. He had no father who begot him and said: "This is I". Building his own egg, a daemon mysterious of birth, he who created his (own) beauty, the divine god who came into being by himself; all gods came into existence after he began to be...

> Amun is One, hiding himself from them, concealing himself from the gods, so that his colour is unknown. He is far from heaven, he is far from the underworld; no gods know his true form. His image is not described in writings. No-one bears witness to him . . . He is too mysterious that his majesty might be disclosed; he is too great that he should be asked about, too powerful that he might be known...

> His soul is Shu, his heart is Tefnut. He is Harakhti who is in the sky. His right eye is day [the Sun], his left eye is night [the Moon]... His body is Nun, and he who is in it is the Nile, giving birth to whatever is and making to live what exists.[56]

Note here how the creator-god Amun manifested himself in the sky-god Harakhti, whose eyes were the Sun and the Moon (final paragraph). Thus it would not be incorrect to say that Amun *was* the Sun and the Moon, even though he was fundamentally more than that. In theory, then, Amun could have been a Sun-god, whilst remaining primarily the creator-god, and this I believe to have been the case with Re, who began his career, historically speaking, as a creator-god, and then became specialised in the Sun.[57]

The Pyramid of Creation

If ancient Egyptian religion was a cult of creation, as I maintain, then it becomes possible to understand the great solemnity, magic and mystery that were ever present in its rituals, along with the durability of its cult practices over thousands of years. Moreover, it becomes possible, for the first time, to perceive a profound motive for the building of the pyramids and temples, at inestimable economic cost to the Egyptian state. Might the pyramids, like the temples, have been monuments to the First Time? Did they too, in their own way, portray the mystery of the creation of the Universe? If so, then a unifying framework would exist within which all of the pyramid's symbolisms – solar, stellar, lunar and chthonian – could be rationalised.

That the true pyramid did have a creational symbolism is established beyond a doubt by the fact that its capstone was called *benbenet*, echoing the Benben Stone, which, as explained earlier, signified the spiritualised seed of the creator-god, which had been ejaculated from the earth into the sky for the conception and birth of the stars, the Sun, and the Moon. The pyramid, like the Benben pillar and the obelisk, is thus to be seen as a phallic symbol, albeit filled out into the broader pyramidal shape.

In support of this interpretation, the pyramid capstone of Amenemhet III, described earlier, bears a wide range of symbolism encompassing the stars, the Sun and the Moon, the god Re, and other gods whose epithets might well be creational ('the Lord of the Horizon', and 'the Great God, Lord of Time').

Is it so controversial to suggest that the pyramid was a symbol of the creation? After all, Egyptology has long known, on the basis of explicit writings, that the Egyptian temple was a simulacrum of creation, its floor signifying the risen land, or primeval mound, its columns signifying the supports of the sky, and its roof signifying the sky (see the quotes in the panel opposite). A precedent therefore exists for an Egyptian building symbolising the creation. So, why not the pyramid?

The Egyptian Temple: a Simulacrum of Creation

The temple was an image of the Universe as it now exists and, at the same time, the land on which it stood was the primeval mound which arose from the waters of the primordial ocean at creation.
(R.T. Rundle Clark, *Myth and Symbol in Ancient Egypt*, 1959)

As *akhet* ('radiant place'), the temple was the place where heaven, earth and netherworld touched. The temple was also the cosmos in microcosm. The enclosure wall and sacred lake were Nun, the sanctuary was the place of First Creation, the hypostyle hall and the bases of walls were the liminal swamp, the columns were plants, the ceilings were sky, the floors were earth, the vaults were netherworld, the pylon was the mountains of the eastern horizon, and the axial way was the path of the Sun. The temple was also the body of god.
(Byron E. Shafer, *Temples, Priests and Rituals: An Overview*, 1997)

Temples were microcosms, realisations in miniature of the landscape of world order. There the visible met the invisible, the human touched the divine, and earth joined sky and netherworld. Obelisks pierced the heavens, and flag masts supported the canopy of the sky; pylons mimicked the horizon, and columns held starry ceilings aloft; sacred lakes teemed with life, like the abyss or primeval swamp, and wells tapped the regenerative powers of creation's waters.
(Lanny Bell, *The New Kingdom Divine Temple*, 1997)

The Egyptian temple (is) a miniature cosmos... the walls surrounding a temple site... symbolise the waves of the primeval ocean surrounding the cosmos... The temple itself is usually located on an elevation... thus, the primeval hill rose from the Nun... From floor level, that is from the ground, one descends into the subterranean crypts, the underworld. Papyrus- and lotus-shaped pillars rise from the floor like papyrus and lotus plants from the primeval swamp. They also serve as symbols for the celestial pillars; they support the temple roof, that is the sky.
(Gunter Burkard, *Conceptions of the Cosmos – The Universe*, 1998)

Here, the modern tendency to compartmentalise things may have acted as a barrier to understanding. The scholar, on learning that the Egyptian temple symbolised the creation, has presumed that the pyramid, having a completely different architectural form, must have symbolised *something else*. However, as certain Egyptologists have now begun to realise, the ancient Egyptians did not think in compartmentalised terms, but rather followed 'a multiplicity of approaches' which allowed a single idea to be rendered in strikingly different, and even contradictory, ways.[58]

There is no reason, therefore, to preclude the possibility that the true pyramid, like the temple, was a simulacrum of creation. On the contrary, there is every reason to view the temple as an important precedent and support for such a hypothesis.

Might the true pyramid represent a variation on the creational theme – a subtly different perspective perhaps? This is indeed plausible, since the temple and the pyramid played significantly different roles in Egyptian religion, the former being a place of ongoing interaction between man and the gods, the latter being a place that was used just once – for the burial of the king's body and the resurrection of his soul – and thereafter sealed up for eternity (at the pyramid, ongoing rituals were performed in the temple that was attached to it, not inside the pyramid itself). The key to the pyramid, then, may lie in the unique personal relationship that it had with the king.

This brings us to the crux of our discussion, namely the burial practice of the Egyptians vis-a-vis the pyramid. Could the king be buried *in* the pyramid, or did he have to be buried *beneath* the pyramid? Was there a hard and fast rule for burial, and if so, might the creational interpretation of the pyramid provide the rationale for it?

The key, I believe, is the king's identity with the creator-god, and the parallel between his death and rebirth and that originally experienced by the creator.

As explained earlier, the Egyptians believed that the king, during his life, embodied the soul, or spirit, of the creator-god – hence his central role in ensuring the perpetual renewal of the events of creation (*creatio continua*). But this personification of the creator-god did not come to an end when the king died; on the contrary, the death of the king echoed the death of the creator-god, and it was therefore the defining moment in the cult.

In life, the king's soul had been divine, his body human. But in death, his soul disappeared (temporarily) into a state of suspended animation, whilst his body became divine. In that one transformative moment, time was not so much halted as returned to the beginning. Suddenly, the light of the world was gone; the laws of *maat* were non-existent; and Egypt was back in the state of darkness and chaos which had prevailed before the First Time. Loud wailing filled the land; there was self-flagellation, fasting and abstinence; and the people smeared mud on their heads and faces as if to signify their return to the subterranean slime. In order that light and life be restored to Egypt, the inert corpse of the king had to be ritually reassembled and revivified – just as the corpse of the creator had been resuscitated at the beginning of time – and a new king, embodying the soul of the creator, had to be installed on the throne.

To this end, the king's body was transformed by magic rituals from an inert corpse into a living Osiris, and then, by further rituals, made to send forth its soul, which would rise up and create the sky, the stars, the Sun, and the Moon, just as the creator-soul had done at the beginning of time. In other words, the king would experience exactly the same body-soul separation that the creator-god (the proto-earth) had experienced at the moment of creation.[59]

Two of the magic rituals are particular noteworthy for the support that they lend to the creational interpretation. First, the wrapping of the king's body in bandages (the final stage in his mummification) is suggestive of the reassembly of the creator's dismembered body, i.e. the proto-earth. And second, the 'opening of the mouth' ceremony that was performed on the mummy is suggestive of the splitting open of the mouth of the earth (we will examine this important ritual further in chapter five). Both of these rituals would thus be re-enactments of creation (in the latter case, the Pyramid Texts state explicitly that this was so),[60] the 'opening of the mouth' being the act that triggered the all-important separation of the soul from the body.

A strong case is thus made that the king's primary identity was with the creator-god (not the Sun-god as Egyptologists imagine), and that the death and rebirth of the king re-enacted that of the creator.

We turn now to a remarkable fact which is well known to Egyptology, but the full significance of which has been missed, namely the identity of the king with the pyramid, this being attested by Utterances 600 and 601 of the Pyramid Texts. In the first of these spells, the creator-god Atum is beseeched to protect the king and the pyramid as if they were one and the same thing:

> O Atum, set your arms about the king, about this construction, and about this pyramid... O Atum, set your protection over this king, over this pyramid of his, over this construction of the king...[61]

Similar verses are then directed to the Great Ennead (the multiplicity of gods who formed the company of Atum) both in Utterance 600 and 601, leaving the reader in no doubt as to the fact that the king and the pyramid were regarded as one.

What does this mean? To Egyptologists, who perceive the king as an ambassador for the Sun-god, it suggests that the pyramid was a symbol of the Sun. Under the creational theory, however, a significantly different theory emerges: since the king personified the creator-god, the pyramid would likewise have been an image of the Great God. Thus we may draw the equation:

king = pyramid = creator-god.

We are now on the verge of a breakthrough as regards the meaning of the pyramidal form. The capstone, as we have seen, represented the creator-god's spiritualised seed. The whole pyramid, meanwhile, represented the creator-god. And so it would seem that the pyramid was a simulacrum of the creation, freezing in stone the moment when the creator-god rose up from the abyss to the sky.

Nevertheless, the exact imagery remains rather vague, for the creator-god personified a fluid concept: as the proto-earth, or proto-Universe, in a state of metamorphosis, he had no permanent abode but rather spanned the realms of the underworld, the earth, the horizon, and the sky. Did his

Figure 7.
THE PYRAMID OF KHAFRE, AERIAL VIEW.
Viewed from above, the pyramid seems designed to thrust its capstone into the sky.

pyramidal form thus incorporate the underworld and the risen earth (the primeval mound) in its lower parts? Or did it stand upon the risen earth, signifying the ascending spirit and the molten seed that had been ejected therefrom? If we are to establish a hard and fast rule for the king's place of burial, then an answer to this question is of paramount importance.

Here, it is all too easy to take a wrong turn.

Firstly, a misconception has arisen that the pyramid is a symbol of the primeval mound, i.e. the risen earth. Egyptologists, for their part, have proposed this identification as an alternative to the solar pyramid theory (an indication of their lack of confidence in that theory). But alternative Pyramid theorists have also suggested the same idea on the grounds that the Great Pyramid's dimensions encode those of the Earth.[62]

To tackle the Egyptologists first, their primeval mound theory relies on a flawed interpretation of the Benben Stone, which they have assumed to be a part of the primeval mound (the risen land), as if the mound were a static concept.[63] Unfortunately, this is categorically not the case, for the Benben Stone rather signified the molten material that had been ejected from the primeval mound – a dynamic concept. Whilst it would not be unthinkable to redefine the mound in recognition of the cataclysm which accompanied its rising, it is better that the term 'primeval mound' be restricted to its present use, namely to describe the risen earth; and this is the approach that is adopted in this book.

Turning to the alternative theorists, there is no need to challenge their view that the Great Pyramid encodes the dimensions of the Earth in order to question their belief in its terrestrial symbolism. Rather it is a matter of asking ourselves what the architect intended when he incorporated those dimensions into the monument. Was it to inform us that the Pyramid was the earth? Or was it to inform us that the creator of the Universe was the spiritual double (ka) of the earth? My point is that the Egyptian creator-god was conceived as a proto-earth that spiritualised itself as a means of creating the present Universe. Thus, if the Pyramid was indeed built as a simulacrum of the earth (the northern hemisphere), it may have signified either the physical earth or the transformative earth (the earth going to its ka). So, if the Pyramid does encode terrestrial data, it would, in fact, be capable of a spiritual, rather than a physical, interpretation.

The second misconception, that might lead to a wrong turn, has arisen from the Pyramid Texts, where an identity is attested between the king, the pyramid, and the god Osiris. In Utterance 600, the creator-god Horus is beseeched:

O Horus, this king is Osiris, this pyramid of the king is Osiris, this construction of his is Osiris; betake yourself to it; do not be far from him in his name of 'Pyramid'...[64]

Now, according to Egyptology, Osiris was the god of the earth and the underworld, with whom the king became identified when he crossed the boundary of death. Thus it is implied, on the authority of Utterance 600, that the pyramid represented the earth and the underworld. But was this really the identity of Osiris? Egyptologists are notably cautious about this passage, for Osiris is seen as the antithesis of the Sun-god, which tends to wreck their theory of a solar pyramid.[65] However, as I argue at length in the companion volume to this book, Osiris was actually a creator-god who became specialised as the god of death and resurrection. Yes, his body did personify the earth, the underworld, and indeed the primeval ocean.[66] But he also possessed a soul, which he had sent forth for the creation of the Universe. Indeed, the Pyramid Texts devote a goodly deal of space to the theme of Osiris-the-king leaving behind his resuscitated body and ascending to the sky as a soul.[67]

Once again, then, we avoid a wrong turn only to face ambiguity. Does the pyramid represent Osiris in his body aspect or in his soul aspect? Did the monument symbolise the body of the creator-god, or the soul of the creator-god?

Fortunately, some reliable clues do exist which can settle this question definitively.

Firstly, there are the names of the pyramids, which take on a particular importance in light of the identification between the king, the pyramid, and the creator, discussed earlier. Are these names mere statements of intent for the king's afterlife, as Egyptologists assume? Or are they, at a more fundamental level, descriptions of the king in his pyramidal form? If the latter, then they provide no support for any chthonian symbolism in the pyramid superstructure, but rather lend emphasis to the creator-soul (*ba*) rising, shining, and enduring, and manifesting itself in the light of the stars, the Sun and the Moon (the latter suggested by 'the Eyes of the Two Lands'). The reader is invited to judge for himself the relevance and significance of these pyramid names, those that are known being listed in the panel opposite. (At the very least, the list illustrates the explanatory power of the creational interpretation.)

Secondly, Utterance 600 of the Pyramid Texts contains a passage that does seem to be decisive on this matter. In the context of the creation by Atum, it asserts that the pyramid was to be filled by the king's *ka*, i.e. his vital spirit:

O Atum-Khoprer, you became the high hill; you rose up as the Benben Stone in the Temple of the Benben in Heliopolis; you spat out Shu,

The Names of the Pyramids

Djoser, Saqqara: 'Horus is the Star at the Head of the Sky'

Sneferu, Meidum: 'Sneferu Endures'

Sneferu, Dahshur (both): 'Sneferu Shines (or Rises/Appears)'

Khufu, Giza: '*Akhet Khufu*', i.e. 'Khufu's Island of Light'

Djedefre, Abu Roash: 'Djedefre is a *Sehed*-Star'

Khafre, Giza: 'Khafre is Great'

Menkaure, Giza: 'Menkaure is Divine'

Userkaf, Saqqara: 'Pure are the Places of Userkaf'

Sahure, Abusir: 'The *Ba* of Sahure Shines (or Rises/Appears)'

Neferirkare, Abusir: 'Neferirkare is the *Ba*'

Neferefre, Abusir: 'Neferefre is the Divine *Ba* (plural)'

Niuserre, Abusir: 'Enduring are the Places of Niuserre'

Djedkare-Isesi, Saqqara: 'Djedkare-Isesi is Beautiful (or Perfect)'

Unas, Saqqara: 'Beautiful (or Perfect) are the Places of Unas'

Teti, Saqqara: 'Enduring are the Places of Teti'

Pepi I, Saqqara: 'Enduring is the Beauty (or Perfection) of Pepi'

Merenre, Saqqara: 'Shining is the Beauty (or Perfection) of Merenre'

Pepi II, Saqqara: 'Enduring is the Life of Pepi'

Amenemhet I, Lisht: 'Shining are the Places of Amenemhet'

Senusert I, Lisht: 'Senusert is the Eyes of the Two Lands'

Amenemhet II, Dahshur: 'Amenemhet is at the Head'

Senusert II, Illahun: 'Senusert Shines (or Rises/Appears)'

Amenemhet III, Dahshur: 'Amenemhet is Beautiful (or Perfect)'

Amenemhet III, Hawara: 'Amenemhet is Life'

(Sources: M. Lehner, *The Complete Pyramids*; J.P. Lepre, *The Egyptian Pyramids*; S. Quirke, *The Cult of Ra*; A. Gardiner, *Egyptian Grammar*.)

you spluttered out Tefnut, and you set your arms about them as the arms of a *ka*, that your *ka* might be in them. O Atum, set your arms about the king, about this construction, and about this pyramid as the arms of a *ka*, that the king's *ka* may be in it, enduring for ever.[68]

Here it is confirmed (final line) that the pyramid represented the spirit of the creator-king (his *ka*).

However, this is not to say that the pyramid signified spirit alone, for the creation also involved an ejection of physical material, namely water and iron (*bja*) which was used for the formation of the sky-ocean and the celestial bodies respectively. In the latter respect, the passage just quoted is most pertinent, for Atum's 'high hill' (*qaa*) almost certainly refers to the molten iron that was blasted into the sky, whilst the twin deities Shu and Tefnut whom Atum ejaculated would personify the twin orbs of the Sun and the Moon (for such is their identity elsewhere).[69] Furthermore, the juxtaposition of these lines to similar lines concerning the pyramid would then tend to suggest that the pyramid *is* 'the high hill' and that the material for Shu and Tefnut, the Sun and the Moon, was contained within the rising pyramid, to be spat out through the *benbenet*, or capstone.

The true pyramid may thus be regarded as an erupting hill of spirit-light (*akhu*) and spiritualised seed (*bnnt*) – the very same symbolism as is found in temples whose generic names included *Akhet* and *Bnnt*.[70]

In conclusion, the true pyramid is to be understood as a memorial to the First Time; a simulacrum of the creator-god rising as a mountain of light to inseminate the nascent sky with his seed; a three-dimensional hieroglyph of the proto-earth, or indeed proto-Universe, in the process of rebirth; and the mystery of beginning, concealed and encoded in stone; whilst the ground on which the pyramid stood is to be viewed as the risen land, or primeval mound, that had emerged from the waters of chaos.

Thus, in building the pyramid, the Egyptians erected not so much a death monument for the king, but rather a life monument that celebrated the existence of the Universe. To build the pyramid was to re-enact the creation, the miracle of the one reflecting the miracle of the other.

What does this imply for the burial of the king?

Working from first principles, I have shown that the king personified the creator-god, that the king's death re-enacted the death of the creator-god, and that the king's corpse was transformed by ritual magic into the corpse of the creator-god, which personified the proto-earth in its time of death crisis. Furthermore, I have demonstrated that the rebirth of the king – the separation of his soul from his body – re-enacted the rebirth of the creator-god, i.e. the spiritualisation of the proto-earth. And, beyond that, I have cited evidence that the pyramid's superstructure represented the ascended spirit and seed of the creator-god, whilst the ground on which it stood signified the earth (this point is corroborated by the symbolism of temples, see the panel earlier). The conclusion, then, is unavoidable. For the Egyptians to bury the king in true re-enactment of the creation, one option – and one option alone – was open to them, namely to inter the mummy in the very earth with which it shared an essential identity. The king, in other words, had to be buried *beneath* the pyramid.

That this was indeed the golden rule is attested emphatically in ancient Egyptian writings, which declare unequivocally that the body of the god, or the king, belonged in the earth, whilst the soul of the god, or the king, belonged in the sky. Some illustrative examples of these statements are listed in the panel overleaf, the most important being Utterance 305 of the Pyramid Texts which confirms that the rule was in operation at the time when the pyramids of the Old Kingdom were built. This axiom, to which I shall refer in abbreviated form as 'the body to earth, the spirit to the sky', provides a hard and fast rule for all Egyptian royal burials, both those with pyramids and those without, but where a pyramid was built it was required absolutely that the king be interred in the earth, i.e. *beneath* the monument (or, if the pyramid in question functioned as a cenotaph, literally 'an empty tomb', then in the ground elsewhere).[71]

This axiom dovetails perfectly with the archaeological record, which confirms the Egyptian custom of burying the deceased at ground level or below, this having been standard practice from the beginning to the end of Egyptian civilisation. As regards the pyramids, the tomb chamber was always placed beneath the monument at ground level or below – subject to one debatable exception which will be examined in a moment – and was accessed by a sloping passage that was generally located to the north of the structure. Figure 8 offers a diagrammatic overview of how this golden rule worked in a sample of pyramids from the Old Kingdom.

Egyptology has long been aware of the Egyptian custom of placing the tomb chamber beneath the pyramid,[72] and has long been acquainted with the saying 'the body to earth, the spirit to the sky'. However, it would not be unduly critical to suggest that its misplaced focus on the Sun cult and misconceived theories of the pyramid's symbolism have blinded it to the full significance of the sub-pyramid burial, with the result that the golden rule has been viewed more as a silver rule that may be flexed and bent as modern circumstances demand. On which note we turn to the mystery of the Great Pyramid. For it is here, in the most famous and enigmatic of all Egyptian pyramids, that the sole exception to standard burial practice is found – according to the theory of Egyptologists.

The Body to Earth, the Spirit to the Sky

O [king], you who are put under the earth and are in darkness!
(Pyramid Texts, Utterance 52)

(The king speaks:) "I come to you, O Nut, I have cast my father to the
earth... my soul has brought me and its magic has equipped me."
(The sky-goddess replies:) "May you split open your place in the sky
among the stars in the sky."
(Pyramid Texts, Utterance 245)

The spirit is bound for the sky, the corpse is bound for the earth.
(Pyramid Texts, Utterance 305)

Let there be praise in heaven to the soul of Re, and let there be praise
on earth to his body; for heaven is made young by means of his soul,
and earth is made young by means of his body.
(The Book of Gates)

The earth is for thy dead body, and the sky is for thy soul... O thou
[Re] whose transformations are manifold, thy soul is in heaven,
thy body is in the earth.
(The Book of Gates)

He is the All-Lord, the beginning of that which is. His soul, they say,
is that which is in heaven. It is he who is in the underworld and
presides over the east [the horizon]; his soul is in heaven, his body is
in the west [the underworld].
(Hymn to Amun)

The heavens rest upon his head, and the earth bears his feet. The
heaven hides his spirit, the earth hides his form, and the underworld
contains his hidden mystery.
(Hymn to Amun)

[O deceased], your soul is bound for the sky, your corpse is beneath
the ground.
(The Book of the Dead, Spell 169)

The heaven holds thy soul, the earth holds thy mummy.
(The Lamentations of Isis)

Figure 8.
PYRAMIDS OF THE OLD KINGDOM (SELECTION).
The Egyptian custom was to place the tomb chamber at ground level or below,
in accordance with the religious axiom 'the body to earth, the spirit to the sky'.

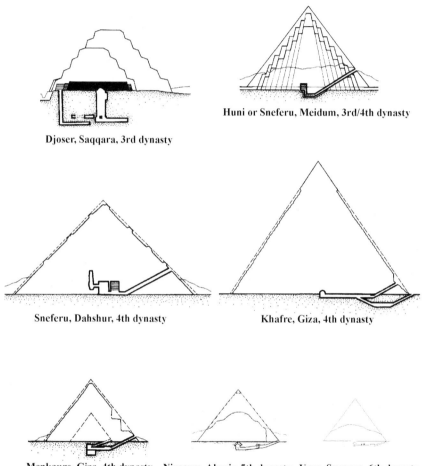

Djoser, Saqqara, 3rd dynasty

Huni or Sneferu, Meidum, 3rd/4th dynasty

Sneferu, Dahshur, 4th dynasty

Khafre, Giza, 4th dynasty

Menkaure, Giza, 4th dynasty   Niuserre, Abusir, 5th dynasty   Unas, Saqqara, 6th dynasty

The Great Pyramid Reconsidered

According to Egyptology, the Great Pyramid of Giza was built by the 4th dynasty king Khufu *c.* 2550 BC, at a time when the cult of Re, the Sun-god of Heliopolis, was reaching its ascendancy in Egypt. Khufu is thus thought to have been a Sun-king, whilst his pyramid (one of the earliest true pyramids) is thought to have been a symbol of the Sun. In the words of Egyptologist Rainer Stadelmann:

> Cheops [Khufu] identified himself with the Sun-god to such an extent
> in his pyramid complex and tomb that his sons and successors referred
> to themselves by the new royal title 'son of Re'.[73]

In keeping with this view, the ancient name of the Great Pyramid, *Akhet Khufu*, is usually translated 'Horizon of Khufu' on the understanding that *akhet* described the horizon upon which the Sun rose.[74]

In accordance with general custom, the Great Pyramid was provided with a northern entrance passage that sloped downward to a subterranean chamber. But, uniquely among the pyramids of Egypt, the Great Pyramid was also furnished with chambers high in its superstructure: the so-called Queen's Chamber at a height of 70 feet, the Grand Gallery at a height of 70-140 feet, and the so-called King's Chamber at a height of 140 feet, as shown diagrammatically in figure 9 opposite. As the reader may see for himself, the Great Pyramid stands in stark contrast to the other pyramid designs shown earlier in figure 8.

What is the meaning of this exceptional architecture?

The answer, according to Egyptologists, is revealed by the smashed granite sarcophagus that is found in the King's Chamber, this box being of just the right size and shape to have contained a human body. There being no other sarcophagi in the Pyramid, and no prima facie evidence of burial in any chamber, Egyptologists have concluded that the king was buried in the King's Chamber, and that the lower chambers represented abandoned tombs, the king having changed his mind twice on his place of burial.[75] Whilst there has been much debate about the exact purpose of these lower chambers, scholars have stuck firmly to their theory that the King's Chamber – the uppermost chamber in the Pyramid – was Khufu's final resting place. Which is basically to say that the Great Pyramid was built as a tomb, and as nothing but a tomb.

However, in reaching this conclusion, Egyptology created for itself a conundrum: for why had Khufu, alone among all of the pyramid building kings of Egypt, decided to place his burial chamber in the superstructure of his pyramid?

According to some Egyptologists, Khufu broke with convention in an

Figure 9.
THE GREAT PYRAMID, VERTICAL SECTION, LOOKING WEST.
Uniquely, the Great Pyramid contains several chambers that are constructed
high in its superstructure.

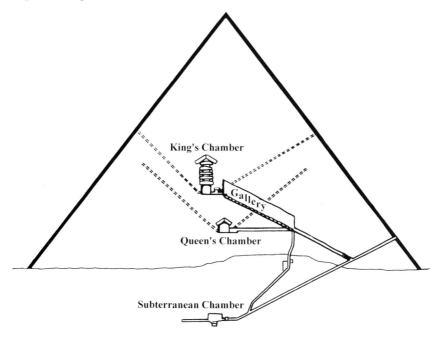

innovative attempt to fool tomb robbers, who had desecrated the graves
of his ancestors. But this theory merely begged another big question: if
security was such a problem, then why had other kings not taken similar
precautions? Answers came there none.

I.E.S. Edwards advanced an alternative theory. Khufu, he suggested,
decided to be buried in a granite sarcophagus, which proved too large to
be introduced to the descending passageway; thus the underground tomb
was abandoned. The Queen's Chamber was then built as a new tomb, at
a height of 70 feet, but it too was abandoned owing to delays in delivery
of the sarcophagus to the site. For this reason, the King's Chamber was
built at a height of 140 feet, and it then received the sarcophagus when it
was finally delivered.[76] It is an ingenious theory, but, for the majority of
scholars, a step too contrived.

Other Egyptologists wondered whether the king had elevated his tomb
chamber for a religious reason, perhaps to become closer to the Sun-god
Re. Zawi Hawass, taking this thought to its logical limits, suggested that
Khufu had appointed himself Re, as opposed to 'son of Re' (the normal
royal title), and had sought burial in the pyramid superstructure in order

to become one with Re in the horizon (*Akhet Khufu*). But this change had marked 'a religious revolution', which had 'violated the idea of *maat*'; and hence had proven short-lived.[77] Mystery solved? "No" say scholars, since there is no reliable evidence for a religious revolution during the reign of Khufu.

There the debate has been parked, stuck in a cul-de-sac one might say, while Egyptologists turn to other, more pressing matters, seemingly not too concerned by their collective failure to solve the conundrum of the raised burial chamber. Khufu, it is supposed, had his reasons; and those reasons might well remain unfathomable to us. It's no big deal.

So much for the orthodox interpretation of the Great Pyramid and its chambers. But what happens when we reconsider the Pyramid in the light of creational mythology?

Firstly, there is no evidence for the assumption that Khufu was a Sun-king. In fact his name alludes to Khnum, who was a well-known creator-god.[78]

Secondly, in the name of the Great Pyramid, *Akhet Khufu*, *akhet* did not refer simply to 'the horizon', but rather to 'the land of spiritual light' – the proto-earth in its process of spiritual transformation. Accordingly, *akhet* was not simply the horizon upon which the Sun rose every day, but rather the primeval earth from which all of the celestial bodies had risen at the beginning of time, initially in the form of spiritualised iron seed.[79] *Akhet Khufu* is therefore to be translated 'Khufu's island (or mountain) of spiritual light', a name which reflects the usual identity of the king, the pyramid, and the creator-god. In this sense, the Pyramid was 'great', but it was no greater than any other pyramid.[80]

In keeping with this interpretation, it is a fact that the Giza plateau – upon which the Great Pyramid stood – was called 'the Splendid Place of the First Time'.[81]

The Great Pyramid thus fits the pattern that I have established in this chapter, the building of the monument re-enacting the rise of the creator-god at the beginning of time, and paving the way for Khufu to further re-enact that great spiritual transformation and journey that the creator had then undertaken. And this journey, as explained earlier, required that the body of the king, like the body of the god, be buried in the earth, i.e. beneath the pyramid.

What, then, of the sarcophagus in the King's Chamber, at a height of 140 feet in the Pyramid's superstructure? Could Khufu really have been buried here?

In contrast to the orthodox approach, which takes this anomaly none too seriously and bends the rules to accommodate it, the creational theory finds it impossible to accept that the anomaly existed at all, since a burial in the Pyramid's superstructure would have destroyed the vital magic of the pyramid building ritual and rendered the entire structure useless from the king's point of view. It would not so much have signified a religious revolution as an annihilation of the fundamental principles of Egyptian religion, which dictated that the body of the king be buried in the earth, *beneath* the Pyramid.

The scene is thus set for a radical reappraisal of the architecture of the Great Pyramid, which is set out in chapters three to eleven of this book.

In chapter three, I scrutinise the many and various problems with the orthodox theory of the king's burial in the King's Chamber. As a finale to this wide-ranging survey, I consider the Queen's Chamber shafts and the evidence for secret chambers located beyond their plugged termini (a subject of tremendous speculation since the robot explorations of 1993 and 2002).

In chapter four, I propose a more plausible location for the burial of the king's body beneath the Pyramid, in accordance with the religious axiom 'the body to earth, the spirit to the sky'.

In chapter five, I suggest that something else of religious significance was enshrined in the sarcophagus of the King's Chamber.

In chapter six, I argue that the Pyramid's upper chambers and passages were sealed off as they were built, rather than being kept open for the burial of the king. Here, I suggest that the Pyramid was built, in its upper parts at least, as a repository for sacred artefacts.

In chapter seven, I probe more deeply into the mystery of the King's Chamber, looking in particular at how acoustics might explain the design of its antechamber, superstructure, and 'airshafts'.

In chapter eight, I offer a new reconstruction of the plundering of the Pyramid in antiquity, making specific suggestions as to the artefacts that may have been removed from the monument at that time.

In chapter nine, I return to the subject of secret chambers, and explain how the discovery of 'doors' and plugs in the Queen's Chamber shafts fits perfectly with my sealed repository theory. I then go on to identify a specific artefact which is likely to have been concealed by the builders in the hypothesised chambers.

In chapter ten, I look at the evidence for yet more undiscovered secret passages and chambers in the Pyramid.

And finally, in chapter eleven, I offer a point by point comparison and contrast between the orthodox Pyramid theory and the new theory that is proposed in this book.

But first, it is absolutely necessary that the reader be made acquainted with the architecture of the Pyramid in a reasonable degree of detail. It is to this task that chapter two of this book is assigned.

Chapter One Summary

- Ancient Egyptian religion was not a Sun cult per se, but a cult of creation, i.e. a cult whose primary aim was to celebrate and re-enact perpetually the myth of the creation of the Universe.

- The true object of worship in ancient Egyptian religion was not the Sun-god but the creator-god, who personified the death and rebirth of the Universe (understood from a geocentric perspective).

- The true pyramid was not a symbol of the Sun, but a symbol of the creation. It was a simulacrum in stone of the creator-god in his ascent from the abyss into the nascent sky for the creation of the stars, the Sun and the Moon.

- The pyramid superstructure was the place of the spirit, whilst the earth beneath it was the place of the body. The pyramid thus signified the separation of the spirit from the body.

- The king embodied the spirit of the creator-god. In life his every act repeated the events of creation, whilst in death he underwent the same transformation as had been experienced by the creator-god at the beginning of time.

- It was a fundamental rule of Egyptian religion that the body of the king be buried in the earth. This practice was intended to establish an identity between the body of the king and the body of the creator, i.e. the primeval earth.

- Where the burial of the king involved the construction of a pyramid, it was an essential precondition that the king be buried beneath the pyramid, at ground level or below.

- From a creational perspective, it is absolutely inconceivable that the builder of the Great Pyramid would have broken the fundamental rule of burial in the earth. Accordingly, this author rejects the orthodox theory that Khufu was buried in the King's Chamber, at a height of 140 feet in the monument's superstructure.

- The purpose of this book is to reconsider the significance of the Great Pyramid's architecture in the context of creational mythology.

CHAPTER TWO

A TOUR OF THE PYRAMID

It should be obvious to even the casual observer that the ancient Egyptian builders – and particularly the master architect of the Great Pyramid – had profound knowledge of certain fundamental principles of both geometry and mathematics. If that were not so, this great monument could never have been so perfectly aligned and oriented.

(J.P. Lepre, *The Egyptian Pyramids*, 1990)

The Great Pyramid is one of the largest buildings that the world has ever seen.[1] With a base 756 by 756 feet square and a designed height of 481 feet, the Great Pyramid had a volume of 91.2 million cubic feet, making it the largest pyramid in Egypt (the next largest having a volume of 78.1 million cubic feet). The exact number of individual stones in the Pyramid may never be known with certainty (since the structure is anchored upon a protruding nucleus of bedrock), but a widely-used estimate suggests that two million, three hundred thousand blocks of stone were raised, whilst a more recent estimate revises that number upwards to nearly four million blocks.[2] With the average weight per block exceeding two tons, a total weight for the Pyramid is indicated somewhere in the region of five to ten million tons.[3]

Such is the difficulty of comprehending these mind-boggling numbers that writers have often made comparisons between the Pyramid and other famous buildings. It has been stated many times, for example, that if the Pyramid were to be viewed as a vast tent, it would be large enough to contain Westminster Abbey and St Paul's Cathedral from London, as well as the cathedrals of Florence, Milan, and Rome.[4] Similarly, it has often been said that the builders of the Pyramid used more stone than was used in all the cathedrals, churches and chapels built in England since the time of Christ. Or alternatively, for the American reader, it has

Figure 10.
THE PYRAMIDS OF GIZA.
Khafre's pyramid (centre) stands to approximately the same height as the Great
Pyramid (right). In the foreground lies the smaller pyramid of Menkaure.

been suggested that the Pyramid corresponds to thirty times the mass
(and twice the volume) of New York's Empire State Building.

At other times, writers have resorted to anecdotes to drive home the
implausible scale of the structure. It has been suggested, for example,
that if the Pyramid's stone blocks were sawn into one-foot cubes and
those cubes were placed in a row, they would stretch two thirds of the
distance around the Earth's equator. Or, again for the American reader,
that the Pyramid's stone could be converted into a wall, six feet high and
one foot thick, that would extend from one side of the USA to the other.

But, if truth be told, neither measurements, anecdotes, nor photographs
can really convey the immense scale of the Pyramid. To really appreciate
its improbable dimensions, one has to go to Egypt and climb it, risking
the wrath of the authorities who forbid such acts. (In the opinion of this
author, to climb the Pyramid is an act of the utmost arrogance, in view of
its symbolism as discussed in this book.)

Why did the builders choose to erect the Great Pyramid on such a
fantastic scale? As important as this question is, we must not forget that
the Second Pyramid of Giza, being built on a slightly higher level of the
plateau, stands to the same height as the Great Pyramid, and rivals it in
size with an estimated volume of 78.1 million cubic feet of stone. Size
alone, then, is not the key to the Great Pyramid's uniqueness. Rather, to
appreciate the unique quality of the Pyramid, we must consider not just

its size but its precision.

The Precision of the Great Pyramid

The reason why so many alternative theorists have been attracted to the Great Pyramid lies not merely in its outstanding size, but rather in the unprecedented precision of its construction, which is rivalled by no other building in the world, whether ancient or modern. It is here that we find the truly unique quality of the Pyramid.

The precision begins with the platform upon which the Pyramid was built. Whilst a natural outcrop of bedrock, about 25 feet high, was left intact, to anchor the monument to the ground, the surrounding plateau was levelled by fitting it with a limestone pavement, carved to match the profile of the underlying bedrock. This pavement was built from fine quality limestone, the blocks varying from 17 to 27 inches in thickness in order to create a platform of uniform height. It extended some 30 feet beyond the Pyramid's boundary on the northern side, and several feet on the other three sides, thus spanning a total area of more than 13 acres. Remarkably, measurements have shown that this limestone pavement is almost perfectly level, even thousands of years after its construction, its height varying by no more than 0.8 inches across the total area. For no other pyramid did the builders undertake such painstaking preparations.

A further amazing example of the Pyramid's precision is found in the consistency of the lengths of its four sides at the base. The measurements are as follows: north 755.43 feet; south 756.08 feet; east 755.88 feet; west 755.77 feet.[5] It may thus be seen that, whilst no two sides were absolutely identical in length, the average difference from the mean length was only 2.3 inches (0.025%), whilst the difference between the longest and shortest sides was only 7.8 inches (0.086%). Nothing like such accuracy is seen in any other pyramid.

Incidentally, this squareness of the Pyramid's base was achieved by cutting the casing stones at the base to an astonishing level of precision. The Egyptologist J.P. Lepre writes:

> The casing stones are without parallel, having been so perfectly cut and squared that their corners were found to be true 90-degree angles to within 1/100th of an inch.[6]

At the four corners of the Pyramid, the deviations from 90° were almost imperceptible: 0° 00′ 02″ (north-west), 0° 03′ 02″ (north-east), 0° 03′ 33″ (south-east), and 0° 00′ 33″ (south-west).[7] Such extraordinary accuracy was achieved in no other pyramid.

Next, there is the alignment of the Pyramid to the cardinal points, its western and eastern sides deviating from true north by only 2.8 and 3.4 arc minutes respectively – on average, about 5% of a degree. This is half the deviation of the next most accurately-aligned pyramid, the Pyramid of Khafre at Giza, and is unrivalled by any other building in antiquity.[8]

Then there is the Pyramid's casing, which consisted of approximately 144,000 multi-angled blocks of polished Tura limestone, arranged in 216 courses from the ground to the capstone.[9] Although only a fraction of these casing stones remain in place today (all at the level of the base), it is clear that they were cut and fitted together with remarkable precision, with jointing so fine that it was almost invisible to the naked eye, and with a cement so superior that it formed an almost unbreakable bond. William Flinders Petrie, who performed the earliest scientific survey of the Pyramid in 1880-81, expressed his utter astonishment in describing the northern casing stones thus:

> The mean thickness of the joints there is 0.020 inches; and, therefore, the mean variation of the cutting of the stone from a straight line and from a true square is but 0.01 inches on length of 75 inches up the face, an amount of accuracy equal to the most modern opticians' straight-edges of such a length. These joints, with an area of some 35 square feet each, were not only worked as finely as this, but cemented throughout. Though the stones were brought as close as 0.002 inches, or, in fact, into contact, and the mean opening of the joint was but 0.02 inches, yet the builders managed to fill the joint with cement, despite the great area of it and the weight of the stone to be moved – some 16 tons. To merely place such stones in exact contact at the sides would be careful work; but to do so with cement in the joint seems almost impossible.[10]

Such a process was replicated on all four faces of the Pyramid, across a total area of about 22 acres – a quite staggering achievement. The effect was to clad the monument from bottom to top in a mantle of fine Tura limestone that resembled a single, flawless, pyramid-shaped slab. When struck by the rays of the Sun, the Pyramid would have dazzled the viewer with a blinding force of light.

Finally, the precision of the Pyramid is seen in the slope of its sides, which rose from ground to apex at an angle of 51° 51′ (+/- 1′).[11] This particular angle is known as 'the perfect angle' in that it embodies the mathematical ratios of pi (π) and phi ($\varnothing$).

As regards pi (π), the relevant formulae are:

$$pi = \frac{2 \times base}{height} \qquad \text{or } pi = \frac{perimeter}{2 \times height}$$

For the Great Pyramid, the second formula here gives a figure for pi of 3023.16 feet divided by 962 feet = 3.142578. This figure differs from the true pi value (3.141593) by only 0.031%. What this means in words is that the Pyramid incorporates the precise geometrical relationship whereby its height stands in the same ratio to its perimeter as the radius of a circle does to the circumference of that circle; thus the monument 'squared the circle' or 'circled the square'.[12] It is for this reason that many writers have described the Pyramid as a simulacrum of a sphere, or rather a hemisphere.[13]

As regards phi (ø), which is otherwise known as 'the golden section', the relevant formulae are:

$$\text{phi} = \frac{\text{apothem}}{\text{base x 0.5}} \qquad \text{or phi} = \frac{1}{\text{cosine x}} \quad (x = \text{the angle of slope})$$

For the Great Pyramid, the first formula here gives a figure for phi of 611.88 feet divided by 377.9 feet = 1.619 (the apothem is the distance from the apex down one face to the centre of a base side).[14] This figure differs from the true phi value (1.618) by only 0.07%. What this means in words is that the slope of the Pyramid is such that each of its four faces embodies the elegant ratio of the golden section.

Several other Egyptian pyramids also incorporated pi and phi in their designs, but none to the level of precision that is found in the Great Pyramid.[15] Incidentally, it is not always realised that the very slope that embodied pi automatically embodied a close approximation of phi. The perfect angle for pi was 51° 51′ 14.3″, and this automatically produced a figure for phi of 1.61767, accurate to 0.02%. For the exact phi figure of 1.618, the slope needed to be a tad less steep, 51° 49′ 48″ to be precise.[16] In practice, it would seem that the builders of the Pyramid focused on pi rather than phi, approximating the perfect pi angle by a 'rule of thumb' principle of fixing the height to the perimeter in the ratio 7:11, namely 280 cubits to 440 cubits in the Egyptian system of measurement.

The precision of the Pyramid is continued, for the most part, inside the structure, where joints routinely measure one fiftieth of an inch, and can be difficult to see unless a powerful flashlight is used. Here, special mention must be made of several structures. Firstly, the Descending Passage, partially built and partially excavated through the bedrock, is the longest and most precisely-built passage of its kind ever constructed in the history of Egyptian pyramid building. Secondly, the Queen's Chamber, built of limestone blocks, is undoubtedly the finest example of its kind in Egypt. Thirdly, the King's Chamber, built of polished granite blocks, is unique and unrivalled in the quality and precision of its finish (it, too, incorporates pi). And fourthly, the Grand Gallery – the sloping hallway at the heart of the Pyramid – is one of a kind, whose splendid engineering is matched only by the majesty of its architectural design.

In summary, the Great Pyramid signifies an undeniable zenith in the history of pyramid building. In the preparation of its pavement; in the laying out of its base; in the alignment to true north; in the jointing of the casing stones; in the slope of its sides; in the precision of its internal passages and chambers; in all of these ways, the Pyramid embodies a degree of precision that would simply not be credited if perchance the monument had been destroyed in antiquity. Fortunately, however, the Pyramid has survived and has been measured and remeasured so many times that the fact of its precision, uncanny though it may be, cannot be denied.

Why this seeming obsession with precision and perfection? To many, it is a sign of a higher intelligence, be it God, the devil, daemons or djinn, a race of extraterrestrials, or the lost civilisation of Atlantis. But to Egyptologists, the explanation is to be found in the religion of ancient Egypt, albeit the exact reason for the precision and perfection remains somewhat obscure. As the pyramid expert Mark Lehner has written in his book *The Complete Pyramids* (1997):

> Why such phenomenal precision? For the royal designers such
> exactitude may have been imbued with symbolic and cultic
> significance that now eludes us.[17]

Could the significance of the Pyramid's precision lie in the 'cult of creation' which I outlined in chapter one? Was the Pyramid intended to be the representation *par excellence* of the Great God, the creator-god, in his moment of creating the Universe? Was it a testament to the perfection of the Great God and the precision of his handiwork? This idea will be discussed further at the end of this book, but suffice to say, for now, that there is a definite pattern here that fits neatly with the cult of creation theory, namely the architect's intent that the building should endure, like the Universe, for eternity. This intent is evident in many of the Pyramid's architectural features, of which the following are especially striking:

- The fact that the Pyramid was built upon the Giza plateau, thus taking advantage of a natural earthquake-resistant platform.[18]

- The fact that the Pyramid was anchored on a 25-feet-high outcrop, or hillock, of bedrock.

- The fact that the Pyramid's corner stones were given unusual mortise and tenon joints, to provide added stability.[19]

- The fact that the Pyramid's sides were built with a subtle concavity, apparently to provide additional inward thrust.[20]

- The fact that the Pyramid's casing stones were cut, fitted, and cemented together to create an exceptionally strong hermetic seal.

So much for the size and precision of the Pyramid. Let us now turn our attention to a third attribute that has been responsible for the many far-fetched theories of the monument's purpose: its highly unusual interior design.

The Interior Design of the Great Pyramid

As noted in chapter one, the Great Pyramid has a complex interior design that is unique among the Egyptian pyramids. In particular, its upper system of passages and chambers is highly anomalous vis-a-vis the usual burial practice, and many of its features there are inexplicable, or at least puzzling, under the orthodox point of view. The big problem, it must be emphasised, is that the Pyramid contains no inscriptions that might shed light on the purpose of its passages and chambers, and the interpretation of these features thus becomes a matter of tremendous subjectivity. The resultant problem, as discussed in the Preface to this book, is that the researcher's impressions of the architecture are clouded by his personal preconceptions and predilections. Inevitably so.

In the remainder of this chapter, therefore, I shall attempt to describe the Pyramid's interior in terms that avoid any theoretical bias (such as the tomb hypothesis) so that the reader might appraise the design for himself, without being influenced unduly by the assumptions of others. By means of photographs, diagrams, measurements, and a commentary that is, for the most part, completely neutral, the Pyramid will be allowed to speak for itself via its own language of architecture, the only barrier being the inevitable preconceptions that the individual reader has brought to this book.

At this point, the reader who is already familiar with the layout of the Pyramid may wish to press on into the next chapter. However, I would highlight the fact that the description below incorporates new data on the Queen's Chamber shafts, which came to light from the second round of robotic explorations in 2002, and here I permit myself the indulgence of offering a prosaic, functional and non-controversial explanation for the mysterious metal-handled 'doors', which are fitted, one apiece, into the two shafts.

Figure 11.
THE GREAT PYRAMID, VERTICAL SECTION, LOOKING WEST.

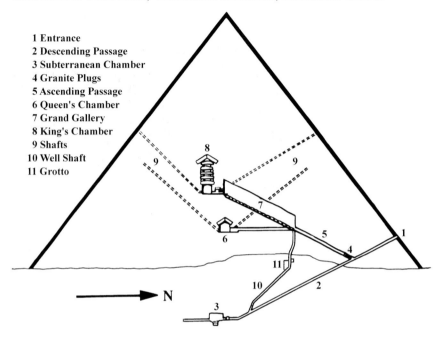

1 Entrance
2 Descending Passage
3 Subterranean Chamber
4 Granite Plugs
5 Ascending Passage
6 Queen's Chamber
7 Grand Gallery
8 King's Chamber
9 Shafts
10 Well Shaft
11 Grotto

We shall now explore the Pyramid, according to a threefold division of its features:

1 The Entrance and Lower Section.

2 The Upper Section.

3 The Well Shaft and Grotto (a system that spans the lower and upper parts and links them together).

The Entrance and Lower Section

Today, the Pyramid is entered through a rough tunnel, about 5 feet wide and 8 feet high, that was supposedly dug by the Arab ruler Abdullah al-Mamun in AD 820.[21] This tunnel begins in the 6th course of masonry in the exact centre of the monument's northern face, and runs due south for about 100 feet, before veering south-eastwards for a further distance of 20 feet, upon which it debouches into a huge man-made chasm in which further tunnels have been cut to the Ascending Passage and Descending Passage respectively.

The original entrance to the Pyramid is located in the 19th course of its northern face,[22] about 39 feet above the al-Mamun tunnel, and is offset to

Figure 12.
THE GREAT PYRAMID, ANCIENT AND MODERN ENTRANCES.
The photograph shows both the original entrance passage (arrowed) and the
rough tunnel which serves as a modern-day entrance to the monument.

the east of centre by 24 feet (it was thus placed, it would seem, so as to
prevent its detection). Unfortunately, owing to stone quarrying in Arab
times, the entrance and the initial part of the passage (to a depth of about
8 feet) have been destroyed. However, the same quarrying has exposed
an imposing set of limestone blocks, arranged in an inverted V-shaped
gable, which would not otherwise have been seen and which provide a
foretaste of the marvels that are to be found inside the monument.[23]

Today, the entrance passage aperture is protected by a metal gate. But
according to the Roman geographer Strabo, who visited Giza *c*. 25 BC,
the passage was originally fitted with a movable door – 'a stone that may
be taken out, which being raised up, there is a sloping passage'.[24] This
door may have consisted of a thin limestone slab, which could have been
removed and replaced at will with the aid of a specially-designed ladder
and platform.[25] Some Egyptologists, however, have visualised a pivoting

Figure 13.
MAIN ENTRANCE AND BEGINNING OF DESCENDING PASSAGE.
The diagram shows the extent to which stone has been plundered from the north
face.

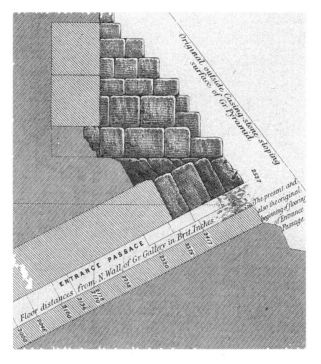

door, the exact pattern of which remains a matter of dispute.[26] Whatever
the design, the door, upon being closed, would have fitted perfectly into
the Pyramid's face and been almost impossible to detect.

In answer to the argument (sometimes heard) that the Pyramid would
not have needed a door,[27] the principle of the 'unlocked suitcase' may be
cited, to the effect that a sensible person, when faced with an intruder
who is determined to break in to a container, allows that intruder to gain
access to the container without causing it serious damage. The principle
is followed by airport travellers and commercial truck drivers, and is
unlikely to have been a modern invention. In view of the stable nature of
human behaviour and psychology, an original door to the Pyramid would
certainly make sense.

Entering the Pyramid via its notional door, we must crouch to enter the
Descending Passage, which measures 3 feet 11 inches high by 3 feet 5
inches wide (the width is two cubits in the original unit of measure). This
passage descends at an angle of 26° 34' and extends for about 138 feet
through built masonry and a further 207 feet through the solid bedrock.[28]

Whilst it is similar in concept to the entrance passages of other Egyptian pyramids, the Descending Passage of the Great Pyramid is altogether more precise, deviating no more than half an inch in angle or orientation throughout its entire length of 345 feet. When the English Egyptologist William Flinders Petrie surveyed the passage in 1880-81, he could hardly contain his astonishment:

> The average error of straightness in the built part of the passage is only 0.02 inches, an amazingly minute amount in a length of 150 feet [sic]. Including the whole passage the error is under 0.25 inches in the sides, and 0.3 inches on the roof, in the whole length of 350 feet, partly built, partly cut in the rock.[29]

There is no evidence that the Descending Passage was ever plugged (i.e. filled with stone blocks), as some authors have speculated. If such plugs had been fitted and removed, there would be chisel marks on the walls, floor and ceiling of the passage, and yet there are none.[30] On the contrary, the passage was seemingly left open in its angular descent, and met its first obstruction at the point where it levelled out (there are signs here of a false bottom that has been broken through, see figure 14).[31]

Figure 14.
JUNCTION OF THE DESCENDING PASSAGE AND SUBTERRANEAN PASSAGE.

Beyond this point, the passage runs horizontally for 29 feet, a notable feature of this section being a roughly-excavated recess in the west wall, measuring approximately 6 feet by 6 feet by 4 feet, apparently designed to hold one or more granite portcullis blocks (crude blocking systems of this kind are known to have existed in the underground passages of other pyramids).[32]

Beyond this portcullis recess, the Descending Passage debouches into the Subterranean Chamber, the entrance lying precisely on the Pyramid's central east-west axis. This remarkable cavern-like room, unique among Egyptian pyramids, has been dubbed 'the chamber of chaos' on account of its haphazard shape – its flat ceiling and walls contrasting with an uneven floor of lower and upper levels, the latter supporting weird and wonderful protrusions that rise up toward the ceiling like stalagmites.[33] The bedrock may have been carved this way by the hand of man, or it may have been eroded by the waters of an ancient aquifer.[34] Whichever, this chamber, lying some 100 feet below ground level, is by far the largest of all known chambers in the Pyramid, measuring 46 feet east-west by 27 feet 1 inch north-south, with a maximum height of 11 feet 6 inches.

In the far south-east corner of the Subterranean Chamber, opposite the entrance, a tunnel about 2 feet 6 inches square heads due south through the bedrock, but terminates in a dead end after 53 feet. This curious shaft, apparently part of the original construction, is often referred to as 'the blind passage'.

Figure 15.
THE SUBTERRANEAN CHAMBER.

Figure 16.
PLAN OF SUBTERRANEAN CHAMBER AND PASSAGE.

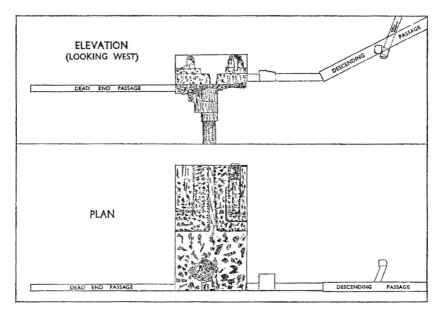

In the floor of the Subterranean Chamber, there is an eight-feet-square Pit, sunk at an oblique angle to the walls, and cut to an original depth of 50 to 60 feet (it is nowadays filled partly with rubble, giving it a depth of only 15 feet or so).[35] It was semi-excavated by explorers during the 19th century, but nothing of significance was found. Curiously, it contains a ledge, some 10 feet down from the top, upon which stands a large block of squared granite, its source and purpose unknown.[36]

We exit the Subterranean Chamber through the horizontal passage set low in its north-east corner, and retrace our steps back up the Descending Passage.

The Upper Section

At a distance of about 22 feet up the Descending Passage, a hole and rough-hewn passage in the west wall marks the lower entrance to the Well Shaft, which will merit our close attention in due course. For the moment, however, let us continue to a point 95 feet short of the main entrance, where we find the junction with the Ascending Passage. Above our heads, there is a multi-angled hollow, once filled by a prismatic stone which formed part of the ceiling of the Descending Passage and which camouflaged the entrance to the Ascending Passage. This 'prism stone',

Figure 17.
THE BEGINNING OF THE ASCENDING PASSAGE, BLOCKED BY A
GRANITE PLUG.
The plug was originally hidden by the prism stone.

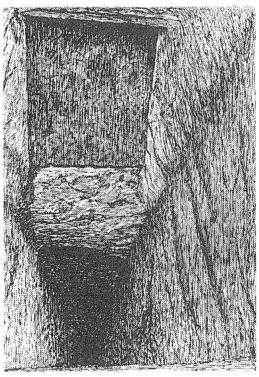

which may, in fact, have been a pivoting door (see discussion in chapter
three), was supposedly dislocated when the Arab ruler Caliph al-Mamun
forced an entry into the Pyramid in AD 820. The whereabouts of the stone
today is unknown.

Above the prism stone aperture, a granite plug seals the mouth of the
Ascending Passage. To bypass it, we must climb down the Descending
Passage a few feet, and crawl through a rough-hewn tunnel in its west
wall. This brings us into a large chasm that was supposedly dug by al-
Mamun. Here, we see all three of the granite plugs which once sealed the
Ascending Passage. They still fit the passage tightly and abut against one
another, although formerly there was a gap of 4 inches between the lower
two. The plugs are tapered slightly to fit the tapered mouth of the passage
(see passage measurements below) and are about 5 feet 6 inches long,
except that the uppermost plug has been broken forcibly at its top end,
reducing its length by about 2 feet. Originally, each granite plug weighed
between 5 and 7 tons.

Figure 18.
THE GRANITE PLUGS, SEEN FROM THE CHASM OF THE ROBBER'S
TUNNEL.

Having bypassed the plugs, we stoop to enter the Ascending Passage –
a unique feature that is found in no other major pyramid.[37] It ascends at
an angle of 26° 2′ for a distance of 124 feet, at which point it debouches
into the Grand Gallery. The average size of the passage is 4 feet high by
3 feet 5 inches wide (this width is exactly two cubits in the original unit
of measure, as with the Descending Passage). However, the passage
tapers significantly from top to bottom, as the following table shows.

The Narrowing of the Ascending Passage

(inches)	Height	Width
Measurements at top	53	42
Measurements at mid-point	48	41.5
Measurements at bottom	47.25	38.5

(Source: J.P. Lepre, *The Egyptian Pyramids*, pp. 73, 77.)

Figure 19.
THE AUTHOR IN THE ASCENDING PASSAGE.

This narrowing of the passage is probably explained by the presence of the granite plugs, which, it is believed, were lowered into the passage from the Grand Gallery above.

A further remarkable feature of the passage is the use of special 'girdle stones', located strategically along its length. In these places, the builders eschewed the use of individual small stones in favour of single monoliths which were hollowed out so as to provide the ceiling, walls and floor of the passage in one integral unit. There are four of these girdle stones in all, plus another three 'half-girdles' which comprise two pieces, split at their midsections. Of this girdle stone design, the Egyptologist J.P. Lepre commented as follows:

> This assembly represents yet another ingenious architectural feature characteristic of the Great Pyramid alone, and which serves as additional proof of this pyramid's individuality and superiority to all others.[38]

Evidently, the idea was that the Ascending Passage be made extremely strong and durable, perhaps in view of the stresses that would be caused by the lowering of the granite plugs. Or the builders may have intended to fill the entire passage with further plugs, either of granite or limestone (but there is no evidence that further plugs were ever fitted; if they had been, there would be chisel marks along the sides of the upper passage,

Figure 20.
THE GRAND GALLERY AND THE PASSAGE TO THE QUEEN'S
CHAMBER.

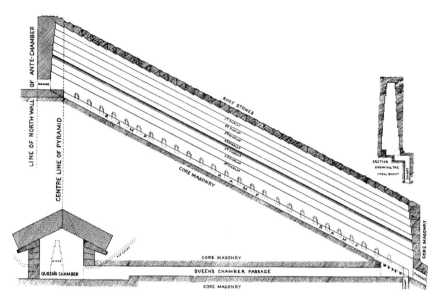

but there are none).

We emerge from the Ascending Passage into the Grand Gallery, which continues to slope upwards into the heart of the monument. The Gallery, the largest and most elaborate chamber in the Pyramid, will be described in due course. But let us first direct our attention to a horizontal passage that lies in front of us – the Queen's Chamber Passage – which marks the twenty-fifth course of the Pyramid's masonry.

The first thing to notice about the Queen's Chamber Passage is that it would originally have been hidden beneath the Grand Gallery's sloping floor. A bridging slab, which no longer exists, once spanned the passage opening and extended the Gallery's smooth floor to the upper mouth of the Ascending Passage – a design that was required for the lowering of the granite plugs into the Ascending Passage. This limestone slab, about 17 feet long and 9 inches thick, rested on a lip at its southern end, and was supported by five cross-beams (of wood or stone) which were fixed into sockets in the side walls. The height to which the sockets were cut indicates that the bridging slab incorporated 9-inch-thick protrusions which fitted into the sockets above the cross-beams (see illustrations in chapter three). There is also evidence that the slab was fixed into place using cement.[39]

Passing through this sub-floor hallway, we stoop once again to enter

Figure 21.
THE QUEEN'S CHAMBER PASSAGE.

the horizontal passage that is the Queen's Chamber Passage en route to
the Queen's Chamber itself. The passage is constructed of fine limestone
blocks and measures 3 feet 9 inches high by 3 feet 5 inches wide. After a
distance of 109 feet, the floor level drops suddenly to give the passage a
height of 5 feet 8 inches. Then, after another 18 feet, the passage gives
way to the Queen's Chamber.

The Queen's Chamber, so named by the Arabs purely on account of its
gabled roof,[40] is made from fine limestone and is so subtly jointed that it
looks to have been carved out of a single block of stone. It is let down
only by its rough floor, the original floor slabs having probably been dug
up and removed in antiquity. The chamber measures 18 feet 10 inches
east-west by 17 feet 2 inches north-south, and its walls rise to a height of
15 feet 4 inches, but at the apex of the roof it has a maximum height of
20 feet 5 inches. The roof gable lies exactly on the Pyramid's central
east-west axis.

The Queen's Chamber's most prominent feature is a large corbelled
niche, 15 feet 4 inches high, let into its east wall to a depth of 3 feet 5
inches. This niche – a unique feature found in no other pyramid – has a
corbelled design, rising in five sections from a width of 5 feet 2 inches at

Figure 22.
PLAN OF THE QUEEN'S CHAMBER.

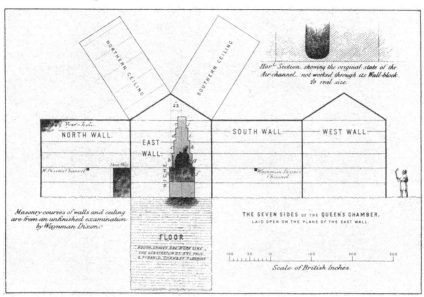

the bottom to just 20 inches at the top. It is the only major feature of the
Pyramid to be aligned east-west and is doubly unusual in that it is offset
by 25 inches from the wall's centre axis. Its purpose is unknown, and no-
one knows what, if anything, it originally contained. At the back of the
niche, treasure-hunters have hacked a tunnel that extends for a depth of
about 38 feet, culminating in a bulb-shaped cavern.

There is also a rough excavation in the top north-west corner of the
chamber; this is attributed to the English explorer Colonel Richard W.
Howard Vyse in 1837.

The other significant feature of the Queen's Chamber is a pair of small
channels or shafts, roughly 8 inches by 8 inches square, which are cut in
the centre of the north wall and south wall respectively to a height of 5
feet 8 inches (the same height as the entrance passage and the first corbel
of the niche). These channels are often called 'airshafts', but at no time
did they ever convey air to the chamber, for they were not built all the
way to the outside of the Pyramid and their mouths to the chamber were
left uncut. They were discovered in 1872 by Waynman Dixon, a British
engineer, who at first observed a crack in the south wall and managed to
insert a length of wire, thus discovering the cavity there. He chiselled out
the uncut plate of stone (some 5 inches deep) to expose the mouth of the
southern shaft. Then, playing a hunch, he measured off an equivalent
point in the north wall, and cut through another 5-inch left to reveal the

Figure 23.
APERTURE OF THE SOUTHERN SHAFT IN THE QUEEN'S CHAMBER.

mouth of the northern shaft. In this latter shaft, Dixon discovered some relics of the builders – a bronze hook, a broken wooden tool handle, and a stone ball.[41]

Since 1872, it has been known that the Queen's Chamber shafts run horizontally into the walls for a distance of over six feet (76 inches in the case of the northern shaft and 77 inches in the case of the southern shaft), prior to turning upwards at steep angles, to terminate somewhere inside the body of the Pyramid. In 1883, William Flinders Petrie measured the angles of the shafts as 37° 28′ (northern) and 38° 28′ (southern).[42]

During the late-19th and early-20th centuries, the shafts were explored by various methods – firing pistols, lighting fires (to send smoke up the shafts) and probing with rods – all to little effect. The lengths of the shafts and their destinations remained shrouded in mystery, as did their purpose.

In 1993, this mystery became even more perplexing when the German engineer Rudolf Gantenbrink sent a remote-controlled robot, Upuaut II, up the shafts, fitted with a video camera and a live feed. In the northern shaft, the robot was blocked by a broken rod lying across the floor (see later). But in the southern shaft, the robot proceeded unhindered for a distance of 213 feet (65 metres), where, to Gantenbrink's astonishment, its progress was blocked by a limestone slab, fitted with two metal latches or handles, one of which had corroded and snapped in two, its end piece lying on the floor. Strangely, the slab was raised off the floor by about 0.2 inches, and appeared to have a tiny gap at its bottom right hand corner.[43]

Close examination of the metal-handled slab showed that it overlapped the width of the shaft, at the left and right sides, by about 0.2 inches, and overlapped the top of the shaft by an indeterminable length.[44] Later tests revealed that it was securely fitted in the shaft, and could not easily be moved.

The two metal handles are thought to be copper or bronze, although one Egyptologist has suggested that they may comprise meteoritic iron (a religiously significant metal) with a copper coating.[45] These fittings were apparently inserted through drill holes in the slab, and then hammered downwards to form a 90° angle.[46] The drill holes seem to be filled with a 'black, tarry mass', as Gantenbrink calls it, whilst the metal fittings seem to be covered in part by a white gypsum-type cement.[47]

Gantenbrink's discovery caused a great deal of excitement, because to modern-day eyes the metal-handled slab looked just like a door that was meant to be opened. Despite the protestations of Egyptologists, who insisted that the slab was insignificant or symbolic, alternative writers began to call it 'the Gantenbrink door', and this name has stuck to the present day.

Figure 24.
THE SO-CALLED 'GANTENBRINK DOOR', 8 INCHES SQUARE,
DISCOVERED INSIDE THE QUEEN'S CHAMBER SOUTHERN SHAFT.

Despite all the controversy and speculation, however, the Gantenbrink 'door' has a mundane explanation.

As the Pyramid was constructed from the ground level upwards, the rising structure was, in effect, a vast building site. From the height of the Queen's Chamber upwards, the inclusion of the two 8-inch-square shafts, sealed at their lower ends, ran the risk that detritus or other objects (e.g. masons' tools) might fall into the shafts and be irretrievable. Moreover, it was possible that living creatures, such as scorpions, spiders, snakes and rodents, might crawl into the shaft, never again to see the light of day. For such reasons, the builders would have used small aperture covers, which prevented detritus, tools and creatures from falling into the shafts. These covers would have been kept in place most of the time, but would have been taken out while the shaft was being worked upon, i.e. at each new stage of construction. That such covers were used is evident from the fact that, with the exception of the builders' relics found in the northern shaft, the shafts were found empty and clean: no dead spiders; no dead scorpions; no dead snakes; and no detritus.

Given that covers would certainly have been necessary for the shafts, it strikes me as highly likely that 'the Gantenbrink door' is one of the original artefacts. Exactly how it fitted into place is not yet entirely clear, but two possibilities spring to mind. Firstly, the cover may have been shaped like a stopper, with a protruding section and a lip, so that it was *inserted into* the mouth of the shaft, with the handles easing the tasks of removal and reinsertion. If this was the case, then we are almost certainly looking at the original upper side of the cover, which has been turned upside down at the time of sealing the shaft (although it is not clear why inversion would have been necessary). Secondly, the cover may have been flat, so that it was placed *on top of* the mouth of the shaft. In this case, the handles on the upper side would have been connected to latches on the lower side, such that they could have been twisted into the 90° position, as shown in figure 25. In favour of this possibility, the latches are of exactly the right length to cut lightly into the soft limestone walls when twisted from above into the 90° position.[48] This method of fitting, whilst somewhat crude, would have held the cover in place while work on the Pyramid continued.

The exact method of fitting the cover may become clearer when the reverse side of the slab has been examined (i.e. by telescopic camera). In the meantime, it should be noted that the slab which we see today is not the original removable slab but a sealed-in version, which may have been altered accordingly. For example, three edges of the slab may have been trimmed to the size of the shaft, whilst the fixing of the handles in the

Figure 25.
POSSIBLE FIXING MECHANISM FOR APERTURE COVER DURING
CONSTRUCTION OF SHAFT (SUGGESTED BY LENGTH OF THE
LATCHES).

vertical position by means of gypsum-type cement has the hallmark of
some kind of ritual act.

On the basis of this theory, I predicted publicly that a matching metal-
handled cover would be fitted at the upper end of the northern shaft, and
was proven correct by a discovery in 2002, as we shall see in a moment.

Aside from the 'door', Gantenbrink collected an unprecedented set of
data on the Queen's Chamber shafts.

On a general note, he found that the shafts were constructed according
to a consistent pattern, in which an inverted U-shaped block, forming the
roof and walls, was placed on top of a flat block, forming the floor. Thus,
as a general rule, the joints in the shafts ran perpendicular to the floor.

Gantenbrink also discovered, to the surprise of many people, that the
walls of the shafts were quite rough, and that the quality of workmanship
varied considerably, several blocks being either scratched, flawed or
unfinished.[49] The latter blocks, he supposed, were the result of 'Monday
morning syndrome'. (Similar variations in quality were also found in the
King's Chamber shafts, to be considered later.)

As regards the northern shaft, Gantenbrink discovered that the angle of
ascent was not a simple 37° 28′, as reported by Petrie, but rather varied
between 33° 18′ and 40° 6′.[50] He explored this shaft to a length of 79 feet,
where his robot's progress was thwarted by a length of iron rod and a
length of wooden rod, both of which had become stuck in the shaft at a
point where it veered sharply to the north-west, at an angle of 45°. These
broken rods are generally thought to be remnants of the exploration by
Waynman Dixon in 1872.[51] However, the robot also found, at a slightly

lower level in the shaft, a broken wooden handle and, lower still, a metal hook – both reminiscent of the relics which had been found inside this shaft by Dixon in 1872.[52] These objects are widely assumed to be original builders' artefacts.

As regards the southern shaft, Gantenbrink discovered that the angle of ascent was not a constant 38° 28′, as reported by Petrie, but rather 39° 36′ on average.[53] His findings in this shaft have already been discussed.

Nine years later, in 2002, the Egyptian authorities, in conjunction with the Boston company iRobot and the National Geographic Channel, sent a new cable-controlled robot, Pyramid Rover, up the southern shaft, in an attempt to resolve the mystery surrounding 'the Gantenbrink door'. The new robot found that the limestone slab was fixed firmly in position, not movable as some had hoped, and was 3.25 inches thick. The go-ahead was then given to drill a hole, 0.75 inches in diameter, through the slab and insert a fibre-optic camera, fitted with a light. In a live television programme, *Pyramids Live: Secret Chambers Revealed*, screened by the National Geographic Channel on 16th-17th September 2002, the robot revealed an upward continuation of the shaft for a further distance of at least 8 inches, where it became blocked by a stone plug, a hollow cavity thus being formed of dimensions 8 by 8 by 8 inches. Zawi Hawass, the project director and head of the Supreme Council of Antiquities in Egypt, has vowed to drill through this second 'door' (as he calls it) as soon as it is practicable. At the time of writing, it is not clear whether the new stone plug is made of limestone or granite.

As a follow-up to the *Pyramids Live* programme, it was announced on 23rd September 2002 that the Pyramid Rover had overcome the obstacles

Figure 26.
THE STONE PLUG IN THE QUEEN'S CHAMBER SOUTHERN SHAFT, AS SEEN LIVE ON NATIONAL GEOGRAPHIC CHANNEL IN SEPTEMBER 2002.

Figure 27.
SECOND 'DOOR', DISCOVERED IN QUEEN'S CHAMBER NORTHERN
SHAFT IN SEPTEMBER 2002.

in the northern shaft and ascended to a distance of 213 feet (65 metres) where its progress had been halted by a metal-handled 'door' identical to that found in the southern shaft in 1993. This fulfilled the prediction that I had made several weeks earlier on the basis of my theory that the first 'door' was one of the original shaft aperture covers.[54]

These are the facts as currently known, all speculation being saved for the following chapter, except to say that future drilling of the aperture cover in the northern shaft will almost certainly reveal, in the near future, a continuation of that shaft, blocked by a stone plug, as with the southern shaft described earlier.

It remains only to say that these shafts are unique, and it is not at all apparent why the builders would have bothered to construct them, only to keep them sealed at both ends. The enigma of the Queen's Chamber shafts must be ranked as one of the most challenging mysteries of the Great Pyramid.

Such are the puzzles of the Queen's Chamber. Let us now retrace our steps through the Queen's Chamber Passage to emerge in the Grand Gallery. And let us try to imagine it as it once was, with the bridging slab fitted in place to provide a smooth continuation of the floor to the mouth of the Ascending Passage.

The Grand Gallery may be viewed as a continuation of the Ascending Passage in that it maintains the angle of 26° 2′ and continues upwards for a length of 153 feet, to provide a smooth floor 3 feet 6 inches in width, sandwiched between two raised ramps (the original design being totally without the steps and hand rails that are fitted today). It is possible that this smooth floor was intended as a storage place and slipway for stone

Figure 28.
THE AUTHOR IN THE GRAND GALLERY.

plugs, to facilitate the blocking of the Ascending Passage. Theoretically, twenty-five plugs could have been stored here. However, archaeological evidence supports the use of only the three plugs that may still be seen *in situ* today at the bottom of the Ascending Passage.

But there is much more to the Grand Gallery than a continuation of the Ascending Passage. Rather, it opens out to a width of 6 feet 10 inches, and expands to a height of about 28 feet, to form a magnificent corbelled vault which sweeps majestically upwards at the same time as its walls close in on themselves in awesome fashion. This splendid hallway has a possible antecedent in the corbelled chambers of Sneferu's pyramids at Dahshur (the Bent Pyramid and the Red Pyramid), but these are not built on an incline, nor on such a commanding scale. Also, it has a possible antecedent in an upward-sloping corridor of the satellite pyramid to the Bent Pyramid, but this is not built with corbelled architecture, nor on any great scale. One is therefore justified in referring to the Grand Gallery of the Great Pyramid as a unique feature. The pyramid expert J.P. Lepre felt moved to write:

> There is nothing quite like this Gallery in any of the other pyramids of Egypt... As the Great Pyramid represented the apogee of pyramid building and design, so the Grand Gallery represented the apogee of architectural development within the pyramid itself... Not before or since has such a hall been so simply yet exquisitely designed and executed. The degree of excellence which has long been associated with ancient Egyptian civilisation has been forever locked in the measurements and jointing of this superb gallery.[55]

The walls of the Gallery are constructed of fine quality limestone blocks, fitted together with great precision. They rise initially to a height of 7 feet 6 inches, then step in by about 3 inches on each side to form the first corbel. This pattern is repeated six times, at intervals of just under 3 feet, thus making seven corbels in all, until the roof is reached at a height of about 28 feet. At that point, the width of the Gallery is reduced from 6 feet 10 inches to 3 feet 6 inches, matching the width of the passage floor below.

An innovative feature of the Gallery's walls is that the stones are all tilted at 26° 2′ in alignment with the tilt of the Ascending Passage. The enormous weight which thus presses downwards throughout its length of 153 feet makes the Gallery a remarkable architectural and engineering achievement by any standards. Even more remarkable is the fact that not a single stone has slipped even a fraction of an inch, despite the passing of millennia in which the Pyramid has been subjected to earthquakes, gunpowder, and tourists by the coach load. Such was the perfection of the Gallery's design and its execution.

The roof of the Gallery, as already stated, is 3 feet 6 inches wide and is spanned by forty roof slabs, not thirty-six as some authors report.[56] These slabs are large and heavy stones in their own right, having a mean length of 3 feet 8 inches (as strange as it may seem, the builders did not use a standard size). Unusually, the roof stones do not rest against one another, as one might expect, but are rather fitted individually into notches in the top of the side walls. According to William Flinders Petrie, this plan was adopted in order that 'no stone can press on the one below it, so as to cause a cumulative pressure all down the roof'.[57]

A most curious feature of the Gallery is a pair of grooves, situated 5 inches above the third corbel in the lower part of the third overhang, at a height of 14 feet from the floor (approximately the mid-height of the Gallery). These grooves, measuring approximately 7 inches high and 1 inch deep, run along the entire length of each wall, and bear rough chisel marks along their lengths, as if something once fitted between them was

Figure 29.
THE GRAND GALLERY.

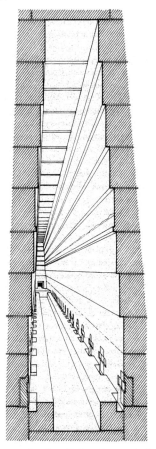

removed by robbers in antiquity.[58] In the opinion of J.P. Lepre: 'It is certain that something did traverse the Gallery'.[59] However, there are no clues at all to suggest what that 'something' might have been.

Another curious feature of the Gallery is the rectangular niches that are cut down into the side ramps, adjacent to the walls. There are fifty-four of these niches in total, twenty-seven in the west ramp and twenty-seven in the east ramp. Oddly, the length of the niches alternates on both sides of the Gallery, as does the pattern of the cut, a 'long hole' of 23.3 inches and horizontal bottom being followed by a 'short hole' of 20.5 inches and an inclined bottom (parallel with the floor of the Gallery); then another 'long hole', and so on and so forth. As Petrie has observed, the measurements follow a pattern in that 'the horizontal length of a long hole is equal to the sloping length of a short hole, both being one cubit.'[60] In keeping with this, the niches vary in depth between 8 and 11 inches,

Figure 30.
PLAN OF INSET STONE IN WALL OF GRAND GALLERY.

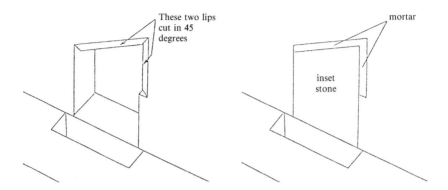

but their width is a consistent 6 inches.

In the side walls immediately above each niche (with the exception of the two lowest niches on each side), a stone measuring approximately 13 inches wide and 18 inches high has been inserted into the wall, as if to fill a vacant hole, each being sealed into place by an inverted L-shaped groove that was filled with cement.[61] These inset stones, fifty in number, are characterised, in forty-eight instances, by a transverse, rectangular, shallow incision, that measures about 10 inches high and 30 inches wide, thus cutting into the wall on both sides of the inset stone. These incisions are between 1 and 2 inches deep. Lepre has observed that all of the inset stones in the east wall, except for one, are in a slightly slanted position from true vertical, whilst all of the inset stones in the west wall, except for one, are in a true vertical position. The twenty-sixth set in the east wall, he notes, is on the vertical, whilst the thirteenth set in the west wall is slanted.[62]

The niches, the inset stones, the L-shaped grooves, and the rectangular incisions are unique features and their purpose has yet to be satisfactorily explained.

At the top of the Gallery, the floor level rises abruptly to become the Great Step – a large limestone block measuring 3 feet high by 6 feet 10 inches wide by 5 feet 2 inches deep. The sole feature of this Great Step is a pair of rectangular niches, 21 inches long, 6 inches wide, and 5 inches deep, cut down into the corners against the south wall (these bring the total number of niches in the Gallery to fifty-six). Old drawings show that the Step suffered a brutal assault in antiquity, the damage of which has been repaired in modern times.

At the Great Step, one may catch one's breath, turn around, and survey

Figure 31.
THE GREAT STEP IN THE GRAND GALLERY, AT THE ENTRANCE TO
THE KING'S CHAMBER PASSAGE.

the full glory of the Gallery, stretching far above and below. As J.P.
Lepre has observed, it is as if this Step was designed as a high platform
specifically to afford this splendid view:

> From this locale [the Great Step], one can take the time to truly
> appreciate the awe that the architect was doubtless seeking to inspire
> in the curious observer. Here, as in no other place in the pyramid, one
> is cast in a position to concentrate on the most glorious achievement of
> the ancient builders. From this unique vantage point the streamlined
> architectural perfection of design [of the Grand Gallery] can be fully
> comprehended.[63]

It is worthy of note that the Great Step stands exactly on the Pyramid's
central east-west axis and marks the fiftieth course of its masonry at a
height of about 140 feet, where the horizontal section has an area equal
to half that of the monument's base.[64]

Passing over the Great Step, we cross from the northern half of the
Pyramid to the southern half, and stoop to enter a low passage, 3 feet 8

Figure 32.
THE KING'S CHAMBER PASSAGE AND ANTECHAMBER.

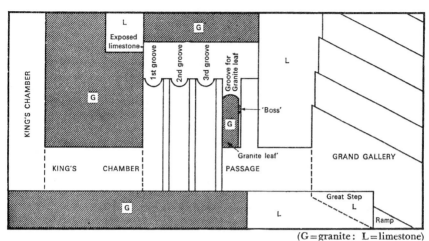

(G = granite : L = limestone)

inches high and 3 feet 6 inches wide, in the south wall. This is the King's
Chamber Passage.

After a short distance of 4 feet 4 inches, the King's Chamber Passage
emerges into the Antechamber to the King's Chamber. Immediately, one
is struck by a change of building material, from limestone blocks to, for
the most part, granite blocks. One also notes that the floor, unusually, has
been inserted between the side walls (a design that continues all the way
into the King's Chamber).

The pattern of the Antechamber is unique among Egyptian pyramids,
and almost beggars description.

The basic dimensions, for the record, are length 9 feet 8 inches, width
6 feet, height 12 feet 6 inches.

The room is fitted with wainscots on both sides, the east wainscot
rising to a height of 8 feet 7 inches, and the west wainscot rising to a
height of 9 feet 4 inches. These wainscots are fitted with four pairs of
grooves that are separated by pilasters. The first pair of grooves (at the
northern end of the room) descend only to half height, whilst the other
three pairs run from top to bottom. The first pair is 17.1 inches wide and
3.2 inches deep; the latter pairs 21.6 inches wide and 3.2 inches deep.
The pilasters, badly damaged by ancient intruders, are 5.3 inches wide.

Above the wainscots, there is on the east side a flat ledge, 12 inches
wide, but on the west side a series of three semi-hollows, of radius 8.75
inches, cut through a distance of about 12 inches to the west wall.

Another interesting feature of the Antechamber is a series of four
vertical, rounded grooves, 4 inches wide and 2.8 inches deep, that run

Figure 33.
PLAN OF THE ANTECHAMBER.

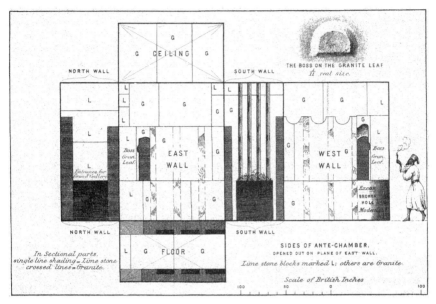

from top to bottom in the south wall, as far as the mouth of the passage.

It is often stated as a matter of fact that the Antechamber housed a portcullis, consisting of three granite blocks, each weighing around half a ton. However, these three granite blocks are absent, and the design of the chamber is, in fact, most unsuitable for a portcullis, as will be discussed in the next chapter.

However, in the first pair of grooves in the side walls, there is a double block of granite, popularly known as 'the granite leaf', which rests upon ledges, the slabs thus being suspended as if in mid-air, 3 feet 8 inches above the floor. This leaf consists of two blocks of granite, apparently cemented together to form a single block. Its combined dimensions are: width 4 feet, maximum height 4 feet 3 inches, thickness 15.5 inches. I say maximum height because the top of the leaf is rough and irregular (perhaps broken in antiquity), and its height thus varies between 3 feet 10 inches and 4 feet 3 inches (and was perhaps originally higher still). Its thickness varies, too, in that its vertical edges bear protruding ridges, 1 inch thick, on its northern face.

Also on the northern face of the granite leaf, on its upper section, we find an unusual feature that is generally described as 'the raised boss'. It is a chiselled protrusion, shaped like a protractor, 4 inches high and 5 inches wide, with a depth that varies from one inch at its horizontal bottom to nothing at all at its arched top. It is positioned approximately at eye level, as one stands in the space at the Antechamber's northern end, but, curiously, it is offset by an inch from the centre of the block.

Before leaving the Antechamber, mention must be made of the very odd fact that this predominantly granite room is laced with limestone blocks. At the entrance, for example, part of the floor is limestone; there are then eight limestone blocks in the side walls at the northern end, one limestone block in the top south-east corner, and a protruding edge of a limestone block at the top of the south wall.[65] Was this merely careless work by the builders, as Petrie surmised, or was it done deliberately, perhaps for some obscure symbolic reason?[66] It is all highly strange. But then again, the Antechamber does seem to be the very personification of anomaly.

Continuing past the Antechamber, we stoop to enter the second section of the King's Chamber Passage, noting the ancient damage to its mouth at the bottom of the grooved wall (this has been filled in by a modern repair). After a distance of 8 feet 5 inches, this passage debouches into the north-east corner of the King's Chamber.

The King's Chamber is the highest known chamber of the Pyramid (at the time of writing), and, perhaps significantly, straddles the monument's central north-south axis. This impressive chamber is in a class of its own, both as regards this pyramid and all other Egyptian pyramids.

As one enters the King's Chamber, one is immediately struck by the

Figure 34.
THE AUTHOR IN THE KING'S CHAMBER.

elegant simplicity of its design and its ability to resonate in harmony with every transient sound, be it a murmur or a footstep. The key to these aesthetic qualities is the builder's use of granite for the walls, floor, and ceiling, and the dimensions of the room, which follow a mathematical pattern incorporating pi (π).[67] For the record, the chamber's dimensions are 34 feet 4 inches east-west and 17 feet 2 inches north-south, with a height of 19 feet 1 inch; and it comprises nine roof stones, twenty-one floor stones, and a hundred and one wall stones.[68] These stones are, for the most part, fitted together precisely, but several joints have opened up and all of the roof beams have cracked, these joints and cracks being daubed with cement, apparently applied in ancient times.[69] The structural damage, which extends also into the King's Chamber Passage and the Antechamber, is generally attributed to an earthquake of exceptional force.

The floor of the King's Chamber is unusual in that it has been fitted between the walls and thus forms an independent structure, standing a full 5 inches above the baseline of the walls. Acoustical analysis of the floor suggests that the stones may be underlaid by corrugated rather than solid masonry.[70] A rough excavation in the floor in the north-west corner goes down to a depth of 30 feet and is attributed to the Arab explorer al-Mamun (the floor here was repaired in 1999).

The roof of the King's Chamber is particularly remarkable, consisting

Figure 35.
PLAN OF THE KING'S CHAMBER.

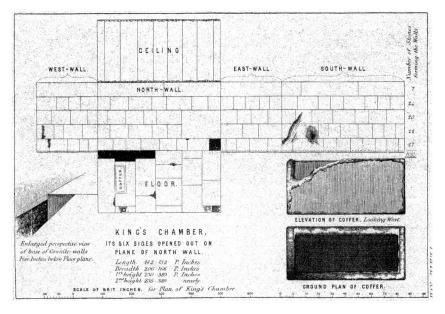

of nine monolithic beams which traverse the room from north to south. Not only is this design unique in the history of pyramid building, but the size and weight of the roof beams is phenomenal: each measures about 27 feet long (they extend beyond the walls on which they rest) and the average width is about 4 feet 8 inches. According to the latest estimates, the beams weigh in the region of 25 to 45 tons each, making a total roof weight of more than 300 tons. In no other pyramid did the builders ever span such a large space with such immense stone beams. We will return to this roof in a short while, as it has a very interesting superstructure.

Inside the King's Chamber, resting upon the floor in the middle of the room, we find a lidless granite box, with external measurements of 7 feet 6 inches long, 3 feet 3 inches wide and 3 feet 5 inches deep. This box or coffer, often referred to prejudicially as a sarcophagus, is made from the same red granite as the chamber, but has taken on a chocolate hue supposedly as a result of 'the accumulated grime of thousands of years'.[71] It is devoid of decorative features or inscriptions, and its design is noticeably different from other Old Kingdom sarcophagi, but it does bear a passing resemblance to the granite box in the Pyramid of Khafre at Giza. The box is positioned on the Pyramid's central north-south axis,[72] and is famous for its resonance when struck.

The interior of the granite box has the following dimensions: 6 feet 6 inches long, 2 feet 3 inches wide, and 2 feet 10 inches deep. In contrast to the exterior, which was left 'in the rough', the interior was cut and polished with great precision, such that the internal volume of the box stands to its external volume in the exact ratio 1:2.[73]

Although the granite box is lidless today, there is evidence that it was once fitted with a lid. This evidence consists of faint traces of grooves, cut inside the upper edges, and a series of three almost imperceptible circles, each the size of a coin, spaced equidistantly along the top of one of its long edges. These circular marks are, in fact, holes in which broken granite bolts are tightly imbedded. Apparently, the lid was slid into the box sideways, and cemented into the grooves, whereupon the bolts were dropped into place and sealed with a hot resinous glue.[74] The thickness of the lid is estimated to have been 10-12 inches and its weight would have been around 2.25 tons. The total weight of the box, including the lid, is estimated at 6 tons.

A rough breakage in one of the box's upper corners testifies to the fact that the lid was removed forcibly by intruders in antiquity, probably at the time when the Pyramid was first breached (perhaps during the period of chaos at the end of the Old Kingdom).[75] Unfortunately, there is no reliable evidence as to what, if anything, the box contained. The lid, it

Figure 36.
FITTING THE LID ONTO THE GRANITE BOX.

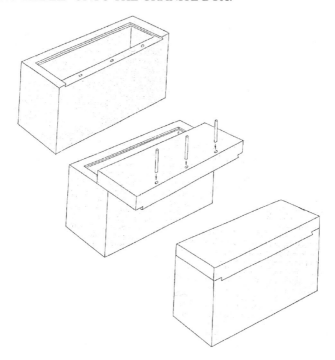

would seem, was removed from the monument for use elsewhere.

The King's Chamber contains one other noteworthy feature: a pair of small shafts cut into the north wall and south wall, respectively, at the height of the entrance passage, i.e. 3 feet 8 inches. Oddly, these shafts are not located in the centre of the chamber, nor on the Pyramid's central north-south axis, but are offset to the east at a distance of 9 feet or so from the east wall. Unlike the shafts in the Queen's Chamber, these were not concealed, nor terminated in the body of the Pyramid. Rather, they were cut through to the outside of the monument, and in theory allowed a free passage of air thence into the chamber.[76] In other respects, too, the shafts of the King's Chamber differ noticeably from those of the Queen's Chamber.

Each of the King's Chamber shafts must be described separately.

To begin with the northern shaft, it begins with a height of 5.5 inches and a width of 8.25 inches and heads horizontally into the wall for a distance of 8 feet 7 inches. Then, at the second block, it turns upwards at an angle of 19° 30′ and simultaneously bends to the north-west, whilst rising in height to about 8.5 inches. From blocks 3 to 5, the shaft changes its angle three times in quick succession, from 19° 30′ to 39°, then to 36°

30′, and then to 34°, whilst also changing its course twice, from north-west to north, and then to north-east. Then, from block 6 onwards, the angle and orientation become more or less constant, 32° 36′ northwards, with the height varying between 8 and 9 inches. Even then, however, the orientation is altered slightly at the beginning of block 20, whilst from block 26 to 32 there is a reduction in angle from 32° 36′ to an average of 31° 12′.[77] Beyond this point, the shaft has been completely destroyed by vandalism, but it is estimated that it would have debouched at the 102nd course of masonry in the Pyramid's northern face, in line with the central north-south axis.[78] The total length of the northern shaft would originally have been about 235 feet.[79]

Turning to the southern shaft, its first section has a peculiar dome shape, which narrows as it heads horizontally into the wall for a distance of 5 feet 8 inches. In the chamber itself, the aperture measures 2 feet 4 inches in height and 1 foot 6 inches in width (it is nowadays fitted with an electric fan to reduce the humidity in the chamber),[80] but after a few feet this narrows to a dome that is 1 foot 6 inches in height and 1 foot in width, before it narrows again to a dome of dimensions 12 by 8 inches.[81] At block 2, the shaft turns upwards at a steep angle of 39° 12′, and bends simultaneously to the south-west, taking on an oval shape. Then, at block 3, the shaft inclines more steeply at 50° 32′, and bends still further to the south-west, taking on a rectangular shape, still of dimensions 12 by 8

Figure 37.
APERTURE OF THE NORTHERN SHAFT IN THE KING'S CHAMBER.

inches. At block 5, the shaft reduces its angle to 45° and heads true south, its height now varying between 8 and 9 inches, but its width constant at 8 inches. It maintains this angle and cross-section all the way to the outside of the Pyramid, but turns slightly to the south-east at block 18.[82] Beyond block 25, the original stones are missing, but it is estimated that the shaft would have debouched at the 101st course of masonry in the Pyramid's northern face, in line with the central north-south axis.[83] The total length of the southern shaft would originally have been about 174 feet.[84]

A curious discovery pertaining to the southern shaft was made in 1837 by Howard Vyse. In an attempt to clear debris from the outer mouth of the shaft, he blasted apart some core blocks, using gunpowder, and found a fragment of an iron plate, apparently dislodged from the masonry.[85] The suggestion has been made that this iron plate once functioned as a cover, or gate, for the shaft.[86] However, although the shafts would have needed covers to prevent the ingress of birds, bats, insects, and rainwater, this particular iron plate was found too deeply imbedded in the masonry, and is thus unlikely to have formed part of a cover. Therefore, whilst there is little doubt that the iron plate was contemporary with the construction of the Pyramid, its exact position and purpose (if any) in the southern shaft remain a mystery.[87]

All in all, it is evident that the architect of the Pyramid was obsessed with these shafts and particularly with the idea that they should exit at the same height on the monument's central north-south axis. Yet, in no other pyramid do we find anything like these shafts. The question, then, of "why here and here alone" is clearly a question of supreme importance to our understanding of the Pyramid.

This completes our tour of the King's Chamber. However, it remains to describe the astonishing and complex superstructure that lies above its roof.

In 1765, the English explorer Nathaniel Davison, perhaps following a rumour that was circulating at the time, investigated a curious echo that came from the height of the Grand Gallery above the Great Step.[88] Upon climbing a ladder, he discovered a small tunnel, about 2 feet square, that led into the Gallery's east wall at its southernmost edge, just below the roof. Braving the bat dung that partially blocked the tunnel, he followed its path, which turned immediately south into a straight section of about 24 feet, and then turned back to the west to debouch into a hollow and empty space, directly above the roof of the King's Chamber. This hollow space was the first of the so-called 'construction chambers' or 'relieving chambers', and thenceforth became known as Davison's Chamber, after its discoverer.

In 1837, Colonel Richard W. Howard Vyse discovered four further construction chambers above Davison's Chamber, which he christened Wellington's Chamber, Nelson's Chamber, Arbuthnot's Chamber and Campbell's Chamber respectively. In these chambers, there is found the only known examples of writing in the Pyramid – graffiti by the work gangs which refers to the divine names Hor-Medjedu, Khnum-Khuf, and Khufu (the last two names encircled in a cartouche). The significance of these inscriptions lies beyond the scope of this book.

It is important to realise that the five 'construction chambers' are not really chambers per se, but rather hollows formed by the arrangement of the superstructure. It is this superstructure, rather than the hollows, which must now be described.

The superstructure of the King's Chamber is perhaps best described as a series of five 'raised roofs', the first four being flat granite structures, virtually identical to the roof of the King's Chamber, and the fifth being a gabled limestone structure. Whilst the roof of the King's Chamber is

Figure 38.
THE KING'S CHAMBER AND ITS SUPERSTRUCTURE, LOOKING WEST.

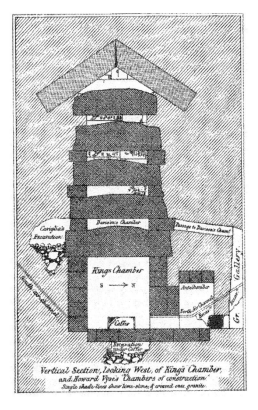

Vertical Section, looking West, of King's Chamber, and Howard Vyse's Chambers of construction. Single shade-lines show lime-stone, & crossed ones granite.

Figure 39.
THE KING'S CHAMBER AND ITS SUPERSTRUCTURE, LOOKING
NORTH.

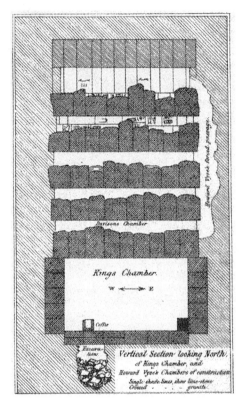

constructed of nine granite beams, the first raised roof comprises eight
beams, the next two roofs comprise nine beams each, and the next roof
eight beams, giving a grand total of forty-three granite beams, all of them
oriented north-south. These raised roofs are, in the first three cases,
separated by walls of granite blocks to the south and the north, but the
fourth roof, exceptionally, is supported there by walls of limestone.
Above these flat granite roofs, the gabled roof comprises twenty-four
cantilevered beams made of limestone, again oriented north-south. This
uppermost roof was apparently designed to distribute the superincumbent
weight to the surrounding limestone and to minimise the load borne by
the multiple granite roofs.[89]

This entire superstructure, standing 49 feet high (measured from the
roof of the chamber to the apex of the gabled roof), was fitted between
two huge limestone walls to the east and the west, which did not form
part of the superstructure per se. As Petrie has observed:

Figure 40.
THE SO-CALLED 'RELIEVING CHAMBERS' IN THE KING'S CHAMBER
SUPERSTRUCTURE (THE LOWERMOST CHAMBER IS NOT SHOWN).

> On the east and west are two immense limestone walls wholly outside of, and independent of, all the granite floors and supporting blocks. Between these great walls all the chambers stand, unbonded, and capable of yielding freely to settlement.[90]

Such is the general design of the superstructure, but the granite roofs are worthy of some additional comment.

Firstly, it is to be noted that the raised roofs contain the largest and heaviest known stones in the Pyramid. Whilst the length and width of the granite beams is equivalent to those in the roof of the King's Chamber, some are considerably thicker, such that the thickest – the central beam in the third raised roof – has been estimated to weigh as much as 70 tons.[91] It is astonishing that such huge megaliths have been used at this height in the monument.

Secondly, the appearance of the granite beams, both in the roof of the King's Chamber and in the four raised roofs, is unusual to say the least. Whilst the beams are perfectly flat on their undersides, having been 'rough dressed' (but not polished), their upper surfaces are extremely rough and uneven in thickness. Why would the builders have dressed the undersides of these beams but not their upper surfaces? It is a mystery.[92] Another puzzling observation is that the beams in some cases bear odd features on their upper surfaces. In the third raised roof, for example, three of the beams contain deep grooves that run breadthwise across their tops, whilst in the fourth raised roof, four of the seven beams have had deep bowls, or basins, cut into them at their ends. It is, as Lepre has put it, 'a strange phenomenon indeed'.[93]

This entire superstructure is a unique work of architecture which is not to be found in any other pyramid. The pyramid expert Mark Lehner has justifiably called it 'an innovative and ingenious arrangement, for which there are few parallels and no precedent'.[94]

This completes our description of the Pyramid's upper parts. However, it remains to describe the Well Shaft that connects the monument's upper passage system to its lower passage system.

The Well Shaft and Grotto

The Well Shaft is a rough-cut passage, approximately 28 inches square throughout, that connects the Descending Passage to the Grand Gallery via a number of oblique and vertical sections. We will begin at the Well Shaft's lower aperture and work our way up to its upper aperture.

The entrance to the Well Shaft is a rough-hewn tunnel in the west wall of the Descending Passage, lying about 22 feet up from the bottom of its

Figure 41.
THE WELL SHAFT.

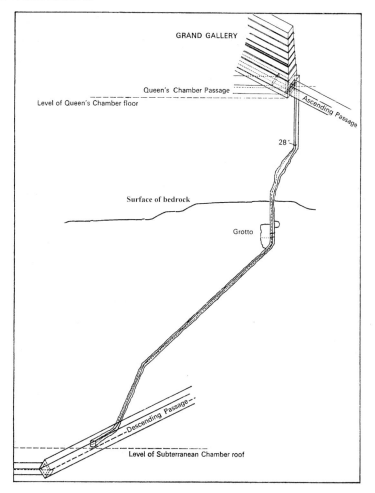

sloping section. It is surmised that this entrance was at one time blocked by a removable plate of stone, but this blocking stone has long been lost.

Initially, the Well Shaft heads west for about 10 feet; then, it turns sharply upwards and heads northwards for a distance of about 30 feet. At this point, the gradient reduces, but the shaft carries on northwards for a straight run of about 100 feet. Throughout this total length of 140 feet, the shaft is cut through the bedrock beneath the Pyramid.

The Well Shaft then enters a perpendicular section, 13 feet high, in which, for the first time, we find ourselves surrounded by regular blocks of limestone. A few feet up, in the south wall of this section, an aperture 28 inches square leads into a low cavern of irregular shape that lies just below ground level in the rocky outcrop on which the Pyramid was built. This small cavern, the so-called Grotto, contains nothing of significance except for a stray granite block measuring 42 by 25 by 20 inches. The room itself will be described further in chapter four.

Continuing up the perpendicular section of the Well Shaft, we reach the lowermost layer of the Pyramid's masonry, which was originally laid over the top of the shaft. Here, a rough tunnel has been hacked through this masonry, and it takes us upwards and northwards, obliquely and steeply, for a further distance of about 35 feet, at which point it enters another built, perpendicular section of the Well Shaft.

This final section of the Well Shaft rises for 25 feet and then takes a sideways turn to run eastwards for about 7 feet to a point directly below the north-west bottom corner of the Grand Gallery. Here, one is able to climb up out of the Well Shaft into the Gallery through an aperture about 2 feet 4 inches square that was once filled by a ramp stone. The said ramp stone is now missing but the surrounding stones bear witness to its forcible removal.

Chapter Two Summary

• The uniqueness of the Great Pyramid lies not so much in its size, but in its unprecedented precision of construction and highly unusual interior architecture.

• In its unique precision of construction, the Pyramid may be interpreted as a representation *par excellence* of the Great God, the creator of the Universe, and a testament to the perfection of his handiwork. Like the creator-god, the Pyramid would endure for eternity.

• The Pyramid is built to a unique architectural plan, involving a series of chambers placed high in its superstructure. Many of its features are unique and therefore difficult to interpret.

CHAPTER THREE

NOTHING BUT A TOMB?

Theory must be supported by fact or lose credibility. Everyone has at some time formulated an idea, or a host of ideas, regarding a particular subject; but can those ideas be supported by the evidence?
(J.P. Lepre, *The Egyptian Pyramids*, 1990)

Since the very beginning of Egyptology in the 1820s, there has been widespread agreement on the idea that the pyramids were built as tombs for the kings, each major pyramid protecting for eternity the mummy of the pharaoh, enshrined in its coffin within the tomb chamber. The Great Pyramid, despite its complex design and precision of build, has never been treated as an exception to this basic rule, at least by mainstream Egyptology. In response to those alternative writers who suggested that the Pyramid might be something more than a tomb, or something other than a tomb, the Egyptologist E.A. Wallis Budge wrote:

> The present writer is convinced that the Great Pyramid was built not to serve as an astronomical instrument or as a standard of measurements for the world, but as *a tomb* and as *nothing but a tomb*.[1] (original emphasis)

Why do Egyptologists feel so confident that the Pyramid can be nothing but a tomb? The simple answer is to be found in the King's Chamber – the highest known chamber in the monument – where a granite box of the right size and shape to contain a human body has been installed in a grandiose and well-protected environment.

An excellent illustration of how this logic goes is found in J.P. Lepre's book *The Egyptian Pyramids*. Here, Lepre, to his credit, considered the possibility that the granite box might be a 'symbol of a sort' and that the Pyramid might actually have been a cenotaph, Khufu's body having been

Figure 42.
THE KING'S CHAMBER SARCOPHAGUS.
The broken granite box encapsulates the mystery of the Pyramid. Did it really
contain the body of the king?

buried elsewhere, perhaps in the city of Abydos, 250 miles to the south.[2]
However, having mused on this idea, Lepre then set down a detailed
rationale for the burial of Khufu in the King's Chamber of the Great
Pyramid at Giza. Firstly, he observed that the King's Chamber, built of
granite and majestic in design, was the crowning achievement of the
builders, 'which for all practical purposes would qualify to be a chamber
fit for the burial of a king.'[3] Next, he observed that the granite box was
the ideal size to house 'three large wooden coffins, with one set into the
other'.[4] Then, he outlined the great lengths to which the builders had
gone to seal the granite box and protect the King's Chamber, and asked:
'What could have been of such great value in ancient Egypt?'. To this
vital question, he then furnished the answer:

> Two things come to mind: a great treasure, and a great pharaoh's
> remains. The former was protected inside the sealed burial chamber,
> and the latter inside the sealed sarcophagus.[5]

Finally, to clinch his case, Lepre observed that the coffer – originally a
hermetically-sealed unit – had had one of its corners smashed and its lid
removed, this proving that it had once contained something of immense
value:

> Once a sizeable hole was made in the corner of the sarcophagus,

thieves could better view its contents. If the sarcophagus was empty, then the intruders would have left us a sarcophagus that, despite a gaping hole in one of its top corners, would still have had its lid relatively intact... But because the lid was removed – at great additional cost – we can only assume that when the tomb robbers looked through the gaping hole they had made, they saw the outer wooden coffin of Khufu with the gold mask...[6]

In this way, Lepre arrived at his unavoidable conclusion:

Is it not logical, in light of this evidence, to conclude that Khufu was in fact buried in his pyramid, and that his body and treasure were stolen...?[7]

This, he felt sure, was 'a reasonable conclusion', even though it fell short of being an absolute proof.[8]

But this theory, which had been reached by numerous earlier pyramid experts before Lepre, begged a crucial question. If the King's Chamber had been the burial chamber, then what had been the intent behind the other chambers in the Pyramid – the Subterranean Chamber, the Queen's Chamber, and the Grand Gallery?

The initial explanation, derived in the early days of Egyptology, ran as follows. Khufu, or Cheops as he was known to the Greek historians, had at first decided to be buried underground, to which end the Descending Passage had been dug and the Subterranean Chamber excavated from the bedrock. But then the king had changed his mind, perhaps on the view that this arrangement was vulnerable to tomb robbers.[9] Accordingly, he had ordered his architects to amend their plans and build the Ascending Passage – a unique development at the time – and above it, hidden in the heart of the monument, a new burial chamber, which we know today as the Queen's Chamber. But even then, the king was not satisfied with the security arrangements. Once again, he had instructed his architects to revise their drawings. This time, they should build a magnificent sloping hallway – the Grand Gallery – and beyond it, still higher in the Pyramid, a new chamber made of granite and protected by a portcullis in the same material. This chamber – which we know today as the King's Chamber – had then met with the king's satisfaction; and thus he came to be buried in the uppermost of three chambers, all of which had been intended as tomb chambers, whilst the Gallery provided a glorious passageway to the king's tomb of choice.

In favour of this 'change of mind' theory (or 'evolutionary' theory, as it is sometimes called), Egyptologists long ago honed the argument that the Subterranean Chamber and the Queen's Chamber had been left in an

Figure 43.
THE GREAT PYRAMID, VERTICAL SECTION, LOOKING WEST.

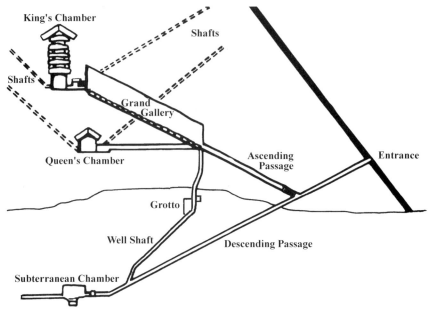

unfinished state, and furthermore alighted on the fact that the walls of the Ascending Passage in its lower part had been constructed of horizontally-laid blocks, in contrast to its upper part which had been constructed of blocks laid in line with the incline of the passage.[10] This latter point, it was claimed, proved that the Ascending Passage had been driven through the existing masonry as a constructional afterthought, when the king first changed his mind about the burial chamber.

This was the theory adopted wholeheartedly by Egyptologists during the 19th and 20th centuries. And yet, eventually, a careful analysis of the evidence turned up a number of serious objections.

Crucially, the theory that the Ascending Passage represented a change of plan was shown to be quite incorrect. In fact, the passage had been tapered towards the bottom to provide a tight fit for the granite plugs, and half-girdle stones had been fitted there to lend the passage additional strength.[11] It was therefore evident that the Ascending Passage had not been driven through the masonry as an afterthought, but rather had been anticipated from the very beginning.[12] Significantly, Vito Maragioglio and Celeste Rinaldi maintained that the blocks in the lower part of the Ascending Passage had been laid horizontally in order to create a strong bulwark at the junction with the Descending Passage, thus anchoring the Ascending Passage in the Pyramid's substructure.[13]

Furthermore, by virtue of the fact that the Ascending Passage had been designed from the beginning to hold granite plugs, it was evident that the Grand Gallery too must have been part of this original design, at least to an extent, for a slipway would have been required for the lowering of the plugs.[14] This view is further supported by the so-called 'trial passages' that were cut into the bedrock 300 feet to the east of the Pyramid, these anticipating the links between the Descending Passage, the Ascending Passage and the Grand Gallery, as well as making provision for the passageway to the Queen's Chamber.[15]

Finally, it has been demonstrated conclusively that the Grand Gallery, Queen's Chamber and King's Chamber all belonged to a unified design in which geometry dictated the architectural arrangements. This point has been explained well by William Flinders Petrie, although his proof is somewhat too complicated to be recited here.[16]

Such is the evidence and logic that has persuaded most Egyptologists to abandon the change of mind theory and recognise the existence of a unified design – a harmonised architectural plan that was used from the beginning. In recent years, confident statements to this effect have begun to appear from pyramid authorities such as Zahi Hawass, Mark Lehner, Alberto Siliotti and Rainer Stadelmann, these being summarised in the panel overleaf.[17]

This is an important development, since it has necessitated a partial revision of Egyptology's ideas concerning the significance of the various chambers. If the lower chambers were not abandoned tomb chambers, then what were they, and why were they required? How is the Pyramid to be understood as a unified design?

The general consensus is as follows.

The Subterranean Chamber, it is believed, may have been intended as a decoy tomb chamber, the aim being to persuade tomb robbers that the Pyramid had already been robbed. Its rough and 'unfinished' design is nowadays viewed as symbolic of the underworld, which was extremely important both in the myth of creation and in the cult of the afterlife. The room might thus have served some ritualistic, chthonian function for the departed king, but it was *not* his burial chamber.

The Queen's Chamber, it is widely believed, was built as a serdab for the king's *ka*-statue, i.e. the statue that was possessed of the king's spirit or life force.

The Grand Gallery, it is assumed, was a glorious passageway to the tomb chamber, functioning also as a slipway for the granite plugs that would block the mouth of the access passage below.

And the King's Chamber, it is held, was the king's final resting place

The Unity of the Great Pyramid's Design

Borchardt saw the three different chambers as an indication of two changes in planning the location of the king's burial place. However, that line of thinking has been altered by later observations that tend to connect a religious motivation to the structural anomalies of the burial chambers inside the Great Pyramid.

(Zahi Hawass, An Update to *The Pyramids and Temples of Gizeh*, 1990)

Many Egyptologists have long accepted Borchardt's suggestion that the pyramid's three chambers represent two changes in plan... Several clues, however, combine to make it probable that all three chambers and the entire passage system were planned together from the outset... that the entire inner complex was conceived and built according to a unified plan. Old Kingdom pyramids frequently have three chambers. Here, the two lower rooms were probably planned from the outset to cater for different aspects of the king's spiritual welfare.

(Mark Lehner, *The Complete Pyramids*, 1997)

The three vertically aligned chambers (the underground chamber, the Queen's Chamber and the King's Chamber) do not appear to be related to changes in design, which have never been proven, but rather serve a ritual purpose.

(Alberto Siliotti, *The Pyramids*, 1997)

To the present day, scholars have tried in a broadly positive spirit to attribute the pyramid's three chambers to three successive changes in the design. But it does not do justice to the architects who designed and executed this unique building so perfectly to suggest that, in the essential element of the pyramid's construction, that is the system of tomb chambers, they had proceeded without concept or design.

Against this view is a conclusive argument in that the exterior construction and the layout of the chamber system work in perfect accord, and that neither inside nor out is there any suggestion of a change in plan.

(Rainer Stadelmann in *Egypt: The World of the Pharaohs*, 1998)

– the Pyramid's raison d'etre. Hence the superior finish of the chamber (in granite), its height in the monument, and the inclusion of the granite sarcophagus.

This, then, is the unified design theory as it is currently envisaged, although, in fairness to the minority view, it must be said that certain 'old school' Egyptologists have found it difficult to jettison the old change of mind theory. Thus, in the final edition of *The Pyramids of Egypt* (1993), the late I.E.S. Edwards held to the view that the Subterranean Chamber had been abandoned for the simple reason that Khufu had set his heart on a granite sarcophagus and the passageway to the chamber could not be enlarged to receive it; and further that the said sarcophagus had then been delivered late to the site, by which time the builders had completed the Queen's Chamber and begun a new tomb chamber, the King's Chamber, to accommodate the all-important sarcophagus when it finally turned up.[18] Whilst few Egyptologists today would actually support this fantastic scenario, it does illustrate the kind of convoluted thinking that dominated the Great Pyramid debate for much of the 20th century.

In any event, whichever approach is taken – the evolutionary theory or the unified design theory – there is universal agreement on the point that the King's Chamber was the eventual burial chamber, and that Khufu's body was buried in the sarcophagus in that room, whence it was stolen by tomb robbers during antiquity. This idea, indeed, is widely lent the status of a fact rather than a theory.[19]

And yet the harsh truth is that no trace of Khufu's mummy has ever been found in the Pyramid, no direct evidence exists of a human burial in the King's Chamber, and no reliable record has ever been unearthed of Khufu having being buried in, or removed from, either the sarcophagus or the Pyramid. And furthermore, as explained in chapter one, the idea of the king being buried at a great height in the Pyramid's superstructure goes against a fundamental principle of Egyptian religion which required that the mummy be buried at ground level or below ('the body to earth, the spirit to the sky'). It therefore follows, incontrovertibly, that Khufu's burial in this room is a theory, not a fact, and a rather dubious theory to boot. And this theory, like any other in Egyptology, should be regarded with a healthy dose of scepticism and subjected to tests, including the ultimate test of good common sense.

In this chapter, then, I shall reconstruct the royal burial scenario, as proposed by Egyptology, and examine its plausibility, both in a logistical and a conceptual framework. Just how strong is the case for the burial of the king in the King's Chamber?

The Orthodox Burial Scenario

According to the orthodox theory, the king's mummy was protected by no less than five levels of security:

1 The sealing of the granite sarcophagus with a 2.25-ton lid.

2 The blocking of the King's Chamber Passage by a triple granite portcullis, located in the Antechamber.

3 The blocking of the Ascending Passage by three granite plugs.

4 The concealment of the mouth of the Ascending Passage by the so-called 'prism stone'.

5 The concealment of the Pyramid's entrance in its northern face by a limestone slab, or perhaps a pivoting door.

In addition, it is possible that the Subterranean Chamber functioned as a decoy burial chamber, to distract tomb robbers from seeking any further passages and chambers in the Pyramid.

In order for this scheme to work, the various protection devices had to be prepared in an open position and be movable, such that they could be closed immediately after the burial procedure. In reverse order, then, the practical arrangements would have been as follows.

Firstly, the granite sarcophagus would have been placed inside the King's Chamber but with its lid in an open position. It is to be surmised that the lid of the box, 10-12 inches thick and weighing 2.25 tons, was placed with one of its long edges resting upon the box and the other supported by props, allowing it to be slid into position after the wooden coffin (or coffins) containing the mummy had been placed inside. Such a procedure would have been necessary owing to the extreme difficulty of manoeuvring the heavy lid in the confines of the chamber. Incidentally, it is known for certain that the granite box was set in place at the time of the Pyramid's construction (i.e. before the King's Chamber was roofed), because the size of the box exceeds the width of the Ascending Passage by half an inch.[20]

Secondly, the granite portcullis in the Antechamber would have been installed with its blocks in an open, i.e. raised, position. It is presumed that the blocks were held in the upper part of the Antechamber by means of ropes, so that the funeral cortege could pass unhindered through the passage into the King's Chamber.

Thirdly, the three granite plugs would have been positioned in the Grand Gallery, ready for their release into the Ascending Passage after the funeral. It is supposed that these plugs were placed upon the smooth central floor, where they were held in check by wooden wedges or struts.

Fourthly, the prism stone would have been kept to one side, allowing unhindered passage of the cortege up through the Ascending Passage. This prism stone was a large block, which completely filled the mouth of the passage, whilst at the same time providing part of the ceiling of the Descending Passage (see figure 53 later in this chapter). It was possibly held back outside the Pyramid and introduced following the funeral, at which time it would have been fitted into the aperture in the passage ceiling. However, it may have been built into the passage to pivot like a door between open and closed positions.

Fifthly, and finally, the main entrance to the Pyramid would have been opened in preparation for the funeral, perhaps by removing a limestone slab, or perhaps by pushing on a pivoting door. For this task to have been performed some 60 feet above the base of the Pyramid, it would have been necessary for a wooden ladder or platform (a kind of tower) to be constructed against the monument's face.[21]

The scene is now set for the funeral of the king, the logistics of which are our primary concern.

The cortege – presumably comprising the absolute minimum number of people, for security reasons – would have set off towards the Pyramid,

Figure 44.
POSSIBLE DESIGNS FOR A PIVOTING MAIN ENTRANCE DOOR.
ABOVE BY W.M.F. PETRIE, BELOW BY J.P. LEPRE.

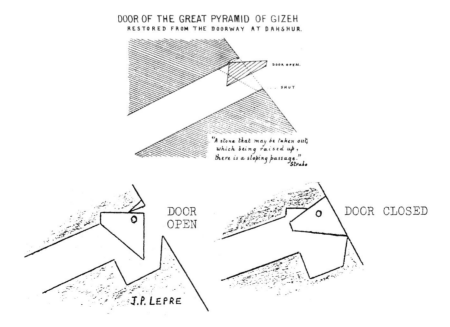

bearing the king's mummy in a wooden coffin, or possibly in a nest of up to three coffins. For convenience, I shall henceforth speak of 'the king' in referring to the wooden coffin, or coffins, and the mummified body within.

Arriving at the Pyramid, the first requirement was to lift the king up to the entrance, some 60 feet above ground level, and then lower him into the Descending Passage. A pivoting door design might well have made this procedure impossible (see figure 44), in which case we must assume access via a removable limestone slab.

Next, the king would have been lowered 95 feet down the Descending Passage as far as its junction with the Ascending Passage, whereupon he would have been manoeuvred through the aperture in the passage ceiling. Such a task would not have been easy in view of the passage's smooth, slippery floor and its 26° 34′ incline (it did not benefit from the steps and hand rails with which it is fitted today), and it is to be surmised that the coffin was controlled by ropes held by men who stood on the temporary platform outside.

At this stage, two men would have climbed ahead of the party up the Ascending Passage into the Grand Gallery, and ropes would have been fastened to the coffin once again, this time to facilitate its lifting into the Pyramid's upper reaches. The rest of the cortege would have followed behind the coffin in the cramped ascent of 129 feet, before emerging into the Gallery.

Arriving in the Grand Gallery, the funeral procession would have been confronted by a central floor, measuring 3 feet 5 inches in width, and two side ramps, each measuring 20.5 inches in width, this design extending upwards for a distance of 153 feet at an angle of 26° 2′. We may presume that the central floor was chosen for the ascent. However, this route did contain an obstacle in the form of the three granite plugs. At some point, the cortege would have been forced to mount these plugs and clamber over them for a distance of 15 feet, before climbing back down to the central floor. Presumably, two men stood at the top of the Gallery upon the Great Step, where they pulled upon ropes to control the ascent of the coffin.

At the Great Step, it is to be surmised, the torch-bearers took up their stations (for it must be remembered that the interior of the Pyramid was almost totally dark), whilst the rest of the cortege passed through one low passage, then through the Antechamber beneath the raised portcullis blocks, and then through another low passage into the King's Chamber. There, the high priest and the coffin-bearers would probably have been greeted by cool, fresh air, which flowed into the room via its two tiny 'airshafts'. Amidst the flickering light and semi-darkness, the king was then sealed inside the granite sarcophagus. Firstly, the men would have pushed the 2.25-ton lid sideways into the sarcophagus, fixing it into its precut grooves by means of a liquid cement. And secondly, they would have dropped three bolts into one of the lid's long edges, and used a hot resinous glue to create an unbreakable hermetic seal.

Next, the coffin-bearers would have returned to the main entrance to collect the funerary furniture, which was intended for the king's use in the afterlife. Once again, ropes would have been used to lower the items down the Descending Passage, and then haul them up through the 129 feet of the Ascending Passage and the 153 feet of the Grand Gallery as far as the passage to the King's Chamber. In order that the furniture be conveyed through the narrow passages, many of the pieces would have to have been dismantled.

This task having been completed, the priest would have conducted the rituals and magic spells that transformed the deceased king into a spirit (*akh*) and despatched him to the sky. At the climax of this ceremony, the king's soul is thought to have ascended to the sky through the airshafts, to the circumpolar stars via the northern shaft and to the constellation of Orion via the southern shaft (this supposedly being the main purpose of the shafts, a theory to which we will return in due course).

The King's Chamber would then have been vacated and sealed by the lowering of the granite portcullis blocks in the Antechamber.

The mouth of the Ascending Passage would then have been sealed by means of the granite plugs that had been stored in the Grand Gallery. The great difficulty of this job required that the three stones, each weighing approximately six tons, be lowered and manoeuvred into position by men who laboured from above, these men thus becoming trapped inside the Pyramid. According to Egyptologists, these workmen escaped by means of the Well Shaft that connected the Gallery to the Descending Passage.

Next, the mouth of the Ascending Passage, directly beneath the granite plugs, would have been sealed and camouflaged by means of the prism stone. According to the orthodox theory, this multi-faced stone, probably weighing more than a ton, was lifted and inserted into the mouth of the passage. However, it is more credible perhaps that the prism stone took the form of a built-in door that could be pivoted shut at the end of the proceedings.

Finally, the main entrance in the Pyramid's northern face would have been sealed by means of a thin limestone slab or a pivoting door, which was indistinguishable from the rest of the casing stones, and the wooden ladder and platform would have been removed and perhaps dismantled.

Thus the Great Pyramid became a hermetically-sealed structure, with the exception of the King's Chamber shafts, which were supposedly kept open to permit the king's soul (*ba*) to travel back and forth between the tomb and the 'other world'.

This, then, is the orthodox funeral scenario. But is it plausible? In the following pages, we shall consider a number of problems with it – some of a practical nature, others of a conceptual nature; some that have been well aired over the years, and others that have never had a proper hearing – which collectively cast substantial doubt on the theory that the King's Chamber was the tomb of the king.

The King's Chamber Airshafts

We begin with a conceptual issue, namely the purpose of the 'airshafts' in the King's Chamber. As mentioned in chapter two, these two shafts provided open passage to the exterior of the Pyramid and thus could have functioned as airshafts, unlike the two shafts in the Queen's Chamber which were terminated inside the Pyramid and blocked at their bottom ends. In this author's view, it is essential to steer clear of the assumption that these two pairs of shafts were of like kind, and instead appraise each pair of shafts on its own merits.

My first observation is that the King's Chamber airshafts are a unique feature among the Egyptian pyramids, and thus almost certainly require a special explanation.[22] Prima facie, this special explanation is likely to be found in the fact that the King's Chamber was positioned high up in the superstructure of the Pyramid – itself a unique phenomenon.

Originally, Egyptologists supposed that the King's Chamber shafts were ventilation channels, designed to supply air to the burial chamber in order to regulate its temperature. This climate control system, it must be stressed, would not have been for the benefit of the deceased king – there is absolutely no precedent for such an idea – but rather for the benefit of the funeral party, who required fresh air to breathe while they performed their practical tasks and magic rituals inside the chamber. A modern-day supporter of this ventilation theory is J.P. Lepre, who justified his view on two pertinent facts: (a) that the King's Chamber lies 350 feet distant from the air supply at its entrance – a much greater distance than is found in any other pyramid; and (b) that the King's Chamber is located at an unusual height which, in the absence of ventilation, would have resulted in a temperature 10 to 20° F higher than the typical subterranean burial chamber (owing to the fact that warm air rises).[23] In Lepre's opinion, then, the Pyramid's architect had good reason for constructing the shafts for ventilation purposes.

This ventilation theory, however, has long been abandoned by most Egyptologists, on the basis that it contains a fatal flaw. The problem with it is this: if ventilation was the objective, then why did the builders not construct the shafts horizontally from the chamber to the outside of the Pyramid? Why instead did they build the shafts obliquely, at significant additional trouble and cost? The problem was summarised by Alexander Badawy in 1964 as follows:

> To ventilate the burial chamber of Cheops, channels running horizontally at the level of the ceiling would have been more adequate than the inclined shafts that start at about one metre [3 feet 4 inches] from the floor, at the level of the lid of the sarcophagus. One should add to this inadequacy in the design all the constructional problems involved of the building of the two inclined shafts through all the courses, a process which could have been avoided by building them through one horizontal course.[24]

To press this point home, it is worthwhile quoting Rudolf Gantenbrink, the German engineer who has invested considerable time in examining the shafts' physical structure. In Gantenbrink's opinion, the construction of the shafts at precise sloping angles through the masonry involved an incredible amount of additional work:

> The shafts, despite their small dimensions, greatly complicated the construction and required massive static changes, endless additional work, time and energy. Any builder forced to penetrate vast horizontal layers with diagonal structures faces enormous challenges and headaches.[25]

Here, we have a serious, and perhaps fatal, objection to the ventilation theory. If air was required to be conveyed to the King's Chamber, then there was a much simpler way of fulfilling the remit. Unless we are to credit the architect of the Pyramid with a certain degree of stupidity – surely an unacceptable premise – then there must have been an ulterior motive behind his design of the shafts. And furthermore, notwithstanding this objection, it may be doubted whether it was even necessary at all to improve the environment of the King's Chamber for tasks and rituals that were brief and transitory in nature (unfortunately, we do not know how much flexibility was involved in the recital of the spells, nor how long a typical set of rituals would have taken).

All things considered, then, there are good reasons why the majority of pyramid experts do not generally subscribe to the ventilation shaft theory

(Lepre being the exception).

Instead, a consensus has formed around the view that the shafts of the King's Chamber had a religious purpose, connected with the despatch of the king's soul to the sky, the theory being that the soul ascended via the shafts to the northern and southern skies, and thereafter returned at will to its body in the tomb. This 'soul-shaft' theory was first suggested by the Belgian Egyptologist J. Capart in 1924 and the German Egyptologist G. Steindorff in 1929, but was fleshed out in much greater detail by the Americans Virginia Trimble (an astronomer) and Alexander Badawy (an Egyptologist-architect) in 1964.[26] Trimble and Badawy suggested that the northern shaft had been aligned with the circumpolar stars whilst the southern shaft had been aligned with the constellation of Orion, both c. 2600 BC when the Pyramid was supposedly built. This theory has since met with widespread approval, not just among pyramid experts such as I.E.S. Edwards and Mark Lehner, but also among independent thinkers, such as Ed Krupp, and alternative theorists, such as Robert Bauval (the latter's theory of the three Giza pyramids representing the three stars of Orion's belt complemented neatly the theory of the Pyramid's Orion star-shaft).[27]

An immediate objection to the soul-shaft theory is that the soul of the king, according to the rules of ancient Egyptian metaphysics, could pass through solid masonry; hence the lack of doors in early tombs and the presence of 'false doors' in Old Kingdom pyramid-temples.[28] The idea that hollowed-out shafts were somehow required for the king's ascent to the sky is therefore ridiculous, since the great magic of the soul rendered them unnecessary. Furthermore, it should be recalled that the King's Chamber shafts are unique, nothing like them having been found in any other Egyptian pyramid or tomb. So, why would Khufu alone, among all the kings of the pyramid age, have felt it necessary to build hollow shafts via which his soul might ascend to the heavens?

A possible rationale, according to the orthodox tomb theory, lies in Khufu's decision to raise the burial chamber from underground to high in the body of the pyramid, thus upsetting the traditional arrangement. In the customary pyramid design, the body would be buried in a chamber at ground level or below, and a passage leading down to this tomb chamber – a practical necessity for the burial – would function also as a passage of ascent to facilitate the flight of the king's soul from the underworld to the northern circumpolar stars.[29] But when Khufu raised the burial chamber into the superstructure of his pyramid, he lost the traditional use of the entrance passage, and for this reason, so the thinking goes, he ordered the northern airshaft to be constructed as a substitute. The concept of the soul-shaft in the Great Pyramid therefore originated from the fact that all pyramids required entrance passages for practical reasons, said passages being used for the ascent of the king's soul not as a matter of necessity, but rather because they happened to be there, oriented in the appropriate direction. As I.E.S. Edwards explained:

> The northern shaft was evidently a replica in miniature of the traditional downward-sloping entrance corridor. And so we see another example of an architectural element being reproduced out of its original context.[30]

In accordance with this line of thinking, Egyptologists refer to the King's Chamber shafts as 'mock corridors' or 'model passages', on the view that the soul, strictly speaking, did not have need of them.

All of this is plausible, but unfortunately it offers a rationale for the northern airshaft only, and fails to explain the presence of the southern shaft. How is that shaft to be explained according to the orthodox tomb theory? On the face of it, the southern shaft seems to throw a spanner in the works.[31]

And there is another problem too. Why would Khufu have needed to build a substitute passage, when his pyramid already contained the main passage (the Descending Passage) which his soul could have used for its ascent to the northern stars? Was it really beyond the soul's capability to descend from the King's Chamber to the Subterranean Chamber and then ascend to the skies through the main entrance? This point was made by J.P. Lepre in his argument against the theory of soul-shafts:

> If there were any association to be made between the pharaoh and the north pole star, that association could surely have been brought about through the use of the Great Pyramid's descending passageway. It would not have been necessary for that passage to have been directly connected with the burial chamber.[32]

If the soul-shaft theory is to be salvaged, then Lepre's argument must be swept aside, and two additional hypotheses must be invoked: firstly, that the southern shaft was oriented deliberately towards the constellation of Orion (as posited by Trimble and Badawy); and secondly, that the king's soul ascended to the northern and southern skies *directly* from the King's Chamber (as opposed to an ascent via the Subterranean Chamber and the Descending Passage).

As regards the hypothesis that the southern shaft was aimed at Orion, a good case can be made, despite the lack of any precedent or rationale for the idea. We will return to this point in a moment, where I will propose a slight modification to Trimble and Badawy's scenario.

However, as regards the hypothesis that the king's soul ascended to the northern and southern skies *directly* from the King's Chamber, there is a big problem. Now, the chief advocate of the 'direct ascent' theory is the German Egyptologist Rainer Stadelmann, who has argued with the full weight of his authority that the Pyramid Texts support the idea of the king's soul ascending directly to the sky, foregoing its perambulation through the underworld.[33] But unfortunately, this argument relies on an out-of-date interpretation of the Pyramid Texts by James Henry Breasted, and represents a fantasy and a distortion of what the Texts actually say.[34] The Texts, in fact, describe the burial of the king's body in the earth, or underworld, and the stirring of the king's soul there, whereupon the soul navigates through the chthonian region en route to the eastern horizon (a projection of the underworld), and emerges thence into the sky for the creation of the Universe. This entire journey, as I explained in chapter one, re-enacted the death and rebirth of the creator-god (the proto-earth), and as such was a fundamental and immutable scheme, which was not to be altered at the whim of any king or high priest. To suppose, as Stadelmann does, that Khufu's soul ascended *directly* to the northern and southern stars without passing first through the underworld goes against the very essence of the myth and its re-enactment. In other words, the Egyptians of the pyramid age had no concept whatsoever of a 'direct ascent' to the sky.

Where does this leave us? As noted earlier, the theory that the King's Chamber shafts were ventilation shafts suffers from a fatal flaw in the fact that they were built obliquely, not horizontally, greatly complicating the task of construction. Alternatively, the soul-shaft theory – that the soul ascended through the shafts to the circumpolar stars and Orion in the northern and southern skies respectively – offers a possible solution, but lacks a valid theoretical basis, for it was a fundamental concept that the king's soul should awaken in the underworld and pass thence to the sky, and this it could have done by descending from the King's Chamber and then ascending into the sky via the main entrance passage. Therefore, the existence of the northern shaft – and by implication the southern shaft too – is not explained by the premise of the king's burial in the King's Chamber.

There is a wider problem here, namely that Egyptologists lack a sound theoretical basis for the interpretation of the pyramid. According to the orthodox theory, the true pyramid (the smooth-sided pyramid) is a solar symbol, representing the pyramidal shape of the rays of the Sun, and Egyptian religion generally is regarded as a fully-fledged Sun cult from the time of the true pyramid age onwards. And yet, in this solar pyramid of Khufu, in what is supposed to be the burial chamber, the soul of the king is visualised as ascending not to the Sun but to the circumpolar stars and the constellation of Orion.

My own research offers a way out of this paradox. As I see it, ancient Egyptian religion was a 'cult of creation', in which temples and pyramids were constructed as simulacra of the creation, the pyramid symbolising the ascent of the creator-god's spirit to the sky for the creation of the Universe. Within this framework, the alignment of the King's Chamber shafts towards the northern and southern skies might well have recalled the creation of the heavens in their entirety, with the circumpolar stars and Orion signifying both the fixed and rotating parts of the celestial vault (see further discussion in chapter seven). It is therefore possible that the shafts symbolised the ascent of the spirit, or soul, *of the creator-god*, who brought into existence not only the stars, but also the Sun and the Moon. In this way, a solid theoretical basis may be found for the idea of soul-shafts. However, it must be stressed that the suggested scenario requires that the soul-shafts be used by the joint soul of the creator-god and king, *their body being buried at ground level or below*.

Thus the paradox of the shafts may be solved, but in contradiction to the orthodox theory.

Even so, it is an uncomfortable fact that the King's Chamber shafts are a unique feature among Egyptian pyramids, and we would do well to ask ourselves why, if the shafts represented creational symbolism, did no other pyramid contain such a feature. Might the shafts have performed some other obscure and hitherto overlooked function? We will return to this question in a later chapter, but it is worth noting, ahead of time, that several aspects of the shafts' construction have yet to receive an adequate explanation. These aspects are as follows: the position of the shafts in the King's Chamber walls; the fact that the shafts are not entirely straight but contain bends and kinks; and the fact that the shafts exit the Pyramid at approximately the same height. In order to account for the entirety of the shafts' design, it may be that a supplementary or replacement hypothesis is yet required.

The Magic Portcullis

So much for the idea that the king's soul departed to the sky through the King's Chamber shafts. We turn now to a more practical objection to the orthodox burial scenario – the case of the magic portcullis.

As discussed earlier, the Antechamber to the King's Chamber was supposedly fitted with a granite portcullis that could be lowered after the funeral to block access to the burial chamber. Upon closer examination, however, it turns out that whilst the Antechamber did incorporate three granite portcullis slabs, those slabs could *not* have been suspended and lowered as the orthodox theory requires. As we shall now see, the design of the Antechamber is really rather mystifying.

On the face of it, the Antechamber does look as if it was designed to house an opening-and-closing portcullis (see figure 45). The wainscots in the east and west walls, for example, have vertical grooves running from top to bottom, as if intended for the lowering of portcullis slabs (that some kind of slabs were originally fitted here is proven by damage to the pilasters between the grooves, the slabs themselves having been removed during antiquity).[35] Then there is the series of semi-hollows at the top of the west wainscot, as if intended for a system of rollers, and the four vertical grooves in the south wall, as if intended for the passage of ropes.

Figure 45.
THE ANTECHAMBER TO THE KING'S CHAMBER.

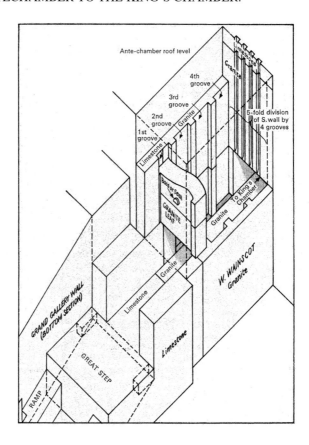

Figure 46.
BORCHARDT'S RECONSTRUCTION OF A PORTCULLIS IN THE
ANTECHAMBER.

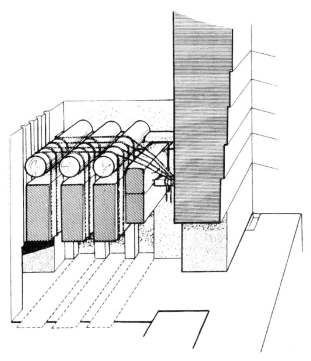

Finally, the impression of a portcullis is strengthened by the presence of
the so-called 'granite leaf', raised off the floor in the forward set of slots,
as if acting as a counterweight to the portcullis slabs. All in all, one may
be forgiven for thinking that the Antechamber once housed an opening-
and-closing portcullis system as envisaged by the German Egyptologist
Ludwig Borchardt in figure 46.

The devil, however, is in the detail.

Firstly, the shelf of the west wainscot stands approximately 9 inches
above the shelf of the east wainscot.[36] It is therefore difficult to see how
the hypothesised system of rollers (suggested by the semi-hollows on the
western side) could have functioned in practice.

Secondly, the grooves in the south wall are quite inconsistent with the
functioning of portcullis ropes. Quite apart from the fact that they run
unnecessarily high, as far as the ceiling, it is unclear how they were used
as rope-guides for a functioning portcullis. They must surely have some
other explanation.

And thirdly, it is difficult to see how the granite leaf, comprising two
blocks of granite, could have worked in practice as a counterweight to

the other granite blocks.

Remarkably, Borchardt's diagram of the portcullis ignores all of these problems. Neither he nor any other Egyptologist has deigned to build a fully-functioning model of the hypothetical device.

One Egyptologist to have spotted the flaws in the portcullis theory and aired his doubts about the whole scenario is J.P. Lepre. In his book *The Egyptian Pyramids*, Lepre cited the standard theory of how the portcullis had operated, but then found himself plagued by misgivings. He wrote:

> Yet although the several parts come together rather cohesively, there is a very serious flaw in this hypothesis – a missing piece of the puzzle – which contradicts the supposed validity of the theory. For while the semi-hollows supposed to have received the wooden rollers are indeed present at the top of the west wainscot, they are missing on the east wainscot. The ledge of this east wainscot is entirely flat and therefore could not have received the edges of the rollers said to have spanned the width of the chamber. Not only this, but the west wainscot is nearly 9 inches higher than the ledge of the east wainscot.

> These facts seem to negate the only logical theory for the interaction of the various components of this strange little compartment. For how could rollers be used when one side of those rollers would have had no semi-hollows within which to be set, and they would furthermore be tilted to such a degree as to make the manipulation of the portcullis slabs a quite impossible task? Why the master architects designed the elements of this chamber in such a contradictory manner presents a unique and puzzling problem for all serious pyramid scholars.[37]

Lepre then went on to question the conventional wisdom concerning the raised boss on the upper part of the granite leaf, arguing that it was not a simple protuberance or construction boss, as Petrie had argued, and nor could it have functioned as part of a portcullis, as Borchardt and others had imagined. Rather, in Lepre's opinion, the raised boss was a 'three-dimensional symbol', akin to the shape of a protractor (see figure 48).[38]

Now, for Lepre to interpret the boss as a symbolic feature was a brave move in the face of widespread antipathy among his colleagues towards the ranks of the 'pyramidiots' who had long adopted this boss as a sign of a high scientific intention behind the Pyramid. But he might well have been on the right track, for it strikes me that the Antechamber contains several features that were principally symbolic and decorative rather than components of an operable portcullis.

For example, the vertical grooves in the Antechamber's south wall, which were supposedly designed for the ropes of a portcullis, actually

Figure 47.
THE SOUTH WALL OF THE ANTECHAMBER COMPARED TO THE 1ST
DYNASTY PORTCULLIS SLAB AT TOMB 3035, SAQQARA.

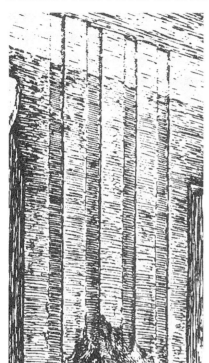 

bear a striking resemblance to *a decorative pattern* on a 1st dynasty tomb
portcullis found by the British archaeologist Walter Emery (see figure
47).[39] As Emery's photographs and diagrams demonstrate, holes were
drilled in the top of the portcullis slab for the purpose of lowering it into
position from above, and thus it is evident that the grooves in its face
must have been purely decorative.[40] A good case can therefore be made
that the grooved wall of the Antechamber is a mock-up of an ancient
portcullis slab, right down to its matching size and dimensions, the wall
symbolising the boundary of the dwelling place of the Great God. As for
the grooves' significance, it is possible that they represented a flattened
form of the fluted column, which itself symbolised the stem of a sacred
plant. That Egyptologists should have missed the decorative nature of
this wall speaks volumes about how a wrong assumption – here, that the
Antechamber housed a working portcullis – can blinker the scholar to a
truth that is terribly obvious.

So, if the grooved wall of the Antechamber is decorative, then why not
the granite leaf? Here, once again, I am struck by the resemblance of the

Figure 48.
THE GRANITE LEAF IN THE ANTECHAMBER.

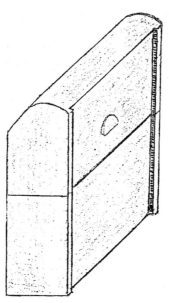

leaf – as far as it may be determined, since the top of it has been broken off – to an architectural feature that was primarily symbolic, in this case the rolled-up reed-mat curtain that was carved from Old Kingdom times onwards over the entrances to tomb chapels and over the elaborately-carved 'false doors' that were erected inside tombs and mortuary temples (both of these signifying the entrance to the 'other world').[41] This feature, which may be compared to a cylindrical drum, varied considerably in style, but it invariably featured a gap above the drum, exactly as is found with the granite leaf in the Antechamber. Moreover, this pattern is found in the 4th dynasty pyramid of Menkaure (the 'third pyramid' of Giza), where a door lintel in the first antechamber has been made in the shape of the rolled-up drum, the antechamber walls being carved with stylized false doors motifs (see figure 49b opposite). In summary, a compelling case can be made for the granite leaf representing an archaic, stylized version of the rolled-up reed-mat curtain symbol, based on its shape, its position in the Antechamber and King's Chamber Passage, its height in the Antechamber, and its juxtaposition to the fluted wall.

Of course, this theory increases the probability that the raised boss on the granite leaf was a symbol, just as Lepre speculated – perhaps a sign of the rising of the spirit of the Great God, to whom the chamber beyond may have belonged.[42]

In summary, the more one considers the Antechamber, the more one is

Figure 49.
ABOVE: A FALSE DOOR FEATURING THE ROLLED-UP REED-MAT
CURTAIN MOTIF. BELOW: THE SAME MOTIF IN A LINTEL FROM
THE THIRD PYRAMID OF GIZA.
(For comparison to the Granite Leaf in the Antechamber, figures 45 and 48).

struck by the symbolic aspects of its design, not just in the granite leaf
and the grooved south wall, but also in the three granite portcullis slabs
that once stood upon its floor. As regards these slabs, other authors have
observed that they would have had limited practical effect in blocking
access to the King's Chamber; an intruder could simply have climbed up
over the granite leaf, dismantled the upper portcullis mechanism (if there

was one), and attacked the third slab from a position of advantage, the other two slabs thus offering no practical obstacle to his progress.[43] In the light of this scenario, a good argument can be made that the number of granite slabs was dictated by religious symbolism, as was perhaps also the case with the three granite plugs in the Ascending Passage.

However, despite all this religious symbolism, implying as it does a religious purpose for the King's Chamber, it does not necessarily follow that the chamber was the burial place of the king. On the contrary, whilst a system of granite slabs almost certainly did exist in the Antechamber, the evidence, as we have seen, refutes the assumption of a mechanism that could have raised these slabs during the funeral procession and then lowered them immediately afterwards, and it may rather have been the case that the slabs were positioned on the floor from the outset, to form a symbolic, or magical, barrier to the King's Chamber.

Meanwhile, several features of the Antechamber remain inexplicable, either by the tomb theory or any other theory.

The Grand Gallery

We turn now to a further practical problem with the burial scenario, this time involving the funeral procession through the Grand Gallery and the plugging of the Ascending Passage after the interment of the king.

At the outset, the reader is reminded that the Grand Gallery is a unique chamber, of a type found in no other Egyptian pyramid, its great size and grandiose design standing in stark contrast to the low, narrow passages that were built in other pyramids. Thus, from a funerary perspective, the Gallery represents a dramatic and inexplicable anomaly, as J.P. Lepre has observed:

> There is nothing quite like this gallery in any of the other pyramids of Egypt... Technically speaking, the Grand Gallery should not be in the Great Pyramid. Most of the passageways in this pyramid and others conformed to a height and width ratio approximately 4 feet high by 4 feet wide... In all other pyramids, the corridor systems merely represented an avenue through which to transport the mummy and coffin of the king, along with other miscellaneous funerary equipment, from the outside of the monument to the burial chamber; they were simply access routes... The Grand Gallery, on the other hand, was so high, and so elaborately contrived, that one wonders whether it served a dual purpose.[44]

Leaving aside, for the moment, the question of what this ulterior purpose might have been, let us consider what was supposed to be the Gallery's

Figure 50.
THE MAGNIFICENT ARCHITECTURE OF THE GRAND GALLERY.

primary function: to facilitate the conveyance of the king's body, in its coffin(s), to the burial chamber.

In the first instance, let us recall the scenario, recounted earlier, of the funeral party advancing up the Grand Gallery. Their task, it must be said, was a formidable challenge. The side ramps, just 20.5 inches wide and dotted with niches, would have made awkward staircases, whilst the central floor way, despite its width of 3 feet 5 inches, was hardly more suitable, comprising smooth and slippery limestone on a slope of $26^\circ\ 2'$, with no handholds provided. In choosing the latter as the least difficult route up the Gallery, the cortege would have been forced to clamber over the three granite plugs for a distance of some 15 feet, before climbing back down to the central floor to continue their 153-foot ascent to the Great Step. To bear the king upwards in this manner would have been extremely undignified to say the least.

Since the earliest days of pyramidology, the design of the Gallery has indeed raised doubts in the minds of investigators. One of the earliest advocates of the tomb theory, the English mathematician and astronomer John Greaves, expressed his very great surprise at its pattern, which was too steep to be a chamber and yet too slippery to be a staircase. Whilst he marvelled at the Gallery's aesthetic quality, he observed that the acclivity and rise 'makes the passage the more slippery and difficult'.[45]

In 1883, the English Egyptologist William Flinders Petrie likewise expressed his astonishment at the Gallery's design vis-a-vis the funeral procession:

> But we are met then by an extraordinary idea, that all access to the King's Chamber after its completion must have been by climbing over the plug blocks, as they lay in the Gallery, or by walking up the ramps on either side of them. Yet, as it is a physical impossibility for the blocks to have been lying in any other place before they were let down, we are shut up to this view.[46]

In the 1930s, the German Egyptologist Ludwig Borchardt described the granite plugs as an 'undignified obstacle' to the funeral procession, and tried his hardest to find an alternative location for them. Noting the existence of the niches in the side ramps and the pair of grooves in the side walls, he theorised that the Gallery had once contained a wooden platform upon which the plugs had temporarily been stored. According to his scenario, the cortege passed unhindered beneath the plugs, which had afterwards been lowered from the wooden platform in order to seal the Ascending Passage.[47]

Whilst Borchardt may have been justified in connecting the niches to the grooves, his theory of a wooden platform for the plugs received short shrift from his Egyptological colleagues. I.E.S. Edwards spoke for many when he wrote that it 'is open to some clear objections, one being the formidable mechanical difficulty involved in lowering the plugs some 14 feet from the platform to the floor of the corridor.'[48] Lepre concurred, writing of Borchardt that 'he fails to adequately describe the unique architectural features within the Gallery upon which the scaffolding would actually have been built, or how they would have lowered the stones. As a result, the theory is neither practical nor workable'.[49] Lepre also observed that it would have been unnecessary to build a platform 150 feet long to support just three granite plugs with a combined length of only 15 feet.[50]

The plugs were thus an obstacle to the funeral procession, and there is no getting around that fact. But the point that jars more with this author is the fact that the architect failed to incorporate even a single feature in the Gallery to ease the passage of the cortege that supposedly bore the

Figure 51.
THE GRAND GALLERY, SHOWING THE GROOVE IN THE THIRD
CORBEL OF THE WEST WALL.

mummy of the king. Why no steps? Why no handholds? If the Gallery
was intended to be a glorious passage to the tomb, then it was designed
very badly indeed, apparently without a thought for the difficulties that
would confront the funeral party. And yet all our instincts tell us that the
architect was a genius, who would have planned the construction down
to the very last detail.

The mystery only deepens when we ponder the function of the pair of
grooves in the walls, at a height of 14 feet, that Borchardt tried to explain
with his platform theory. As Lepre has pointed out, chisel marks running
along these grooves testify to the fact that something originally spanned
the Gallery's width (5 feet 4 inches at this height) and traversed its entire
length, prior to being removed by intruders in antiquity. Lepre suggested
that this something must have been valuable, perhaps taking the form of
'cedar panels inlaid with gold'.[51] But the crucial point that Lepre failed to

spell out was that this ceiling – for it would, in effect, have been a low ceiling or roof – would have halved the Gallery's height and rendered its full splendour invisible to the cortege as it transited with the body of the king.

But if the Grand Gallery was not intended to be seen at the time of the funeral, then what was the point of its elaborate design? In search of an explanation, Lepre hinted at an ulterior, symbolic purpose, suggesting that 'the architect decided to seize upon the opportunity... to display his talents on a grandiose scale never before equalled.'[52] But to display to whom? To his peers? Surely not. To the living king, or the all-seeing God? Perhaps. However, if the architect's intention was to put on such a majestic display, then why would he have divided the Gallery's space into two parts by fitting a roof in its middle? It is an intriguing mystery, to which a possible solution will be proposed in the later chapters of this book.

For now, the reader must be satisfied with two observations: firstly, that the Gallery was ill-suited as a passageway to a burial chamber; and secondly, that its architecture remains inadequately explained by the 'tomb and tomb only' theory. The extent of the mystery is reflected by the comments of the various experts in the panel opposite.

If this seems ominous for the orthodox tomb theory, then worse is to come, as we turn our attention to the plugging of the Ascending Passage immediately following the burial of the king in the King's Chamber.

Plugging the Ascending Passage

The plugging of the Ascending Passage, according to Egyptologists, was an astonishing achievement, the three granite plugs being slid down with minimal clearance especially in the lowermost section where the passage was tapered to the exact dimensions of the plugs. In the words of I.E.S. Edwards:

> To have succeeded in moving even three plugs into position was a remarkable achievement, because they are rather less than half an inch narrower than the corridor and the gap between the top of the plugs and the ceiling of the corridor is only about 1.25 inches.[53]

Similarly, J.P. Lepre has written:

> When one considers the tremendous size and weight of these blocks, the distance they had to travel in their descent, and the precision with which they would have had to have been slid into place – allowing for near-zero tolerance at their final place of rest, without their having

The Mystery of the Grand Gallery

The Grand Gallery in this edifice, so sublime in height, so abrupt in beginning and termination, so different from all the other passages before or beyond it, so elaborately and peculiarly contrived and finished in every part, is absolutely incomprehensible on the tomb theory or on any other, save that of a high astronomical, historical and spiritual symbolism...
(J. Seiss, *The Great Pyramid: Miracle in Stone*, 1877)

No author on the pyramids – Borchardt and myself included – has yet given an adequate rendition of the way in which all the peculiarities of the Grand Gallery come together in a working order to explain the purpose of the Gallery in its relationship to the pyramid as a whole.
(J.P. Lepre, *The Egyptian Pyramids*, 1990)

In a somewhat different vein, several authors point to the possibility that the Gallery possessed a high spiritual symbolism. Perhaps this theory is not far from the truth... I do feel that a high symbolism was intended by the architect when he so perfectly fashioned this extraordinary corridor in the very centre of the pyramid's massive superstructure...
(J.P. Lepre, *The Egyptian Pyramids*, 1990)

This is in many ways the most elaborate and mysterious feature of the whole internal system of the Great Pyramid... There is a quasi-inhuman quality about the Grand Gallery that is hard to explain, as though it were not intended for people to walk up and down but to serve some other specialised or specific function. Many have remarked that the Grand Gallery looks like part of a machine, whose function is beyond us... No-one has the answer to the riddle of the Grand Gallery and perhaps no-one ever will.
(Robert Bauval, *The Orion Mystery*, 1994)

The Great Gallery is one of the architectural masterpieces of ancient Egypt... The exact significance of this magnificent structure is still not clear.
(Alberto Siliotti, *The Pyramids*, 1997)

jammed – it is truly staggering to comprehend.[54]

So staggering indeed that many alternative pyramid theorists have argued that the granite plugs were built *in situ*, i.e. constructed in the bottom of the passage where they sit today – an idea that would really foul up the 'tomb and tomb only' theory if it were true.[55] There is, however, good evidence against the 'built *in situ*' theory, most notably the fact that the Ascending Passage is tapered towards its bottom, and strengthened there by partial-girdle stones, the plugs themselves having been tapered to fit there. Such elaborations would hardly have been necessary if the plugs had been built *in situ*. But they would have been desirable if the plugs had been lowered into position from above, as Egyptologists maintain they were.[56] Incidentally, a chip of granite cemented to the passage floor, just above the broken-off end of the uppermost plug, does not offer proof of the 'built *in situ*' theory, as some alternative theorists assert, but, on the contrary, surely testifies to the fact that the plugs were slid down the passage using liquid mortar as a lubricant.[57]

This is not to argue in favour of the tomb theory, however, for it is still possible that the plugs were slid into place during the construction of the Pyramid, i.e. years before any burial took place.

All things considered, therefore, it is virtually certain that the granite plugs were held initially on the Gallery's smooth floor, where they were secured by wooden wedges or chocks (or, as some have proposed, by wooden cross-beams whose ends were somehow secured via the niches in the side ramps). From this position, the plugs were then slid down into the Ascending Passage.

But how exactly was this done? In the opinion of Egyptologists, it would not have been feasible to lower the three plugs simultaneously from below, since one or more plugs might have jammed prematurely in the passage and become impossible to move. Instead, it is believed that the plugs were lowered individually from above, this method allowing much greater control over the descent of each plug. From the observed fact that all three plugs were fitted perfectly into the passage mouth with near-zero clearance, the experts have concluded that this was, without a doubt, the actual method that was used.[58]

This is a very important conclusion, since it implies that a number of workmen were forced to bury themselves alive in the Pyramid's upper reaches – an idea that finds no precedent in the entire history of pyramid building. It was to this anomaly that I.E.S. Edwards was referring when he wrote with splendid understatement that: 'Owing to its upward slope, the blocking of the Ascending Corridor of the Great Pyramid after the funeral presented unusual difficulties.'[59]

In answer to this conundrum, Egyptologists found a convenient patch to their theory. They assumed that the trapped workers had escaped from the Grand Gallery via the Well Shaft, which led down to the Descending Passage, and thence to the main entrance (see figure 52 overleaf). As I.E.S. Edwards explained:

> From the moment when the first plug was introduced into the upper end of the Ascending Corridor, the workmen who were charged with the task of transferring the plugs to their final position would have been unable to leave the pyramid by the normal way. They had, however, provided themselves with a means of escape down the shaft which leads from the bottom of the Grand Gallery to the Descending Corridor... The shaft would have been completely concealed at the time of the funeral by the lowest stone in the western ramp, which is now missing. The removal of the stone would have presented no difficulty to the workmen when the time came for making their descent. After the last of the workmen had reached the bottom of the shaft, the opening in the west wall of the Descending Corridor would have been covered with a slab of stone so that it would have been indistinguishable from the remainder of the corridor.[60]

In explanations such as this, Egyptologists give the impression that the entire Well Shaft was cut in anticipation of the eventual need to evacuate the workmen from the Gallery. And yet this idea is open to two serious objections.

Firstly, it is clear that when the earliest layers of masonry were laid the decision had already been taken to build an Ascending Passage and fit it with stone plugs (this being evident from the tapering of the passage at its bottom and the provision of half-girdle blocks to strengthen the passage at that point). Already, at this time, it would have been apparent to the architect that the workmen who lowered the plugs would become trapped inside the monument. And yet for a distance of about 35 feet in the vertical the builders failed to provide any connection at all to the pre-existing Well Shaft.[61] Only above this point did they begin construction of a vertical section of shaft which may, or may not, have been intended for the escape of the workers;[62] and it was only some time later (we know not when) that this vertical shaft was connected to the lower part of the Well Shaft by means of a rough tunnel through the masonry (see figure 52). Thus it is perfectly clear that the architect had no original intention to connect the Gallery to the lower Well Shaft, and that the connecting tunnel was dug as an afterthought. The case for the Well Shaft having being planned as an evacuation route for the workmen is thus weakened

Figure 52.
THE WELL SHAFT.

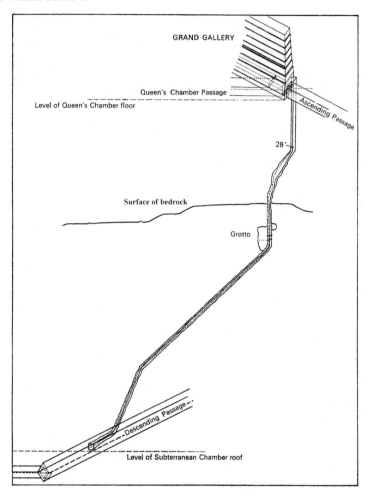

GRAND GALLERY

Queen's Chamber Passage

Level of Queen's Chamber floor

Ascending Passage

28°

Surface of bedrock

Grotto

Descending Passage

Level of Subterranean Chamber roof

considerably.

Secondly, it is vital to realise that the Well Shaft, when connected to the Gallery, provided a back door route to the upper chambers, where the tomb of the king supposedly lay. It thus in effect doubled the risk of the burial chamber being discovered and robbed. Would the king really have sanctioned the construction of this shaft and its tunnel for the use of the workmen who sealed his tomb, or indeed for any other purpose? Some Egyptologists indeed acknowledge this doubt. As I.E.S. Edwards put it: 'It is idle to speculate whether this shaft was constructed with or without the knowledge of Cheops, but the burial of living persons was certainly not practised by the Egyptians of the pyramid age'.[63] In other words, we are given no choice but to suspend our disbelief: the Pyramid was a tomb and nothing but a tomb; the king was buried in the King's Chamber; the plugs in the Ascending Passage were released from above; the workers were trapped inside; burial of living persons was not practised; *Q.E.D.* the Well Shaft was built to facilitate their escape.

But this scenario, nonetheless, is extremely disturbing, for it involves either a flawed plan and a forgetful architect, or else a sacrilegious act of vandalism and a reckless disregard for the security of the tomb, or else, in the last resort, a deliberate burial of workmen alive, in conflict with our understanding of ancient Egyptian culture. The objections, one way or another, are serious.

Meanwhile, Egyptologists have overlooked an alternative solution to the conundrum: that the king was never buried in the Pyramid's upper chambers, that the plugs were lowered at the time of construction (when the Gallery had not yet been roofed), that the lower section of the Well Shaft was built to provide access to the Grotto – a pre-existing natural cave feature in the plateau bedrock – and that the rough tunnel was dug for the purpose of inspecting the King's Chamber, long after the Pyramid had been built. We will discuss this scenario further in the next chapter.

But now we come to yet another baffling problem: the sealing of the mouth of the Ascending Passage by means of the prism stone.

The Mystery of the Prism Stone

In order to conceal the Ascending Passage where it branched off from the Descending Passage, a multi-angled stone, the so-called prism stone, was inserted into the mouth of the passage just below the granite plugs, such that it filled the aperture, its lower face becoming indistinguishable from the ceiling of the Descending Passage. This was supposedly done at the close of the funerary proceedings, and yet Egyptologists are extremely vague as to how it was done. How was it possible to lift this multi-angled stone, weighing at least a ton, and fit it into the ceiling, whilst working in the cramped confines of the Descending Passage? How was it possible to fix the stone into place with the precision and durability that the Pyramid elsewhere required? For this stone was important, more than any other, in concealing the passage to the monument's upper chambers.

J.P. Lepre, one of the few Egyptologists to address the matter of the prism stone, has provided us with a telling clue:

> This lower end of the passage was originally sealed or camouflaged by a removable ceiling stone which was indistinguishable from the other stones comprising the lengthy descending passageway. This specially

cut stone is referred to as the 'prism stone', as it is thus shaped. It was held into place by small protrusions at its sides which were received by hollows cut into the ceiling at the point where it meets with the the uppermost corners of the east and west wall sections of the corridor. The prism stone has since disappeared, but the shallow hollows can still be seen to this day.[64]

Lepre here observed that the prism stone had protrusions on two of its sides, which allowed it to be located securely in the aperture – this being evidenced by two hollows in the walls. However, he failed to realise that such a stone could not have been slotted into place after the funeral, since its protrusions made it wider than the walls of the passage. Such a stone could have been slotted into the aperture only while the passage was in the course of construction.

This observation is not fatal to the tomb theory, but it requires that the stone was able to pivot on its protrusions, thus forming an opening-and-closing door to the Ascending Passage. The archaeological evidence here does seem to be decisive, leaving Egyptology no option but to suppose that the prism stone was indeed a pivoting door (as opposed to being a fixed stone, which would wreck the 'tomb only' theory). In fact, when I sketched this multi-angled stone (there being no diagrams of it in the textbooks at my disposal), I was struck by its resemblance to the pivoting stone which Lepre had envisaged as the main door to the Pyramid.

There is, of course, a problem with this pivoting door to the Ascending

Figure 53.
THE PRISM STONE.
Note: The drawing assumes that the stone filled the entire aperture at the bottom of the Ascending Passage.

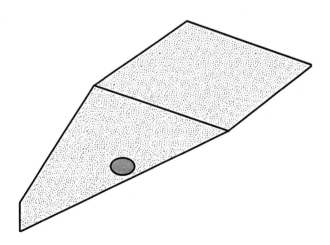

Passage, namely that it limited the space available for the passage of the king's coffin(s) and funerary furniture. By pivoting in the midst of the passage, it would have had the effect of halving (at least) the height of the entrance at that point. My calculations suggest that the passage height of 3 feet 11 inches would have been reduced to around 1 foot 9 inches, allowing for the thickness of the door itself. In other words, the workmen would have had to manoeuvre the coffin through an aperture measuring just 1 foot 9 inches high by 3 feet 5 inches wide. Would this hypothetical manoeuvre have been possible? In view of the likely size of the coffin and the difficulties caused by the sloping T-junction with the Descending Passage (itself just 3 feet 11 inches high and 3 feet 5 inches wide), I very much doubt it.[65]

Does this finding disprove the orthodox burial theory? Not quite. The wooden coffin is, after all, an assumption; we have no real evidence that an inner coffin (or set of coffins) was actually used. The important thing is the king's body, and here the pivoting door would have provided just enough of a gap for the mummy to be passed through. The orthodoxy is thus saved by the presumption that Khufu's mummy was placed directly into the stone sarcophagus.

Even so, assumptions and presumptions must be avoided, for there is no hard evidence that the prism stone actually pivoted on its protrusions. It is possible, on the contrary, that the protrusions were permanent fixing points, the stone having been cemented into place when the Pyramid was being built. However, in the absence of the prism stone itself (which has not been seen since medieval times), it is impossible to say for certain whether or not this was the case.

In this regard, there is one final clue to be considered. In 1865, Piazzi Smyth, the astronomer-royal of Scotland, discovered an unusual joint in the floor of the Descending Passage directly beneath the prism stone, and having no conceivable purpose other than to indicate the existence of the prism stone and the secret passage concealed above it. Smyth wrote:

> When measuring the cross joints in the floor of the entrance-passage in 1865, I went on chronicling their angles, each one proving to be very nearly at right angles to the axis, until suddenly one came which was diagonal; another, and that was diagonal too; but after that, the rectangular position was resumed. Further, the stone material carrying these diagonal joints was harder and better than elsewhere in the floor... Why?... The answer came from the diagonal joints themselves, on discovering that the stone between them was opposite to the butt-end of the portcullis of (the) first ascending passage, or to the hole whence the prismatic stone of concealment, through 3,000 years, had

dropped out almost before al-Mamun's eyes. Here, therefore, in a peculiar relation of position to something concealed, was a secret sign in the pavement of the entrance-passage, appreciable only to a careful eye...[66]

Whilst Smyth is today reckoned as one of the earliest 'pyramidiots' on account of his far-fetched theory that the Great Pyramid was a divinely-inspired compendium of weights and measures, and a chronicle of man's past and a prophecy of his future, his discovery of this anomalous joint is not to be gainsaid. Thus J.P. Lepre wrote approvingly:

This particular line – a joint set opposite to the other floor joints – was discovered by Smyth in his inspection of the descending corridor. He correctly referred to it as 'a sign in the floor for the wise'. For here, at that point immediately above the unorthodox joint, lay the lower end of the pyramid's ascending passage which gave access to the upper reaches of the monument.[67]

This is indeed a remarkable little fact. For, on the one hand, the architect went to great lengths to conceal the Ascending Passage, and yet, on the other hand, he left a subtle sign as if to betray its location. Why would the architect have done this if, as Egyptologists suppose, the Ascending Passage led upwards to the tomb of the king in the King's Chamber? It makes no sense at all. If the 'tomb and tomb only' scenario is correct, then the 'secret sign in the pavement', as Smyth put it, simply should not be there.

This completes our critique of the funeral scenario, as presented earlier in this chapter. However, we have yet to discuss the funerary role that has been assigned to the Queen's Chamber.

The Queen's Chamber

Earlier, I outlined the two orthodox theories for the Queen's Chamber: firstly the evolutionary theory, that it had been built as the king's tomb chamber but then abandoned upon completion of the King's Chamber; and secondly the unified design theory, that it had been built, along with all the other chambers, as part of a single harmonious scheme. Today, the second of these two theories has preferred status, the first having been rejected by the vast majority of Egyptologists. Nevertheless, for the sake of completeness, we must continue to explore both possibilities. In doing so, the reader will be apprised of yet another conceptual difficulty in the 'tomb and tomb only' theory.

To begin with the abandoned tomb theory, this idea owes its existence to a number of observations, some pertaining to the Queen's Chamber itself, and others pertaining to the wider design of the Pyramid. We will examine here the former points only, the latter points having been dealt with earlier in this chapter. The points basically comprise clues that the Queen's Chamber was left in an unfinished condition, these clues being fivefold:

- The passage to the chamber has an abrupt drop of 1 foot 11 inches some 18 feet before the entrance to the room.[68]

- There are red ochre lines in the passageway which one would expect to have been rubbed out by the builders.[69]

- The floor of the chamber is very rough.[70]

- The mouths of the 'airshafts' were left uncut.[71]

- The 'airshafts' were terminated inside the Pyramid, apparently at the level where the King's Chamber was completed, i.e. at the apex of its roof.[72]

These points can be dealt with briefly.

Regarding the first point, it is possible that the drop in the passage was planned, and that the builders inserted something in this space.

Regarding the second point, this is, frankly, no big deal. If one was minded to, one could highlight all sorts of imperfections in the Pyramid's other chambers (in the Grand Gallery, for example, did someone forget to fill in the niches in the side ramps?). Such imperfections, in my view, stemmed from the strict use of deadlines by the architect as the Pyramid rose up, stage by stage, from the ground. These deadlines affected the Queen's Chamber as much as any other chamber – no more, no less.

With regard to the third point, the extreme roughness of the floor does *not* indicate that the floor was left unfinished. Rather, it may be the case that the original floor slabs were torn up and removed by intruders. J.P. Lepre is one of the few Egyptologists to embrace this possibility, writing: 'the finely cut limestone blocks which once comprised this chamber's floor are now missing, presumably having been violated [at the hands of despoilers].'[73]

Finally, we come to the question of the 'airshafts', the theory being that the small channels in the walls of the Queen's Chamber are of a kind with the small channels in the walls of the King's Chamber, the former being abandoned versions of the latter. According to this theory, the shafts were cut as high as the level of the King's Chamber lest that room (a pioneering development) prove to be a disaster, in which case the

Queen's Chamber would have been used as the tomb. In that eventuality, the builders would have finished off the Queen's Chamber by extending its shafts to the exterior of the Pyramid and cutting open the mouths of the shafts in the room. There is, however, a problem with this theory in that the bridging slab that sealed off the passage to the Queen's Chamber was *fitted permanently* into the walls beneath the Gallery's side ramps, this being evidenced by the fact that the sockets in these side walls are cut too high to receive support beams, but are at the appropriate height to have received 9-inch-thick protrusions from the bridging slab itself (see figure 54).[74] In fact, the height of the sockets would suggest that cross-beams (of wood or stone) were used *in addition to* the support offered by the slab's protrusions. The conclusion is therefore unavoidable that the bridging slab was *sealed into the walls at the time when the Pyramid was built*, making it impossible for workmen to have returned to the Queen's Chamber. From this observation, it may be deduced that the mouths of the shafts in that room were left uncut upon the deliberate instructions of the architect.[75]

In any event, it has now become apparent from robot explorations in 1993 and 2002 that the Queen's Chamber shafts extend above the level

Figure 54.
THE BEGINNING OF THE QUEEN'S CHAMBER PASSAGE.
The photograph demonstrates that the sockets in the walls are aligned to the lip on which the bridging slab sat (the lip is just visible at the top of the picture). See also the diagram in figure 55.

Figure 55.
THE PLACEMENT OF SOCKETS FOR THE BRIDGING SLAB.
For comparison to the photograph in figure 54.

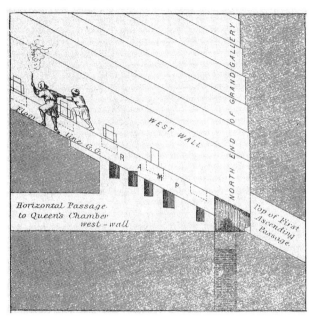

of the King's Chamber per se to a point in line with its uppermost roof, where they are then plugged in a manner suggestive of secret chambers beyond. I will comment further on this idea in a moment, but suffice to say for now that these shafts look less and less like abandoned airshafts.

Let us turn, then, from the unfinished chamber theory, which receives dwindling support these days, to the unified design theory, which is now accepted by most Egyptologists. According to this theory, the Queen's Chamber served a special role pertaining to the burial or afterlife of the king. In the opinion of some, the chamber housed a chest containing the king's embalmed entrails (an unlikely idea in view of the evidence, just discussed, that the passage to the chamber was sealed off at the time of construction). The consensus, however, is that the chamber functioned as a serdab.

A serdab is defined in the general dictionary as 'a secret chamber in an ancient Egyptian tomb', but in the specialist dictionary as 'a room in the mastaba tombs of the Old Kingdom, where statues of the *ka* of the deceased were usually placed'.[76] The idea was that the king's statue was a representation of the king's otherworldly double, the *ka*, and that this *ka* – a spiritual energy – remained ever present both in the tomb and in the sky. A notable example of the *ka*-statue in the serdab may be seen at

Figure 56.
THE SERDAB OF KING DJOSER AT SAQQARA.

Saqqara, to the north of the Step Pyramid, where a life-size statue of king Djoser, contained in a tilted enclosure, gazes through peepholes towards the northern stars (see figure 56).

In the Great Pyramid, the idea of the *ka*-statue and serdab is suggested to some by the Queen's Chamber, which was not only sealed off, as we have seen, but also dominated by a corbelled niche which has long been suspected of housing a statue of the king (said statue having been broken up and removed in antiquity).[77] Mark Lehner spoke for the majority of Egyptologists when he wrote in 1997:

> The so-called Queen's Chamber was certainly not for the burial of a queen. Very probably it was a sealed room for a special statue of the king, representing his *ka* or 'spiritual force'.[78]

This serdab theory offers a plausible (if unprovable) theory for the large corbelled niche, and does fit well with the archaeological evidence, cited earlier, that the Queen's Chamber Passage was sealed off at the time of its construction. However, there are a number of problems with it, which the pyramid experts have generally overlooked.

Firstly, the niche in the Queen's Chamber faces to the west whereas a *ka*-statue ought to face to the north for eternal life in the circumpolar stars, or to the east for eternal rebirth with the rising Sun.[79]

Secondly, the Queen's Chamber was a totally sealed room, whereas in serdabs the *ka*-statue was usually provided with open peepholes or a slit, through which the *ka* could establish contact with the sky. The peepholes were known as 'the eyes of the *ka*-house'.[80]

And thirdly – here is the most fundamental objection – the serdab/*ka*-

statue concept belonged to the realm of the tomb and the underworld. In order for it to work in a pyramid, therefore, it would have been essential to bury the *ka*-statue in an underground chamber. The *ka*, i.e. the king's spiritual energy, would then have been able to rise up, by magic, to fill the pyramid in re-enactment of the time when the creator-god's *ka* had filled the Universe (Pyramid Texts, Utterance 600).[81] According to this interpretation of the pyramid, the Queen's Chamber, lying at a height of 70 feet in the Pyramid's superstructure, could not have been a serdab for the *ka*-statue of the king. Egyptologists, of course, are unaware of this problem, being ignorant of the pyramid's creational symbolism.

Even so, let us put our scepticism to one side, and subject the serdab theory to a critical test, namely to explain the significance of the Queen's Chamber shafts. These 8-inch-square shafts are arguably the Pyramid's most baffling and challenging feature. Why were their mouths left sealed at the time of construction? And why were they terminated somewhere in the body of the Pyramid? If we accept that the Queen's Chamber was a

Figure 57.
THE NICHE IN THE EAST WALL OF THE QUEEN'S CHAMBER.
The corbelled niche stands to a height of 15 feet 4 inches.

serdab, and *not* an abandoned tomb chamber (for which the evidence is slender), then it follows that the shafts represent the intended design of the architect, rather than being an abandoned feature. The questions then arise of why the builders went to the great trouble of building the shafts upwards only to stop them with metal-handled covers, and then build the shafts yet further upwards for the insertion of stone plugs (I am assuming here that a plug system will also be found in the northern shaft). These are indeed questions to tax the most ingenious mind.

So, how do proponents of the serdab and *ka*-statue theory explain the existence of the Queen's Chamber shafts? What insights, if any, emerge from their analysis?

According to Egyptology, the *ka* was a spiritual energy that remained resident in the tomb and the statue, despite its conjugations with the *ka* in the wider Universe. In this respect, it differed from the king's *ba*, or soul, which was thought to travel back and forth between the confines of the tomb and the limits of the Universe. In short, the *ka* (spirit) was a static concept, whereas the *ba* (soul) was a dynamic concept. In recognition of this difference, Mark Lehner has proposed that the *ka* was confined in the Queen's Chamber by its sealed shafts, in contrast to the *ba* which was allowed free passage from the King's Chamber (the tomb) via its open shafts. In an interview for a London newspaper, *The Sunday Telegraph*, Lehner expressed his idea as follows:

> The open shafts in the larger chamber [the King's Chamber] allow the *ba* [the king's soul] to come and go from the mummified body. But the statue [in the Queen's Chamber] represents a substitute body, a repository for the *ka* force, and the blocked shaft symbolically stops the *ka* from leaving.[82]

This is an ingenious idea, and yet it really begs the question of why the architect would have gone to the trouble of constructing the shafts at all if he had intended the *ka* to be trapped inside the chamber. It simply does not make sense. In addition, it is questionable whether physical restraints on the *ka* were necessary, for other serdabs, or *ka*-houses, were provided with open peepholes or slits, as mentioned earlier (see, for example, the Djoser serdab in figure 56). Finally, an argument may be mounted that the *ka*, like the *ba*, had the magical ability to pass through solid matter, in which case the sealing of the shafts could not have impeded its passage, had it been minded to travel forth to the sky, as Lehner himself concedes in respect of the *ba*:

> A blocked passage would be no problem for a king's soul. It didn't have to be open for the king to ascend. The principal means of going

into the 'other world' in any normal Egyptian tomb was what we call a 'false door'...[83]

Lehner's serdab and *ka*-statue theory thus runs into a number of serious problems.

In what is perhaps a telling commentary on Lehner's *ka* theory, other pyramid experts, for example Stadelmann and Hawass, have advocated a quite different theory, namely that the shafts of the Queen's Chamber anticipated those of the King's Chamber, and were thus intended for the comings and goings of the *ba*, the king's soul. Interestingly, Stadelmann has gone on record to suggest that the *ba* ascended through the southern shaft and opened the so-called 'door' by turning its metal handles, which he referred to as 'magical instruments'.[84] (Compare this interpretation to my own suggestion in chapter two that the 'door' is one of the original shaft aperture covers that were used during construction of the Pyramid to prevent the ingress of detritus and living creatures, the metal handles being nothing but mundane latches or lifting handles.) This *ba* theory, it must be said, is a hangover from the old, and now discredited, theory that the Queen's Chamber was built as the king's tomb, only to be abandoned in the course of construction.

In summary, the Queen's Chamber shafts are a major anomaly to the orthodox tomb theory, and place scholars in something of a quandary. On the one hand, the abandoned tomb chamber theory fails to convince; the shafts do not appear to be abandoned airshafts, nor conduits for the king's soul. But on the other hand, the serdab and *ka*-statue theory sheds very little light on the question of why the shafts were built only to be sealed at both ends. It makes no sense. And nor am I able to furnish any ideas that might extricate Egyptologists from their sticky predicament, at least not from an orthodox perspective.

What is more, the problems for orthodoxy grow ever greater when we consider the evidence for a secret chamber, albeit of small size, lying just beyond the stone blockage in the southern shaft.

Secret Chambers?

The evidence for a secret chamber above the Queen's Chamber southern shaft is compelling.

Firstly, the blocks forming the southern shaft change from rough-hewn limestone to fine, white, Tura limestone in the uppermost section just before 'the Gantenbrink door'; Tura limestone was generally reserved for special applications, such as lining chambers.[85]

Secondly, the southern shaft is constructed of vertically-laid blocks in the vicinity of the 'door'. This building technique indicates a need for stress relief, as would be required, for example, if there were a complex structure overhead.[86]

Thirdly, and finally, there is evidence of structural complexity in the southern shaft *of the King's Chamber*, about 39 feet *directly above* the aforementioned features of the Queen's Chamber southern shaft.[87] Rudolf Gantenbrink offers the engineer's view of these structural anomalies as follows:

> Between block no. 15 and 16 [in the King's Chamber's southern shaft] we discovered a vertical joint. In the shafts, such joints, which have a distinct static function, otherwise occur only proximate to the chambers. It is a complete anomaly to find a vertical joint fully isolated in the nucleus of the pyramid. Since it requires much greater effort to shape and fit the blocks in such an arrangement, we can assume that the builders must have had significant structural justification for going to the trouble of deflecting forces into the horizontal plane. This vertical joint is located about 12 metres [39 feet] above a point in the lower southern shaft [i.e. the Queen's Chamber] which is subject to extraordinary static influences... For a construction engineer, this is a significant clue to the possible existence of an as yet undiscovered structure in the vicinity of these static anomalies.[88]

All in all, a compelling case can be made for an undiscovered chamber, located beyond the plugged end of the Queen's Chamber southern shaft. This chamber, according to calculations of the shaft's trajectory, would lie some 50 feet from the southern face of the pyramid (although some authors state 20 feet), and would therefore be relatively small compared to, say, the King's Chamber.[89]

It should be added, in response to those who believe that the shaft has been plugged and abandoned, that the plugging stone (I refer here to the stone block, not to the metal-handled 'door') finds a precedent in the three-part granite plug which sealed the lower end of the Ascending Passage; this plug, of course, signified the entrance to a higher system of undreamed-of passages and chambers. At the time of writing, it is not yet clear whether the shaft plug is made of limestone or granite, but the latter in particular would be an unmistakable 'sign for the wise' and might well signal a triple plug arrangement (note how three was also the number of the granite slabs in the King's Chamber Antechamber; it would seem that the number '3' was of some religious significance to the builders).[90]

It should be added that a second secret chamber, this one beyond the

Figure 58.
THE GREAT PYRAMID, VERTICAL SECTION, SHOWING THEORISED
LOCATION OF SECRET CHAMBERS ABOVE THE SHAFTS.

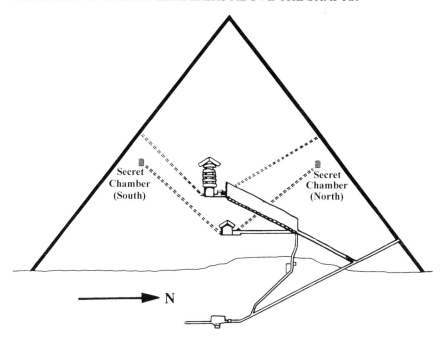

Queen's Chamber *northern* shaft, also looks likely on the basis of that shaft's similarities to the southern shaft. This shaft, too, is blocked by a metal-handled cover, and it is highly likely that a plugging stone (or a set of three, as discussed) will be found beyond it in the near future. It is not known, as yet, how close this second chamber would be to the northern face of the Pyramid. But, for the purpose of the illustration in figure 58, a distance of 50 feet is assumed.

Does the orthodox theory of the Great Pyramid have any explanation that would account for these hypothesised secret chambers, built in such inaccessible locations? Surprisingly, perhaps, several Egyptologists have lent support to the secret chamber theory and, in some instances, even speculated about what such a chamber might contain.

Pride of place must go to J.P. Lepre, who mooted the idea of a secret chamber above the Queen's Chamber southern shaft in his 1990 book *The Egyptian Pyramids*, on the basis of the 1872 experiment performed by John and Waynman Dixon. The Dixon brothers had sent smoke up the southern shaft, but had failed to detect the emergence of said smoke from the outside of the Pyramid. The idea of the secret chamber thus occurred to Lepre at least three years prior to Gantenbrink's 1993 discovery of the metal-handled 'door' in the shaft.[91] However, he had no explanation of why such a chamber might have been built at this location, and made no suggestion as to what such a chamber might contain.

After Gantenbrink's discovery in April 1993, a secret chamber became a more tangible possibility. I.E.S. Edwards, who viewed the southern shaft as a soul-shaft, was drawn to speculate on the existence of a small serdab, containing 'a statue of the king gazing towards the constellation of Orion' (it should be noted that alignment of this shaft to Orion has not been proven; Bauval believes that the shaft was aligned to Sirius).[92]

At around this time, too, Zawi Hawass, then Director General of the Giza Pyramids, told a German television crew that the 'door' might lead to a small chamber containing written records of the builders, perhaps pertaining to their religious beliefs.[93] In later years, Hawass backed away from this speculation, but then in promoting the National Geographic Channel *Pyramids Live* extravaganza in September 2002, he resurrected the idea, speaking of the possibility of a secret chamber containing the 'Sacred Book' that had been written by Khufu.[94] Undaunted by the new discovery of the stone plug in the southern shaft, Hawass exclaimed live on air that the stone was 'another door', i.e. an entrance to a secret chamber, and that 'something important is hidden here'.[95]

Finally, there is Mark Lehner, who was also involved in promoting the *Pyramids Live* show on the National Geographic Channel. Lehner has wavered on the point of whether there is, or is not, a chamber behind the 'door', and he has ruled out the possibility of a large chamber (owing to its proximity to the southern face of the Pyramid), but he does accept the possibility of a small compartment. As for its purpose and contents, he told the London newspaper *The Daily Mail* on 14th September 2002:

> What do I think is there? I think it may be a serdab. A serdab is a sealed room for a *ka*-statue – a statue of the dead king which embodied his *ka*, or life spirit.[96]

This, essentially, is the same speculation as made by Edwards in 1993.

What are we to make of these various pronouncements? Does it make sense, according to the orthodox theory, that the hypothesised chamber is a serdab containing a statue of the king, or a repository for the Sacred Book of Khufu? Is it plausible that a soul-shaft – for this is the theory suggested by Edwards, Hawass, and, in a manner, Lehner – would lead to a serdab or a repository?

As regards the serdab idea, it must be remembered that Egyptologists have already identified the Queen's Chamber itself as a serdab (a shaky theory, for the reasons mentioned earlier). It is thus being suggested, in effect, that there are two serdabs, a large lower one and a small upper one, connected to each other by the shaft. But why on earth would a soul-shaft, *sealed at both ends*, lead from one serdab to another and then *fail to exit on the outside of the Pyramid*? Such an arrangement would be unique in the history of Egyptian architecture, but, more to the point, it would make no sense.

As regards the repository idea, it likewise makes no sense that a soul-shaft, sealed at both ends, would lead to a cache of sacred writings, and then fail to exit on the outside of the Pyramid. Hawass, who advocates the repository theory in parallel with the soul-shaft theory (he believes that the southern shaft conveyed the king's soul to the barque of the Sun-god), does not explain this, and neither does Robert Bauval who made a similar speculation in his 1999 book *Secret Chamber*.[97] Bauval, like Hawass, subscribes to the soul-shaft theory, but with the southern shaft being oriented towards Sirius, but does not rationalise why such a shaft would lead to a library of ancient writings. In short, the repository idea, as it has been expressed by Hawass and Bauval, remains altogether too vague and lacks a theoretical basis.

In summary, we have a weird situation in which certain Egyptologists lend support to the secret chamber hypothesis, but upon speculating as to its contents find themselves in a nonsensical or paradoxical position. In short, the existence of the secret chamber is inconsistent with the soul-shaft theory, and inconsistent with the orthodoxy that the Pyramid is 'a tomb and nothing but a tomb'.

It must be emphasised, however, that Hawass and Lehner do not speak for the majority of Egyptologists. To these scholars, the idea of a secret chamber is anathema, for they recognise, quite rightly, that it contradicts the theory that the Pyramid was a tomb (hence all the denials of a secret chamber when 'the Gantenbrink door' was first discovered in 1993).[98] To them, the Queen's Chamber was either a serdab or an abandoned burial chamber, and the shafts must be abandoned features – either unfinished airshafts or unfinished soul-shafts. According to these scholars, nothing of interest lies beyond the 'doors' and stone plugs. Rather, the shaft is 'disused' and, to quote the archaeologist Aidan Dodson, 'all that is on the other side is the main body of the pyramid.'[99] This, it must be said, is almost certainly the majority view among Egyptologists, although few would pretend to be experts on the subject of the pyramids in general or the Great Pyramid in particular.

In summary, as things stand, there is compelling evidence for a secret chamber lying beyond the plugged end of the Queen's Chamber southern shaft, and the presence of such a chamber is inexplicable according to the orthodox theory of the Pyramid. If, or when, the existence of this secret chamber (and indeed its northern counterpart) is confirmed, it will bring the problems of the 'tomb and tomb only' theory into even sharper focus.

Chapter Three Summary

- There is no hard evidence for the supposition that Khufu was buried in the sarcophagus of the King's Chamber; indeed, such a hypothesis runs counter to a fundamental axiom of ancient Egyptian religion which required that the body be buried in the earth, i.e. in this case *beneath* the Pyramid.

- The 'tomb and tomb only' theory has no adequate explanation for the southern airshaft in the King's Chamber.

- There are major problems with the assumption that the Antechamber to the King's Chamber housed an operable portcullis. In particular, it would seem that several of the supposed portcullis features were in fact decorative and symbolic.

- The design of the Grand Gallery is ill-suited for a passageway to a burial chamber. Several aspects of its architecture remain inexplicable under the 'tomb and tomb only' theory.

- The orthodox theory that the Well Shaft was cut for the evacuation of the workmen who had lowered the plugs into the Ascending Passage is most implausible. Much doubt is therefore cast on the whole scenario of burial in the upper chambers.

- The prism stone was fitted into the walls of the Ascending Passage at the time of construction. On the assumption that the stone pivoted open, there would have been insufficient space for the passage upwards of coffins or funerary furniture. In addition, the marking of the prism stone's location by the 'sign in the floor for the wise' is inconsistent with the hypothesis of a secret burial in the upper chambers.

- The purpose of the Queen's Chamber remains inadequately explained by the orthodox theory. The 8-inch-square shafts represent a particular difficulty, which is compounded by the evidence that secret chambers are located above their plugged ends.

CHAPTER FOUR

THE BODY TO EARTH

The very best minds of ancient Egypt were given the task of designing these complicated monuments; and it is this intelligence and this challenge which we are up against if we ever hope to penetrate the secret crypts of those pharaohs.
(J.P. Lepre, *The Egyptian Pyramids*, 1990)

Egyptologists are adamant that Khufu's mummy was laid to rest in the granite sarcophagus of the King's Chamber. However, whilst this stone box is indeed the right shape and size for a human body, there is no hard evidence that a human burial ever took place there, and the theory runs into a number of serious problems, as discussed in chapter three. Above all, the idea that the king was buried in the King's Chamber, at a height of 140 feet inside the Great Pyramid, conflicts with a fundamental axiom of Egyptian religion: 'the body to earth, the spirit to the sky'.

As discussed in chapter one, the true pyramid symbolised the creation of the Universe, orchestrated by the creator-god whose spirit had risen up to the sky whilst his body had remained behind in the earth. The building of the pyramid re-enacted this supreme moment, just as the death of the king re-enacted the death of the creator-god. Whilst the body of the king became the body of the creator-god, 'the body to earth', his soul became the soul of the creator-god, 'the spirit to the sky'. The most fundamental principle of Egyptian religion thus dictates that we look for the king's tomb at ground level or below, 'ground level' corresponding to the 'risen earth' or 'primeval mound', 'below' corresponding to the subterranean abyss whence the earth emerged at the beginning of time.

In the Great Pyramid, therefore, we are faced with three possibilities for a royal burial:

1 The Subterranean Chamber.

2 Another, as yet unknown, chamber, concealed in the basement of the Pyramid.

3 The Grotto.

As regards the first possibility, the rough finish and irregular shape of the Subterranean Chamber have long persuaded Egyptologists to believe that it was abandoned by the builders in favour of a tomb chamber higher up in the Pyramid. Accordingly, no-one has given much serious thought to the idea that the king might have been buried here. However, whilst the chamber in certain respects does seem to be incomplete,[1] its rough finish and irregular shape almost certainly symbolised the underworld, which was said to have been in a state of chaos prior to the creation.[2] In this sense, the Subterranean Chamber would have represented the perfect location for the burial of the king, and would have justified the great time and trouble which the builders evidently took to reach this point, 100 feet beneath the bedrock. Incidentally, the finishing off of its access passage (the Descending Passage) throughout its 350-feet length, argues strongly against the abandonment theory.

Might the king have been buried in the Subterranean Chamber? Whilst

Figure 59.
THE GREAT PYRAMID, VERTICAL SECTION, LOOKING WEST, WITH SUBTERRANEAN FEATURES HIGHLIGHTED.

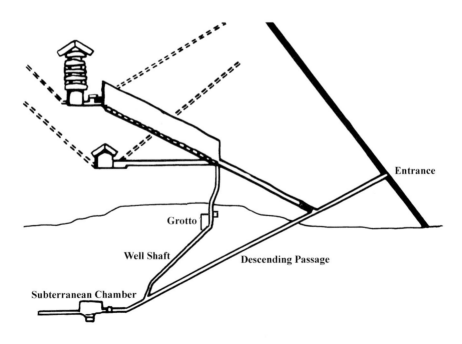

Entrance

Grotto

Well Shaft

Descending Passage

Subterranean Chamber

no hard evidence has been found, it is perfectly possible that the king's mummy and coffin were removed in antiquity, or that the burial remains here undiscovered, perhaps beneath the Pit which has been only partially explored.

However, there is a major problem with the idea that the Subterranean Chamber was a tomb, namely its vulnerability to robbers, for as Michael Hoffman observed in his book *Egypt Before The Pharaohs* (1979): 'tomb robbery was already a well-established national pastime a thousand years before Khufu'.[3] In the event that such robbers had located the entrance to the Great Pyramid and proceeded down the Descending Passage, they would have proceeded forthwith to the location in question, where the tomb of the king would surely not have eluded them. On balance then, whilst the Subterranean Chamber was suitably symbolic for a tomb, it seems unlikely that the king would have sanctioned his burial here, since it was altogether too vulnerable. Nevertheless, for this precise reason, the chamber would have made an ideal decoy tomb, to throw intruders off the scent, as the Egyptologist J.P. Lepre has noted:

> This chamber was ideally situated to act as a ploy, to make the unsuspecting mind believe that a pharaoh had once been buried here.[4]

Not all Egyptologists would support this view, since many still believe that the Subterranean Chamber was unfinished and abandoned, making it a less than convincing decoy chamber.[5] But one cannot help thinking that if Egyptologists could only recognise that the rough finish and irregular shape of the chamber were deliberately symbolic of the underworld, then this decoy theory could emerge as a definite consensus.

Turning to the second of the possibilities listed above, might the king have been buried in some other, as yet undiscovered, chamber, concealed in the basement of the Pyramid? Here, one is reminded of the report of the Greek historian Herodotus (5th century BC), who was informed by the Egyptian priests that Cheops (Khufu) had been buried beneath the Great Pyramid in subterranean chambers 'built on a sort of island, surrounded by water introduced from the Nile by a canal.'[6] Unfortunately, this report matches no part of the Pyramid that we know, but it seems to imply an excavation deep in the bedrock. In this regard, there have been several unsuccessful explorations of the Pit in the Subterranean Chamber,[7] but a better prospect perhaps would be an independent subterranean chamber accessed via a separate tunnel, the entrance to which would be concealed somewhere on the Giza plateau. The possibility of secret tunnels will be addressed in a later chapter, but at this juncture it takes us 'off the map' into the realms of what is unknowable at the present time, and cannot provide the solid basis for a theory.

This leaves us with the third possibility (3), that the king was buried in the Grotto. It is to this small cave-like sanctuary, situated approximately at ground level, that I wish to direct my investigation in this chapter.

The Grotto

The first thing to be noted about the Grotto is that very few people have ever visited it on account of its inaccessible location. To reach it, one must engage in a long and perilous climb, either 133 feet upwards from the bottom of the Descending Passage or 70 feet downwards from the bottom of the Grand Gallery. J.P. Lepre, one of the few Egyptologists to have visited the Grotto, has written:

> It represents that area of the pyramid which, more than any other, has been so neglected by nearly all researchers and explorers... although so many authors have mentioned the Grotto in passing within the context of their treatises on the subject of the Great Pyramid, very few have actually had the opportunity to visit it for themselves.[8]

In the following pages, we will be indebted to Lepre for his descriptions of the Grotto.

First, the basic facts. The Grotto lies just below the highest point of the rocky outcrop on which the Pyramid is anchored, the upper entrance to it having been sealed off by the first layer of the Pyramid's masonry. It thus lies at ground level theoretically, although in practice it is about 15 feet above the exterior base.[9] In the horizontal plane, meanwhile, the Grotto is located about 120 feet north of the Pyramid's central east-west axis, but exactly straddles the central north-south axis (the main passage system being offset to the east). An interesting fact that no-one has ever recorded, to the best of my knowledge, is that in the Pyramid's original design the Grotto lay further from the entrance than any other chamber in the Pyramid, at a total distance of about 466 feet (comprising 323 feet of the Descending Passage and a 143 feet segment of the Well Shaft) – a distance not far short of the height of the Pyramid (481 feet).

The Grotto is essentially a natural cave. Before the Pyramid was built, it must have been an earthen oasis in the midst of the plateau bedrock, as Lepre explains:

> The Grotto of the Great Pyramid, situated just below the monument's ground level, constitutes what appears to be the hollowing-out of a once-smaller natural pocket of earth at the centre of the pyramid plateau. Unusual as it may seem, being uniquely located in the very

middle of an otherwise solid rock foundation, no other explanation can be given.[10]

The Grotto may be described as a low cavern of irregular shape with its floor on three levels. Lepre describes the shape of the room as follows:

> The shape of the Grotto is unorthodox, displaying several levels. Only at its centre is it high enough for the average man to barely stand erect. It curves or bends in its configuration, and forms a rough L-pattern.[11]

This L-pattern is visible in the ground plan, figure 60. The main feature here is the Well Shaft, a vertical shaft approximately 28 inches square, which provides the entrance and exit to the room. It is constructed of roughly-squared limestone blocks in ten layers, its uppermost layer abutting against the core masonry of the Pyramid. In the south side of this shaft, at its bottom, an aperture, again 28 inches square, provides a doorway into the room. It is possible that this 10-feet high section of the Well Shaft was originally independent of the Pyramid and predated its construction by centuries.

In the west side of the Grotto is the lowest floor level, in which a deep hole has been dug, for a purpose unknown. In the centre of the room the floor level rises, and then it rises again. The relative floor levels and the depth of the excavation are revealed by the profile view in figure 61.

Figure 60.
THE GROTTO, GROUND PLAN.
Compare figure 61.

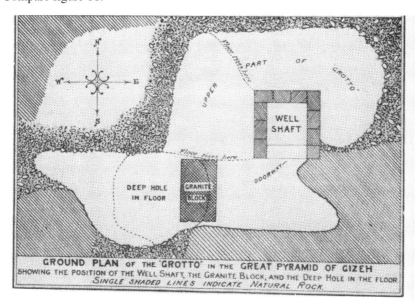

GROUND PLAN OF THE 'GROTTO' IN THE GREAT PYRAMID OF GIZEH
SHOWING THE POSITION OF THE WELL SHAFT, THE GRANITE BLOCK, AND THE DEEP HOLE IN THE FLOOR
SINGLE SHADED LINES INDICATE NATURAL ROCK.

Figure 61.
THE GROTTO, VERTICAL SECTION, LOOKING NORTH.
Compare figure 60.

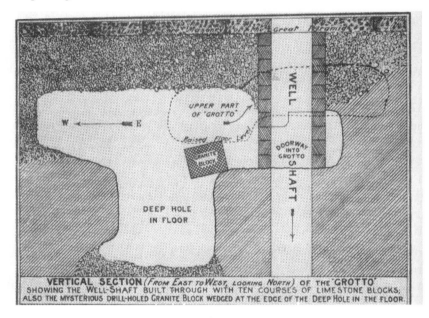

VERTICAL SECTION *(From East to West, looking North)* of the 'GROTTO'
SHOWING THE WELL-SHAFT BUILT THROUGH WITH TEN COURSES OF LIMESTONE BLOCKS;
ALSO THE MYSTERIOUS DRILL-HOLED GRANITE BLOCK WEDGED AT THE EDGE OF THE DEEP HOLE IN THE FLOOR.

   Inside the Grotto, resting on the floor near the deep hole, is a block of
granite, measuring 42 by 25 by 20 inches, with a 3.5-inch hole bored
through it, perhaps to facilitate its lowering into the room.[12]
   The ceiling of the Grotto is low, fairly flat and highly unusual. Lepre
comments:

> Even more curious than the presence of this earthen cavity is the fact
> that its ceiling is composed, not of packed earth as would be expected,
> but of gravel packed in damp, caked sand. Whereas the earthen walls
> of this cavity are relatively hard to the touch, the ceiling of small
> stones is so loosely packed that one has only to reach up and dig in
> with one's fingers in order to extract whole handfuls of this material.
> M. Edgar collaborates this observation by stating that this ceiling
> 'crumbles when touched'. This is a very unusual configuration, and
> one which would lead us to believe that perhaps the ceiling might
> represent an impromptu fill-in by the builders.[13]

Lepre then notes something even more peculiar about this ceiling:

> The ceiling is also unusually damp to the point where there is actually
> a perceptible coating – like a light frost – over the pebbles themselves.
> This unusual composition naturally tempts one to speculate about the

existence of a nearby water source. Yet a water source – and especially one so very cool – does not seem likely in the middle of a solid rock foundation at the edge of a barren section of desert.[14]

What was the purpose of this strange room? As Lepre has noted, many Egyptologists have referred to the Grotto in passing, but few have ever visited it, and it has not figured prominently in their explanations of the Pyramid. As far as the orthodoxy is concerned, this cave-like enclosure is a primitive feature, possibly dating back centuries to the earliest days of Egyptian civilisation.[15] Then, like many caves, it was probably regarded as a holy sanctuary – the dwelling place, perhaps, of the 'dead gods' who had assisted the creator in his act of creation.[16]

In the context of the Great Pyramid, however, the Grotto has been all but ignored by Egyptologists, who have focused all their attention on the more sophisticated, well-finished and larger chambers. Having decided long ago that the King's Chamber was the tomb of Khufu, they have deemed the Grotto to be unworthy of detailed study.

But Lepre, whilst supporting the orthodox point of view, sensed that the Grotto may have had a hitherto overlooked purpose. He wrote:

> Although seemingly insignificant when compare to the other, much more commanding, apartments of the Great Pyramid, the Grotto nevertheless had a special purpose which we are not presently familiar with.[17]

Could this 'special purpose' have been the burial of the king? Might it be possible that Khufu was buried in the Grotto? If the reader will indulge me, I would like to explore this hypothesis. And the key to it is the Well Shaft.

The Well Shaft

The Well Shaft was described briefly in chapter two, and was mentioned in chapter three in the context of the hypothetical escape of the workmen who had been buried alive in the Pyramid. However, it is now imperative that we take a much closer look at the Well Shaft, and consider how and why it was constructed.

To begin, a more thorough description of the Well Shaft is warranted, and to this end I have labelled the various sections of the shaft according to a system that will soon become apparent. In this system, the shaft is formed of two segments that were originally separate: an upper section X-Y-Z, and a lower section A-B-C-D-E. At a later date, these two original segments were joined together by a roughly-hewn and irregular

Figure 62.
THE WELL SHAFT, WITH KEY SECTIONS LABELLED.

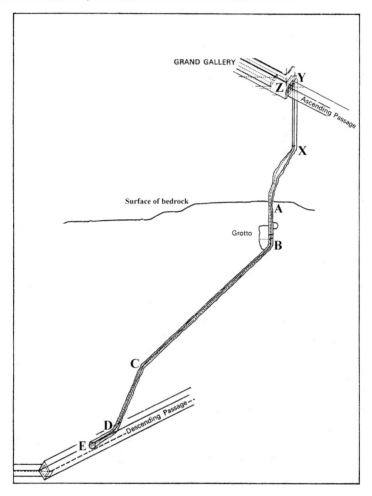

tunnel A-X (designated after the axe that was used in its cutting).

We will consider the two original segments of the Well Shaft in turn, beginning with the lower one A-B-C-D-E, which may be summarised as follows:

A-B = 13 feet vertical.
B-C = 100 feet oblique, north-south.
C-D = 30 feet oblique, north-south.
D-E = 10 feet horizontal, east-west.

(Note: all sections of the shaft are approximately 28 by 28 inches square.)

Section A-B comprises a 10-feet length of built shaft, at the bottom of which is the door to the Grotto (see description earlier), and an additional 3-feet length that has been cut vertically into the bedrock below. Exiting from the Grotto, we drop down this short length, whereupon the passage turns southwards and runs obliquely, in an accurate straight line, for a distance of 100 feet through the bedrock (section B-C). In the uppermost part of this passage, two large fissures can be seen – evidence perhaps of earthquake activity.

Next, the passage drops away more steeply, and runs obliquely, again in a straight line, for a further distance of 30 feet in a southerly direction (section C-D).

Finally, the passage turns sharply eastwards and runs horizontally for a distance of about 10 feet (section D-E), where it connects into the wall of the Descending Passage. Today, this connection is marked by a gaping hole in the west wall of the Descending Passage. But in ancient times, this aperture would have been filled by a camouflaging stone. (This is evidenced by the fact that Greek and Roman explorers who visited the Subterranean Chamber knew nothing about the upper system of passages and chambers; if the lower entrance to the Well Shaft had been open, then they would surely have explored the passage, or at least mentioned its existence in their writings, but they did not.[18] It is thus probable that the Well Shaft's lower entrance was still concealed at those times.)

What was the design of the camouflaging stone? Egyptologists speak of a limestone block or slab 'which would have been indistinguishable from the other stones comprising the west wall of that corridor';[19] it may have been cut out and prepared before the king's funeral, or it may have been cut out immediately after the funeral by the workmen who used the Well Shaft to escape their own entombment. One way or the other, it was then refitted into the wall, perhaps permanently using cement, or perhaps in a way that the priests could use it as a movable door to enter and exit the Well Shaft at will.[20] But one can only speculate on the mechanics of opening and closing this entrance, since the camouflaging stone has long disappeared from the Pyramid.

Let us turn now to the upper section of the Well Shaft X-Y-Z and the tunnel A-X that joined it to the lower section. This segment may be summarised as follows:

A-X = 35 feet oblique, north-south, a roughly-hewn tunnel.
X-Y = 25 feet vertical.
Y-Z = 7 feet horizontal, east-west.

(Note: all sections of the shaft are approximately 28 by 28 inches square.)

Beginning once again from the Grotto, we climb up the vertical, built section of the Well Shaft, described earlier, to the level of the Pyramid's core masonry, at which point the passage becomes a rough-hewn tunnel that has been hacked through the masonry.[21] This irregular tunnel A-X winds its way upwards quite steeply in a northern direction for about 35 feet, until it connects with a vertical section of passage, built of neatly-squared limestone blocks (section X-Y).

Section X-Y extends perpendicularly for 25 feet, at which point it turns sideways to run eastwards for about 7 feet to a point directly below the north-west bottom corner of the Grand Gallery (section Y-Z). Here, one is able to climb up out of the Well Shaft into the Gallery through an aperture about 2 feet 4 inches square that was originally filled by a ramp stone. This ramp stone is now missing but the surrounding stones bear witness to its violent removal.

Figure 63.
THE MISSING RAMP STONE AT THE BOTTOM NORTH-WEST CORNER OF THE GRAND GALLERY.

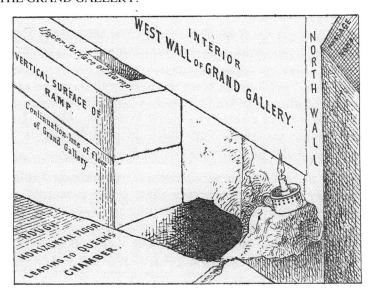

The Well Shaft Mystery

When we consider the Well Shaft as a whole, it emerges as a remarkable and impressive construction, indeed the second longest passage in the Pyramid. With a total length of 217 feet, much of it through the bedrock, the builders evidently went to a lot of trouble. But the question is why? Why was it necessary?

In addition to the mystery of the Well Shaft proper, two further sub-mysteries require to be solved. Firstly, there is the mystery of the rough tunnel A-X, which connected the upper and lower sections of the Well Shaft. Who dug this tunnel, when, and why? And secondly, there is the mystery of the missing ramp stone. Who forcibly removed it, when and why? Was it broken out from above, or was it broken out from below? All of these questions are undoubtedly interrelated.

In an attempt to solve these mysteries, two observations provide us with a good starting point:

1 The lower section of the Well Shaft A-B-C-D-E was cut *downwards*.

2 The lower section of the Well Shaft A-B-C-D-E was cut *at the same time as the Descending Passage was cut.*

The evidence for these two observations is as follows.

As regards (1), the bottom section of the Well Shaft C-D extends slightly below the level of the passage that connects it to the secret door in the Descending Passage. This is a crucial piece of evidence, as J.P. Lepre has explained:

> The well shaft was dug out from the top down. This is indicated by the fact that its bottom end penetrates a few feet below its lowermost doorway. If it had been hewn from the bottom up, this bottom section would surely have been level with its doorway at that point.[22]

As regards (2), the vertical built shaft, section A-B, was evidently used in conjunction with the Grotto, which probably predated the Pyramid by several centuries. From here, section B-C runs straight like an arrow until it takes a sudden turn downwards at point C. Why? The only plausible explanation is that the Well Shaft was being cut at the same time as the Descending Passage, and that the plan for the latter was changed, to cut short its length, perhaps by about 25 feet. Then, the builders of the Well Shaft, wanting for reasons of security to make a connecting door some way up the sloping section of the Descending Passage rather than in the horizontal section that was now planned, were forced to cut the Well Shaft much more steeply. Hence the angle of section C-D. The fact of this sudden turn, then, argues strongly for the cutting of the entire Well Shaft at the same time as the Descending Passage was being cut. The builders were thus digging on two fronts simultaneously, with the clear intention that the two shafts should intersect beneath the Pyramid.

None of this is particularly controversial, but it helps to set the scene for a reconstruction of what happened.

The big question, of course, is why the builders went to all the trouble of seeking a conjunction of the two passages so deep underground.

Egyptologists have suggested two possible explanations. Firstly, that the Well Shaft was cut to supply air to the workmen at the bottom of the Descending Passage and in the Subterranean Chamber. Or secondly, that the Well Shaft was cut to facilitate the escape of the workmen who had become trapped in the Grand Gallery following the king's funeral.

Each of these two theories must now be considered briefly, in turn.

The Ventilation Theory

The Well Shaft ventilation theory was first suggested by the Italian archaeologists Vito Maragioglio and Celeste Rinaldi in an eight-volume study of the Egyptian pyramids entitled *L'Architetettura delle Pyramidi Menfite* (1963-77).[23] In their opinion, the workmen at the bottom of the Descending Passage had experienced difficulties in breathing, and it was therefore decided to provide them with air by sinking the Well Shaft. On the face of it, the theory seemed plausible, for the workmen were indeed digging at an unprecedented depth. Many eminent Egyptologists thus lent their support to this idea. For example, I.E.S. Edwards argued in the final edition of his book *The Pyramids of Egypt* (1993) that the Well Shaft had been designed originally as a ventilation shaft, which had then been used, at the time of the king's funeral, to evacuate the workers from the Grand Gallery:

> Initially, it [the Well Shaft] may have served to ventilate the bottom end of the Descending Corridor and the Subterranean Chamber when they were being constructed...[24]

Mark Lehner took the same view in his book *The Complete Pyramids* (1997). The workmen had escaped through the Well Shaft, he said, but it had originally been cut for the purpose of ventilation:

> This was no robber's tunnel as some have believed, but was probably cut to conduct air down to the bottom of the Descending Passage, so that work could continue on the Subterranean Chamber.[25]

Unfortunately, however, the Well Shaft ventilation theory is open to a number of serious objections.

Firstly, it may be disputed whether the workmen in the Subterranean Chamber would have been so desperately short of air, to the extent that a 140-feet-long shaft was required to be cut for that purpose, and for that purpose alone.

Secondly, it may be argued that the builders would have devised a much less onerous means of providing air to the Subterranean Chamber; for example, a manually-operated pump system that could have forced air down the Descending Passage.

Thirdly, as Peter Tompkins has pointed out, there is some irony in the fact that the diggers of the 'ventilation shaft' would have experienced conditions every bit as cramped and airless as the workers whom they were trying to assist.[26] By the time the problem had been identified and the relieving shaft completed, the workers in the Subterranean Chamber might well have finished their tasks.

Fourthly, the ventilation theory requires that the Descending Passage had already been cut to a considerable depth, perhaps even as far as the Subterranean Chamber, at the time when it was decided to sink the Well Shaft. However, if this were so, it becomes difficult to explain the kink in the Well Shaft at point C, since one would expect the Well Shaft to have been cut directly in a straight line from the Grotto to its junction with the Descending Passage.

Fifthly, if the Well Shaft was designed to ventilate the Subterranean Chamber and the Descending Passage for the completion of the work there, one would expect it to have been kept open for as long as possible. However, when the builders began to construct the Pyramid, they laid the first courses of masonry directly over the Well Shaft's upper mouth, and thus sealed off the supposed air supply.

In summary, whilst none of the above five points may be decisive in its own right, the cumulative weight of argument tends to throw serious doubt upon the ventilation hypothesis.

The Evacuation of the Workmen Theory

The second theory is that the Well Shaft was cut to facilitate the escape of the workmen who had lowered the granite plugs into the Ascending Passage and thereby trapped themselves in the Grand Gallery after the king's funeral. According to Egyptologists, the builders of the Pyramid had foreseen this eventuality, and had therefore cut the Well Shaft so as to offer the workmen an escape route. Firstly, the builders had precut the lower section A-B-C-D-E; then they had dug the rough tunnel A-X through some 35 feet of the Pyramid's masonry, apparently having forgotten to extend the shaft upwards (!); and finally, they had built the upper section of the Well Shaft X-Y-Z. The retiring workmen could thus lift the ramp stone at the bottom of the Gallery, slip down sections Y-Z and X-Y of the Well Shaft, pass through the tunnel A-X (or dig it if it had not already been dug), navigate the remaining depths of the Well

Shaft, and then use the Descending Passage to exit the Pyramid.

This scenario, frankly, is ludicrous. Not only is it incredible that the builders would have forgotten to extend the Well Shaft from point A to point X, but it also beggars belief that the king would have authorised the construction of a shaft that effectively provided a back door route to his tomb in the King's Chamber (as noted in chapter three, the Well Shaft, if constructed in this way, would have doubled the risk of the tomb being discovered and robbed); finally, for good measure, a much shorter shaft could have served the purpose of the hypothetical evacuation. For these reasons, the theory is a non-starter.

Egyptologists are nevertheless keen to explain how the workmen, who lowered the granite plugs, escaped from their entombment in the Grand Gallery. They have therefore retained this theory by hybridising it with the ventilation theory. It is now widely believed that the lower section of the Well Shaft A-B-C-D-E was designed as a ventilation shaft, and that the upper section X-Y-Z and the connecting tunnel A-X were designed for the escape of the workmen, possibly without the knowledge of the king (thus circumventing one of the main objections above). This is the view taken by the pyramid experts I.E.S. Edwards and Mark Lehner.

Again, serious objections may be raised. Firstly, the ventilation theory is itself open to question, as already noted. And secondly, it strikes this author as preposterous that the builders would have kept from their king the existence or purpose of sections X-Y-Z and A-X, given the risk that the Well Shaft as a whole would have posed to the tomb (and it is even more preposterous that the king would actually have approved these sections of the shaft).

In defence of the 'evacuation of the workmen' theory, Egyptologists often cite the 'fact' that the missing ramp stone at the north-west bottom corner of the Gallery (see figure 63) was removed *from above*. Who else but the workmen, they say, would have had the knowledge of the Well Shaft's upper entrance there, along with the incentive to open it?

This idea was advocated by Noel Wheeler in 1935, and subsequently by Vito Maragioglio and Celeste Rinaldi in 1965. They argued that it would have been extremely difficult to dislodge the ramp stone from below, in addition to which chisel marks on the upper sides of the stones that surrounded the aperture indicated that the ramp stone had been removed from above.[27] According to the authors Ian Lawton and Chris Ogilvie-Herald, writing in 1999,[28] this view is nowadays supported by the majority of scholars, which is, of course, no surprise since the orthodox burial theory virtually demands that this view of the ramp stone be taken.

Other authorities, however, dispute that the ramp stone was broken out from above.

In 1865, Piazzi Smyth, the astronomer-royal of Scotland, carried out a close inspection of the masonry around the ramp stone, and came to the considered view that the stone had been broken out *from below*. In his 1880 book *Our Inheritance in the Great Pyramid*, he expressed his deep scepticism about the 'evacuation of the workmen' theory:

> In what state would they [the escaping workmen] have left the ramp stone over the Well's mouth? Certainly not blown from within outwards, as if by uncontrollable explosive force, breaking off part of the wall with it, and leaving the hole's mouth exposed; for that would have defeated the whole object. They would, on the contrary, have contrived a temporary support for the stone... such that when the last man had come away, the prop would be easily withdrawn, and the stone would fall neatly into a seat already cut for it, and cemented round the edges with freshly applied lime to make the work permanent and secure... The original builders, then, were not those who knocked out, from within on the well side, that now lost ramp stone... no-one could have done it except by entering the Well from the very bottommost depths of the subterranean region.[29]

Smyth's opinion was shared by the English structural engineer David Davidson, who carried out a detailed study of the Pyramid in the early-20th century. He, too, was persuaded by the fractured appearance of the stones in the vicinity of the missing ramp stone, which suggested that the said stone had been forced upwards and outwards.[30] But by whom and for what reason? In Davidson's view, the Pyramid had been damaged by an unusually strong earthquake, and this had prompted the guardians of the monument to enter the upper chambers in order to ascertain the damage and carry out any necessary repairs. These guardians, having possession of the Pyramid's design blueprint, had ascended the lower section of the Well-Shaft A-B-C-D-E (Davidson claimed rashly that they had dug it as they went) and dug the rough tunnel A-X in the precise direction of the upper section X-Y-Z. In this way, they had gained access to the upper chambers in an inconspicuous way, and avoided any damage to the system of plugs in the Ascending Passage.

Davidson's earthquake theory, of course, begs the question of why the Well Shaft, sections A-B-C-D-E and X-Y-Z, existed in the first place. But it is an interesting theory nonetheless, to which we shall return in a later chapter.

At this juncture, however, our greater concern is the conflict of views surrounding the manner of the ramp stone's removal. Was it broken out from above, in accordance with the 'evacuation of the workmen' theory, or was it broken out from below, in accordance with the kind of scenario envisaged by Davidson?

As I see it, there is an awkward problem here in that the broken ramp stone is liable to be interpreted by researchers in accordance with their predilections about the design and purpose of the Pyramid.[31] But, whilst I have no desire to fall into the same trap, it nevertheless seems to me that a number of important points have been overlooked in the heat of the argument.

Firstly, it should be pointed out that the evidence for the ramp stone having been broken out from below, as cited by Smyth and Davidson, does not automatically invalidate the orthodox tomb theory. It is possible (although I am not advocating it) that the workmen did release the ramp stone in the controlled manner discussed by Smyth and then evacuated the Pyramid via the Well Shaft; and that, at a later date, the guardians of the Pyramid forcibly removed the ramp stone from below (it having been cemented into place) in order to inspect the upper chambers, perhaps following an earthquake. Thus Smyth and Davidson's view of the ramp stone is not inconsistent with the orthodox theory.

Secondly, concerning the chisel marks on the upper sides of the stones around the ramp stone aperture, it is perfectly possible that these were made at the time of *enlarging* the aperture rather than cutting it for the first time. Such a task might have been performed by the guardians of the Pyramid to facilitate transit in and out, or by unauthorised intruders who may have used the Well Shaft subsequently to remove artefacts from the Pyramid. Or, alternatively, it is possible that the ramp stone was blown out from below, then restored by the guardians of the Pyramid, and later chiselled out from above by intruders. Thus, the chisel marks in no way prove that the ramp stone was removed from above, but are consistent with a scenario in which the ramp stone was removed from below – by someone with intimate knowledge of the Pyramid's design.

In summary, the fact and manner of the ramp stone's removal neither proves nor disproves the orthodox theory of the workers' evacuation, and it permits the two possibilities that the stone was broken out from above or that it was broken out from below (a difficult but not impossible task). The only way to resolve these issues is on the balance of probabilities pertaining to the various scenarios. Here, the theory of the workmen's evacuation suffers from the serious problems outlined earlier: firstly, the lack of an adequate explanation for the length and shape of the lower Well Shaft A-B-C-D-E (i.e. the shortcomings of the ventilation theory); secondly, the absurd suggestion that the builders forgot to extend the

Well Shaft from point A to point X; and thirdly, the bizarre notion that the king would have sanctioned the construction of shafts and a tunnel that provided a back door route to his tomb in the King's Chamber (or, equally bizarre, that the builders would have kept secret from their king the existence or purpose of said tunnel and shafts). In view of all these problems, then, there is every incentive to look for an alternative, more plausible, theory that is consistent with the physical evidence inside the Pyramid.

The Secret Burial Scenario

So far, no theory of the Well Shaft has had the ring of plausibility. We know, with reasonable certainty, that the shaft was cut downwards; and we know, with reasonable certainty, that the shaft was cut downwards at the same time as the Descending Passage was being cut. Could there be another explanation as to why it was necessary for these two passages to intersect 80 feet underground?

Let us now take a different approach to the problem, this time putting the cave-like Grotto at the heart of the proceedings. Let us suppose, as some Egyptologists have suggested, that the Grotto was a sacred site for centuries before the Pyramid was built; and let us suppose that access to it was gained via the vertical shaft A-B, point A being the entry point at the level of the Giza plateau.

Let us now spring forward to the time of the Pyramid's construction, a few centuries later. And let us suppose, quite reasonably, that the priests wished to retain access to the Grotto – this most ancient and hallowed of sites. But how would this access have been achieved when the Pyramid

Figure 64.
THE GROTTO, PRIOR TO CONSTRUCTION OF THE PYRAMID.

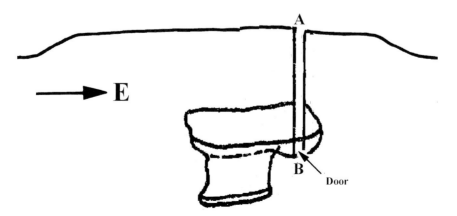

was to be built upon that spot?

The first possibility was to create a new entrance shaft, leading down from the northern end of the Grand Gallery to the Grotto's old shaft at point A. But we know for a fact that the builders did not take this option, but rather laid 35 feet of masonry over the entrance to the Grotto. Let us suppose, quite reasonably, that this was *not* a mistake. In which case, we are left with the second possibility.

The second possibility was to connect the Grotto's old shaft to the new Descending Passage that was being cut for the Pyramid. This is indeed consistent with what we see in the downward extension of the Well Shaft from point B to point E, and the secret door in the Descending Passage at point E.

In other words, I am suggesting that the Well Shaft's lower section B-C-D-E was cut for the sole purpose of providing a means of access to the Grotto after the Pyramid had been built. Not an unreasonable idea in view of the likely sanctity of the Grotto, and very different from the two orthodox theories which we examined earlier.

But what exactly did the priests want with this secret passage to the Grotto? One possibility is that they sought to use the cave for ongoing rituals, perhaps at certain times of the year. But another possibility is that they required a one-off access to the Grotto for the funeral ceremony of the king.

Whilst not dismissing the first possibility, it is the second possibility that I would like to explore in the remainder of this chapter. Was the king buried secretly in the Grotto?

If the reader will indulge me, I would like to outline a scenario.

The Giza plateau is devoid of its pyramids. But work is about to begin. A team of specialist workers is preparing to sink the Descending Passage of the Great Pyramid approximately 258 feet into the bedrock, where it will debouch into a subterranean chamber at a point directly under the Pyramid's central east-west axis. As they do so, however, a second team of workers has set up base on top of the rocky outcrop, about 100 feet to the south and 10 feet to the west of the first team's position. This second team, given privileged access to the holy site of the Grotto, is preparing to sink into the bedrock a shaft about 168 feet long, which, unbeknownst to the first team, will intersect with the Descending Passage some 25 feet short of the latter's terminus.

Each day, as the first team cuts the Descending Passage southwards at an angle of 26° 34′, the second team slips down the vertical shaft past the Grotto, and cuts the so-called Well Shaft southwards at an angle of about 43°.

Then, one day, the architect decides (for a reason unknown to us) to shorten the Descending Passage by about 25 feet, and replace this length by *a horizontal passage* to the Subterranean Chamber. In keeping with this decision, he orders the second team to alter the angle of their passage from 43° to a much steeper 68° so that the second passage will intersect with the first passage in its sloping section, about 22 feet above the terminus, as originally planned. This change in angle is considered to be essential, since otherwise the second passage will meet the first passage in the horizontal section, where tomb robbers would be more likely to discover the secret door.

The second team extend their passage southwards at its new angle for a distance of about thirty feet. Then, having taken careful measurements of their position relative to the Descending Passage, they cut a 10-feet-long connecting passage eastwards to intersect the Descending Passage in its west wall. As they get closer and closer to the first passage, they work more and more carefully, until a reed can be poked through into the passage beyond. Then, with the utmost care, the workmen perform their most difficult and precise task: they chisel away at the rock to form a thin slab that can be removed and replaced in the wall. Having completed this task, they reinsert the secret door in the wall, ready for later use during the king's funeral.

The existence of this connecting passage and door, we may surmise, was known only to members of the second team, and to as few of them as possible. The first team, who dug the Descending Passage, would have known nothing of the secret entrance, work on their passage having been completed or suspended at the time when the final secret linkage was made.

As work begins on the Pyramid's superstructure, the priests make the final preparations for the secret funeral in the Grotto, lowering into the sacred cave any necessary ritual objects and perhaps assembling there a wooden coffin for the king. Soon afterwards, the Pyramid's masonry is laid across the entrance to the Grotto's shaft, to block off that entrance for ever. From this moment on, the Grotto becomes inaccessible, except via the Well Shaft and its secret door in the Descending Passage.

The Pyramid is completed, and the funeral of the king takes place. To outside observers, the king's mummy is conveyed into the Pyramid's main entrance, whence it will be lowered through the Descending Passage into the Subterranean Chamber. Perhaps a burial ritual is indeed performed in that chamber, in order to bring the mummy to life. But a secret plan is now to be executed, on the orders of the late king, of which only a very few people have knowledge. Two or three of these people,

Figure 65.
THE GROTTO AND WELL SHAFT, ORIGINAL DESIGN, SHOWN
IMMEDIATELY AFTER COMPLETION OF THE PYRAMID.

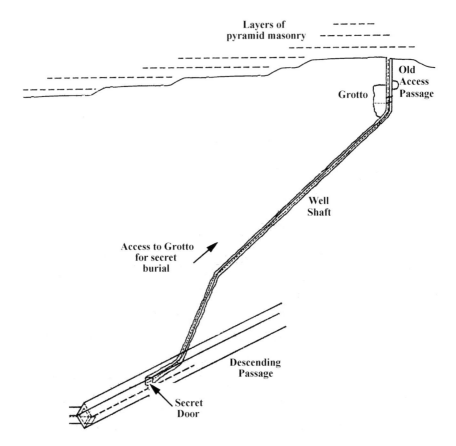

we may surmise, are those who remain behind in the chamber to perform the last rites.

These trusted priests backtrack up the Descending Passage and gently prise open the secret door to the Well Shaft. With as much respect as it is possible to display in the circumstances, they remove the king's mummy from the coffin in the Subterranean Chamber (for reasons that will soon become evident), carry it through the horizontal passage, and then haul it 22 feet up the Descending Passage to the secret entrance to the Well Shaft. There, having manoeuvred the mummy through the hole in the wall (in a space too cramped to permit the coffin's insertion), the priests convey it all the way up the Well Shaft to the Grotto. And there they perform the last rites for the king, whose soul is forthwith translated into the Pyramid above, and to all four corners of the Universe.

Now, the priests make their way back down the Well Shaft and into the Descending Passage, where they refit the secret door, cementing it into place and camouflaging its joints. Having made any final necessary adjustments to the Subterranean Chamber, which is to perform the role of a decoy burial chamber, they vacate the chamber, block the passage to it with the portcullis slabs, and exit the Pyramid through the Descending Passage, leaving outside observers none the wiser as to the secret plan that has been executed.

Is this scenario plausible?

Before we discuss the wider merits of the idea that the Grotto was the king's burial place, we must first consider whether it was practical for the priests to introduce the king's mummy to the Well Shaft, to haul it up that shaft for a distance of about 143 feet, and to manoeuvre it into the Grotto. Do the physical dimensions of the shaft permit the envisaged scenario?

To begin with the hole in the west wall of the Descending Passage, its dimensions are about 28 inches square – large enough for a human body to be inserted. But, in addition, we must take into account the cramped confines of the Descending Passage, which measured 3 feet 11 inches high by 3 feet 5 inches wide. Again, this would have provided enough space, just, to manoeuvre the king's mummy into the Well Shaft (though perhaps not a coffin).[32]

Inside the Well Shaft, the first turn upwards at point D would have required a difficult manoeuvre. Once again, however, the shaft contains just enough space for the mummy to be tilted and passed through (see figure 67).

Figure 66.
THE SECRET ENTRANCE TO THE WELL SHAFT.

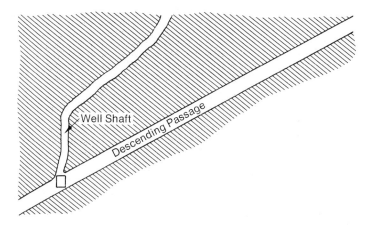

Figure 67.
THE ENTRANCE TO, AND FIRST TURN INSIDE, THE WELL SHAFT.

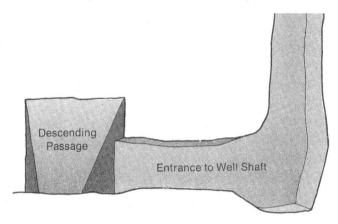

Figure 68.
THE FIRST TURN INSIDE THE WELL SHAFT.

From this point, the main challenge facing the priests would have been to convey the king's mummy up section C-D of the Well Shaft, which, as we have already seen, was cut more steeply than planned at an angle of about 68°. If the priests could navigate this section, then the next section B-C would have been a doddle.

So, how difficult was it? Not too difficult, it would seem, for several researchers have managed the ascent in modern times.

Mark Lehner, who climbed up as far as the Grotto in the early-1980s, recalled his impressions as follows:

This is best done with a rope, which I lacked at the time. There are cup-shaped footholds in the sand-covered floor of the dusty passage.[33]

In the late-1980s, J.P. Lepre made the same climb and also observed the footholds. But he did comment on the difficulty of the ascent:

It is approximately 28 inches square throughout and is lined at intervals with rough footholds, apparently fashioned there by the pyramid builders. This shaft is the area of the pyramid least frequented by visitors and explorers alike. Devoid of any artificial or natural lighting, with steep and vertical turns throughout, it presents a very real element of danger to even the most adept of climbers.[34]

The real danger of the ascent was also emphasised by the investigator Amargi Hillier, who climbed the Well Shaft in 1998 in order to discount rumours of a secret tunnel and chamber:

With an inspector assisting, I personally climbed up the treacherous Grotto in the currently closed Great Pyramid. Now I fully understood why this shaft is off limits to the public. It is a very dangerous climb and descent, and I myself even became extremely nervous as I got high into it... with my back and elbows harshly rubbing against the walls of this very narrow, almost vertical, shaft [section C-D], my hands and feet grasping sweatily to the crumbling stone foot holdings all the way up... Much to the inspector's concern for my safety, I continued on up for the sake of informing the worldwide public that there was absolutely no entrance to any secret room. This is exactly what I found inside the entire length of the Grotto shaft: nothing.[35]

By all accounts, then, the ascent of the Well Shaft is quite difficult and even dangerous in parts. Furthermore, it may be granted that the ascent would have been even more difficult and dangerous if the climbers had had to bear the king's mummy. Nevertheless, the fact remains that all of our intrepid explorers, Lehner, Lepre and Hillier, did made it up to the Grotto and back without loss of life or limb, as did other explorers before them (I am unaware of anyone sustaining death or serious injury in this pursuit). Moreover, as regards the additional burden of hauling the king's mummy up the shaft, this could surely have been achieved, without too much difficulty, by using a rope, perhaps anchored around the granite block in the Grotto.

Finally, the priests would have had to manoeuvre the king's mummy

Figure 69.
THE DOORWAY INTO THE GROTTO.

into the mouth of the Grotto from the vertical shaft A-B. This 90° turn
would have been one of the trickiest of all, the shaft measuring about 28
inches square and the aperture about the same. Once again, however, it
would seem that there is just enough room for a mummy to have been
turned and passed through (though probably not a coffin).

One day, I hope to visit the Pyramid to reconstruct this burial scenario,
to prove beyond any doubt that a mummy could have been conveyed into
the Grotto via the various twists and turns in the Well Shaft. But, in the
meantime, the manoeuvres can be tested by means of paper diagrams and
models, and with positive results it must be said.

The plausibility of the Grotto burial theory is thus established, as far as
it can be at present. But let us keep our sceptic's hat on, and probe for
possible holes in the theory. What objections might be raised against the
idea that the Well Shaft was cut specially for secret access to the Grotto?

One possible criticism is the lack of any explanation for section X-Y-
Z. The theory as it relates to the lower section of the Well Shaft is fine,
but what about the upper section, comprising the two built shafts below
the ramp stone on the Grand Gallery's western side? My feeling is that
this section of the shaft is a red herring in the sense that its purpose was
disconnected from the main length of the Well Shaft below (as evidenced
by the fact that there was no planned link between these two sections of
the Well Shaft). Perhaps the vertical hollow X-Y was required for some
purpose of construction (perhaps there is a similar hollow under the floor
on the eastern side).[36] Perhaps it was filled with sand, for some obscure
religious purpose.[37] Or perhaps it was a secret cavity for objects that were
long ago removed.[38] These ideas are admittedly a little vague, but my
point is that the purpose of section X-Y-Z may well have no bearing at

Figure 70.
THE DOGLEG SECTION OF THE WELL SHAFT AT THE BOTTOM
NORTH-WEST CORNER OF THE GRAND GALLERY.

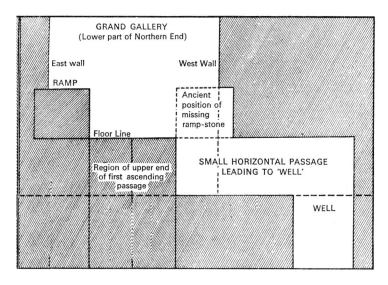

all on the matter of the Well Shaft leading up to the Grotto.

This response also covers any criticism pertaining to the rough tunnel
A-X. As I see it, this tunnel was not part of the Well Shaft's original
design, but was dug upwards for the purpose of gaining access to the
Gallery via the shafts X-Y and Y-Z, in the process linking together two
sections of the Well Shaft that were non-related in function. A possible
explanation for the rough tunnel lies in the need for an inspection of the
Pyramid's upper chambers, perhaps following an exceptional earthquake
as suggested by Davidson. Evidently, the person that directed the digging
had a precise knowledge of the Pyramid's interior design.

Another possible criticism is that if the architect wanted secret access
to the Grotto, he could have saved himself time and trouble by planning a
much shorter passage, running more or less vertically to the Descending
Passage below. I would reject this criticism, however, because a vertical
passage would have been impractical for access to the Grotto, whereas a
sloping passage would have been ideal. In addition, sloping passages,
oriented northwards, were generally favoured by the Egyptians for their
religious symbolism. And a further point, admittedly more speculative, is
that the sloping design of the Well Shaft made the distance from the
Pyramid's main entrance to the Grotto almost exactly the height of the
monument itself. Perhaps this amazing little fact did not go unnoticed in
the mind of the architect.

Finally, the sceptic might argue lack of evidence for the Grotto's use as a ritual or burial chamber. Where are the ritual objects? Where is the king's coffin and mummy? Or, alternatively, where are the fragments of the coffin and mummy, left behind by the tomb robbers? The criticism is, of course, unfair, since evidence of this kind would have been removed long ago, as has happened, so it is claimed, with the burial of the king in the King's Chamber. Or, then again, it may be that no traces have been found because the king's coffin and mummy are still hidden and intact in the Grotto. We will consider this possibility further in chapter ten.

In conclusion, we have now established the plausibility of two things: firstly, that section B-C-D-E of the Well Shaft was cut specifically for access to the Grotto; and secondly, that the purpose of that access could have been the concealment of the king's mummy, with the Subterranean Chamber acting as a decoy tomb.

It now remains only to summarise the attractions of this hypothesis.

The Power of the Grotto

The great attraction of the Grotto burial theory is the room's location, just below the surface of the plateau outcrop on which the Pyramid was anchored. As noted earlier, whilst it lies about 15 feet above the exterior base, it theoretically lies at ground level. A burial here would thus have accorded with the fundamental rule for royal burials in Egypt: 'the body to earth, the spirit to the sky'.

But this is only the half of it.

Egyptologists believe that the Grotto lies exactly in the upper centre of the rocky outcrop on which the Pyramid was built, and that this outcrop takes the form of an artificially-levelled mound, resembling a low, squat step pyramid (see figures 59, 62, 64, 65).[39] Now, the significance of this design lies in the creation myth, according to which the first dry land emerged from the waters of chaos in the form of – you guessed it – a low, squat step pyramid, which Egyptologists refer to as the 'primeval hill' or 'primeval mound'.[40]

This primeval mound was incorporated symbolically in the temples of ancient Egypt, whose architecture enshrined the myth of creation. The floor of the temple was the primeval mound; the ceiling was the sky; and its pillars and obelisks froze the mythical moment when the sky had been separated from the earth.[41] Beneath the temple's floor was the primeval ocean and the underworld. Outside, the enclosure wall symbolised the celestial ocean that bounded the Universe. Inside, a complex of halls, courtyards and chambers, arranged in zones of increasing sacredness,

Figure 71.
RECONSTRUCTION OF THE TEMPLE OF KHONS AT KARNAK,
SHOWING THE STEPPED FLOOR IN THE SHAPE OF THE PRIMEVAL
MOUND.
For comparison to the plateau outcrop beneath the Great Pyramid.

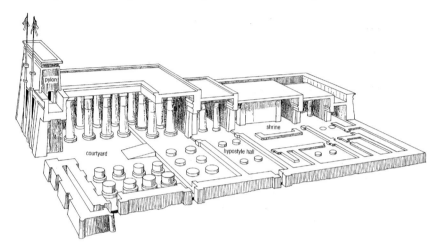

rose in the form of a stepped platform, representing the primeval mound,
on which stood the inner sanctum or naos. There, in the 'holy of holies',
shrouded in mystery, stood the statue of the Great God and his barque.

In his book *Ancient Egyptian Religion* (1948), the great explorer and
scholar Henri Frankfort wrote:

> The basic plan of an Egyptian temple is logical and comprehensible.
> The holy of holies was a small dark room in the central axis of the
> temple towards the back. It thus appears as at the end of a long road
> which passed through the forecourts and narrowed through porticos
> and halls until the hidden shrine was reached. This road also mounted,
> steeply in the case of pyramid temples and the rock temples, less
> noticeably in other cases. But at every door we find a few steps or a
> ramp to mark the rise. For the holy of holies was ideally conceived as
> the primeval hill, the first land to arise from the waters of chaos on the
> day of creation. Since all that exists had gone forth from this spot, it
> was a centre of immeasurable potency well suited for the
> manifestation of a divinity.[42]

But the primeval mound was not just a prominent feature of temples; it
was also the basic form of the royal tomb, for it signified the place where
the creator-god's body had been revivified. As Frankfort wrote in *The
Intellectual Adventure of Ancient Man* (1946):

But the coalescence of temples with the primeval hill does not give us the full measure of the significance which the sacred locality had assumed for the ancient Egyptians. The royal tombs were also made to coincide with it. The dead, and, above all, the king, were reborn in the hereafter. No place was more propitious, no site promised greater chances for a victorious passage through the crisis of death, than the primeval hill, the centre of creative forces where the ordered life of the Universe had begun.[43]

Now, Egyptologists have made the mistake of assuming that the pyramid in its entirety symbolised the primeval mound. However, as explained in chapter one, this is incorrect, as proven by the fact that the capstone of the pyramid, *benbenet*, signified the insemination of the sky.

In the case of the Great Pyramid, then, it is surely the case that the primeval mound – the risen earth of the creation myth – is symbolised not by the Pyramid itself, but rather by the rocky outcrop on which it is built. If this outcrop was levelled artificially into a stepped platform, as is widely supposed, then it would bear an unmistakable resemblance to the primeval mound, and recall the way in which that mound was enshrined in the floors of temples. The Grotto, therefore, standing as it does in the upper centre of the stepped platform, would correspond to the naos or 'holy of holies' – the centre of creation and the dwelling place of the revivified body of the creator-god.

The symbolism was therefore perfect for the burial of the king, for not only did the Grotto conform with the essential requirement for burial of the body at ground level or below, but it also corresponded with the risen earth or primeval mound of the creation myth.[44] (Indeed, in relocating the king's mummy from the Subterranean Chamber to the Grotto, the priests would have re-enacted the rising of the mound at the First Time.)

Contrast this with the orthodox theory, which holds that the king's body was buried in the King's Chamber, at a height of 140 feet inside the Pyramid. Here, it is implied that the king's entire body, identified with the body of the creator, had been ejected from the earth and conveyed towards the sky, in complete contradiction to a fundamental axiom of Egyptian religion.

I could rest my case here, for on symbolism alone the Grotto ranks as the most likely place for a burial chamber in the Pyramid, more fitting than the King's Chamber (and, by the same token, the Queen's Chamber) and arguably more potent than the subterranean chambers considered earlier. But in addition to this, the Grotto burial theory benefits from a significant practical advantage vis-a-vis burials in the King's, Queen's or Subterranean chambers.

This practical advantage is, in a word, security.

As explained in chapter three, the orthodox theory of the king's burial in the King's Chamber suffers from a number of practical problems pertaining to the funeral procession and the closure of the Pyramid after the funeral. Of these, the most serious is the sealing of the Ascending Passage by plugs that had to be lowered from above, the workmen thus becoming trapped inside the Grand Gallery. It has thus been theorised that the Well Shaft, initially designed for ventilation, was extended by sections X-Y-Z and A-X in order to provide a means of evacuating the workmen. This scenario, however, stretches one's credibility to the limit, for in the first instance there are doubts about the ventilation shaft theory, and, in the second instance, it is difficult to believe that the king would have sanctioned the construction of a passage and a tunnel that would have jeopardised the security of his tomb.

In the Grotto burial scenario, in contrast, the Well Shaft terminated at section A-B, and, far from jeopardising the security of the king's tomb, offered an exceptional opportunity to bury him in a well-concealed place by means of a simple (and symbolic) relocation of his body from the Subterranean Chamber to the Grotto. This was ideal from the security point of view, since the Subterranean Chamber, itself an obvious target for tomb robbers, made an ideal decoy chamber, whilst the Grotto lay at the furthermost distance from the entrance of any chamber in the Pyramid (a distance of about 466 feet). Moreover, the secret entrance to the Grotto was expertly camouflaged and situated in the most unlikely of places (in the wall of the Descending Passage). But most important of all, the transference of the king's body from the Subterranean Chamber to the Grotto would have been a quick and inconspicuous procedure, and therein lay the key to the security of the burial. The scenario is just about perfect from a practical point of view.

In summary, the theory that the Grotto was the king's burial chamber is logical, makes sense, accounts for all the physical data, contains no serious flaws (unlike rival theories), is in keeping with the fundamental religious axiom 'the body to earth' (again, unlike rival theories), and is highly attractive in regard to its primeval mound symbolism. Here, in the Grotto, we surely have the best protected, most sacred and ancient room of the Pyramid, which, owing to its inaccessibility, has been overlooked by explorers and scholars who have focused their attention instead on the monument's more grandiose and precision-built chambers.

This theory, I expect, will be difficult for some people to swallow. If the reader belongs to the orthodox school, he will be naturally hostile to a theory that departs from the 'party line'. On the other hand, if the reader belongs to the alternative school, he will be naturally hostile to any notion that a king was buried in, or beneath, the Pyramid. However, it must be borne in mind that it is not my aim to argue dogmatically that the king *was* buried in the Grotto, but rather to argue the plausibility of this scenario, in order to prepare the ground for the hypothesis that is yet to come in the later chapters of this book.

On this note, let us turn to the next stage of our enquiry: the King's Chamber and its sarcophagus. For, if the king was buried underground, in the Grotto, then it behoves me to explain what, in the name of Amun!, was being protected in the Pyramid's highest and most elaborate room. This is the task for the next chapter.

Chapter Four Summary

- In order to ensure the successful despatch of Khufu's soul to the sky, it was essential that his body be buried in the earth, i.e. *beneath* the Great Pyramid, in accordance with the fundamental axiom 'the body to earth, the spirit to the sky'.

- The Subterranean Chamber, being too vulnerable to tomb robbers, was almost certainly a decoy tomb. The only other known subterranean compartment is the rarely-visited Grotto – a cave-like room, accessed via the Well Shaft, that was probably held to be sacred for centuries prior to the construction of the Pyramid.

- Orthodox theories for the Well Shaft are unsatisfactory. A more likely explanation is that the builders cut the lower section of the shaft B-C-D-E solely to provide access to the Grotto after construction of the Pyramid.

- The Grotto, being accessed via a secret door in the Descending Passage, would have made a perfect burial chamber from a security point of view.

- The Grotto also made an ideal burial chamber from a symbolic point of view. Its position amidst the height of the stepped plateau outcrop would have corresponded to the head of the primeval mound (i.e. the risen earth) of the creation myth. A burial there would have been in perfect harmony with the religious axiom 'the body to earth, the spirit to the sky'.

CHAPTER FIVE

THE IRON OF CREATION

He [the king] has appeared upon the Stone, upon his throne, he has sharpened the iron by means of his spirit.

(Pyramid Texts, Utterance 667A)

If Khufu was buried underground, perhaps in the Grotto, then what was the purpose of the granite sarcophagus in the King's Chamber? As noted in chapter three, this granite box evidently once contained something of sufficient value that intruders went to the trouble of breaking open its lid in order to remove its contents. But what exactly were those contents?

The Great Pyramid, unfortunately, remains mute on this question; as with all the early pyramids, its interior is bare and uninscribed. However, during the late-5th and 6th dynasties, from *c.* 2350 to 2100 BC, five royal pyramids at Saqqara (those of Unas, Teti, Pepi I, Merenre and Pepi II) had their interior chambers and corridors inscribed with hieroglyphics – the oldest known surviving corpus of religious writings in the world. It is here, in the so-called Pyramid Texts, that the crucial clues are found for the solution of the sarcophagus mystery. For, even though the Great Pyramid predates the Pyramid Texts by at least two centuries, there is ample evidence that religious beliefs remained broadly unchanged in the Nile Valley during this time.

The Pyramid Texts constitute a collection of magical spells aimed at the successful translation of the king to the 'other world' in the form of a spirit (*akh*). In the eyes of Egyptologists, the Texts comprise a mishmash of conflicting ideas, embracing solar and stellar cults, as well as older, primitive beliefs such as animism and fetishism. A confused picture thus emerges, which sheds frustratingly little light on the significance of the pyramid. In my view, however, all of these supposedly conflicting ideas actually belonged together in a 'cult of creation', and the Pyramid Texts may be understood in this light as *a ritualistic re-enactment of the events of creation.*

It worked like this.

Upon death, the inert body of the king became identified with the inert body of the creator-god, their decaying flesh representing the earth in its primeval condition of darkness and lassitude. The king's body was then mummified and revivified, just as the creator-god (the earth) had been reassembled and brought back to life at the beginning of time. At this, the king's soul separated from its body and ascended to the sky, just as the soul of the creator-god had originally done, and brought the Universe into being in all its diverse splendour: the celestial ocean, the stars, the Sun and the Moon.

The transformation of the king in the Pyramid Texts is thus to be read as an allegory of creation, following the basic principle 'the body to earth, the spirit to the sky', whilst the pyramid itself, in which the Texts are inscribed, encapsulates the story of creation in a single hieroglyphic image, its capstone, *benbenet*, recalling the rising of the creator's seed into the womb of the sky.

Here, in this story of creation, is the big clue to the object (or objects) which the King's Chamber sarcophagus contained.

The Iron of Creation

One of the recurrent images in the Pyramid Texts, which no reader of these Texts can overlook, is the 'iron of creation', or *bja* as the Egyptians used to call it. This iron seems to turn up everywhere, in all parts of the king's journey, beginning in the earth and culminating in the sky, as well as in the rituals that triggered this magical metamorphosis. If the reader will indulge me, I would like to illustrate the ubiquity of this iron in the Pyramid Texts.

To begin, it is said that the king's body is constituted of iron. A typical passage reads:

O king, raise yourself upon your iron bones and golden members, for this body of yours belongs to a god.[1]

Again and again, the deceased king is exhorted to gather together his iron bones and sit on his iron throne:

O king! Raise yourself, receive your head, gather your bones together, shake off your dust, and sit on your iron throne...[2]

In sitting upon the iron throne, the king acquires power over the gods – 'those whose seats are hidden' – and thereby becomes the master of his own resurrection:

> Sit on this iron throne, give commands to those whose seats are hidden. The doors of the sky are opened for you...[3]

The iron throne is a moveable feast. It may be located in the west, in the land of the dead, but it may also be located in the east, in the *akhet* or 'Land of Spiritual Light', and it may also be located in the sky, as we shall see in a moment. But here, the iron throne is in the east, where 'the doors of the earth' and 'the doors of the sky' are located. And fittingly, since the throne will soon split open the earth, it is said to be made of 'sharpened iron':

> He [the king] has appeared upon the Stone, upon his throne, he has sharpened the iron by means of his spirit.[4]

A general cataclysm now occurs. The earth quakes and splits open, and the king ascends into the sky, to the accompaniment of a mighty storm and the rising of the iron. Utterance 669 of the Pyramid Texts uses the metaphor of a boat, the *Hnw*-barque of Sokar, to visualise the creation of the starry sky by the god and the king:

> The designate king ascends in a great storm from the inner horizon... The gods say: "You [Isis] have borne him [the king]; you have shaped him, you have ejected him, but he has no legs he has no arms; how can he be knit together?" Isis replies: "This iron shall be brought for him, the *Hnw*-barque shall be brought that he may be lifted up into it." Sokar shall come for him... it is he who will break the egg and split the iron... Behold, the king comes into being; behold, the king is knit together; behold, the king has broken the egg. The gods ask: "How can the king be made to fly up?" Isis replies: "There shall be brought to you [the king]... the *Hnw*-barque and the *kdmw* of the *hn*-bird. You shall fly up therewith and alight...[5]

We now have 'lift off' for the iron throne:

> The earth speaks, the gate of the earth-god is open, the doors of Geb are opened for you in your presence, and your speech goes up to Anubis... may you remove yourself to the sky upon your iron throne.[6]

> May I soar to the sky... May Orion give me his hand, for Sothis has taken my hand... I sit on my iron throne, my iron sceptre in my hand.[7]

In some passages, the king traverses the iron in the sky, or cleaves it in two, as if to suggest that the sky was filled with the stuff:

> I ascend to the sky, I cross over the iron... I ascend to the sky among the Imperishable Stars. My sister is Sothis, my guide is the Morning

> Star, and they grasp my hand at the Field of Offerings. I sit on this iron throne of mine, the faces of which are those of lions and its feet the hooves of the Great Wild Bull.[8]

> There is tumult in the sky... Horus is in the light. He sits on the throne of the Lord of All. The king takes possession of the sky, he cleaves its iron.[9]

Whilst in the sky, the king finds a mysterious set of iron doors, which apparently lead him to the Egyptian equivalent of Heaven:

> The doors of *Ba-ka*, which is in the firmament, are opened for me, the doors of iron which are in the starry sky are thrown open for me, and I go through them... my (iron) sceptre is in my hand.[10]

In keeping with the concept of re-enacting the creation, the king can, at the same time as finding a fixed abode in the sky, also circulate around the earth from the western horizon to the eastern horizon. And, in doing so, he crosses the iron once again:

> Go up... you shall bathe in the starry firmament, you shall descend upon the iron bands on the arms of Horus in his name of 'Him who is in the *Hnw*-barque'.[11]

The 'arms of Horus' are here perhaps a metaphor for the two 'supports of the sky' that kept it fixed firmly above the earth.[12]

The iron theme is continued and amplified considerably in the Coffin Texts – the successors to the Pyramid Texts – which were inscribed on the inner sides of coffins during the Middle Kingdom, from *c.* 2000 to 1850 BC.

In the Coffin Texts, the Field of Reeds – a supernatural region of the land of the eastern horizon – is given an enclosure wall of iron.[13] Also, there is mention of 'a great plain of iron on which the gods stand', this being located in the northern sky among the circumpolar stars (the so-called 'Imperishables').[14] To reach this place, the king's celestial barque is towed across the waters of the sky by the Imperishable Stars and the Unwearying Stars, pulling upon 'ropes of iron'.[15] The Coffin Texts also expand on the themes of the king 'breaking the iron egg' and 'splitting the iron', and refer to the iron itself 'splitting open the earth'.[16]

What does all this mean? Why are the Pyramid Texts and Coffin Texts littered with references to iron – iron in the west, iron in the east, and iron in the sky?

The explanation lies in the myth of creation, which I outlined briefly in chapter one. According to Egyptian beliefs, the earth was at the centre of the Universe, and all things had been born from a primeval proto-earth which comprised both solid material and a watery abyss. For reasons that are alluded to in dark and opaque terms, this primeval earth underwent a terrible crisis, from which it then recovered, only to expand, split open, and eject a combination of spiritual and material elements into the sky (the sky itself being formed of spiritualised water ejected from the mass of the proto-earth). From these spiritual and material elements, the stars, the Sun, and the Moon were formed. But what was the material element of which these bodies were made? It was – you guessed it – iron, or *bja* as it was known to the Egyptians. Hot and molten iron, blasted out of the earth by the force of the cataclysm. Hence the fact that certain Egyptian inscriptions describe the sky as being made of *bja*.[17]

Behind this mythical cataclysm stood the creator-god, personifying the entire sequence of events, although strictly speaking the creation was brought about by two powers, the Great God and the Great Goddess, who acted in union. The event was allegorised by the Egyptians in numerous ways: by the God masturbating his phallus and ejaculating seed into the womb of the sky-goddess, who then conceived and bore the stars, the Sun and the Moon; by the God manufacturing a Great Boat, made up of his constituent parts, namely the gods, and containing iron in its bow; by the God raising up his iron throne from the primeval earth to the sky; and by numerous other mythical and allegorical ideas.

And in lieu of the creator-god, in Egyptian ritual, stood the king – the very embodiment of the divine spirit – re-enacting the moment when the iron of the earth had become the iron of the sky, as Utterance 684 of the Pyramid Texts makes clear:

> This king ascended when you ascended, O Osiris; his word and his *ka* are bound for the sky; the king's bones are iron, and the king's members are the Imperishable Stars.[18]

So far, so good. The ubiquity of the iron is explained. But how do we get from the molten iron of creation to the contents of the King's Chamber sarcophagus? The answer, as we shall now see, is via meteorites.

The Fall of the Sky

The molten iron of creation, having been ejected into the sky, circulated in primeval clouds of chaos, prior to forming the bodies of the stars, the Sun and the Moon. But, in a remarkable anticipation of modern asteroid theory (albeit from a geocentric perspective), some of the iron continued to circulate in loose, leftover fragments. These were destined to fall back to earth periodically and from time to time, but the heaviest shower came immediately in the aftermath of the creation; and it was this fall of *bja* to the earth that fertilised the newly-risen land and sowed the seeds for the beginning of life.

These events are alluded to in fragmentary and disjointed fashion in numerous passages of the Pyramid Texts and the Coffin Texts. Here, we read of 'the day of the storm over the Two Lands' – a day of unspeakable chaos and violence, when the sky became 'choked and stifled' and 'big with gods'.[19] The events were allegorised by the myth of the battle of the gods, in which the creator-god went forth against his foes, the forces of darkness, and destroyed them utterly in a 'day of great slaughter'.[20] In a representative passage in the Coffin Texts, the king is identified with the creator-god Re, who took the form of a Great Cat to destroy his enemies:

> I am that Great Cat who split the *ished*-tree on its side in Heliopolis on that night of making war and warding off the rebels, and on that day in which were destroyed the foes of the Lord of All. *What is that Great Cat? He is Re himself... he was cat-like in what he did... As for the splitting of the ished-tree on its side in Heliopolis, it was when the Children of Impotence did what they did. As for the day of making war, it means that they entered into the east and war broke out in the whole of the earth and in the sky.*[21]

In another popular myth, the parties to the cosmic conflict were Horus and Seth, who personified the forces of order and chaos respectively. Their dispute had begun in the depths of the earth and the abyss, but had erupted thence into the sky, where they continued to wage war upon one another. In recognition of this, Horus and Seth were recalled as 'the two who would destroy the sky'.[22] Eventually, Horus prevailed, and the chaos in the sky was brought to a state of order (*maat*).

In the Pyramid Texts and Coffin Texts, the king re-enacts the role of the creator-god in bringing peace to the sky and order to the Two Lands (the latter was a metaphor for Egypt but representative of the whole earth).[23] Numerous passages refer to the king calming the sky, dispersing the storm, scattering the clouds, dispelling the darkness, clearing the sky, clearing the vision of Horus (an allusion to the god's two eyes, the Sun and the Moon), opening the paths in the sky, making a road through the celestial expanses, and opening the way from horizon to horizon.[24] In his guise as Thoth, he is able to pacify and reconcile the combatants Horus and Seth.[25]

That the battle of the gods led to the fall of iron to the earth is evident from the damage that the warring sky-gods inflicted upon the earth. The splitting of the *ished*-tree in Heliopolis is but one example of this idea (see the earlier citation). Elsewhere, in Spell 7 of the Coffin Texts, we read of the fiery origin of a crater in Heliopolis:

> The earth was hacked up when the Rivals [Horus and Seth] fought; their feet scooped out the sacred pool in Heliopolis. Now comes Thoth, adorned with his dignity... So the fighting is ended, the tumult is stopped, the fire which went forth is quenched, the anger in the presence of the Tribunal of the God is calmed, and it sits to give judgement in the presence of Geb.[26]

Here, the 'feet' of Horus and Seth is a metaphor for the iron of the sky, just as elsewhere the 'hands of Horus', the 'finger of Horus', the 'fingers of the four sons of Horus', the 'finger of Seth', the 'foreleg of Seth' and the 'fingers of Thoth', were all metaphors for the iron of the sky.[27]

The fall of the iron and the seeding of the earth was held to be a sacred secret by the Egyptians, and it was therefore not described in the kind of explicit prose that we might like to see. Rather, the myth was conveyed by way of metaphors and allusions that only made sense to the initiated. In Utterance 233 of the Pyramid Texts, for example, the iron that had been ejected from the earth fell back to the earth in the form of a fiery serpent:

> Fall, O serpent which came forth from the earth! Fall, O flame which came forth from the abyss! Fall down, crawl away![28]

Whilst elsewhere, in Spell 80 of the Coffin Texts, the iron of the sky fell back to the earth apparently in the form of the creator-god's saliva:

> I am the soul of Shu at the head of the celestial kine, who ascends to the sky at his desire, who descends to earth at his wish... the storm-cloud of the sky is my efflux; hail-storms and half-darkness are my sweat... I am he whom Atum created [from his mouth], and I am bound for my place of eternity. I am Everlasting, who fashioned the chaos-gods, whom the spittle of Atum produced, which issued from his mouth when he used his hand. His saliva [?] will be made to fall to the earth.[29]

Here, the translation 'saliva' is uncertain, but there is a clear allusion to the creation myth in which Atum masturbated his phallus and spat out semen from his mouth into the sky (his 'mouth' being the mouth of the earth). It was therefore the seed of the creator-god that fell back to the earth, and that seed was iron.

Exactly the same idea lies behind the Egyptian tradition that the earth had been inseminated by the blood of the gods. At Busiris, it was said that Seth and his followers had been put to death in the form of goats, whose blood had fertilised the earth.[30] Similarly, in the Book of the Dead, it is written that Seth threw himself to the ground in despair when the judgement of the gods went against him, and that agriculture began from the blood that spurted from his nose.[31]

Ancient Greeks writers corroborate this interpretation of the Egyptian myths.

In the 5th century BC, the philosopher Anaxagoras expressed the view that meteorites fell from a whirling mass of stones in the sky, and that the Sun and the Moon were the largest of these stones.[32] All animal life on earth, he said, had been created by 'seed' that fell down from the sky.[33] According to Ammianus Marcellinus, a Roman historian living in the 4th century AD, it was in Egypt that Anaxagoras derived his knowledge about meteorites.[34]

Similarly, in another echo of the myths recited earlier, the philosopher Plutarch (1st century AD), on the authority of Eudoxus (4th century BC), reported the following belief among the Egyptians:

> They believe the vine to have first sprung out of the earth after it was fattened by the bodies of those who fell in the wars of the gods.[35]

Plutarch observed that when the Egyptians drank the juice of the vine, they were partaking of the blood of their own ancestors.

In summary, then, whilst the Sun, Moon and stars had been formed by the molten iron of creation, some leftover iron had fallen back to earth, and seeded the beginning of life. This iron, which is known in modern terminology as meteoritic iron, was held to be sacred in Egypt, not so much as a 'messenger of the gods', as some have expressed it, but rather as an actual sample of the creator-god's seed, which had inseminated the sky and created the Universe. And this leftover iron, it was believed, was still infused with the creator-god's spirit. It was, as the Egyptians called it, 'spiritualised iron'.

Meteoritic Iron in Egyptian Religion

Our knowledge of the meteorite cult in ancient Egypt is not as good as it ideally ought to be, for a number of reasons. Firstly, because the cult was wrapped in secrecy. Secondly, because iron meteorites have a tendency to rust and eventually disintegrate (more on this problem in due course). And thirdly, because iron meteorites were a primary source of iron for secular objects, such as axes, swords and other ancient weapons of mass destruction. Our knowledge of the meteorite cult in Egypt is thus gained necessarily from textual references, including the writings of the Greeks, and modern archaeological reports. Together, these sources attest to the existence of a profoundly important religious cult.

On account of its intimate connection with the creation, meteoritic iron was credited with magical powers, and was thus used in the production of ceremonial objects, ritual tools and protective amulets. Many of these artefacts ended up in tombs, an example being a dagger of meteoritic iron which was found, reportedly, among the treasures of Tutankhamun's tomb.[36] Significantly for our study of the Great Pyramid, meteoritic iron objects have been found in tombs of the pre-dynastic and early dynastic periods.[37]

Alternatively, iron meteorites were kept in their natural forms and worshipped directly in temples as manifestations of the creator-god, not so much as a symbol of his presence, but rather as an actual sample of his presence.

One of the best attested cases of meteorite worship in Egypt is the so-called Benben Stone of Heliopolis. Although it is not described explicitly as being made of *bja*, its name meant literally 'the stone that flowed out', which certainly recalled the molten iron of creation. Oddly enough, the best evidence for the Benben's meteoritic credentials comes not from Heliopolis but from Thebes, where an inscription in the temple of Khons connects the term *benben* to the seed of the creator-god Amun-Re. In the following quotation of the relevant passage, I have inserted some of the original terms in brackets in order to convey the word puns that were so beloved by the Egyptians:

> Amun-Re is the god who begat (*bnn*) a place (*bw*) in the primeval ocean, when seed (*bnn.t*) flowed out (*bnbn*) the first time... it flowed out (*bnbn*) under him as is usual, in its name 'seed' (*bnn.t*).[38]

Here, it may be seen that the Benben Stone was a 'flowed-out' stone, the nature of that stone being the seed of the creator-god.

Some Egyptologists have indeed described the Benben Stone as the 'solidified seed' or 'petrified semen' of the creator-god Atum,[39] whilst others, on the basis of its conical shape, have identified it outright as a meteorite.[40] The latter include E.A. Wallis Budge in 1926, Jean-Philippe Lauer in 1978, Robert Bauval in 1989 and 1994, and Toby Wilkinson in 2001.[41] Of these, Bauval was the first to highlight the fact that the conical shape of the Benben matched a certain class of iron meteorites known as 'oriented' meteorites (on account of the shape that is formed when the meteorite passes through the Earth's atmosphere). According to Bauval, the Benben Stone was probably an oriented iron meteorite within the 1 to 15 ton range, although he later revised this estimate to 6 to 15 tons.[42]

Perhaps the second most famous case of meteorite worship in Egypt is the *ka-mut-ef* cult object of Thebes. In an in-depth study of the *ka-mut-ef* object in 1932, the Egyptologist G.A. Wainwright concluded that it was almost certainly a small iron meteorite, sacred to no less than three gods, Amun, Min and Horus, each of whom was the subject of a meteorite cult:

> A series of studies has proved Amun and Min to be closely connected with meteorites and thunderbolts, which are the same thing. These gods were two of the partners in the *ka-mut-ef* object of Thebes, and Horus was the third.[43]

Bearing in mind this identification of the *ka-mut-ef* as a meteorite, it is worthwhile asking why these three gods, in particular, had a stake in the *ka-mut-ef* object. The intriguing answer lies in the literal meaning of *ka-mut-ef*, 'bull of his mother', and by the fact that Amun, Min and Horus had each inseminated and impregnated their own respective mothers in Egyptian myth. Of Amun it was said: 'he is the bull of his mother, who rejoices in the cow, the husband impregnating with his phallus.'[44] Of Min it was said: 'Hail to Min, who impregnates his mother! How mysterious is that which you have done to her in the darkness.'[45] And of Horus it was said: 'Behold, Horus violates his mother', and 'the heart of Horus united with his mother Isis when he violated her and turned his heart toward her.'[46]

What does this mean? As Henri Frankfort pointed out in his book *Kingship and the Gods* (1948), 'bull of the mother' (*ka-mut-ef*) was an ancient Egyptian euphemism for engaging in violent sexual intercourse with the mother.[47] But this was no profane act of incest. Rather, it was an allegory for the act of creation in which the Great God was, in a sense, borne by the Great Goddess in the primeval ocean, but then rose up to impregnate her, she having become spiritualised as the sky.[48] Amun, Min and Horus were thus parallel forms of the One Great God, whilst their respective mothers were parallel forms of the One Great Goddess, now turned sky-goddess. In each case, the god had been bull-like in injecting his seed into the womb of the sky-goddess, who was often conceived in Egyptian religion as a great cow, and this cosmic seed had returned to the earth in the shape of the *ka-mut-ef* cult object of Thebes.

Wainwright thus hit the nail bang on the head when he identified the *ka-mut-ef* as an iron meteorite.

A third Egyptian meteorite city, in addition to Heliopolis and Thebes, was Letopolis, situated about 11 miles due west from Heliopolis and about 10 miles due north from Giza. The Greek name Letopolis meant 'Thunderbolt City', and its Egyptian name Khem was indeed written with the thunderbolt hieroglyph of the god Min (one of the gods of the *ka-mut-ef* meteorite).[49] In a detailed article *Letopolis*, published in 1932, Wainwright presented considerable evidence for thunderbolt worship at Letopolis and described it as 'a meteorite city'.[50] Of all cities in Egypt, he said, it was the one most specially linked to the meteorite material *bja*:

> *Bja* was iron, the thunderbolt material which is obtained from meteorites, and very specially belonged to Letopolis.[51]

Almost certainly some kind of meteoritic iron object was worshipped at Letopolis.

A fourth meteorite city was Abydos. According to the Roman writer Pliny (1st century AD), the priests there worshipped a 'stone fallen from the Sun'.[52] This description would certainly fit a meteorite, since it was believed in antiquity that the Sun was a blazing mass of stone. It also fits the Egyptian tradition that placed 'the head of Osiris' at Abydos;[53] Osiris, as we have already seen, was the god of iron members.

On the subject of Osiris, various Egyptian cities claimed to possess his body, or a part thereof, which was either kept in a holy shrine or buried in the ground. According to the various traditions, his head was kept in Abydos; his phallus in Heliopolis; his backbone in Busiris (Djedu); his left arm in Letopolis; a leg in Avaris; another leg in Elephantine (in the sanctuary of Abaton); his eyebrows in Tanis (Pelusium); the list goes on, reflecting the myth that Osiris had been dismembered by Seth.[54] Other cities claimed the entire body of the god; these included Heliopolis, Memphis, Rostau (south Giza), Herakleopolis, Abydos, Elephantine and Philae.[55] In view of the tradition that the body of Osiris comprised iron members, it is likely that some of these traditions recall authentic cases of meteorite worship.

Undoubtedly, there were many other places of meteorite worship in ancient Egypt. Several cities claimed, at various times, to have benben stones, modelled after the original Benben Stone of Heliopolis (the term *benben* apparently became a generic term for meteorites).[56] And several cities possessed a *baetylus* or *omphalos*, i.e. a sacred stone that purported to mark the place of creation and the axis of the Universe. These *baetyli* and *omphaloi* may, or may not, have been meteorites, but at the very least they symbolised meteorites and, in many cases, it is probable that the object was modelled after a meteorite that had once been worshipped on that spot.[57] Examples that we know of are the *omphalos* of Horus at Hierakonpolis, and the *omphaloi* of Amun at his shrines of Napata and Siwa.[58]

Meteorites and the Opening of the Mouth

In addition to the direct worship of iron meteorites, the Egyptians also smelted the iron and forged it into tools for ritual use. Here, the prime example is the tools used for the 'opening of the mouth' ceremony. This ritual – perhaps the most fundamental of all Egyptian religious acts – is worthy of our very close attention, for it provides a unique insight into the significance of meteoritic iron in ancient Egypt.

Firstly, the tools. There was the adze – a kind of chisel – shaped in the pattern of the northern stars, whose blade was made ideally from *bja*.[59] There were the two *neterti*-blades, 'the iron of the south' and 'the iron of the north', which were principally made from *bja*.[60] And finally, there was the *pesesh-kef* knife, which was ideally made from *ds*, a material which, according to Wainwright, signified either flint or a special kind of *bja* (*ds* was associated with the sky, storms, thunderbolts and fire).[61]

Secondly, the ritual use of the tools. The 'opening of the mouth' was a ritual performed on royal mummies and statues of the gods, either by the designate king or by the priests, to whom authority had been delegated by the king. The ritual involved the striking of the mouth of the mummy or statue with a force suggestive of a violent act, and was intended to bring the mummy or statue to life, in the sense that the divine spirit,

Figure 72.
THE OPENING OF THE MOUTH RITUAL.

resident within, would be released. In the case of the royal funeral, the 'opening of the mouth' was the crucial act which translated the king as a spirit to the sky.

But why the violent striking of the mouth? And why the tools made of meteoritic iron?

In the Pyramid Texts and other Egyptian books of the afterlife, it is made perfectly clear that the 'opening of the mouth' ritual re-enacted a myth in which the creator-god, and the gods who made up his company, had had their mouths opened at the beginning of time, thus bringing him, and them, to life. In Utterance 21 of the Pyramid Texts, for example, the priest recites the following spell whilst performing the ritual upon the mouth of the deceased king:

> I split open your mouth for you, I split open your eyes for you. O king, I open your mouth for you with the adze of Upuaut, with the adze of iron which split open the mouths of the gods. O Horus, open the mouth of this king [your father]!... Horus has split open the mouth of this king [Osiris] with that wherewith he split open the mouth of his father, with that wherewith he split open the mouth of Osiris, with the iron which issued from Seth, with the adze of iron which split open the mouths of the gods.[62]

Here, the king's mouth is opened by the meteoritic iron of Upuaut and Seth, but elsewhere it is opened by the iron of Horus, the four sons of Horus, Shu, Ptah, or Osiris.[63] In addition, the iron is used to split open the king's eyes.

What does this mean? In the myth of creation, the creator-god's body had experienced a mysterious crisis and had then been reassembled, to form the first mummified body. The splitting open of his mouth had then released his spirit, which had departed from his body and ascended to the sky. But the creator-god's body was nothing but a personification of the primeval earth. Therefore, the earth was the archetype of the bound and mummified body. The meaning of the myth is that the primeval earth had been spiritualised, so to speak. Amidst a violent cataclysm, the mouth of the earth had split open, and spirit and seed had been ejected into the sky, thereupon to bring about the creation of the Universe.

Now, the implication of this interpretation is that meteoritic iron was instrumental in the act of creation, specifically in the splitting open of the mouth of the earth. And, sure enough, the ancient Egyptian texts confirm this supposition. In Spell 816 of the Coffin Texts, we read an explicit account of how the adze of iron fell from the sky and was subsequently used in the 'opening of the mouth' ritual to re-enact the splitting open of the earth, here referred to as 'the West' and 'the land of the West':

> The iron is broken by Anubis in the sky. Ho, iron which opened up the
> West! This is the iron that is on my mouth, which Sokar spiritualised
> in Heliopolis, which makes the water of my mouth to rise. The iron is
> washed, and it is sharp and strong. This is the iron which Sokar raised
> on high in the name of 'Great One in it in Heliopolis'; (this is) the
> iron which raises me up, which lifts me up, so that I may open the land
> of the West in which I dwelt.[64]

This passage merits a careful reading. It is not the falling iron that splits
open the land of the West. Rather, it is the rising iron – the iron that is
spiritualised. To visualise this, one has to picture a reservoir of molten
iron in the heart of the earth, forcing its way upwards, causing the earth
to split apart, and erupting into the sky, where it then coagulates into the
stars, the Sun and the Moon. Spell 816 picks up the story at the point
where the leftover iron has fallen back to the earth in its meteoritic form,
whereupon it can be used in ritual by the priests to re-enact the events of
creation.

Incidentally, Spell 816 provides the most explicit description we have
of the primeval terrestrial iron being 'spiritualised', and provides crucial
support for my suggestion that the sarcophagus in the King's Chamber of
the Great Pyramid contained iron meteorites, in accordance with the
axiom 'the body to earth, the spirit to the sky'.

To return to the 'opening of the mouth' ritual, it was the opinion of
G.A. Wainwright that it might have heralded from the city of Letopolis,
'Thunderbolt City', which was especially associated with the meteoritic
materials *bja* and *ds*. There, the high priest went by the name of *Wn-ra*,
'the Opener of the Mouth', and bore the titles 'the Opener of the Mouth
in Letopolis' and 'the Opener of the Mouth upon Earth'.[65] According to
Wainwright, the key to this opening was the thunderbolt or meteorite,
which not only opened the mouth of the deceased king, but also opened
the doors to the sky which were located in Letopolis, as well as the doors
of Heaven that were *in* the sky. As he put it:

> The thunderbolt is a potent means of blasting open that which is
> closed... the opening of heavenly gates was one of the powers of the
> meteorite in Egypt... the idea that the thunderbolt could open not only
> the dead man's mouth but even Heaven itself was familiar to the
> Egyptians.[66]

Now, it is well known to Egyptologists that the king's ascent to the sky
was marked by a quaking of the earth and a great storm in the sky, but

Meteoritic Iron in the Opening of the Mouth

The *Wn-ra* was the high priest of that city [Letopolis]. His title means 'The Opener of the Mouth', and this mystical opening was effected through the blasting virtue of a thunderbolt. The thunderbolt in ancient Egypt, as elsewhere, was a piece of iron, a substance first obtained from meteorites. The divine pattern for the earthly openers of the mouth was Horus, and others were his Four Children. Each of them used *bja*; Horus an instrument of *bja* (iron), and his Four Children 'their fingers of *bja* (iron)'...

(G.A. Wainwright, *Letopolis*, 1932)

A significant peculiarity of the *neterti*-blades is their composition. They are said in all the textual sources to be of... a material thought to be meteoritic... Except for the initial human little fingers, all the tools used in the 'opening of the mouth' ritual are associated with iron, meteoritic material, or stars... The adze itself theoretically had a blade of meteoritic iron and was originally and most frequently called the *dua-ur*, a name that is written with a star and is clearly related to the *duat*...

(Ann Macy Roth, 'Fingers, Stars and The Opening of the Mouth', in *JEA*, 1993)

Iron was the traditional magical material used for the blades and points of the various sacred implements used in the 'opening of the mouth' ceremony. These were almost certainly made originally from meteoric iron, metal from the sky which was considered to be the magical gift of the gods.

(Hilary Wilson, *People of the Pharaohs*, 1997)

The symbolic blade of this tool [the adze] was a small bit of meteoric iron – a magical metal, associated with the heavens, that had provided the first spark or lightning strike that brought the first generation of beings into existence.

(Lanny Bell in B.E. Shafer ed., *Temples of Ancient Egypt*, 1997)

Wainwright suggested, in effect, that the latter storm was equivalent to the thunderbolt or meteorite, which had provided the means of ascent to the sky. He wrote:

> Seeing, therefore, that there is already much evidence that Letopolis was a meteorite city, there can be little doubt that the way into heaven, which was offered there by rope ladder, was derived from the flight of a meteorite. It might even have been a thunderbolt, which primitive religion does not distinguish from a meteorite.[67]

Wainwright even suggested that the rope ladder, by means of which the kings ascended to the sky from Letopolis, was a metaphor for a meteoric rise:

> In enquiring into the nature of the Letopolite rope ladder, those other ropes which the dead man used in heaven will be remembered. They were 'ropes of *bja*'... They were, therefore, stellar ropes and were associated with the Letopolite stars. *Bja* carries on the idea, for it proves to have been meteoric material and to have been specially connected with Letopolis and the Great Bear constellation. The meteorite gives the clue to the meaning of the ropes, for shooting stars have been widely connected with the passage of a soul from this world to the next.[68]

> Thus both the idea of ascent into heaven in a thunderstorm and that of heavenly ropes which are likely to have represented shooting stars were well established in Egypt. It is, therefore, hardly possible to doubt that the rope ladder on which the soul mounted from Letopolis to heaven was either a flash of lightning itself or a shooting star, a meteorite, which non-scientific man does not differentiate from a thunderbolt. The rope ladder would, therefore, be one more variation of the thunderbolt theme so often encountered at Letopolis, the thunderbolt city.[69]

Modern language, unfortunately, obscures Wainwright's point. To us, a meteorite (or thunderbolt) is something that falls from the sky. It makes no sense to imagine the meteorite opening the doors of the sky, nor the king ascending to the sky aboard a meteorite. But the Egyptian concept of the meteorite was different from ours. In their world, meteoritic iron had originated in the earth, and had been blasted out of the earth into the sky at the time of creation. Sure, leftover fragments of iron fell back to the earth. But their significance lay in the myth of creation, in which the iron had erupted from the earth into the sky. It is in this context of the creation myth, and the ritual re-enactment of it, that the use of meteoritic iron tools in the 'opening of the mouth' ceremony makes sense.

So, we have now discussed the evidence and rationale for the sanctity of meteorites and meteoritic iron in ancient Egypt. It remains only to justify the idea that meteorites were enshrined in the King's Chamber sarcophagus. To do that, we must consider the various ways in which the Egyptians used meteorites to symbolise and celebrate the act of creation, and consider some specific examples of how meteorites were enshrined in stone boxes and sarcophagi.

Meteorite Shrines

In seeking to establish how meteorites were used to celebrate the act of creation, we run up against the problem, mentioned earlier, of the secrecy that surrounded the meteorite cult. Since the meteorite was the cosmic trigger, so to speak, for the miracle of creation, it was not the done thing to speak openly of its nature, nor of its presence in the temples. Rarely, if ever, do we find an explicit reference to meteorites per se, and even the word *bja* (iron) is generally mentioned in an indirect or roundabout way. Instead, the Egyptian texts speak cryptically and in highly metaphorical language of such things as an egg (*swht/mtwt*), or seed (*bnnt*), or relics (*iht*), and there are many references to the 'secret form' or 'secret image' of the Great God, this being regarded as *sheta*, i.e. hidden, mysterious, and inaccessible.

To reconstruct the Egyptian meteorite cult, therefore, is like trying to assemble a giant jigsaw puzzle, where many of the pieces are faded with age, others are long lost, and still others were never intended to be seen. Even so, it is possible to piece together a broad picture, and that picture suggests a threefold treatment of the meteorite, which commemorated the act of creation in the following ways:

1 The meteorite was buried in the earth, either in a temple's crypt, or beneath the foundations, or in a separate burial site annexed to the temple. This buried meteorite could symbolise one of two things: (a) the molten iron in its pre-creation phase; or (b) the leftover iron that had fallen back down and fertilised the earth.

2 The meteorite was maintained in a shrine inside a temple, perhaps inside the naos, or 'holy of holies'. This enshrined meteorite symbolised the risen earth, or primeval mound, of creation.

3 The meteorite was raised upon a pillar inside a temple's boundaries. This raised meteorite symbolised the 'spiritualised iron', the seed of the creator-god, which had inseminated the sky.

It is the third of these treatments that is of particular interest to us here, in connection with the King's Chamber in the Great Pyramid. Nevertheless, it is important that the reader should understand the broader picture, and so we shall look at each of the three treatments in turn.

To begin with the buried meteorite, one of the best examples of this treatment is recorded in Spell 1080 of the Coffin Texts, which forms part of the Book of Two Ways. Here, we find an unusually explicit account of a meteorite fall, the said meteorite being termed 'the efflux of Osiris'. The fallen object, we are informed, was sealed and hidden in a place called Rostau:

> This is the sealed thing which is in darkness, with fire about it, which contains the efflux of Osiris, and it is put in Rostau. It has been hidden since it fell from him [Osiris], and it is what came down from him on to the desert of sand. It means that what belonged to him was put in Rostau.[70]

Where was Rostau? Geographical considerations aside, Rostau was the name of a subterranean realm, presided over by the god Sokar, who was closely associated with Osiris in Egyptian myth. Its name meant 'mouth (or gate) of the passageways', signifying a mythical (and perhaps even real) labyrinthine realm.[71] According to the Coffin Texts, Rostau was the place of the suffering Osiris, and the home of various anonymous beings (gods or serpents) whose places were secret;[72] the Texts mention a day of concealing the mysteries deep in Rostau,[73] and at one point the deceased says: "I have come to Rostau in order to know the secret of the *Duat* into which Anubis is initiated."[74] Anubis was the jackal-headed god, who had supposedly mummified the body of the creator.

It is therefore evident that Rostau was a part of the underworld, and that the meteorite, termed 'the efflux of Osiris', was buried in some kind of underground crypt.

Remarkably, a stylistic representation of the Rostau meteorite appears in the fifth chapter of the Book of the Hidden Chamber. In figure 73, we see the beginning of the creation, as if it were frozen in time. In the lower register is the body (or flesh) of Sokar, contained within an ellipse of sand, representing his 'hidden land'. He is about to put on his wings of transformation. Above him, in the middle register, a pyramid-shaped hill represents the body (or flesh) of Isis, whose head is seen at the apex of the mound. Above the head of Isis, in the upper register, there appears a dark, bell-shaped chamber, flanked by two falcons and surmounted by the hieroglyphic sign for 'night'. From the bottom of this chamber, a scarab beetle – symbolic of rebirth – descends towards the head of Isis in

Figure 73.
THE MYTHICAL SUBTERRANEAN REALM OF SOKAR IN ROSTAU.

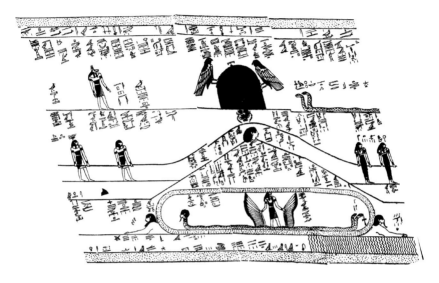

order to converse with Sokar below, but is menaced by a two-headed serpent who 'sets himself in opposition to the scarab'. Between the beetle and the head of Isis, there runs the rope by which the barque of Re is towed through the underworld by seven gods and seven goddesses.[75]

Of all the features in this Sokarian subterranean landscape, the bell-shaped chamber alone goes unexplained by the hieroglyphs, as if its role were too secret and awesome to be divulged. What is it meant to be? The answer is furnished by Sokar's intimate association with iron (his *Hnw*-barque contained iron in its bow, and it was he who spiritualised the iron in Heliopolis, as we saw earlier), by the bell shape of the chamber which reflected both the primeval hill and the *omphalos*, and by the myth that the efflux of Osiris (an iron meteorite) had been buried in Rostau. What we see, then, is a snapshot of creation: Sokar has undergone the mystical union with Isis in the flesh, and his spirit now prepares to break out from the underworld and ascend to the sky. The chamber, then, unmistakably, represents the iron seed of Sokar, which as yet remains in the darkness of night, but will soon be ejected from the earth into the sky. The falcons perhaps symbolise the idea that the chamber of iron seed is about to take flight, i.e. to be spiritualised. The Sokarian realm thus encapsulates the complete mystery of transformation that lay at the heart of Egyptian religion.

Such was the meteorite cult of Sokar/Osiris at Rostau.

Elsewhere in Egypt, numerous traditions existed of gods being buried beneath temples, but begged the question of what those gods actually were. The best known of these buried gods was Osiris, whose body was claimed by various cities, and whose body parts were interred throughout the land. But Osiris was by no means the only such god.

All over Egypt, cities and temples claimed to be the actual burial sites of the creator-god or his 'children', the latter conceived as the limbs of his body. At Heliopolis, a hidden tomb was said to house the body of Atum, or variously Shu or Re.[76] At Hermopolis, a group of eight gods, the Ogdoad, who had been instrumental in the act of creation, were said to be buried beneath the temple of Medinet Habu on the west bank of the Nile.[77] And near to Edfu, at the foot of the cliffs by the edge of the desert, there was a necropolis dedicated to 'the dead gods of Edfu', the children of Atum (or variously Re), who had assisted him in his act of creation; 'His Majesty Re', we are told, 'ordered that their bodies be mummified on the very spot on which they had been active; they were bandaged in Edfu, and it was there that their bodies were made inaccessible.'[78]

What was the form of these mysterious buried gods? In the case of Osiris, his body was often said to comprise members of *bja*, the iron of creation. As regards the other gods, in the light of their contribution to the act of creation, it may be surmised with reasonable certainty that their bodies too comprised, in theory, the secret substance *bja*. It is very likely, therefore, that many, if not all, of these traditions of buried gods recall authentic meteorite burials in the land of Egypt.

Finally, on the subject of buried meteorites, mention must be made of a 4th century BC inscription in the tomb of Petosiris at Tuna el-Gebel. In it, Petosiris, the high priest of Thoth at Hermopolis, states that vandals had damaged a part of the temple known as 'the birthplace of every god', where 'the relics of the cosmic egg' had been buried.[79] The vandals had apparently dug up and removed the relics, for it had been necessary to replace them with an image of Re breaking out from the egg. The whole of Egypt had been outraged at the desecration of this sacred shrine. What were these 'relics of the cosmic egg'? In the light of parallel references to these relics of the egg (in the Edfu creation myth),[80] and in the light of statements in the Coffin Texts that an 'egg of iron' had been split open at the time of creation, it is a fairly safe bet that these relics of Hermopolis were meteorites or artefacts made of meteoritic iron. In all probability, we have here a unique record of how a meteorite was removed from the archaeological record.

Turning now to examples of meteorites being kept inside temples, as opposed to being buried beneath them, there is little to be said. In most cases, it must be acknowledged, the temple enshrined a cult image of the god, usually in the form of a statue. However, there were exceptions, and these have already been mentioned: the *ka-mut-ef* cult object of Thebes; the thunderbolt objects of Letopolis; the 'Sun-stone' of Abydos; and the *omphaloi* of Hierakonpolis, Napata and Siwa. In addition, it is likely that an *omphalos* of Sokar was enshrined in Giza or Saqqara, representing the daylight form of the 'night' *omphalos* that lay hidden underground in Rostau. This class of cult object signified the iron that had risen from the abyss to form the crust of the primeval earth – the primeval mound as it is often called.

This brings us to the third form of meteorite worship, and the most significant for our purposes – the raised meteorite.

The best known example of a raised meteorite is the Benben Stone of Heliopolis, which we discussed earlier. According to Egyptologists, this conically-shaped stone was raised toward the sky upon a broad pillar, as shown by the artist's reconstruction in figure 74.

That the Benben Stone commemorated the act of creation is proven by Utterance 600 of the Pyramid Texts, which recalls how the creator-god Atum rose up in the form of the Benben Stone in Heliopolis, spat out Shu, and spluttered out Tefnut.[81] That the pillar was a phallic symbol is proven by Utterance 527 of the Pyramid Texts, in which Atum created

Figure 74.
THE TEMPLE OF THE BENBEN IN HELIOPOLIS.
Note: the drawing is a reconstruction of how the temple may have looked in archaic/early dynastic times.

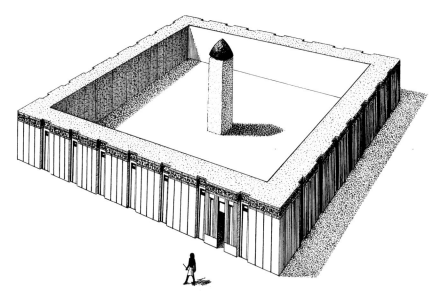

the same deities, Shu and Tefnut, by masturbating and ejaculating them from his phallus.[82] The image of the Benben meteorite on its pillar thus symbolised the creative moment when the iron was ejected into the sky, for the conception and birth of the stars, the Sun and the Moon. The Benben meteorite thus represented the spiritualised seed of the creator-god.

Significantly, the Benben Stone on its pillar was the archetype for the obelisk – the tall slender column which was known to the Egyptians as a 'sky-splitter'.[83] In the obelisk, the meteorite was substituted by a stone replica named *benbenet* after the Benben Stone, this term being generally translated as 'pyramidion'.[84] The obelisk, like the Benben pillar, was thus a memorial to the act of creation.

Even more significantly, the *benbenet*, or 'little *benben*', was the name given to the capstone of the true pyramid, where the meteorite, as far as we know, was eschewed once again in favour of a stone substitute.

In summary, it may be argued that all these architectural forms – the Benben Stone, the obelisk, and the true pyramid – froze in stone the primeval moment when the earth burst open and blasted the molten iron of creation into the sky.

Figure 75.
THE BENBEN PILLAR, THE TRUE PYRAMID, AND THE OBELISK.
The shared benben symbolism recalled the seeding of the sky with the iron of creation.

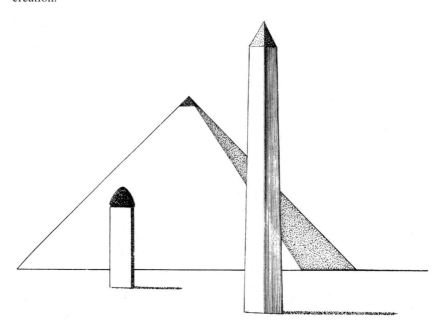

The Benben Stone

This object was already sacred as far back as the middle of the 3rd millennium BC, and will doubtless have been vastly older. We may conjecture that it was one of those sacred stones, which gained their sanctity in times far back of all recollection or tradition, like the *Ka'aba* at Mecca.
(J.H. Breasted, *Development of Religion and Thought in Ancient Egypt*, 1912)

The most sacred object within the temple [of Heliopolis] was the Benben, probably a conically shaped stone which was thought to symbolise the first phenomenon in the creation of this earth.
(I.E.S. Edwards, *The Pyramids of Egypt*, 1947)

The first solid substance was a stone, the Benben; and it had originated from a drop of the seed of Atum... The determinative in the Pyramid Texts shows a tapering, somewhat conical shape for the Benben Stone, which became stylised for use in architecture as a small pyramid, the pyramidion.
(Henri Frankfort, *Kingship and the Gods*, 1948)

Taking into account... the Benben Stone's supposedly cosmic origin and most particularly its 'conical' shape, it is justified to conjecture that this sacred stone was an 'oriented' (conical) iron-meteorite... Many meteorites often retain their orientation in the direction of flight; this causes the front part to melt and flow towards the rear. The result – especially for the iron variety – is a meteorite having the characteristic shape of a rough cone. These are known as 'oriented' meteorites.
(Robert Bauval, 'Investigations on the Origins of the Benben Stone', in *Discussions in Egyptology*, 1989)

I'm not a geologist, and wouldn't claim to be, but there is a particular kind of meteorite, a rare kind of meteorite, which as it enters the atmosphere, is formed into a shape that startlingly resembles a pyramid. Could the Benben Stone have been such a stone?
(Toby Wilkinson, Bloomsbury lecture, 2001)

And the Great Pyramid, *Akhet Khufu*, was in no way an exception to this basic story.

Egypt, then, was full of monuments commemorating the raising of the meteorite and the insemination of the sky, all stemming from the original Benben Stone of Heliopolis, which was probably erected in archaic, pre-dynastic times.[85]

But the Benben may not have been the only raised meteorite in archaic Egypt. In addition, the city of Abydos possessed a fetish object, said to represent the 'head of Osiris', which was crowned with a pair of feathers and mounted on a pole. This strange object was bell-shaped, and bears a striking similarity to the *omphalos* of Sokar, except that in this case it has been removed from the underworld and raised towards the sky. What did this 'head of Osiris' signify? To Egyptologists, it is a representation of the primeval mound of creation;[86] but the primeval mound, in its raised form, was equivalent to the meteoritic seed with which the creator-god

Figure 76.
THE FETISH OF ABYDOS.
The bell-shaped object represents 'the head of Osiris'.

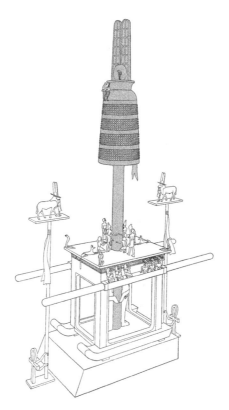

had inseminated the sky. The 'head of Osiris' would thus have been an iron meteorite. But, intriguingly, Abydos was also the place where the head of Osiris had been buried.[87] It seems likely, therefore, that Abydos celebrated the meteorite in its dual aspects – both the concept of the iron in the earth, pre-creation, and the concept of the iron in the sky, mid-creation.

Again, like the Benben Stone of Heliopolis, the 'fetish of Abydos' is dated to the earliest phase of Egyptian history.[88]

In summary, meteorites were enshrined in three places: underground, at ground level, and at high elevations; and these three placements were complementary in their creational symbolism. In the first instance, the iron had flowed forth in the underworld. In the second instance, the iron had risen from the abyss to form the crust of the earth. And in the third instance, the iron had been blasted out violently from the earth into the sky. And finally, last but not least, leftover iron had fallen back to its source, sowing the seeds of life in the earth, and thus closing the circle, so to speak. Thus did the Egyptian meteorite cult follow a coherent and cohesive system, reflecting the entire cycle of the creation.

So far, so good. In principle, there can be no objection to the idea that the Great Pyramid, itself a symbol of the creation, may have contained meteorites at the elevated height of the King's Chamber. However, if we wish to make this argument convincing, we must take it to the next stage, and justify the idea that meteorites may have been sealed inside boxes or sarcophagi. What evidence is there for that?

The Meteorite Problem

Iron meteorites, for all their sanctity, have a weakness, which must have greatly exercised the minds of the Egyptian intellegentsia: once exposed to the elements on Earth, the iron begins to rust. As the meteorite expert Phil Bagnall has observed, the collection of iron meteorites can therefore be a risky business:

> The truth is it's hard to keep them in pristine condition. Many contain iron that's spent most of its history in the ultra-dryness of space. Once in contact with Earth's water-rich atmosphere, it rusts quickly.[89]

The rust problem, in the first instance, is merely aesthetic, but in the final analysis it can become more serious, causing the meteorite to crack, split apart, and eventually decompose into a pile of loose fragments.

I can vouch personally for the rusting phenomenon, though thankfully of the less serious kind. In 2000, I purchased two iron meteorites – a 33 kg Gibeon and an 11 kg Campo del Cielo – Phil Bagnall acting as my

Figure 77.
THE AUTHOR WITH AN IRON METEORITE FROM HIS PERSONAL
COLLECTION.

broker. The Gibeon came from a fall in Namibia of uncertain date; upon
acquisition, it bore a few minor flecks of surface rust; and since then, it
has remained reasonably stable. The Campo del Cielo, meanwhile, came
from a fall in Argentina around 4,000 to 6,000 years ago; it came with
some surface rust; and it has since taken to shedding small, thin flakes of
rusted iron, like a snake shedding its skin. Such has been the reaction of
these two irons to the less-than-ideal environment in my study, and it
underlines the fact that each type of iron meteorite (a type represents a
particular fall/location) has its own specific characteristics, the Gibeon
being renowned for its longevity, the Campo del Cielo being known for
its tendency to rust gradually.

As a general rule, however, all meteorites do rust in the long term, as
Bagnall points out in his standard information pack:

> Rust develops on all iron meteorites at some stage. Iron meteorites
> have spent most of their 4.55-billion-year history in the ultra-dryness
> of space. The Earth's water-rich atmosphere is a particularly hostile
> environment for irons. Meteorites should be checked regularly – at
> least once a month – for signs of rusting.

This information pack also contains some useful advice on handling and
storing meteorites. The following key points are of particular interest vis-

a-vis our study of ancient Egyptian meteorites:

- Try to keep storage temperature reasonably stable, and do not heat.

- Do not use hot spot lights.

- Keep out of direct sunlight.

- Avoid water.

For the professional meteorite collector, this means not only keeping the iron meteorites at a constant temperature, but also at an acceptably low degree of humidity. Thus, for example, Rob Elliott, who runs Fernlea Meteorites in Fife, keeps his showroom at a constant temperature of 19° C (66.2° F) in order to achieve a relative humidity (RH) of no more than 30%, this having been identified as a practical ideal for retarding rusting (oxidisation) of the iron. (A temperature higher than 19° C allows more moisture in the air, increasing the RH to above the critical threshold of 30%.)[90]

The ancient Egyptian priests must have been all too familiar with the problems of rusting iron meteorites. For example, if the original Benben Stone was an iron meteorite, as is widely believed, then its position atop the pillar at Heliopolis would have broken the four cardinal rules that are listed above. It is no wonder, then, that the Benben Stone is no longer with us. It would probably have become structurally unsound long before the pyramids were built. This would explain why the Egyptians turned to an imitation meteorite (the *benbenet*) in the manufacture of obelisks and pyramids. No such problem of corrosion with a pyramidion made of granite.

What about an iron meteorite enshrined in the temple's holy of holies? Here, the meteorite would have been less exposed, but it would still have suffered from temperature variations, again causing the iron to become unstable and decompose over the long term. This would go some way toward explaining why so few Egyptian meteorites have survived to the present day, and it would certainly explain why the Egyptians – and other ancient peoples – turned to the worship of substitute stones, i.e. the *baetyli* and *omphaloi*.

Finally, what of the iron meteorite that was buried underground? In this case, the meteorite would have survived longer, since subterranean chambers benefit from almost constant temperatures all the year round.[91] Nevertheless, the humidity of the air would have posed a problem, and there may have been an additional risk of water run-off and damp.

Might there have been an even better solution? The reader may, by now, suspect where this is heading.

In the light of the sanctity of iron meteorites, and knowing, as we do, the ancient Egyptian obsession with preserving bodies for eternity, we can predict with confidence that the priests would have sought a better way to protect and preserve the iron, in effect to 'mummify' it. Was there a way of reducing, or eliminating, the corrosive effect of the humidity of the air? In the absence of a modern air-conditioning system, what could be done?

There was indeed an obvious solution: to deposit the iron meteorites in hermetically-sealed boxes or sarcophagi, and then, for good measure, to install these boxes in places of little or no temperature fluctuation.

In Egypt, such hermetically-sealed boxes are indeed found, both in the pyramids and in underground vaults.

Meteorites in Boxes

In 1851, the French Egyptologist Auguste Mariette made an astonishing discovery – a huge underground vault containing twenty-four sarcophagi, some made of basalt, some made of granite, individually weighing up to 70 tons. This was the Serapeum at Sakkara, so named in the belief that an Apis bull, worshipped at nearby Memphis as a manifestation of the Great God, had been mummified and buried in each of the sarcophagi. The fact is, however, that these sarcophagi were found sealed but empty, and their original contents remain a matter of speculation.

One of the most remarkable things about these sarcophagi, apart from their size and weight and sculpture from individual blocks of stone, is the precision of their finish. Christopher Dunn, an alternative researcher who carried out a close inspection of some of these boxes in 1995, found that their outer and inner surfaces were absolutely flat, and he was astonished to discover that the lids had been so cut as to form perfect airtight seals. He wrote:

> Checking the lid and the surface on which it sat, I found them both to be perfectly flat. It occurred to me that this gave the manufacturers of this piece a perfect seal – two perfectly flat surfaces pressed together, with the weight of one [around 10 tons?] pushing out the air between the two surfaces.[92]

It later occurred to Dunn that the Saqqara sarcophagi had been finished off underground, inside the Serapeum itself, in order to achieve the level of precision:

> The builders of these relics, for some esoteric reason, intended for them to be ultra precise. They had gone to the trouble to take the

Figure 78.
A MULTI-TON SARCOPHAGUS IN THE SERAPEUM AT SAQQARA.

unfinished product into the tunnel and finish it underground for a good reason... To finish it with such precision at a site that maintained a different atmosphere and a different temperature, such as in the open under the hot Sun, would mean that when it was finally installed in the cool, cave-like temperatures of the tunnel, the workpiece would lose precision. The granite would give up its heat, and in doing so change its shape through contraction. The solution, then as now, of course, was to prepare precision objects in a location that had the same heat and humidity in which they were going to be housed.[93]

Now, this decision to finish off the sarcophagi underground, rather than outside in the open air, meant that the workers had to endure cramped and dusty conditions. The precision of the boxes, then, was clearly the driving factor. But why? Did the builders have some 'esoteric reason', as Dunn put it? Or might the aim have been purely practical? Perhaps to form a perfect airtight seal, so as to protect meteorites from the corrosive effect of the air?

It is indeed tempting to think that the Saqqara sarcophagi never did house mummified Apis bulls, but rather the iron of the creation, which, by coincidence or not, was known to the Egyptians as the semen of the bull. As noted earlier in this chapter, the *ka-mut-ef* meteorite was named after the creator-god who had inseminated the sky-goddess as 'the bull of his mother'. The sky-goddess, in like manner, was compared to a great cow, whilst her offspring, the Sun, was described as a calf. Similarly, in the Pyramid Texts and Coffin Texts, the king ascends to the sky with the power and the seed of the bull.[94] One cannot help wondering, therefore, if the tradition of the Apis bulls buried in the Serapeum may have stemmed from an earlier tradition of a metaphorical kind of bull.

Not only this, but the site of Saqqara appears to take its name from the god Sokar, who, as we saw earlier, was a deity of the underworld and of meteoritic iron.

Figure 79.
THE HNW-BARQUE OF SOKAR.
According to Egyptian texts, the barque carried iron in its bow.

But, speculations aside, the main lesson to draw from the Serapeum is that it contained sarcophagi which were not only perfectly airtight, but also located in a subterranean chamber of virtually constant temperature all the year round. Perfect conditions for the storage of iron meteorites.

Is there any real evidence that meteorites were housed in stone boxes or sarcophagi in Egypt? As we shall now see, the ancient Egyptian texts contain several intriguing clues to such a practice.

One such clue appears in Spell 1119 of the Coffin Texts, where Osiris is praised for driving off uproar. This is then followed by an intriguing reference to the god Seth: 'I speak of the content of the chest of red stuff of him who is spiteful'.[95] Might this recall a reddish or rusty meteorite sealed inside a chest?

Another clue was mentioned earlier in passing. In Spell 1080 of the Coffin Texts, it is said that 'the efflux of Osiris', which had fallen down from the god onto the desert of sand, was hidden in Rostau 'in the sealed thing'. This 'sealed thing' sounds remarkably like a hermetically-sealed sarcophagus (the 'fire about it' may refer to the granite material of the box).[96] Indeed, in another spell of the Coffin Texts, it is written that 'Osiris has placed his efflux in his coffin'.[97] By this, it was surely meant that the iron efflux of the god – the meteorite – had been placed in the coffin.[98]

In Spell 1087 of the Coffin Texts, 'the efflux of Osiris' is held to be synonymous with 'the Word',[99] a metaphor which brings us neatly to our second example of a meteorite in a box – the myth of 'the seven words' that became trapped in a chest. According to a popular story, the creator-god had brought about the creation by uttering seven words, one after the other. These words had structured the world geographically, but had been translated into 'dead gods' who were shut up inside a chest.[100] There they remained for eternity, with the proviso that repetition of the words would bring about the cataclysmic end of the world. Now, in the light of the connection to 'the efflux of Osiris', it can hardly be doubted that these seven words or dead gods were meteorites. Indeed, as if to confirm this, the seven words appear in a related tradition as 'the seven arrows' which the fiery Eye-goddess had fired in her wrath.[101] As G.A. Wainwright has rightly observed, the term 'arrow' was a metaphor for the meteorite.[102]

In the example just cited, the shutting up of the words inside the chest may well allude to a practice of storing meteorites in a sealed box, but at the same time the term 'chest' is used as a metaphor for the whole earth. This metaphor is best illustrated by the image of Anubis reclining on his chest (figure 80), where the chest represented the 'western mountain', 'the sacred land', and 'the booth of the god' (a reference to Osiris, the lord of the underworld).[103] This image was used as an ideogram in the title *hry sesheta*, 'keeper of the secrets', which referred not only to Anubis, who guarded the secrets of the earth in a metaphorical chest, but also to certain priests who presided over real chests in which the secret relics of Osiris were housed.[104]

This brings us back to the question of Osiris' body and its connection with iron. If the reader will accept that the body of the creator-god was a metaphor for the primeval earth, which, in large part, comprised the iron of creation, then it follows logically that the widespread references to the god's body being buried in a sarcophagus provide further examples of meteorites being sealed in stone boxes. And this argument applies not

Figure 80.
ANUBIS UPON HIS CHEST.
The chest represented the earth and the underworld, and hence contained the
mysteries of Osiris.

only to Osiris, but to the creator-god in all of his names.

In the books of the afterlife, the motif of the creator-god buried in his
sarcophagus is ubiquitous, as a few examples will suffice to demonstrate.

In the Coffin Texts, Spell 647, the deceased is made to say: "I have
lifted Maat on to the altar of Shu who is in the coffin".[105] The reference
here is to Shu as the body of Atum, whose corpse was held to have been
buried in Heliopolis.[106]

In the Enigmatic Book of the Netherworld, section A, two oval-shaped
sarcophagi are pictured, one containing the mummified body of Osiris,
the other containing the mummified body of Re.[107]

In the Book of the Hidden Chamber (otherwise known as Am Duat),
four rectangular-shaped sarcophagi are depicted, each containing a form
of the creator-god, concealed within a mound of sand.[108] The four forms
of the god are Tem (Atum), Khoprer, Re, and Osiris (see figure 81).

In the Book of Caverns, there are numerous scenes of gods buried in
sarcophagi, some oval-shaped and some rectangular.[109] Usually, the god
is Re or Osiris, but on several occasions the artist has depicted in their
coffins the children, or followers, of Re and of Osiris respectively. Of
particular interest here is a scene in the first cavern, in which Osiris is
represented by a round object containing a relic of his body,[110] and a
scene in the fifth cavern, in which an upright oval-shaped coffin contains
'the sceptre of Atum', with which he 'created the *Duat* and brought forth
the realm of the dead'.[111]

Finally, in the Book of the Earth, there is an unusual picture of Osiris,
mummified, standing between two *omphalos*-shaped mounds, beneath

Figure 81.
THE CREATOR-GOD IN THE FORMS OF ATUM, KHOPRER, RE AND
OSIRIS, BURIED IN MOUNDS OF SAND IN SARCOPHAGI.
A scene from the seventh division of the Book Am Duat.

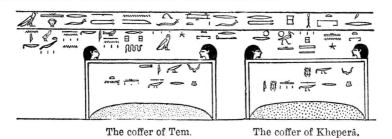

The coffer of Tem.   The coffer of Kheperâ.

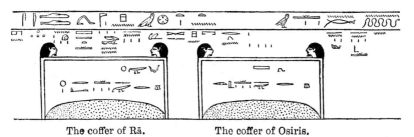

The coffer of Râ.   The coffer of Osiris.

which lies his 'mysterious coffer', his corpse therein being invisible.[112]
And, in the lowest register of the same scene, there is a huge mummy-
shaped sarcophagus in which, remarkably, the entire realm of the dead is
buried, personified by 'the corpse of Shetit'.[113]

In summary, it needs to be restated that these weird and wonderful
scenes of the underworld do not portray the burial of human beings, but
rather the burial of the gods of creation at the beginning of time. It may
thus be argued that the concept of burial in a sarcophagus is based upon a
divine archetype, in which the sarcophagus contained the very essence of
the creator-god and his followers. And this essence was none other than
meteoritic iron.

This argument may strike the reader as too conceptual. What is needed
is a more specific and detailed textual record of a meteorite being placed
in a sarcophagus. Fortunately, there is one example: the remarkable story
of the stone box in the Temple of Aart. The story is inscribed on a granite
shrine, dating to the Ptolemaic period, and is known to scholars as 'the
Legend of Shu and Geb'.

The inscription tells how, in the olden days, Shu had fought a cosmic
battle against the forces of chaos, aided by Ankhet, the serpent of Re. In
the aftermath of this battle, the victorious Shu had then placed the fiery
serpent on his head. But Shu had eventually grown old and decrepit, and

the gods had revolted against him. Shu had therefore departed from the earth and ascended to the sky amidst a cataclysmic storm. But, when the storm had died down, Geb, the son of Shu, had appeared on the throne.

Geb then announced: "I will set the serpent on my head as my father Shu did." Accompanied by his followers (the gods), he went into the Temple of Aart, where he found the serpent concealed in a chest. Putting his hand to the chest, Geb began to remove the serpent, which is here referred to as the 'son of the earth'. As he did so, however, the serpent breathed forth venomous fire which burned Geb and killed many of his followers. At this, Geb retreated from the temple, and retired, badly hurt, to the Field of the Henna Plants. His followers thereupon brought to him the Aart of Re (His Majesty's Great Eye), at the sight of whose mysteries the injured god was healed. Immediately, Geb returned to the Temple of Aart, where he was able to place the other Aart there upon his head. The text then states:

> And he caused a great coffer of real stone to be made for it. It was hidden in a secret place in the Temple of Aart near the divine Aart of the Majesty of Re.[114]

What was this fiery serpent or Aart, 'Great Eye'? To the reader who is unfamiliar with Egyptian religion and mythology, terms such as 'serpent' and 'Eye' will mean little. However, to the reader who is conversant with these subjects, these terms are metaphors for the Great Goddess, who was widely associated with cataclysm and fire; hence the burning of Geb when he handled the serpent.[115] Moreover, the Eye, in its manifestations as the twin 'eyes', the Sun and the Moon, was said to be composed of *bja* or *ds*, i.e. meteoritic iron.[116] It is therefore quite clear – as far as anything can ever be said to be clear in Egyptian mythology – that the story of the serpent in the stone box in the Temple of Aart recalls an authentic burial of a meteorite in a sarcophagus in an Egyptian temple.

Boxes on High

Thus far, we have seen that iron meteorites were buried underground, enshrined in temples, and raised on pillars. And we have seen evidence that such meteorites were sealed in sarcophagi, both underground and in temples. But what about the idea of raising a sarcophagus of meteorites above ground level, as perhaps in the case of the King's Chamber in the Great Pyramid? At first sight, it seems unlikely that corroboration for this practice may be found. After all, the Great Pyramid is a unique case. No other pyramid contained (or contains), as far as we know, a sarcophagus at an elevated height. Nor are we likely to find a raised sarcophagus in any other form of Egyptian architecture. The final proof of the theory is surely likely to elude us.

And yet, there are a couple of clues that do lend corroboration to the idea that the Great Pyramid raised a sarcophagus of meteorites toward the sky.

The first piece of evidence is admittedly circumstantial. In Utterance 506 of the Pyramid Texts, there is an intriguing reference to 'the coffer of the sky' in the context of a creator-god named *Zwntw*. The speech is that of the deceased king:

> I am *Ztty*; I am *Zty-zty*; I am the *Zw-zw* water; I am *Zwntw* the coffer of the sky; I am the double-maker... I am the creator who created this land... I am the Great Word... O men and gods (place) your arms under me! Lift me up, raise me up to the sky, just as the arms of Shu are under the sky when he raises it. To the sky! To the sky! To the great throne among the gods![117]

Taking these passages at face value, it would seem that 'the coffer of the sky' is literally raised to the sky. Is this the proof that we are looking for? Who was this coffer-god *Zwntw*? Elsewhere, he is described as the god who 'crosses the sky nine times a night' – an allusion perhaps to his role as 'double-maker' during the act of creation;[118] and in two other spells the departed king is said to traverse or circumambulate the sky 'just like *Zwntw*'.[119] Evidently then, *Zwntw* was a god of the sky. Yet, even so, his epithet 'the coffer of the sky' is both unusual and unique. One therefore feels reluctant to burden old *Zwntw* with the full weight of the hypothesis under consideration.

But a stronger piece of evidence is yet to come.

Earlier, in our discussion of the raised meteorite, it was noted that the 'head of Osiris' was worshipped at Abydos in the form of a fetish object that was placed atop a pole. But, according to Egyptologists, the fetish object, whilst symbolising the head of Osiris, was not the head per se, but rather a box containing the head. In the words of E.A. Wallis Budge:

> Tradition affirmed that the head of Osiris was preserved at Abydos in a box, and a picture of it became the symbol of the city.[120]

> The object under the pair of horns [or feathers] was the coffer which contained the head of Osiris.[121]

For the reasons outlined earlier, the 'head of Osiris' was almost certainly a metaphor for the iron of creation. It may thus be hypothesised that the bell-shaped box in the 'fetish of Abydos', began its career as a reliquary for an iron meteorite.

Figure 82.
VARIANT FORMS OF THE FETISH OF ABYDOS.

In summary, if Wallis Budge is right, the 'fetish of Abydos' offers a powerful precedent for the idea of a box of iron meteorites being raised towards the sky, in commemoration of the act of creation.

A Brief Summary

It is time to summarise what has been covered thus far.

Firstly, it is a known fact that the Egyptians, along with other ancient peoples, used meteorites as their primary source of iron, knowing full well that this iron had fallen from the sky.[122]

Secondly, no-one in Egyptology would dispute the fact that the ancient Egyptians held iron meteorites to be sacred. The original Benben Stone of Heliopolis was almost certainly an iron meteorite, as was the *ka-mut-ef* cult object of Thebes, and, furthermore, it is known that meteorites or meteorite substitutes (*baetyli* and *omphaloi*) were worshipped at several other cities besides.

Thirdly, it has been demonstrated that iron (*bja*) is ubiquitous in the Pyramid Texts and the Coffin Texts, appearing both in the depths of the primeval earth and in the heights of the sky. The reason for this, I have argued, is that the deceased king was re-enacting the myth of creation, in which molten iron had been blasted from the abyss into the sky, where it had coagulated to form the stars, the Sun and the Moon. This iron was regarded as the seed of the creator-god, with which he had inseminated the womb of the sky-goddess. Later, leftover iron had fallen back to the earth and had fertilised it with the seeds of life.

Fourthly, it is a known fact that meteoritic iron tools were used in the 'opening of the mouth' ceremony. The reason for this, I have argued, is that the ritual was a re-enactment of the myth of creation, in which the mouth of the earth had been split open at the time of the ejection of the iron. In accordance with this myth, it was believed that the thunderbolt, or meteorite, had the power to blast open the doors to the sky, as well as the doors *in* the sky, thus carrying the king to his heavenly destination.

Fifthly, it has been shown that meteorites were revered in a number of ways: some were buried underground, some were enshrined in temples, and some were raised on pillars towards the sky. All of these treatments were complementary, in that they commemorated the journey of the iron at the time of creation, from the earth to the sky, and, for some of it, back to the earth.

Sixthly, it is a fact that iron meteorites are susceptible to oxidisation (rusting) and, in the long run, disintegration. In order to preserve these meteorites in pristine condition, it is necessary to store them at a constant temperature and in a humidity-free environment. Sure enough, there is evidence to suggest that the Egyptians stored meteorites underground (where temperatures are virtually constant all the year round) and sealed them inside boxes, or sarcophagi, thus shutting out the air. The precision finish of the sarcophagi in the Serapeum at Saqqara, the original contents of which are unknown, is entirely consistent with the desire to create an airtight seal for exactly such a purpose.

Seventhly, whilst it was admittedly unusual for the Egyptians to raise a box containing meteorites to an elevated height, as is hypothesised in the case of the King's Chamber sarcophagus, there is a precedent for the idea in the 'fetish of Abydos', where a bell-shaped box containing 'the head of Osiris' – almost certainly an iron meteorite – was raised towards the sky atop a pole.

Eighthly, it is beyond question that the true pyramid was a symbol of the creator-god and his creation of the Universe. In keeping with this, the capstone of the pyramid was known as *benbenet*, 'little *benben*', after the original Benben meteorite of Heliopolis. The pyramid, therefore, was a phallic symbol, commemorating the creator-god's act of inseminating the sky with his iron seed. The Great Pyramid, *Akhet Khufu*, is no exception to this rule. Incidentally, it is worth noting, in this regard, that the Great Pyramid and the Second Pyramid of Giza were aligned to the meteorite cities of Heliopolis and Letopolis.[123]

Ninthly, finally, there is little doubt that meteoritic iron was known and used in Egypt at the time when the Great Pyramid was built. For the most part, the evidence covered in this chapter relates to the latter part of the Old Kingdom, just a few centuries after the reign of Khufu. But, in

Meteorites in Egypt and the Ancient World

It is known that the archaic preliterate peoples, as well as the prehistoric populations, worked meteoric iron long before they learned to use the ferrous ores occurring on the earth's surface... When Cortez asked the Aztec chieftains where they got their knives, they pointed to the sky. And in fact excavations have revealed no trace of terrestrial iron in the prehistoric deposits of the New World. The paleo-Oriental peoples presumably held similar ideas. The Sumerian word AN.BAR, the earliest vocable designating iron, is written with the signs 'sky' and 'fire'. It is generally translated as 'celestial metal' or 'star metal'. For a long period the Egyptians knew only meteoric iron. The same is true of the Hittites: a text of the fourteenth century states that the Hittite kings used 'the black iron of the sky'. Iron, therefore, was scarce (it was as precious as gold), and its use was principally ritual.
(Mircea Eliade, *A History of Religious Ideas*, 1978)

Iron was metal of mythical character. According to legend, the skeleton of Seth... was (made) of iron. Iron was called the 'metal of heaven' because for a long time the Egyptians knew only meteoric iron, which has a high nickel content. Because of its supposedly divine origin, meteoric iron was used in particular for the production of protective amulets and magic model tools which were needed for the ritual called the 'opening of the mouth'.
(Bernd Scheel, *Egyptian Metalworking and Tools*, 1989)

Meteoritic iron has been found in Egypt in burials as early as the predynastic period. It was thought to have a magical significance, since the same word is used to mean 'marvel, miracle'. That this material came from 'falling stars' was apparently well understood...
(Ann Macy Roth, 'Fingers, Stars, etc', in *JEA*, 1993)

The Egyptians came across meteoritic iron, knew it came from heaven, and knew that this metal was not available to them on Earth. They quite naturally assumed that iron was a heavenly substance... occasionally one was tossed to Earth. This rare celestial material was then hammered into adzes in the shape of the constellation known to us as the Great Bear or Big Dipper... and pressed against the mouths of mummies and statues in a ritual meant to 'open their mouths' so that they could, like infants, be born and live again in the world of the dead. It all makes sense if you are an ancient Egyptian.
(Robert Temple, *The Crystal Sun*, 2000)

certain instances, the evidence dates back to the pre-dynastic or early dynastic period, several centuries before the reign of Khufu; for example, the Benben Stone of Heliopolis, and the 'fetish of Abydos'.

I therefore put it to the reader that the burden of plausibility has been discharged. In principle, there can be no objection to the hypothesis that the builders of the Great Pyramid enshrined a sacred iron meteorite, or meteorites, in the sarcophagus of the King's Chamber.

But this is to put the case too modestly.

In fact, there are good arguments why the sarcophagus in the King's Chamber is more likely to have contained iron meteorites than to have contained the mummy of the king.

Firstly, the King's Chamber is situated at an elevated height in the Great Pyramid. According to the fundamental axiom 'the body to earth, the spirit to the sky', the body of the king, identified with the body of the creator-god, did not belong at such a height. Rather, it belonged in the earth below. The meteorite, on the other hand, represented the iron seed of the creator that had been ejected into the sky. It was not part of the creator's body per se, but rather represented the molten iron which had flowed forth from his body, and then become, for the most part, separate from his body, manifesting itself in the celestial bodies, rather than in the body of the earth below. It was, as Spell 816 of the Coffin Texts puts it, 'spiritualised iron'. It did, therefore, belong at an elevated height in the Pyramid, which monument symbolised the spiritualisation of the creator-god and his insemination of the sky.

The axiom of the pyramid may thus be written: 'the body to the earth, the meteorite to the sky!'.

Secondly, a stunningly simple point. There is no precedent for a king's body being buried high up inside a pyramid. But there is a precedent for a meteorite being raised to a height upon a pillar or a pole. Moreover, in 'the fetish of Abydos', a precedent would seem to exist for a meteorite *in a box* being raised towards the sky. This point argues persuasively in favour of the meteorite hypothesis.

Thirdly, a home truth for Egyptologists. In Egyptian religion, the cult of the king was fundamentally secondary and emulative of the cult of the creator-god. Primacy, therefore, lay with the god whose body was made of iron. In this light, it makes sense that the King's Chamber – the most splendid chamber in the Great Pyramid – was reserved for the original god and true god: the god of the iron of creation.

On this note, let us return to the King's Chamber, and put the finishing touches to the meteorite hypothesis.

The Meteorite Chamber

It is surely a significant fact that the King's Chamber and its sarcophagus provided an ideal environment for the storage of iron meteorites. On the one hand, the room benefited from a cave-like situation, being shielded by a minimum of 170 feet of masonry. Here, deep inside this man-made mountain, the temperature would have been virtually constant at all times of the year, and at all times of the day.[124] Secondly, the granite box in the King's Chamber was hermetically sealed, thus preventing the outside air from permeating inside. If an iron meteorite had been placed inside this box, inside this chamber, it would have been ideally situated to withstand the corrosive effects of oxygen, humidity, and fluctuating temperatures. Such a meteorite would have lasted for eternity, effectively in a state of suspended animation, or mummification. (It is acknowledged that these conditions would, by the same token, have benefited the mummy of the king, but that scenario has already been negated, and is not the point at issue here.)

Figure 83.
THE SARCOPHAGUS IN THE KING'S CHAMBER.
This box, originally hermetically sealed, would have kept iron meteorites at constant temperature and free of humidity, in effect mummifying the iron.

    This is an appropriate moment to revisit the question of the King's Chamber 'airshafts'. Were these shafts designed to air-condition the room, in order to keep the temperature constant for the preservation of the iron? It is a tempting thought. After all, there is anecdotal evidence to suggest that, when the shafts are cleared of obstructions, the chamber enjoys a stable temperature of 68° F.[125] However, two arguments militate against this possibility. Firstly, if ventilation had been the objective, then the builders would surely have cut the shafts horizontally, not obliquely, thereby avoiding a lot of unnecessary work. And secondly, the chamber would have benefited from a stable temperature without the shafts, since it was embedded so deeply inside this man-made mountain that it would have taken on all the attributes of an underground cave. Upon reflection, then, modern observations of the chamber's constant temperature, 68° F, may be a little misleading. What was important was not the absolute temperature, but rather its constancy, which would have been achieved anyway, perhaps at a slightly lower figure than 68° F. (As noted earlier, the practical ideal temperature for meteorite storage is 66.2° F, based on a relative humidity of 30%.)

In fact, from the meteoritic perspective, the King's Chamber shafts, far from helping to mummify the meteorite, would actually have conveyed humid air into the room, making the hermetically-sealed sarcophagus all the more necessary, indeed critical, for the conservation of the iron. From this point of view, it would seem that the architect incorporated the shafts for some ulterior purpose. But for what?

In assessing the possible purpose of the shafts, considerable weight must be given to the fact that the shafts rise steeply, on paths of evolving inclines and trajectories, with the apparent aim of exiting the Pyramid at the same height on its centre axis, in the northern and southern faces, respectively. This fact must be explained.

One possible explanation is religious symbolism. Egyptologists hold the view that the king's soul used the two shafts to ascend to the northern and southern skies respectively. However, as discussed in chapter three, the orthodox 'soul-shaft' theory suffers from a number of difficulties, all stemming from the notion (surely misguided) that the king himself was buried in the (inaptly named) King's Chamber.

However, if we relocate the body of the king to its proper place in the subterranean world, and introduce to the King's Chamber the seed of the creator-god, in the form of meteoritic iron, a truly magical thing happens. The soul-shaft theory, in a new and revised version, makes sense.

It works like this.

According to the Egyptian creation myth, the Great God came to life as a spirit in the abyss. Then, in an almighty cataclysm, he spat out both a spiritual essence and a material substance into the sky. The latter, as we have seen, was terrestrial iron, or *bja*. But, without the influence of the spirit, the iron was but inert matter. It is therefore a combination of spirit and iron that is despatched into the sky for the formation of the stars, the

Sun, and the Moon.

The Pyramid not only commemorates this act of creation, but re-enacts it. In the ground below, the body of the king is transformed, through acts of ritual magic, into the body of the creator-god. Then, following the 'opening of the mouth' ceremony, the spirit of the king/creator-god, the *ka*, rises up to fill the entire structure above. The Pyramid, at this point, becomes a simulacrum in stone of the creator-god.

Now, the capstone of the Pyramid (*benbenet*) symbolises the iron seed being thrust into the womb of the sky. But, in the heart of the Pyramid, in the King's Chamber, the real iron, in the form of the meteorite, is ready to be spiritualised and raised to the sky. When the creator's energy hits its peak, the spiritualised iron is blasted into the northern and southern skies respectively via the two shafts, symbolically speaking of course. The northern sky is then able to conceive and bear the circumpolar stars, whilst the southern sky is able to conceive and bear all of the celestial bodies (Sun, Moon and stars) that traverse the eternal circuit from east to west.[126] In both cases, the celestial bodies are formed from spirit and iron, or spiritualised iron.

Figure 84.
THE IRON IS BLASTED INTO THE SKY VIA THE KING'S CHAMBER SHAFTS.

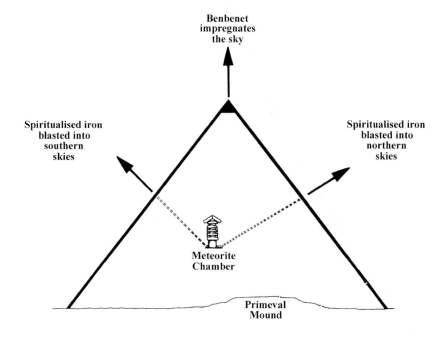

Benbenet
impregnates
the sky

Spiritualised iron
blasted into
southern
skies

Spiritualised iron
blasted into
northern
skies

Meteorite
Chamber

Primeval
Mound

Underworld

The King's Chamber shafts would thus be soul-shafts, but not quite in the way that Egyptologists have assumed. They would not simply have sent the king's soul to certain specific stars, or to the Sun, but rather sent the joint soul of the king/creator-god to all parts of the sky, crucially via the iron seed that was enshrined in the chamber. Hence the instruction to the king in the Pyramid Texts: 'may you remove yourself to the sky upon your iron throne'. In a nutshell, the shafts would have been conduits for the re-enactment of creation.

The shafts thus fit well with the theory that the King's Chamber was a 'meteorite chamber'.

Furthermore, in favour of the meteorite theory, it should be noted that the King's Chamber is built entirely of granite, as is the sarcophagus. Now, granite is an igneous rock, and it is highly likely that the Egyptians held it to be symbolic of fire and the cataclysm of creation (hence its use in obelisks). Its use in the King's Chamber would therefore be perfectly consistent with the concept of a meteorite chamber, or a 'chamber of creation'. Incidentally, it may be no coincidence that the modern word 'pyramid' originates from the ancient Greek *puramis*, which meant 'fire in the middle', from *pur/pura* 'fire'/'hearth', and *misos*, 'middle'.[127] It is not inconceivable that the Greeks invented the word *puramis* following discussions with the priests at Giza, although this would imply that the Egyptians had themselves heard reports of a sacred 'fire chamber' in the midst of the monument. (By coincidence or not, the Egyptians informed the Greeks that Khufu's body lay *under* the Pyramid.)

In closing this discussion, however, it must be pointed out that some features of the King's Chamber remain unexplained. Why, for example, were the shafts not positioned centrally in the walls, or on the Pyramid's north-south centre axis? Why was the mouth of the southern shaft built to such an unusual pattern? And what was the purpose of the 'raised roofs' that are stacked above the chamber? Until all of these questions have been answered satisfactorily, suspicions must remain that something else was going on in the King's Chamber, and that some ulterior function has yet to be identified. We will indeed discuss this possibility further in chapter seven. But for now, the crucial point is that the King's Chamber and its sarcophagus did not protect a human body but rather meteoritic iron – the iron of creation.

Chapter Five Summary

- Meteorites and meteoritic iron were of fundamental importance in ancient Egyptian religion. According to the myth of creation, molten iron (*bja*) had been blasted into the sky to provide the material for the stars, the Sun and the Moon, and some leftover iron had fallen back to the earth and seeded the beginning of life. The meteorite was thus held to be the seed of creation, both in the sky and in the earth. This myth was re-enacted in Egyptian rituals, often using tools made from meteoritic iron, whilst the meteorites themselves were worshipped in temples as actual samples of the creator-god's seed.

- Crucially, the meteoritic iron was said to be infused with the creator-god's spirit. It was therefore described as 'spiritualised iron'.

- All iron meteorites have a tendency to rust over time, but this effect can be mitigated by storage at constant temperature and at a relative humidity of no more than 30%. It is likely that the Egyptian adopted such measures by enshrining the meteorites in hermetically-sealed sarcophagi, and placing those sarcophagi in temple crypts.

- The hermetically-sealed sarcophagus in the King's Chamber, shielded by 170 feet plus of the Great Pyramid's masonry, would have provided ideal conditions for the storage of iron meteorites. Whilst there is no precedent for the king's body being buried at such a height, there is a precedent for meteorites being raised on high, and possibly in sealed boxes to boot. Moreover, the iron meteorite, representing the spiritualised seed of the creator-god, belonged symbolically in the height of the Pyramid. It is thus likely that the sarcophagus in the King's Chamber contained iron meteorites.

- If the Pyramid was a simulacrum of creation and the King's Chamber a meteorite chamber, then it would follow that the so-called 'airshafts' in that room had a symbolic significance, recalling the blasting of the spiritualised iron into the sky for the conception and birth of the celestial bodies. This symbolism would be complementary to that of the Pyramid's capstone, which likewise recalled the impregnation of the sky by the meteoritic Benben Stone.

- It must be remembered that the cult of the king was secondary to that of the creator-god, it thus being appropriate that the Pyramid's most splendid chamber was reserved for the actual seed of the creator-god rather than the body of the king.

CHAPTER SIX

CAPSULE OF ETERNITY

———————— ◁—▷ ————————

Everything fears Time, but Time fears the pyramids.
(Ibn Fadlallah al-Umari, d. 1348)

In chapter four, I argued that the king's body would have been buried beneath the Pyramid, probably in the cave-like Grotto, whilst, in chapter five, I argued that the King's Chamber sarcophagus enshrined meteoritic iron, the seed of creation. Together, these two complementary theories address the crux questions posed by Egyptologists in defiant defence of the orthodox theory: if the king's body was not buried in the King's Chamber sarcophagus, then *where* was it buried; and if the king's body was buried elsewhere, then *what* was buried in the King's Chamber sarcophagus? Significantly, the answers here provided to these questions are not speculations, but have been derived from a coherent and logical theory, namely that ancient Egyptian religion was a 'cult of creation' and that the true pyramid was a creational symbol. The upshot of this is that the Pyramid's unique interior design sprang not from a desire to raise the burial chamber, as Egyptologists have presumed (in contradiction to the fundamental axiom 'the body to earth, the spirit to the sky'), but rather from a desire to create a shrine for iron meteorites and re-enact the iron's spiritualisation to the sky (hence the so-called 'airshafts').

This novel approach eliminates at a stroke the many difficulties with the orthodox funeral procession and burial scenario (see chapter three), and instead opens up a completely new realm of possibility. Until now, it has always been assumed that the Pyramid's upper passageways and chambers were kept open in readiness for the burial of the king. But now that assumption becomes superfluous, and instead it becomes possible that the entire upper system was *sealed off at the time of construction* – a thought that has never, for one moment, occurred to Egyptologists. What I mean is that the passageways and chambers could have been sealed off individually by means of plugs, 'lefts', and camouflaging stones at the time when the Pyramid was being built up from the ground, layer upon layer, towards its apex.

But why build the Pyramid as a sealed system? What possible motive could the architect have had?

Only one answer suggests itself. The Pyramid must have been built, in part, as a giant repository, to protect the sacred relics and artefacts of the early Egyptians. In the Grand Gallery, the Queen's Chamber, the King's Chamber, and perhaps in other, yet-to-be-discovered chambers, precious objects would have been sealed and concealed, perhaps to ensure their survival for posterity, or perhaps to magic them into being in the 'other world'. The meteoritic iron in the King's Chamber sarcophagus would be a prime example of such an object, which could have been sealed into its location while the Pyramid was still being built. But, as for the contents of the other chambers, it is necessary to consider a diverse range of other possibilities, discussion here being reserved for chapters eight and nine of this book.

This sealed repository theory raises many interesting questions. What was the rationale for building it? Why was it incorporated into the Great Pyramid but not into any other pyramids (so far as we know)? And why did the architect anticipate the eventual discovery and retrieval of the hidden objects (as evidenced by his inclusion of connecting passages and a subtle signpost in the Descending Passage marking the place where the hidden passages began)?

These ancillary questions are important, and require to be explored if the plausibility of the sealed repository theory is to be established. But, before we do so, I would first like to present the physical evidence that the Pyramid was indeed sealed, stage by stage, as it was built, as opposed to being kept open for the funeral procession and burial of the king. The evidence, as we shall now see, consists of a pattern of concealment that runs from bottom to top of the Pyramid's interior design (as that design is currently known).

The Art of Concealment

If the reader will turn to figure 85, we may begin. In this diagram, we see the interior of the Pyramid as the first explorers would have seen it.

From the main entrance in the northern face, the Descending Passage leads down into the Subterranean Chamber, which would probably have contained decoy burial arrangements. The earliest visitors to the Pyramid would have emerged from the Subterranean Chamber under the distinct impression that the king's tomb had already been robbed, and they would

Figure 85.
THE GREAT PYRAMID, VERTICAL SECTION, AS THE EARLIEST
INTRUDERS WOULD HAVE SEEN IT.

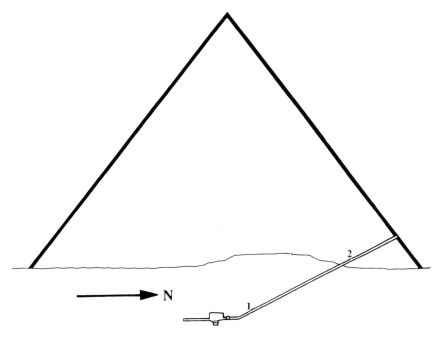

have been entirely oblivious to the fact that the Descending Passage, in
its inclined section, contained concealed entrances to two secret passage
systems. The first of these, at point 1 on figure 85, provided access to the
Grotto via the so-called Well Shaft, and was probably intended for the
secret burial of the king, whilst the second, at point 2, provided access to
the upper chamber system via the Ascending Passage. It is the second of
these hidden entrances that is our concern in this chapter, for it is here
that the pattern of concealment begins in the form of the prism stone that
was fitted into the ceiling of the Descending Passage. As I.E.S. Edwards
has observed in his book *The Pyramids of Egypt*, this prismatic stone had
the purpose of camouflaging the entrance to the Ascending Passage:

> ... the opening [to the Ascending Corridor] was covered with a slab of
> limestone, so that it was not distinguishable from the remainder of the
> ceiling.[1]

As discussed in chapter three, the prism stone had protrusions at its sides
which fitted into the side walls, such that the stone must have been fitted
into place when the Pyramid was built. Whether the prism stone could
have pivoted on these protrusions is a moot point; I actually favour the

possibility of a pivoting stone, since it would have enabled the builders to better control the descent of the first granite plug when it was lowered down the Ascending Passage; later, after the other two plugs had been lowered, the stone would have been swivelled into its closed position and cemented firmly into place.

Remarkably, as noted in chapter three, it would seem that the builders of the Pyramid wanted the camouflaging stone to be found. For, as Piazzi Smyth discovered in 1865, an unusual joint was constructed in the floor of the Descending Passage directly opposite and beneath the mouth of the secret passage. Here, it is worth quoting the Egyptologist J.P. Lepre, whom I cited earlier in chapter three:

> This particular line – a joint set opposite to the other floor joints – was discovered by Smyth in his inspection of the descending corridor. He correctly referred to it as 'a sign in the floor for the wise'. For here, at that point immediately above the unorthodox joint, lay the lower end of the pyramid's ascending passage which gave access to the upper reaches of the monument.[2]

Such is the subtlety of this 'sign in the floor', however, that it evidently was not intended to be discovered by the hurried intruder, but rather by someone who took the time to inspect the monument's interior with the utmost care. (It must be remembered that, even today, with the benefit of electric lighting, many of the fine joints are difficult to discern.)

It may be surmised, then, that the architect of the Pyramid wanted the camouflaging stone in the ceiling to be found by the right kind of person, and, furthermore, it may be surmised that he expected the seeker to break through the prism stone in order to access the secret passage above it.

Whether this scenario is what actually transpired is debatable (see the discussion in chapter eight). But the intention, it would seem, was that the attentive explorer discover and penetrate the prism stone, whereupon he would see the rectangular end of a large granite plug – the lowest of three such plugs – blocking the bottom of the inclined passage, as shown in figure 86.

The purpose of these plugs is a mystery, for the camouflaging stone, by the art of concealment, would itself have provided sufficient security for the Ascending Passage. Also mysterious is the builder's decision to install plugs made of granite, rather than limestone. To the modern mind, this arrangement seems nonsensical, since the hard barrier of granite can be avoided all too easily by digging into the soft surrounding blocks of limestone. What was the builder playing at? Was the granite plug another 'sign for the wise'? Or some kind of initiation test? Was it intended that

Figure 86.
THE BEGINNING OF THE ASCENDING PASSAGE, BLOCKED BY A
GRANITE PLUG.
The aperture below the plug was filled by the prism stone which formed part of
the ceiling of the Descending Passage.

the explorer should cut through the granite plugs rather than taking the
easy route around them? I will return to this perplexing matter in a later
chapter. But, whatever the answer, it is evident that the builders went to a
great deal of trouble, not only to lower the three granite plugs into the
mouth of the passage, but also to build the passage itself to a special
tapered and girdled design for the plugs' containment.

   Here, orthodoxy meets its nemesis in the sealed repository theory.
According to orthodoxy, the difficulty of manoeuvring the plugs to the
bottom of the Ascending Passage required that workmen lowered the
plugs from above, thereby trapping themselves inside the Grand Gallery.
It therefore becomes necessary to assume that the workmen escaped via
the Well Shaft, the cutting of which jeopardised the security of the king's
tomb – a highly contrived and unlikely scenario. According to the sealed
chambers theory, however, the plugs would have been slid down the

passage while the Gallery was still under construction, and the problem of the workmen's evacuation thus does not arise.[3] Let's chalk this one up to the sealed repository theory.

Moving beyond the plugs, the earliest explorer would have discovered the Pyramid's interior as it appears in figure 87. Here, the key points to be noted are the low roof height of the Grand Gallery and the complete absence of the Queen's Chamber and the King's Chamber. The picture is one wholly unfamiliar to us.

Figure 87.
THE GREAT PYRAMID AS IT WOULD HAVE BEEN SEEN FOLLOWING DISCOVERY OF THE ASCENDING PASSAGE.

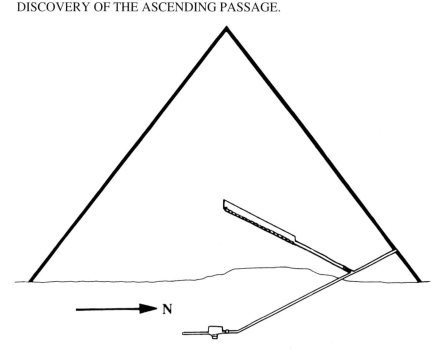

Why is this?

Firstly, the Gallery has its section of 'false floor' intact, concealing the passage to the Queen's Chamber.

Secondly, the Gallery has its 'false roof' intact, concealing the full expanse of its design.

And thirdly, the Gallery terminates at the Great Step, where the mouth of the passage to the King's Chamber is concealed.

Let us consider each of these three concealments in turn.

To begin with the 'false floor', although no trace of it remains, the fact of its former existence is not a matter of controversy. As J.P. Lepre noted in his book *The Egyptian Pyramids*:

> This room [the Queen's Chamber] was permanently sealed off from the Grand Gallery by a camouflaging 'false floor' at the lower end of the Gallery...[4]

This 'false floor', or 'bridging slab' as it is sometimes called, was about 17 feet long, and provided a smooth continuation of the floor between the Grand Gallery and the Ascending Passage. It was by means of this smooth floor that the granite plugs were lowered into the mouth of the Ascending Passage.

Now, the key question is whether this bridging slab was movable or fixed in position at the time of construction. According to Egyptologists, the slab rested on cross-beams (of wood or stone) that spanned the walls immediately beneath it, but was independent of these beams. Up until the time of the king's funeral, it is believed, the slab could have been raised to allow access into the Queen's Chamber, and then lowered afterwards (a number of ritual scenarios are envisioned for the king's mummy in the Queen's Chamber). It was only after the king's burial that the slab would have been cemented permanently into place.

However, as explained in chapter three, the sockets in the side walls are cut too high to receive simple cross-beams, but are at the appropriate height to receive 9-inch-thick protrusions from the bridging slab itself, in addition to the cross beams. This arrangement is clearly visible in figures 54 and 55 (see chapter three). It is therefore apparent that the orthodox theory of the movable slab is incorrect, and that the slab was actually built into the walls at the time of the Pyramid's construction. Let's chalk this up as a second point to the sealed repository theory.

Turning to the 'false roof', although there is no trace of it (as with the 'false floor'), the fact of its former existence is not to be gainsaid. As Lepre has explained, its design is vouchsafed by the pair of grooves into which it was fitted:

> Among the interesting architectural features of the Grand Gallery are two grooves cut into the east and west walls... Hundreds of rough chisel marks are staggered along the top edges of these grooves... It is certain that something did traverse the Gallery... Could it have been cedar panels inlaid with gold?[5]

Whilst the exact nature and form of this 'false roof', or 'lower roof', is uncertain, there is no doubt, as Lepre says, that something did span the width and length of the Gallery, truncating its height from 28 feet to 14 feet. And, once again, it is evident that this roof feature – whatever it was

– was not something movable, but rather something that was fitted into place when the Pyramid was built. It is a puzzling idea in a funerary context, but a concealment of the Gallery's full height might just make sense under the sealed repository theory.

Finally, it remains to be shown that the Gallery originally terminated at the point of the Great Step, the mouth of the King's Chamber Passage being hidden. Here, the evidence takes the form of significant damage to the mouth of the passage, as shown in figure 88. No Egyptologist, to my knowledge, has ever offered an explanation for this damage – not a word as to who might have caused it or why. And it certainly is curious when we stop to think about it. For, if the mouth of this passage was left open by the builders, as has always been assumed, why would it have been necessary for an intruder to inflict violent blows to its mouth? A possible

Figure 88.
THE GREAT STEP AND ENTRANCE TO THE KING'S CHAMBER PASSAGE.
The damage to the mouth of the passage suggests that it was once blocked by a camouflaging stone (compare photograph in figure 31).

explanation – the only one that I can come up with – is that the aperture was originally filled with a limestone block, or covered by a 'left', thus camouflaging the passage to the King's Chamber. In such circumstances, an intruder might well have taken an axe to the wall in order to break out the obstruction. To be fair, the case for the sealed repository theory is less clear cut in this instance, but the clue is there, and it fits the general pattern.[6]

If the reader will now turn to figure 89, he will see the Pyramid as it would have been seen by the explorer who first broke through the 'false floor', the 'false roof', and the camouflaging stone upon the Great Step. In this diagram, we see the full extent of the Grand Gallery, the passage to the Queen's Chamber, and the beginning of the passage to the King's Chamber. But where is the Queen's Chamber itself? The remarkable answer is: behind another camouflaging plate of stone.

The evidence for this further concealment of the Queen's Chamber is shown in figure 90, where a rough protrusion to the wall may be seen at the point where the passage debouches into the chamber. This is another oft-overlooked feature of the Pyramid, but it has been remarked upon by

Figure 89.
THE GREAT PYRAMID AS IT WOULD HAVE BEEN SEEN FOLLOWING DISCOVERY OF THE GALLERY'S FALSE ROOF, FALSE FLOOR, AND CONCEALED PASSAGE ON THE GREAT STEP.

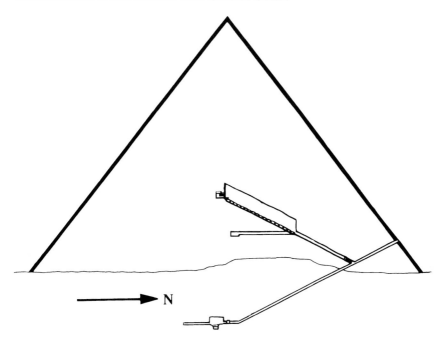

Figure 90.
THE ENTRANCE TO THE QUEEN'S CHAMBER.
The rough 1-inch-thick protrusion at the side of the entrance suggests that the
room was once sealed off by a camouflaging plate of stone.

some researchers. For example, the French consul in Egypt, Benoit de
Maillet, in his detailed examination of the Pyramid between 1692 and
1708, noted the existence of the 'slight projection' at the entrance to the
chamber, and speculated that it may have been intended to retain plug
blocks that were stored in the passage. His remarks are paraphrased by
the English explorer Colonel Howard Vyse as follows:

> (Maillet) is of the opinion that the slight projection, on the right side of
> the entrance into this chamber, was intended to prevent the stones,
> with which the horizontal passage had been filled, from being forced
> beyond the entrance of this room, and that the stone originally placed
> there fitted it exactly.[7]

This protuberance was also commented upon by the alternative theorist
Peter Lemesurier, who wondered whether it had once extended across

the opening to the Queen's Chamber 'like a uterine membrane that needs to be ruptured'.[8] Perhaps it did indeed need to be ruptured, although I would not wish to endorse Lemesurier's symbolic interpretation of this or any other feature of the Pyramid.

Once again, then, we find physical evidence in keeping with the sealed repository theory. Not conclusive by any means (William Flinders Petrie took the view that the builders had simply been in a hurry, and had thus neglected to apply the finishing stokes),[9] but certainly indicative of the pattern of concealment that runs right through the Pyramid.

If we now allow our notional explorer to break through this thin plate of stone into the Queen's Chamber, his view of the Pyramid is extended as shown in figure 91. But, again, a crucial element is missing, this time the Queen's Chamber 'airshafts', for they too were concealed behind a thin plate of stone, as J.P. Lepre observed:

> Unlike the vents leading out from the King's Chamber, these channels terminate just 20 feet short of the exterior. These vents are also different from those in the King's Chamber in that they do not begin their ascent in the chamber proper, but 5 inches in from the north and south wall stones of that chamber. A 5-inch veneer of the wall stones

Figure 91.
THE GREAT PYRAMID AS IT WOULD HAVE BEEN SEEN FOLLOWING DISCOVERY OF THE QUEEN'S CHAMBER.

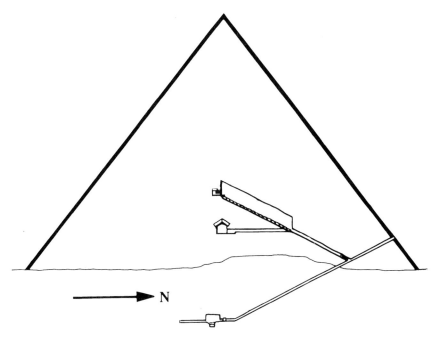

N

Figure 92.
THE MOUTH OF THE NORTHERN SHAFT IN THE QUEEN'S CHAMBER,
PART OF THE ORIGINAL STONE SEAL BEING CLEARLY VISIBLE.

through which these channels were to have entered the Queen's
Chamber was left intact by the architect, camouflaging the channels
from the sight of anyone who might happen to be in the chamber.[10]

This pair of shafts represents a real mystery. Clearly, the builders went to
a great deal of trouble to build them on a steep incline, each to a length
of about 213 feet. But why would they have terminated the shafts so
close to the outside of the Pyramid? And why would they have left the
shafts sealed at their lower ends? What was the point of all this work?

According to Egyptologists, the shafts may have been intended for the
ascent of the king's soul (*ba*), or for the non-ascent (!) of the king's spirit
(*ka*), as discussed in chapter three. But this theory does not really explain
why the shafts were terminated inside the Pyramid, and nor does it
explain why the mouths of the shafts were sealed. Were the soul-shafts
abandoned mid-construction? Even when the theory is patched in this
way, it still does not explain why the mouths of the shafts would have
been left sealed, especially since, according to my earlier analysis, the
builders did not have the option of returning to the Queen's Chamber at a
later juncture to cut the said mouths (the bridging slab having been fitted
permanently into the side walls). In order to save the soul-shaft theory, it
must be patched once again by the assumption of a complete 'cockup' on

the part of the person who was assigned to cut open the shafts. But this merely begs the question of why the chamber's walls were built in such a way that the shafts had to be cut through afterwards? It just doesn't make sense. At least not from an orthodox point of view.

But the concealment of the shafts does fit the pattern of concealment that has been demonstrated elsewhere in the Pyramid, and is therefore consistent with the sealed repository theory. Indeed, the evidence is all the more pertinent in this case since the limestone 'lefts' were penetrated in modern times, by Waynman Dixon in 1872, leaving no room for doubt that the mouths of the shafts were indeed left sealed by the builders.

As for the termini of the Queen's Chamber shafts, the likely presence of a sealed chamber above the southern shaft, just 50 feet short of the Pyramid's exterior (see the evidence cited in chapter three) is difficult to explain by the orthodox theory, but is entirely consistent with the sealed repository theory. Indeed, the stone plug that has been discovered in the shaft beyond the metal-handled 'door' (southern shaft) is reminiscent of the first granite plug that was fitted into the bottom of the Ascending Passage. And that plug, the first in a series of three, barred the access to a system of passages and chambers that exceeded the wildest dreams of the earliest Pyramid explorers.

If a similar plug is discovered soon in the northern shaft, the evidence will be all the more compelling that these two shafts – sealed at their lower ends and plugged at their upper ends – functioned as hidden paths to secret chambers, the intention being that the explorer dig his way up through the masonry (the shafts themselves measuring only 8 inches by 8 inches). Since the sealed repository theory is the only theory to explain satisfactorily the design of these shafts, we may chalk up another point to it, at the expense of the orthodox theory.

Let us continue to follow in the footsteps of our notional explorer, who has now left the Queen's Chamber and returned to the Great Step, at the top of the Grand Gallery, where he has cut through the camouflaging stone and discovered the Antechamber to the King's Chamber.

Here, a change of strategy by the architect becomes apparent. Instead of concealing the existence of the passage and King's Chamber beyond the Antechamber, he rather drew attention to them by placing three huge granite slabs between the pilasters in the Antechamber's side walls as a physical barrier to the explorer's progress (the inclusion of these slabs is attested by the damage to the pilasters, the slabs themselves having been removed during antiquity).

Now, according to orthodoxy, these three granite slabs formed part of a portcullis system, and were lowered onto the passage floor following

the funeral of the king. The fact is, however, that the Antechamber could
not have housed an operable portcullis (for the reasons cited in chapter
three), and, furthermore, the first two granite slabs would have presented
no real obstacle to an intruder, who could have climbed up over them to
attack the third slab from a position of advantage.

The purpose of the three granite slabs is thus a mystery, although it
might well be the case that the architect incorporated them for reasons of
religious symbolism – a suggestion in keeping with my earlier proposal
that the granite leaf and the grooved south wall represent decorative and
symbolic elements in the Antechamber (see chapter three).

In any event, the explorer would have bypassed the first two slabs and
assaulted the third in order to gain access to the passage beyond; and the
evidence that he did just that is the damage to the south wall of the room,

Figure 93.
THE ANTECHAMBER TO THE KING'S CHAMBER.
At this point, the concealment strategy was eschewed in favour of three granite
slabs that blocked access to the passage and chamber beyond.

immediately below the grooves, as seen in figure 93 (note: the breakage might well indicate the height of the third slab). Whilst it is possible that the mouth of this passage was concealed by a grooved plate of stone, the presence of the slabs would have made concealment a redundant idea.

Having forced his way past the third granite slab, the explorer would have discovered the King's Chamber, the Pyramid's design unfolding as in figure 94. This diagram shows the monument as it was known in the early-18th century, prior to the discovery of the superstructure above the King's Chamber's roof (Davison 1765, Vyse 1837), and prior to the discovery of the Queen's Chamber shafts (Dixon 1872).

Figure 94.
THE GREAT PYRAMID AS IT WAS KNOWN TO EARLY-18TH CENTURY EXPLORERS.

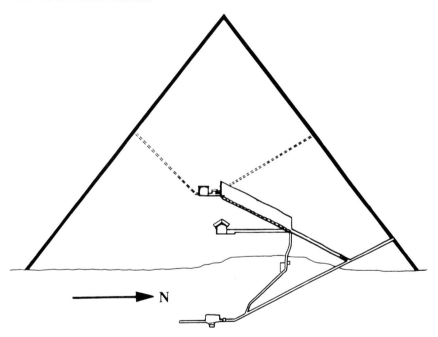

Our investigation of the evidence is now complete, and I trust that the pattern of concealment in the Pyramid, from bottom to top, has become apparent to the reader.

In summary, it seems to me that the Pyramid's upper passages and chambers were not kept open for the funeral of the king, but rather were sealed as they were built, various sacred relics and artefacts being sealed up inside the rooms, the prime example being the meteoritic iron in the King's Chamber sarcophagus. Furthermore, it seems evident to me that the builders of the Pyramid wanted these secret passages and chambers to be found, ideally by someone who would take the time to study the architecture in the minutest detail. Why else build connecting passages behind the camouflaging stones? And why else place an unusual joint – 'a sign in the floor for the wise' – directly beneath the hidden entrance to the Ascending Passage? (This latter point, incidentally, argues against the tomb hypothesis for the upper chambers.)

All of this suggests that the sacred relics and artefacts were not sealed up for eternity, but were sealed up with the intention that they be found and retrieved by someone who would, as it were, play the architect's game of 'hide and seek'.

This game, it would seem, began millennia ago, and remains ongoing in modern times – witness the discovery of the Queen's Chamber shafts by Waynman Dixon as recently as 1872, and the discovery of the 'doors' and plug(s) above these shafts in 1993/2002. The full story, surely, is yet to be told.

Finally, it behoves me to emphasise that I am not suggesting that the Pyramid was a sealed repository and nothing but a sealed repository. Rather, I am arguing that the Pyramid was primarily a symbol of the creation, but that, above and beyond its religious symbolism, it had a dual function: on the one hand, a tomb for a king, and, on the other hand, a reliquary for sacred relics and artefacts; or, to state it simply, a tomb below, and a sealed repository above.

The Time Capsule Theory

At this point, the reader may yet remain sceptical of the sealed repository theory. Why, he might ask, would the architect have required such a structure? Why would he have gone to such inordinate lengths to protect sacred relics and artefacts? And why would he have wanted those objects to be ultimately found and retrieved?

At the risk of sounding a little cranky, this author can think of only one possible answer: that the Pyramid was constructed as a kind of 'time capsule' that would safeguard the material treasures, and perhaps even the spiritual and scientific knowledge, of the builders' civilisation, so as to keep these things in trust for the benefit of a future generation, or race, of men.

But why would the builders have envisaged the requirement for such a time capsule?

Again, only one answer suggests itself to this author: that the builders' civilisation became obsessed by the idea that it would, in the near future, be destroyed by a cataclysm. The rulers of this civilisation, it may be hypothesised, therefore decided to build the Pyramid and conceal inside it all of the crucial relics and scientific knowledge that would be required to initiate a later generation of men. And, moreover, lest an aeon pass before the new generation, or race, of men rose up from the ashes of the destroyed world, the rulers ordained that the Pyramid be built upon an earthquake-resistant platform – the Giza plateau – and constructed to such a degree of precision and exactitude that it would indeed endure for the aeon that might pass until a new age of civilisation could begin.

A controversial theory? Certainly. For it is not the orthodox theory.

But a cranky theory? Whilst it might seem so to the 'old school' reader who believes that the path of ancient history has been a long, ordered and uniformitarian rise from barbarism to civilisation, it will not necessarily seem so to the reader who is versed in the evidence for the punctuation of ancient history by cataclysmic impacts (from comets and earth-crossing asteroids), which have, on at least one occasion, brought civilisation to its knees.[11]

Did such a period of cataclysmic activity precede the construction of the Great Pyramid? Here, we must inevitably speculate, for the textual sources prior to 2550 BC (the time assigned by orthodoxy for the building of the Pyramid) are exceedingly thin. Nevertheless, the scenario is quite plausible, as demonstrated amply by the work of the scientists Victor Clube and Bill Napier.

In a series of studies, Clube and Napier have mounted a persuasive argument that Encke's Comet and the Taurid meteor stream represent the remnants of a huge comet (Proto-Encke) that broke apart in our solar system around eighty thousand years ago. In their 1990 book *The Cosmic Winter*, Clube and Napier plotted a series of periods at which the Earth's orbit would have been intersected annually by the orbit of the cometary debris, producing a high risk of cataclysmic collisions. Clube and Napier described what people on Earth would have witnessed in the skies during these periods:

> The slow evolution of the cometary orbits ensures that, at a few brief epochs in the past, the orbital tracks of the major comet and Earth intersected. Close encounters with a major, active fragment, over those centuries, must have been spectacular if not terrifying, with the comet nucleus, brighter than Venus, crossing the sky in a few hours, accompanied by a complex, striated red tail bisecting the sky. Meteor storms of ferocious intensity, recurring annually when the Earth crossed the debris of the comet, must have taken place during those epochs, the shooting stars blazing out from a small region of sky in

Taurus or Aries. On some such occasions the sky must have been filled with brilliant fireballs, such storms lasting for several hours. Some of these fireballs would on occasion reach the upper atmosphere or the ground, and there would be explosions – there could be no doubting the association of these spectacular phenomena with the supreme being in the sky.[12]

In addition, a large number of meteorites would have fallen to the Earth at the times of these cataclysmic storms.

Did one of these cosmic storms trouble Egypt in the days preceding the building of the Great Pyramid? Unfortunately, Clube and Napier's model for Comet Proto-Encke yields only approximate ranges of dates, and is still subject to revision. But, at the very least, it demonstrates that the hypothesis is plausible.

Comet Proto-Encke, of course, is by no means the only potential threat to the Earth circulating in the heavens.

Intriguingly, the astrophysicist Professor Chandra Wickramasinghe has recently suggested that Egypt was indeed afflicted by cosmic storms in the era immediately preceding the construction of the pyramids. In a newspaper article entitled 'Pyramid to Paradise', he wrote:

The time at which the pyramids were built, from around 2800 BC, may offer the greatest clue to their celestial importance. It was an era when our planet was under attack from the skies in the form of cosmic missiles, meteorites and pieces of comets that crashed through the skies.[13]

As far as I know, the definitive proof for impacts in Egypt c. 2800-2550 BC has yet to be found. But 'smoking gun' or not, Wickramasinghe's statement adds credence to my suggestion that the Great Pyramid was built, exceptionally, as a sealed repository and time capsule, in the face of a cataclysmic threat to Egyptian civilisation.

Let us now turn from astrophysics to ancient Egyptian religion and myth, in search of further corroboration of my hypothesis. Is there any evidence that the Egyptians were obsessed with cataclysms and a fear of the 'end of the world'?

As noted in earlier chapters, the Egyptian religion was founded upon the idea of the creation, which was conceived as an almighty geocentric, cataclysmic event. This mythical cataclysm (pertaining to a time before the birth of mankind) is attested in all periods of Egyptian literature, from the Pyramid Texts, c. 2350 BC, to the Coffin Texts, c. 2000 BC, to the later Book of the Dead, and it lies at the heart of all Egyptian ritual, to the extent that the building of the pyramid and the despatch of the king's soul to the sky re-enacted the cataclysm event. For a full treatment of this idea, which has yet to be fully apprehended by Egyptologists, the reader is referred to the companion volume to this book.

So much for the cataclysm of the creation. But what about prophecies of the 'end of the world'? Here, the references are more fragmentary and sporadic, but some noteworthy examples can be mentioned.

To begin, we find in Utterance 254 of the Pyramid Texts an unusual threat of universal cataclysm, not the cataclysm of creation but rather a kind of cataclysm of anti-creation. The king states:

> O Lord of the horizon [*akhet*], make ready a place for me, for if you fail to make ready a place for me, I will lay a curse on my father Geb [the earth-god] and the earth will speak no more; Geb will be unable to protect himself, and whoever I find in my way I will devour him piecemeal. The *hnt*-pelican will prophesy, the *psdt*-pelican will go up, the Great One will arise, the Enneads will speak, the earth being entirely dammed up; the borders will be joined together, the river-banks will be united, the roads will be impassable to travellers, and the stairways will be destroyed for those who wish to go up.[14]

This end of the world (or possibly non-beginning of creation) prophecy is echoed in Spell 1130 of the Coffin Texts (part of the Book of Two Ways) in which the creator-god 'the Lord of All' bewails the fact that mankind has perpetrated evil deeds in contravention to his edicts. He therefore announces that he will sit in the land of the dead and judge the evildoers, and he utters the following intriguing line:

> And mounds will become cities, and cities will become mounds, and mansion will desolate mansion.[15]

The idea, alluded to obscurely here, is that the world created by the Great God would be annulled in the final reckoning.

Egyptologists have connected Spell 1130 to a similar passage in the Book of the Dead. Here, the deceased asks Atum how long he will live in the realm of the dead, whereupon Atum paints a scenario of the 'end of the world':

> "You shall be for millions on millions of years... (until) I will despatch the Elders and destroy all that I have made. This earth will return to the primeval water, to the surging flood, as in its first state. I will remain with Osiris; I will transform myself into a 'something else'-serpent, which men do not know and the gods do not see."[16]

The clear intent here is that the world will ultimately come to an end in an exact reversal of the process by which it came into being. In other words, the earth and the sky will sink back into the depths of the abyss, amidst a global cataclysm, whereupon Atum will return to his original, mysterious form as the primeval serpent.

In addition to these 'end of the world' prophecies, Egyptian texts also speak of the dangers of an imminent fall of the sky. Let us consider a few of them.

A text entitled 'The Prophecy of Neferti' (18th dynasty) envisages a time in the near future when 'that which has never happened (before) has happened'. The scribe tells the king what he sees in his vision: the Sun disc has become hidden; the rivers have become empty; the winds are in disarray; the land of Egypt has perished completely – it is 'helter-skelter' and 'topsy turvy'; Re has separated himself from mankind; and the Heliopolitan nome, 'the birthplace of every god', no longer exists upon the earth. At that time, the scribe prophesies, Re will found the land all over again, as at the First Time, and a new king will come.[17] The story, intriguingly, is set in the Old Kingdom during the reign of Sneferu, the father of Khufu (the owner of the Great Pyramid).

In the Papyrus Salt (late-19th dynasty), a cataclysm is described in the context of a ritual for the equilibrium of the Universe, performed in the *Per Ankh*, the 'House of Life'. Here, the statuette of the creator-god (Osiris/Re) is addressed as follows:

> You will be protected from sudden death, you will be protected from fire, you will be protected from the sky; it will not fall, and the earth will not founder, and Re will not make ashes with the gods and goddesses.[18]

In the Great Harris Papyrus (20th dynasty), a magician utters a spell of cataclysm against the demon in the cosmic waters. If the demon does not turn away, all gods, demons and men will witness the cataclysmic 'end of the world':

> If the one who is on the water [the crocodile] opens his mouth, or if he shakes with his arms, I shall cause the earth to sink into the primeval water, and the south will become the north, and the earth will be turned upside down.[19]

In the Chester Beatty Papyrus Number 1 (20th dynasty), in a bawdy tale entitled 'The Contendings of Horus and Seth', the goddess Neit attempts to influence the judgement between the two gods Horus and Seth by bringing the sky down upon the earth. She declares:

> "I shall be angry and the sky will fall on the earth."[20]

As a final example, the fall of the sky is mentioned in the magical spells which appear in connection with sacred amulets from the 21st dynasty onwards. Of one such amulet, it is said that the wearer will be protected 'from the seven stars of the Great Bear, from a star that falls from the sky, and from the decan stars'.[21] And, as regards the decan stars, another amuletic spell identifies them as 'they who bombard the lands with fire, at whose approach everyone trembles.'[22]

Now, these Egyptian prophecies of the 'end of the world' and the 'fall of the sky' date, for the most part, to the New Kingdom period, from c. 1550 BC to 1070 BC. To be fair, few such references appear in the earliest texts, namely the Pyramid Texts (c. 2350 BC), where the emphasis is on the re-enactment of the cataclysm of beginning, i.e. the creation of the Universe. During this earlier period, it would seem, the Egyptian scribes had much greater confidence in the ability of the king and the priests to maintain the cosmic order and keep the forces of chaos at bay, by means of their magic rituals and spells.

Even so, it may be that the very nature of ancient Egyptian religion, exemplified by the concept of 'right cosmic order' (*maat*), holds the key to a major historical cataclysm (or series of cataclysms) that preceded the establishment of the religion.

Consider. All Egyptian ritual was aimed at re-enacting the creative act in which the creator had established right order (*maat*) at the beginning of time. By means of magic rituals and spells, performed in the temples on an annual, seasonal, monthly, and even daily basis, the power of the creator-god was rejuvenated and the shackling of the forces of chaos was reconfirmed. The king himself personified this ongoing struggle. As an incarnation of both Horus and Seth simultaneously,[23] he encapsulated in his own personage the judgement of Horus over Seth, and the triumph of order over chaos. By means of the rituals performed by the priests in the name of the king, it was believed that right order would be perpetuated till eternity. In theory, the very nature of the king, as an embodiment of the divine, creative spirit, ensured that the Sun and Moon would always rise, that the celestial vault would always turn, and that the Nile would always flood in its due season. With the king at the helm, the sky would never fall, the Sun disc would never be hidden, the Nile would never run dry, and the land would never sink into the abyss. As one king replaced another, in an unbroken chain of succession, the era of *maat* would be continued for ever.

Why did Egyptian religion take this remarkable form? Could it be that the obsessive need to impose cosmic order stemmed from a traumatic experience with cosmic *disorder*? Might the roots of Egyptian religion

Figure 95.
SHU SUPPORTS THE SKY (NUT) ABOVE THE EARTH (GEB).
Was the principle of cosmic order a psychological reaction to a traumatic
experience of a falling sky?

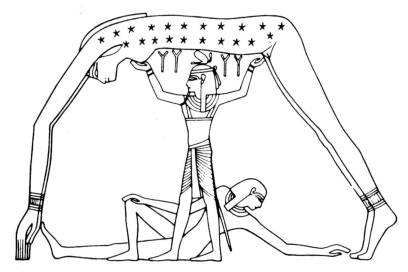

lie in a major historical cataclysm, or perhaps, more plausibly, in a series
of lesser cataclysms that threatened the arrival of the major, world-
ending 'cataclysm of all cataclysms'? Was *maat* a psychological reaction
to a fear of the 'end of the world'?

The answer to these questions may well be found in the Greek myths,
where a close parallel to *maat* may be found in the ideas of the eternal
reign of Zeus and the eternal support of the sky by Atlas. Significantly,
this arrangement of the cosmos came about, according to Greek myth, in
the aftermath of the cataclysmic 'battle of the Titans', when Heaven and
Earth, personified by the gods and the Titans, had arrayed their violent
powers against one another.[24] According to the Greeks, one world after
another had been 'destroyed' by cataclysms, and the inhabitants of each
world had been consigned to ashes. But each time, a new race of beings
had sprung up from the earth (quite literally) and rebuilt civilisation
anew, culminating in the present age of man – the so-called 'iron age'.[25]

On the basis of the Greek model, there is every reason to believe that
cataclysms, of the cosmic variety, played a major role in the formation of
Egyptian religion as we know it. From the fear of the 'end of the world',
it may be surmised, the concept of *maat* was born; and by the enactment
of *maat*, the fear of the 'end time' was banished; only for the real world
to intrude and renew the fear of the 'end of the world'; thereby leading to
the redoubling of efforts to enact *maat* through magic rituals and spells.

And perhaps in the midst of this struggle between the real world and the world of ritual, the king gave the order for the Great Pyramid to be built. Perhaps with the aim of asserting *maat*. Perhaps with the aim of distracting and pacifying his anxious subjects. (Here, one thinks of Kurt Mendelssohn's memorable line: 'what mattered was not the pyramid – it was *building* the pyramid'.)[26] And perhaps also with the aim of building the Pyramid as a repository and time capsule, just in case his worst private fears came to pass. Perhaps, with all of these objectives in mind, the king ordained that the Pyramid be constructed to an unprecedented degree of exactitude and, at the same time, to a demanding set of stage-by-stage deadlines.[27]

According to this scenario, the time capsule element of the Pyramid may have been built as an insurance policy, lest the worst case scenario occur. But, as with all insurance policies, the premiums are paid for years and years before any claim is required. In the case of the Pyramid, then, we should not be bothered in the slightest by the fact that the 'end of the world' did not happen, or at least not on the scale that the king might have envisaged. Egyptian civilisation continued, and it continued via various ups and downs for more than two millennia, its spiritual and scientific knowledge remaining safe in the hands of the kings and priests. And, for all this time, the Pyramid would have awaited the 'end of the world' and the future race of men which was intended to benefit from its hidden contents.

This intriguing scenario provides a potentially important backdrop for our understanding of the history of the Pyramid. If, as I am suggesting, its upper chambers were intended for a future race of men, then it would have been necessary, nay imperative, that the current generation of men be kept from entering and exploring it. The Pyramid would, therefore, have been entrusted to guardians – a tightly-knit family of priests, no doubt – who would have been tasked with preserving the Pyramid intact until the 'end time' (which, as with Christianity, would have been always just around the corner). These guardians, quite conceivably, would have held the blueprint to the monument's upper chambers, but would have balked at the thought of using it. For the Pyramid's secret contents were not aimed at the contemporary race of Egyptians, who already possessed the required sacred knowledge. No. It was aimed at a post-cataclysm race of men, who were expected to rise up from the ashes of the present world – a future race who, lacking civilisation, knowledge and enlightenment, required a guiding hand from their forebears so as to restore the glory of Egypt in the new age of the world. The paradox of the Pyramid would be that it was a time capsule not for our time, but rather for 'a time away from time'.[28]

Legends of Egypt and the Pyramids

To summarise the argument thus far, the Pyramid's architecture fits the pattern of a sealed repository that was designed ultimately to be found and opened; and this makes sense only if the Pyramid was built as a time capsule, to preserve relics and knowledge for a future generation; and this, in turn, makes sense only if the builders of the Pyramid entertained serious fears about the cataclysmic 'end of the world'. In support of this scenario, I have pointed to the possibility of historical cataclysms in the era to which the construction of the Pyramid is attributed, and I have highlighted the importance in ancient Egyptian religion of the cataclysm of creation, together with the corresponding idea of the cataclysm of the 'end of the world'. The fundamental concept of *maat*, I have suggested, bears all the hallmarks of an institutionalised psychological reaction to disorder in the cosmos – the need to restore order, via religious ritual, to a Universe in which the heavens and the earth were being literally shaken by cataclysmic events. It is therefore quite plausible that during the early centuries of Egyptian civilisation a king, in fear of the 'end of the world', decided to build the Pyramid not only as a memorial to the creation, and not only as his tomb, but also as a means of transmitting the gifts of civilisation to a future generation, or race, of men, which was prophesied to emerge in the aftermath of the expected 'cataclysm of all cataclysms'.

This, in a nutshell, is the essence of my sealed repository and time capsule theory. Controversial, yes; cranky, no. For it is, after all, rooted in the hard evidence of the Pyramid's architecture and in the fundamental precepts of Egyptian religion.

There the argument might rest, and perhaps it should rest, subject to our examination of what the objects hidden inside the Pyramid's upper chambers might have been, and indeed might still be (a subject to be discussed in chapters eight and nine). However, it would be churlish of me to ignore the remarkable resemblance that my theory bears to many traditions of antiquity, which speak, as if with one voice, of a time before the Flood when a god-like hero, in precognition of the coming cataclysm, sealed up the great treasures and knowledge of his civilisation in order to preserve these things for a future age of man. Again and again, these traditions refer to the land of Egypt and to hermetically-sealed vaults, located either in its temples or its pyramids, as the place and places where the aforementioned artefacts and knowledge were hidden.

Naturally, these traditions deserve a special mention in this book, in which I am proposing an almost identical idea in respect of the Great Pyramid. However, in providing a summary of these various traditions, I do not wish to suggest that they be counted as evidence in support of my theory. Rather, they are detailed here for the interest and amusement of the reader, and to demonstrate a pattern of thinking that may, or may not, ultimately draw upon a kernel of truth pertaining to the construction of the Great Pyramid.

We shall begin with the Greek philosopher Plato who, in his book *Timaeus* (*c.* 350 BC), suggested that the oldest antediluvian traditions of the Athenians were recorded only in Egypt, at the temple of Neit in the Delta city of Sais. According to Plato, the great sage and poet Solon had received from the priests at Sais an account of how the ancient Athenians had once saved the Mediterranean world by defeating an invading force of Atlantians. The story had been preserved at Sais for nine aeons, during which time there had been three major 'end of the world' cataclysms, culminating in the Flood of Deucalion.[29] The implication is that the story was somehow preserved in Egypt during these cataclysms, perhaps by being hidden in the temple of Neit at Sais. According to the neo-Platonist writer Proclus (5th century AD), a student of Plato's named Crantor had visited Egypt *c.* 300 BC and had seen for himself the antediluvian account 'written on pillars which are still preserved'.[30]

Another intriguing legend is recorded in the Book of Enoch, thought to have been compiled by Hassidic Jewish reactionaries between the 2nd century BC and the 1st century AD. The book recounts the adventures of the biblical sage Enoch, whom God had chosen to witness the secrets of the 'seven heavens' and record everything in a book for the benefit of mankind.[31] According to one tradition, Enoch, forewarned of the coming Flood, had constructed, with the aid of his son Methuselah, nine secret vaults, one stacked on top of the other, and placed therein various sacred artefacts and writings. Having sealed the vaults, he had then built above them a pillar of marble and a pillar of brick such that the first would never burn and the second would never sink (an allusion to the idea of dual cataclysms, one of fire and one of water).[32]

This tradition of the two pillars appears also in the writings of the Jewish historian Flavius Josephus (1st century AD). He described how Adam and his children had lived in bliss in the antediluvian world – 'in a happy condition without any misfortunes falling upon them'. One of his sons, Seth, had taken advantage of this idyllic environment to found the first sciences, which he had taught to his children. Josephus then writes:

> They [the Sethites] also were the inventors of that peculiar sort of
> wisdom, which is concerned with the heavenly bodies and their order.

And that their inventions might not be lost before they were sufficiently known, upon Adam's prediction that the world was to be destroyed, one time by force of fire, and at another time by the violence and quantity of water, they made two pillars, the one of brick, the other of stone, and they inscribed their discoveries on them both, that in case the pillar of brick should be destroyed by the Flood, the pillar of stone might remain, and exhibit these discoveries to mankind; and also inform them that there was another pillar of brick erected by them. Now this remains in the land of Siriad to this day.[33]

In view of the obvious 'two pillars' symbolism in the two giant pyramids of Giza,[34] it is somewhat disappointing to note that Josephus here places the pillar of stone in Siriad, which is thought to correspond to modern-day Lebanon. Moreover, the Christian writer Eusebius (4th century AD) suggested the same idea, reporting that the Egyptian historian Manetho (3rd century BC) had obtained much data for his Kings List 'from the inscriptions which were engraved in the sacred dialect and hieroglyphic characters upon the columns set up in the Siriatic land by Thoth, the first Hermes.'[35] Whilst the 'two pillar' motif may originate from the mythical idea of the two supports of the sky, it nevertheless occurs to this author that the pillar of Siriad may have stood at Baalbek in Lebanon, with the second pillar standing at Heliopolis in Egypt (these two sites having been anciently twinned as 'the Heliopolis of the North' and the 'Heliopolis of the South', the Egyptian name for the latter being *Iunu*, literally 'Pillar City').[36]

We now come to the Hermetic traditions, which are thought to have been composed in Alexandria around the beginning of the Christian era. Here again, we find the idea of a great wisdom of an antediluvian age that needed to be saved from the Flood. But this time, instead of the sage being Enoch or the Sethites, the saviour of the knowledge is Hermes, the Greek god who represented the Egyptian god Thoth. In the *Hermetica*, Hermes appears as the fount of all secret knowledge, and as the teacher and initiator of the deities Isis and Osiris.

Among the various books of the *Hermetica*, one in particular, entitled *Kore Kosmou* (Virgin of the World), is most noteworthy. In this treatise, it is said that Hermes entrusted his 'knowledge of hidden writings' to Isis and Osiris on condition that they keep some of the knowledge secret but transmit the other part to mankind through inscriptions 'on slabs and obelisks'.[37] Much of the text then consists of a dialogue between Isis and Horus in which the goddess initiates her 'son' into the secrets that are permitted to be known. In an oft-quoted section, Isis says:

Such was all-knowing Hermes, who saw all things, and in seeing understood, and in understanding had the power both to disclose and give explanation. For the things he knew, he engraved on stone; yet, though he engraved them onto stone, he hid them mostly... The sacred symbols of the cosmic elements (he) hid away hard by the secrets of Osiris... keeping sure silence, that every younger age of cosmic time might seek for them.[38]

Isis then tells Horus that before Hermes returned to the heavens he cast a magic spell to keep the secret writings safe until the right time came for them to be unveiled:

It is not fitting, my son, that I should leave this report unfinished; I must tell you what Hermes said when he deposited the books. Thus did he speak: "O holy books, who have been made by my immortal hands... remain free from decay throughout eternity, and incorrupt from time. Become unseeable, unfindable, by all who go to and fro upon the plains of this land [Egypt], until the time when Heaven, grown old, shall beget organisms worthy of you."[39]

Here, there is no explicit mention of a cataclysm, but in ancient Egyptian texts, the birth of Horus to Isis (a theme of *Kore Kosmou*) does coincide with a cataclysm.[40] Moreover, the ascent of Hermes to the heavens, after this speech, hints at the idea of cataclysm, as does his name, stemming from the Greek *herma*, 'a pile of stones'.[41]

Where were the sacred books of Hermes concealed? Although *Kore Kosmou* provides no clue (other than to suggest that they were hidden in Egypt), other, non-Hermetic writings assert that the antediluvian wisdom had been sealed up inside the vaults of temples and pyramids in Egypt. Eusebius thus reported that Agathadaemon (a figure corresponding to Osiris or Seth) had deposited scrolls in the libraries of the temples of Egypt three thousand years before the beginning of Christianity,[42] whilst the Roman historian Ammianus Marcellinus (4th century AD) wrote that:

Inscriptions which the ancients asserted were engraved on the walls of certain underground galleries, constructed in the interior of certain pyramids, were intended to preserve ancient wisdom from being lost in the Flood.[43]

All of this is frustratingly vague, and the Great Pyramid has not yet been mentioned explicitly. This void of information, however, was to be filled by the Arabs, who conquered Egypt in AD 642. It is in their traditions that we find the most detailed legends of the pyramids and temples of Egypt.

By general consensus, Arab scholars ascribed the Egyptian pyramids and temples to an antediluvian age.[44] One popular tradition, drawing on Coptic and Hermetic lore, asserted that the builder of the pyramids and temples had been 'the first Hermes' or 'Hermes of Hermes', otherwise known as Hermes Trismegistus on account of his threefold qualities of prophet, king, and wise man.[45] A second popular tradition, drawing on old Arab lore, maintained that the builder of the pyramids had been an antediluvian king named Surid Ibn Salhouk (Surid, for short). And, in the 13th century, it was even suggested by one writer that the pyramids had been built by a pre-Adamite race – inhabitants of an earlier earth.[46] These ideas became merged to the extent that Surid became identified with Hermes (as well as with other antediluvian hero figures such as Enoch and Idris).[47]

Why had the pyramids and temples been built? Many Arabs cited the Hermetic tradition, contained in the books of the Sabaeans,[48] that the two large pyramids at Giza had been built as the tombs of the antediluvian prophets Hermes and Agathadaemon (the latter character was regarded as even older and more famous than Hermes).[49] Alongside this tradition, however, there existed the idea that the pyramids and temples had been built as repositories for the artefacts and knowledge of the antediluvian civilisation, the king of this race having been apprised of the fact that the Flood was imminent.

According to the 14th century explorer Ibn Batuta, it was Hermes who 'having ascertained from the appearance of the stars that the Flood would take place, built the pyramids to contain books of science and knowledge and other matters worth preserving from oblivion and ruin.'[50] Similarly, al-Maqrizi in his book *Hitat* (15th century) reported that:

> The first Hermes... read in the stars that the Flood would come. Then he ordained that the pyramids should be built; and in them he hid treasures, texts and scripts, and everything which might otherwise be lost, so that they might be preserved.[51]

We see here, perhaps, the origin of the modern expression 'hermetically sealed'.

But earlier Arab writers consistently named king Surid as the one who, having learned of the coming Flood in a dream, built the pyramids as vaults for the protection of the antediluvian books and artefacts. Among the reporters of this particular legend are the astrologer Abumasar Balkhi (9th century), the historian Abd al-Hokm (9th century), al-Masudi (10th century), and al-Maqrizi (15th century), the latter asserting that Hermes and Surid were one and the same person. All of these authorities tell basically the same story.[52]

The following is the account of Abd al-Hokm:

The greatest part of chronologers agree that he who built the pyramids was Surid Ibn Salhouk, king of Egypt, who lived three hundred years before the Flood. The occasion of this was because he saw in his sleep that the whole earth was turned over, with the inhabitants of it, the men lying upon their faces, and the stars falling down and striking one another with a terrible noise, and being troubled he sealed it up [the rest of the dream?]. Awakening with great fear, he assembled the chief priests of all the provinces of Egypt, one hundred and thirty in number, the chief of whom was Aclimon, and related the whole matter to them. They took the altitude of the stars, and made their prognostications, foretelling of a deluge. The king said: "Will it come to our country." They answered: "Yes, and will destroy it." But there remained a certain number of years for it to come, and he commanded in the meantime to build the pyramids... He filled them with talismans, strange things, riches, treasures, and the like. He engraved in them all things that were told by wise men, as also all profound sciences, the names of *alakakirs* [magical precious stones], the uses and hurts of them, the science of Astrology, and of Arithmetic, and of Geometry, and of Physics.[53]

Al-Hokm goes on to describe how 'the western pyramid', probably the Pyramid of Khafre, was filled with 'riches and utensils, signatures made of precious stones, instruments of iron, vessels of clay, arms which did not rust, glass which could be bent and yet not broken, strange spells, several kinds of *alakakirs*, deadly poisons, and other things besides'.[54] Meanwhile, in 'the eastern pyramid', probably the Great Pyramid, Surid deposited a mechanism of 'diverse celestial spheres and stars', certain perfumes which were to be used in conjunction with it, and a book, or manual, of how to operate these things.[55] And in 'the coloured pyramid', probably the Third Pyramid of Giza, the king placed 'the commentaries of the priests in chests of black marble, and with every priest a book, in which the wonders of his profession, and of his actions, and of his nature were written; and what was done in his time, and what is and what shall be from the beginning of time to the end of it.'[56]

Al-Masudi records a similar account of Surid's dream three hundred years before the Flood, but adds that the king had a second dream in which he saw 'the fixed stars descend upon the earth in the form of white birds', who 'seizing the people, enclosed them in a cleft between two great mountains, which shut upon them.'[57] Revealing the dreams to his priests and wise men, he was told that a great cataclysm would overtake the earth, but that afterwards 'the sky would resume its former altitude' and the earth would become fruitful again. Thus the king ordained that the pyramids be built. Al-Masudi, however, provides a slightly different version of what was concealed in the pyramids:

> ... the predictions of the priests to be inscribed upon pillars and upon the large stones belonging to them; and he [Surid] placed within them his treasures and his valuable property, together with the bodies of his ancestors. He also ordered the priests to deposit within them written accounts of their wisdom and acquirements in the different arts and sciences... He filled the passages with talismans, with wonderful things, and idols; and with the writings of the priests, containing all manner of wisdom, the names and properties of medical plants, and the science of arithmetic and geometry; that they might remain as records, for the benefit of those who could afterwards comprehend them.[58]

Finally, al-Maqrizi, citing as his authority an earlier writer Usted Ibrahim Ben Wasuff Shah, provides an almost identical account of king Surid's dream three hundred years before the Flood, but adds the prophecy that fire would issue from the constellation of Leo and consume the world.[59] Surid had thus ordered the construction of the pyramids, which he filled with 'talismans, wonders, treasures, idols, and the corpses of kings', and which he inscribed with the secret antediluvian sciences.[60]

Such is the account given for the pyramids, those of Giza featuring prominently. But Arab traditions also refer to the temples of Egypt as being repositories for antediluvian science. The Arab Hermetic text 'The Serpent Book of Hermes Trismegistus', for example, asserts that the first Hermes built the temples of Egypt before the Flood and deposited therein timeless knowledge to ensure its survival.[61] In particular, the temple of Akhmim is mentioned as having been built 'several years before the Flood' (Ibn Duqmaq, c. 1400), its walls having been inscribed with 'all the knowledge of alchemy, magic, talismans, medicine, astronomy and geometry' (al-Maqrisi).[62]

What is to be made of these legends, along with the earlier Hermetic, Jewish and Graeco-Roman traditions?

On the one hand, it must be said that, whilst the legends consistently refer to the concealment of an antediluvian science, they are especially vague as to its whereabouts. Egypt? Yes, but it is a vast land. Pyramids? Certainly, but there are many of them. Temples? Again yes, but they are plentiful too. In which pyramids and temples did Hermes, or Surid, or Idris, conceal his eternal wisdom? And why is the Great Pyramid not singled out, as one might expect, for special attention? (Supporters of the Sphinx 'hall of records' theory will likewise be disappointed at the lack of ancient roots for their beliefs; as an amusing aside, a 14th century Arab manuscript speculates that the Sphinx had formerly sat on top of the Great Pyramid and had been hurled off by the violent force of the Flood;[63] if nothing else, this demonstrates that 'pyramidiocy' is not just a modern phenomenon.)

In view of this vagueness, not to mention the sometimes romantic and fanciful nature of the later Arab accounts, it is all too easy to dismiss this entire corpus of literature as having little or no value to the present-day researcher.

On the other hand, all of the legends cited here exhibit a remarkably consistent pattern of underlying thought. The antediluvian golden age. The prophecy of the Flood cataclysm. The need to protect the artefacts and science of the antediluvian civilisation. The building of two pillars. The construction of the pyramids and temples of Egypt. Virtually all of the stories possess this common core of ideas. Moreover, it is quite likely that this myth has its roots in authentic Coptic and Hermetic beliefs that were circulating in Egypt two thousand years ago, and which may, in turn, have derived from an authentic ancient Egyptian tradition.

On this note, the Egyptologist Mark Lehner has suggested that Surid, the name of the antediluvian king in the Arabian legends, might in fact have been derived from Khufu, via the reading of his cartouche name as Suphis.[64] It is an unproven speculation, of course, but it does give one pause for thought. Could it be that two thousand years of pyramid lore have sprung from an authentic tradition of Khufu and the Great Pyramid? In closing this chapter, it behoves me to highlight two authentic ancient Egyptian texts, which might well provide an affirmative answer to this question. Whilst not wishing, or needing, to rest my argument upon these texts, I nevertheless present them below and encourage the reader to form his own opinion as to whether or not they are relevant.

The Legends of Sneferu and Khufu

Putting to one side all of the legends of post-Egyptian times, it has been my argument in this chapter that the Great Pyramid was built in part as a sealed repository and time capsule, to protect sacred relics and artefacts, and perhaps also the spiritual and scientific knowledge, of the builder's civilisation, in the face of a likely global cataclysm that would herald the 'end of the world'. Now, that builder, according to Egyptologists, was Khufu, the second king of the 4th dynasty, and the successor to Sneferu, his father, who had founded the 4th dynasty *c.* 2600 BC. To Sneferu are credited the two giant pyramids of Dahshur (the Bent Pyramid and the Red Pyramid), the earliest true pyramids ever built.

It is to the time of Sneferu that the first of our two texts refers (though the text itself was composed in the 18th dynasty). In 'The Prophecy of Neferti', Sneferu calls into his court a high ranking scribe named Neferti, and demands to be entertained by a prophecy of the future. Neferti then dictates a vision, which the king writes down (an extraordinary reversal of roles, but then Sneferu was regarded as the archetype of the beneficent ruler). He describes the 'end of the world' in no uncertain terms: the Sun disc is hidden; the rivers are empty; the winds are in disarray; the land of Egypt is 'helter-skelter' and 'topsy turvy'; Re has departed from the earth; and Heliopolis, 'the birthplace of every god', has ceased to be. In short, 'that which has never happened (before) has happened', namely the 'end of the world'. Everything will have to be created anew, when Re returns and appoints a new king, who is named here, anachronistically, as Ameni – a reference to Amenemhet I, the first king of the 12th dynasty, *c.* 2000 BC.[65] Astonishingly, the author of the text has edited out seven dynasties and six hundred years from Egyptian history.

Unfortunately, 'The Prophecy of Neferti' does not state whether or not the prophesied cataclysm occurred during Sneferu's reign. Scholars have therefore taken it to be an anachronistic allusion to the ultimate downfall of the Old Kingdom, *c.* 2180 BC, and the onset of the First Intermediate Period.[66] Sneferu, it is supposed, was used merely as a figurehead for the past glory of the 4th dynasty.

But then again, it is equally possible that 'The Prophecy of Neferti' anticipated the 'end of the world' cataclysm during the reign of Sneferu himself. In which case, Sneferu could have been motivated to build his pyramids in fear of 'the end time', and his son Khufu would have come to the throne with the prophecy of Neferti still ringing in his ears.

Bearing this possibility in mind, let us turn to our second text, 'The Story of Khufu and the Magicians'. This text is contained in the Westcar Papyrus, dating to the early-16th century BC, but copied from an original document dating to the Middle Kingdom, possibly as early as *c.* 2050 BC.[67] But the story itself is set in the reign of the 4th dynasty king Khufu.

One day, we are told, Khufu feels bored and demands that his four sons regale him with tales of magic. The first three sons having dutifully obliged, the fourth son Hordedef then volunteers to demonstrate magic, rather than tell a tale about it, by inviting into the king's court the great magician Djedi. At this point, Khufu becomes quite excited, since Djedi reportedly 'knows the number (*tnw*) of the secret chambers (*ipwt*) of the sanctuary (*wnt*) of Thoth', and he, the king, 'has spent (much) time in searching for the secret chambers of the sanctuary of Thoth, in order to make the like thereof for his *Akhet*'.[68] Djedi then arrives and proceeds to entertain the king with his repertoire of magic tricks, focused initially on restoring decapitated animals to life. But Khufu now broaches the subject of the secret chambers:

> Then said king Khufu (to Djedi): "What of the report (that) you know the number of the secret chambers of the sanctuary of Thoth?" And Djedi said: "So please you, O Sovereign my lord, I know not the number thereof, but I know the place where it is . . ." And His Majesty said: "Where is that?" And Djedi said: "There is a box of flint in a room called 'Revision' (*Sipty*) in Heliopolis. (Well) in that box!"[69]

Djedi then seems to go into a trance, in which he prophesies that the wife of a priest of Re at Heliopolis will soon bear triplets, who are destined to be kings of Egypt (apparently a prophecy for the foundation of the 5th dynasty). Khufu's dynasty, therefore, will soon be ended: "I say this to you: your son, then his son, but then one of them."[70] Strangely, Khufu must wait for the birth of the triplets, the eldest of whom will bring to him the box containing the information which he seeks. The remainder of the text involves Khufu venturing forth to confirm the prophecy, but breaks off before resolution is achieved.

Now, the significance of this tale lies in the fact that Khufu sought the number of the secret chambers 'in order to make the like thereof for his *Akhet*', i.e. for his pyramid, the Great Pyramid, which was known to the Egyptians as *Akhet Khufu*. The text is admittedly a little ambiguous here, since *Akhet* could also mean 'temple', perhaps a temple to be attached to the Pyramid (some scholars prefer this interpretation, perhaps mindful of the fact that the story is set towards the end of Khufu's reign).[71] But most scholars agree that the *Akhet* in question was the Great Pyramid. Alan Gardiner, for example, wrote:

> And, indeed, what ambition could have fired Cheops more than to possess in his own pyramid a replica of the mysterious chambers in the hoary sanctuary of the god of Wisdom? The temple of the Great Pyramid is utterly destroyed, but the inner chambers of the pyramid itself remain a marvel down to the present day... I conclude, therefore, that the word *ipwt* means 'secret chambers', and that Cheops was seeking for details concerning the secret chambers of the primeval sanctuary of Thoth, in order that he might copy the same when building his pyramid.[72]

Gardiner's interpretation is most plausible. After all, the Great Pyramid does have a complex, multi-chambered interior design, and it stands out from all other pyramids (with the possible exception of Sneferu's Bent Pyramid) in having such a design. In view of the stated connections both to Khufu and to his *Akhet*, can there really be any doubt that the Great Pyramid is intended here?

The implications are intriguing. The multi-chambered design of the Pyramid, it would seem, corresponded to the multi-chambered design of 'the sanctuary of Thoth' – a place that almost certainly existed in Egypt (it has been suggested that it lay at *Wnw*, Hermopolis Magna).[73] But why was Khufu, the all-powerful ruler of the land, unable to discover the number of the chambers by inspecting the sanctuary itself? Why did he, instead, need to discover their 'number' via a plan contained in a box at Heliopolis? A likely explanation is that the sanctuary's chambers were sealed up and impenetrable. Indeed, the hieroglyphic text suggests that the chambers were 'sealed up' or 'closed', hence the translation 'secret chambers'.[74]

Now, this sounds remarkably like my sealed repository theory of the Great Pyramid of Giza. But, what is more, it sounds remarkably like my time capsule hypothesis. For Thoth, whose sanctuary provided the model for Khufu's *Akhet*, was the god of *maat*, the god of wisdom, the god of the sciences (notably astronomy), and the god of writing; in short, the god most likely to be associated with the provision of the kind of things that would be sealed up inside a time capsule. It was this very Thoth, indeed, who later became Hermes, the possessor of all secret knowledge, who had initiated Isis and Osiris, and concealed his 'holy books' and 'sacred symbols' in Egypt, to be 'unseeable' and 'unfindable' until a new age of the world. The same Hermes who, according to Arab legends, had built the pyramids of Egypt and been buried beneath the Great Pyramid of Giza.

Coincidences?

Could it be that 'The Story of King Khufu and the Magicians', despite its anachronisms,[75] contains a kernel of historical truth pertaining to the construction of the Great Pyramid?

And could it be that 'The Prophecy of Neferti', recounted earlier, recalls a kernel of historical truth pertaining to the fear of a world-ending cataclysm during the reign of Sneferu, Khufu's father?

Was this the reason why the first giant pyramids were built?

Was this why Khufu spent so much time searching for the number of the secret chambers of the sanctuary of Thoth?

Chapter Six Summary

• There is much evidence to suggest that the Pyramid was sealed, stage by stage, as it was built, rather than being kept open for the funeral procession and burial of the king. The case having already been made for the burial of the king beneath the Pyramid, and the deposition of iron meteorites in the King's Chamber sarcophagus, it becomes reasonable to hypothesise that the Pyramid, in its upper parts, was built as a sealed repository, i.e. a reliquary for the sacred relics and artefacts of the early Egyptians.

• Why build a sealed repository? In view of the evidence that the relics and artefacts were intended to be found (i.e. the 'sign in the floor for the wise' and the inclusion of the connecting passages), only one answer suggests itself: the Pyramid was constructed as a time capsule that would safeguard the material treasures, and perhaps also the spiritual and scientific knowledge, of the builders' civilisation, so as to keep these things in trust for the benefit of a future generation, or race, of men.

• Why build a time capsule? Again, only one answer suggests itself: the builders' civilisation became obsessed by the idea that it would, in the near future, be destroyed by a cataclysm. Accordingly, it deposited inside the Pyramid all of the crucial relics and scientific knowledge that would be required to initiate a later generation of men.

• Ancient Egyptian texts indeed confirm the importance of cataclysm, both in the myth of creation and in prophecies for the 'end of the world'. Moreover, it may be argued that the fundamental religious concept of *maat* ('cosmic order') represented an institutionalised psychological reaction to disorder in the cosmos during the earliest epoch of Egyptian history.

• Certain Egyptian legends pertaining to Khufu (the owner of the Great Pyramid) and his father Sneferu lend support to the hypothesis that the Great Pyramid was built, in part, as a sealed repository and time capsule.

CHAPTER SEVEN

ECHOES OF CREATION

Almost certainly the ancient Egyptians did have an advanced understanding of acoustics which was coupled with an esoteric world view of breathtaking wisdom and complexity.
(Ian Lawton and Chris Ogilvie-Herald, *Giza The Truth*, 1999)

A common trap for the researcher is to use one theory, and one alone, to account for all the evidence that is under consideration – the monolithic approach. I would therefore be following in a long and time-honoured tradition if I were to attempt an explanation of *all* the Great Pyramid's features using the sealed repository theory. But the monolithic approach shuts out other lines of enquiry that often prove complementary to the chosen line, and, for this reason, it tends to produce conclusions that are doomed to fail the test of time. Wise, then, is the researcher who follows a multifaceted approach, keeping a watchful eye on developments in related fields, and incorporating, where necessary, any relevant data and ideas. Already, in this book, I have taken this wide-angled approach in treating the Pyramid as a symbol of the creation and a tomb for a king, as well as a sealed repository and time capsule, these ideas being mutually complementary. Now, in this chapter, I am going to reach out to a theory that has emerged in 'alternative Egyptology' and has not yet crossed over into the mainstream, with the exception of a favourable mention in the pseudo-orthodox book *Giza The Truth* by Ian Lawton and Chris Ogilvie-Herald, published in 1999.[1] This theory pertains to the ancient science of sound and acoustics, specifically in regard to the King's Chamber of the Great Pyramid.

Of course, Occam's Razor, the law of parsimony, demands that we keep things as simple as possible, and invent no unnecessary hypotheses. Having come this far in resolving the mysteries of the Pyramid, it would be a shame to spoil things by unwarranted speculation. Nevertheless, several significant aspects of the King's Chamber's design have yet to be adequately explained, in particular the multi-tiered superstructure, the pattern of the shafts, the positioning of the shafts in the walls, and the Antechamber. If a single hypothesis can explain the purpose of all these unusual architectural features, whilst dovetailing with existing theories pertaining to the King's Chamber and the Pyramid, and making sense in the context of the pyramid building ritual, then that hypothesis should be advanced and tested.

Acoustics, I believe, is the key to such a hypothesis, although I would hasten to add that I am not proposing an advanced science of acoustics in ancient Egypt. Rather, it seems more likely that the builders of the Great Pyramid mastered their sonic art by careful observation of nature, by simple experimentation, and by a trial and error approach to the design of the King's Chamber, perhaps using a small test pyramid that would later have been dismantled or incorporated into one of the larger pyramids on the site. In other words, they had nothing more than a practical working knowledge.[2]

In this chapter, I draw upon published research into the acoustics of the King's Chamber, but reframe the results in the context of the sealed repository theory (as advocated in chapter six of this book) to generate a new acoustic theory that offers a remarkably comprehensive solution to the architecture of the King's Chamber. It must be stated at the outset, however, that this theory is necessarily speculative, since it pertains to an acoustic system that is no longer operational, having been disabled long ago by a major earthquake (the effects of which may clearly be seen in the chamber). Of all the theories in this book, this is the one most likely to be falsified, either by new data or by new arguments.

Having said that, it should be stressed that the King's Chamber is a unique structure and, as such, it warrants a unique explanation, one way or another, preferably one that accounts for *all* of the unusual features in its design.

On this note, let us begin.

King's Chamber Acoustics

In 1581, Jean Palmerme, the French official, visited the Great Pyramid and reported that the granite sarcophagus in the King's Chamber, when struck, 'sounded like a bell'.[3] The same phenomenon was observed by other travellers. In 1610, Sandys wrote of the sarcophagus 'sounding like a bell'.[4] In 1646, John Greaves used exactly the same phrase.[5] And, later in the 17th century, Melton tried in vain to break the sarcophagus with a hammer, and remarked that it 'sounded like a bell'.[6] All of these men had been regaled by the local Arab guides, whose custom, in those days, was to strike the coffer to make it resonate in the room.

This same effect may be witnessed today, but attention is now focused equally on the King's Chamber itself, whose granite construction has the effect of amplifying the bell-like sound. In 1997, the pyramid expert Mark Lehner described the chamber thus:

> The room itself is like a sarcophagus, lined with red granite and
> resonating with every murmur and footstep.[7]

For centuries, little thought has been given to the resonant properties of the King's Chamber and its sarcophagus, and the subject has consisted of little more than anecdotal reports. However, in recent years, researchers from the alternative school (a colourful mix of characters, with a variety of motives) have conducted scientific tests and experiments in the King's Chamber, in order to quantify its acoustic credentials. These tests have sought to measure *inter alia* the chamber's 'reverberation time' and its 'resonant frequency'.

Reverberation time (RT) measures the echo effect in the chamber. It is defined as 'the time in seconds required for a sound event to decay to one millionth of its initial level'.[8] In 1996, the English acoustics engineer John Reid measured the RT of the King's Chamber at 4.47 seconds – a result that is comparable to modern cathedrals and churches (by way of comparison, Newcastle Cathedral has a RT of 3.9 seconds).[9] Reid attributed this long reverberation time to the use of granite in the walls, floor and ceiling of the chamber (granite being a quartz-bearing rock that is renowned for its vibrational properties). Whilst granite had qualities in abundance, such as strength, durability and religious symbolism, Reid wondered whether it might have been chosen primarily 'for its acoustical properties, possibly as an experiment in reverberation enhancement'.[10]

The resonant frequency of an enclosed space, in this case the chamber and the sarcophagus, is the tone at which it becomes acoustically excited. Whilst the granite in the chamber has a unique resonant signature, we are interested here in the chamber and sarcophagus as cavities, in which the dimensions of the cavity are the main factors determining its resonant frequency. Since this concept of resonant frequency will be important throughout this chapter, it is essential that the reader is provided with some suitable definitions and explanations. In particular, it is necessary to understand the terms 'sound', 'frequency', 'resonance', 'resonant frequency', 'prime resonant frequency', and 'harmonics'.

Sound is commonly understood as pressure waves vibrating in the air, or some other medium. External vibrations cause the eardrums to vibrate, producing electrical signals in the inner ear which are interpreted as sound by the brain. The human ear has evolved to detect a range of vibratory frequencies, from about 16 Hz (Hertz), at the bottom end of the scale, to about 17 KHz (Kilohertz), at the top end. Prior to the invention of CDs, all hi-fi systems worked on a vibrational system: the grooves of the vinyl record caused the stylus to vibrate; these vibrations were then converted into an electrical signal; and this signal, having been amplified, emerged from the loudspeakers in the form of vibration of the air.

Frequency, otherwise known as pitch, defines the position of a sound wave in the vibrational spectrum; thus we speak of lower frequencies as 'bass' frequencies and higher frequencies as 'treble' frequencies. The proper definition of frequency, in relation to sound, is 'the number of cycles of a given sound wave which occur each second'. Frequencies of sound are thus measured in 'cycles per second', or Hertz.[11]

Resonance may be defined as 'the reinforcement or prolongation of sound by reflection or synchronous vibration'.[12] It may be defined more simply as 'sympathetic vibration'.

Resonant frequency is a frequency at which a given object, cavity or enclosed space becomes excited, producing a peak of audible vibration. Thus, when we play a hi-fi system at home, it occasionally happens that an object in the room emits an audible buzz in sympathy with a certain sound frequency. This usually happens at low, bass frequencies, and is especially noticeable when the object lacks damping, for example a loose piece of wooden skirting board.

Prime resonant frequency is the frequency at which a given object, cavity or enclosed space becomes *most* excited, i.e. resonates (vibrates) most energetically. This is the frequency at which the maximum acoustic energy is reflected back to the sound source, or, conversely, at which the least acoustic energy is absorbed by the object, cavity or enclosed space. In the case of a cavity, the prime resonant frequency is determined by the size and shape of the cavity.

The term '*prime* resonant frequency' implies the existence of *multiple* resonant frequencies. This brings us neatly to the definition of harmonics and subharmonics.

Usually, an object, cavity or enclosed space will resonate at harmonics of its prime frequency, where the harmonic is an exact multiple of the prime. Thus, for example, if the prime frequency is 16 Hz, there will usually be harmonic resonances at 32 Hz (the second harmonic), 48 Hz (the third harmonic), and so on, up the scale, in diminishing intensity. Similarly, the prime frequency has subharmonics, also at exact multiples of the prime. So, if the prime is 16 Hz, there will be subharmonic (and subaudible) resonances at 8 Hz, 5.3 Hz, and so on, down the scale, in diminishing intensity. This principle of harmonics and subharmonics (otherwise known as overtones and undertones respectively) gives music a quintessential dimension.

So, what are the resonant frequencies of the King's Chamber and its sarcophagus?

One of the earliest experiments in the King's Chamber was performed by the flautist Paul Horn, who tuned his flute to the ringing tone of the sarcophagus at approximately 440 Hz (the musical note A). Horn played a variety of instruments, improvising as he went along, and was struck by the reverberative quality of the chamber, and its remarkable ability to produce harmonics of the notes. The results of his musical experiment were published as an album in 1997.[13]

In 1995, the pyramid researcher Christopher Dunn performed some simple experiments in the King's Chamber using a fairly basic Matrix tuner and a tape recorder, and corroborated the 440 Hz resonance of the sarcophagus. In addition, his tape recorder revealed that the chamber itself resonated to the sound of his every footstep at about 440 Hz, and produced harmonics when that note was hummed. In publishing his results in 1998, Dunn remarked that a similar finding had been made by Robert Vawter, an acoustics engineer who had worked on a tape supplied by the researcher Stephen Mehler.[14]

But was 440 Hz the *prime* resonant frequency, or was it a harmonic of the prime?

In 2001, the English acoustics engineer John Reid published the long-awaited results of his more sophisticated experiments, performed inside the Pyramid in late-1996. He found that the prime resonant frequency of the King's Chamber lay further down the acoustic scale in the range 121-129 Hz (probably at 121 Hz).[15] He was also struck by the fact that the sarcophagus had a resonant frequency, 117 Hz, that was very close to the resonant frequency of the chamber itself. Allowing for the fact that the sarcophagus had sustained damaged at one of its corners, he wondered whether it had originally resonated at exactly the same frequency as the chamber, perhaps by deliberate intent:

> In isolation, I would have probably viewed this similarity as coincidental; however, in the context of other results, it does seem possible that the acoustic resonance of the sarcophagus was engineered to be the same as that of the chamber in order to ensure

maximum coupling...[16]

But, again, we must ask: was 121-129 Hz the *prime* resonant frequency of the chamber, or was it a harmonic of the prime?

In 1996, Tom Danley, an acoustics engineer and consultant to NASA, was commissioned by the Schor Foundation to conduct tests inside the Pyramid using a sophisticated range of equipment – large amplifiers, subwoofers, and vibration monitors.[17] Although the results remain largely unpublished, a brief account did appear in the July/August 2000 edition of *Live Sound!* magazine. There, Danley described what happened when he played bass frequencies inside the King's Chamber:

> What really made everyone get up and run to the exit was the resonance near 30 Hz. At that moment I aborted the test. This was a good resonance; it got nice and strong and scared the wits out of several crew members.[18]

Now, this is the phenomenon to which I referred earlier when I spoke of a room becoming excited and reflecting acoustic energy back toward the sound source. It may be that Danley hit the prime resonant frequency of the King's Chamber at around 30 Hz, or perhaps a strong harmonic of a lower prime, perhaps at 16 Hz or 8 Hz.[19] Whichever may be the case, the figure of 30 Hz is significantly lower than the frequencies mentioned earlier.

Other researchers, to be fair, did not have the benefit of sophisticated equipment. Reid's test loudspeaker, for example, had a roll-off frequency of 63 Hz, and thus he was unable to test the lowest audible frequencies.[20] In his booklet *Egyptian Sonics*, Reid acknowledges this point and lends his support to the possibility that Danley indeed identified the chamber's prime resonant frequency:

> Danley's work was valuable in its own right. His woofer loudspeaker, being of larger dimensions than that which I used, was capable of generating lower frequencies and he was, thus, able to identify a very powerful mode at around 30 Hz, possibly the prime resonant frequency of the chamber.[21]

What is to be concluded from all of these tests?

Firstly, it is possible that the builders' choice of granite for the King's Chamber and its sarcophagus reflected the long reverberation time and special resonant properties of that material.

Secondly, the King's Chamber has a prime resonant frequency that is well down the acoustic scale. Although higher frequencies have been found (121-129 Hz and 440 Hz), these are almost certainly harmonics of the fundamental tone, which may lie at around 30 Hz, or perhaps even lower at 16 Hz or 8 Hz. It is possible that the dimensions of the chamber were chosen deliberately to generate this low frequency response.[22]

And thirdly, there is some evidence that the granite sarcophagus may have been manufactured to resonate in tune with the King's Chamber, i.e. to couple acoustically with the granite room.

Putting all of these observations together, the evidence is suggestive that the King's Chamber and its sarcophagus were designed deliberately for some kind of acoustic purpose.

But what?

Chanting Priests?

The acoustics engineer John Reid believes that the purpose may have been ritualistic. His theory is that the Egyptian priests, by the sound of their voices, caused the chamber to resonate and the sarcophagus to become a bath of vibratory energy. In this manner, the body of the king, entombed in the coffer, could have been stimulated by sound, perhaps for ritual purposes. Or, more controversially, a living person, lying therein, could have been induced to an altered state of consciousness as part of an initiation ritual.[23] Reid's hypothesis is supported by the writer David Elkington, who publicised it in his insightful book *In the Name of the Gods* (2001).[24]

At first sight, this theory seems plausible. In recent years, much good work has highlighted the importance of sound and acoustics in ancient religious rituals and in the architectural design of the buildings in which those rituals took place. Increasingly, it is being realised that singing and chanting energised ancient spaces in temples, pyramids and tombs, just as they invigorate modern spaces in churches, cathedrals, temples and mosques.[25] In Egypt, the Great Pyramid would be but one example of this phenomenon, other pyramids, such as the Red Pyramid at Dahshur, also displaying acoustic properties.[26] In principle, one can think of no reason why Egyptologists would not embrace this theory, at least in regard to the funeral ritual.[27]

However, this ritual theory does suffer from a number of weaknesses.

Firstly, Tom Danley's research has shown that the prime resonant frequency of the King's Chamber is a very low frequency, *c*. 30 Hz or less. Both Elkington and Reid recognise the validity of this finding, and, crucially, have acknowledged that this tone is too low to have been vocalised by the priests.[28]

Secondly, the ritual theory finds no place for acoustical effects arising in the superstructure, despite the fact that its granite beams are laid out in a similar pattern to the roof of the chamber. As Reid put it to me, the male voice would not have been sufficiently powerful to stimulate the massive overhead complex.[29]

Thirdly, the ritual theory, as it currently stands, does not address the fact that granite was used predominantly in the King's Chamber Passage and the Antechamber. Was acoustics important here too? If so, why? Elkington and Reid do not provide the answers.[30]

And fourthly, there is good evidence that the King's Chamber, along with the other upper chambers in the Pyramid, was sealed off at the time of construction, as I have argued in chapter six of this book. If I am right about this, then the chamber could not have been designed for ritual chanting, for the priests would not have had access to the room, whether for a funeral or any other ritual purpose. Elkington and Reid would thus have been working under a false premise.

This is not intended to be a personal criticism of Elkington and Reid, nor indeed a criticism of their ideas about ancient sound and acoustics in general. Rather, it is a critique of these ideas *as applied in the specific instance of the King's Chamber of the Great Pyramid*, where they have had little choice but to follow a questionable orthodoxy. In fact, I regard Elkington and Reid's research, at its most basic level, as important and valuable.

In summary, whilst scientific tests do support the idea that the King's Chamber was built for an acoustic purpose, the chanting priests theory does not persuade this author. Rather, we must open our minds to some other acoustic purpose, taking account of all the evidence that is before us. And foremost among this evidence is the highly unusual structure above the chamber, in which four additional granite-beamed roofs are arranged like a tower above the granite roof of the chamber itself. It is here, in this unprecedented and complex arrangement, that we find the evidence for a more lofty and ambitious scheme.

The King's Chamber Superstructure

Above the roof of the King's Chamber stands an unusual, indeed unique, system of 'raised roofs', as shown in figures 96 and 97. The first four of these roofs are flat and comprise huge granite beams, just like those in the roof of the King's Chamber. Above them, the fifth roof is gabled and made of limestone. Remarkably, this entire superstructure is fitted between two huge limestone walls to the east and the west, which do not form part of the superstructure per se. What we have, then, in effect, is a

Figure 96.
THE KING'S CHAMBER AND ITS SUPERSTRUCTURE, LOOKING
WEST.

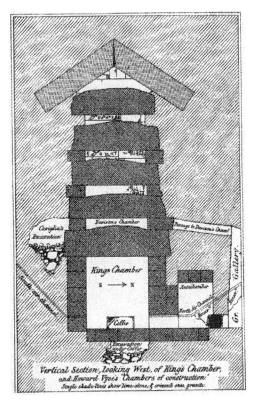

free-standing structure.

It is here in the roof and superstructure of the King's Chamber that we find the heaviest blocks of stone that are known in the Pyramid. The nine granite beams that form the roof of the chamber have a length of about 27 feet and an average width of about 4 feet 8 inches. According to the best estimates, these beams weigh between 25 and 45 tons each, making a total roof weight in excess of 300 tons. But as astonishing as this figure is, it is dwarfed by the weight of the granite beams in the four flat roofs overhead. Here, a further thirty-four beams, comparable in size to the nine below, have a cumulative weight of around 1,200 tons, producing a grand total of 1,500 tons for the granite used in the King's Chamber roof and superstructure. This really is a quite staggering figure.

What was the purpose of this massive megalithic superstructure?

According to Egyptologists, the builders were attempting to protect the flat roof of the King's Chamber from the superincumbent weight of

Figure 97.
THE KING'S CHAMBER AND ITS SUPERSTRUCTURE, LOOKING
NORTH.

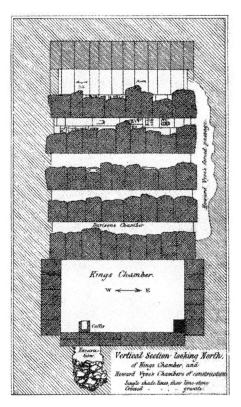

the Pyramid's masonry. They thus refer to the spaces between the roofs
as 'relieving chambers'. This theory has been proffered for more than a
hundred and fifty years, and is repeated uncritically as if it were a self-
evident fact.[31] Only rarely does an Egyptologist attempt to justify it. An
exception is J.P. Lepre, who has offered the following explanation for the
'weight relief' theory:

> There are five relieving chambers... specifically designed to relieve the
> King's Chamber ceiling from the tremendous amount of weight
> pressing down on it from above... The master architect had these five
> support chambers built in such a manner that each had the weight
> bearing down upon it redirected to the walls and not the ceilings. This
> was accomplished by constructing the uppermost relieving chamber
> with a gable (pointed) roof of limestone, so that the weight imposed
> upon it from above would be channelled downward and to the sides.
> This weight would then be distributed to the relieving chambers

beneath. Such a system resulted in the pressure being shifted to the walls, and not the ceilings, of these several compartments, said pressure travelling downward through their wall courses until reaching the walls of the King's Chamber.[32]

Lepre emphasised that this system worked in conjunction with the walls of the King's Chamber, which had been built independently of its floor, and thus could, if overloaded, sink without compromising the integrity of the chamber.

To be fair to Lepre, it is evident that he has at least tried to rationalise the design of the superstructure in his own mind – more than can be said for most other pyramid experts. Nevertheless, this theory of weight relief has been ridiculed by non-Egyptologists, several of whom claim an expertise in structural engineering.[33]

The sceptics' main argument is that the four raised roofs provide no weight relief function, but support only their own weight; hence they are superfluous to the design. If weight relief had been the sole objective, then it could have been achieved more easily by setting the pented roof *directly above* the roof of the King's Chamber, as shown in figure 98.

Figure 98.
A SIMPLER DESIGN FOR THE KING'S CHAMBER ROOF, PROVIDING
SUFFICIENT PROTECTION FROM SUPERINCUMBENT WEIGHT.
The design is after an idea by John Reid, verified by Peter Southern of
Maughan, Reynolds and Partners, Structural Engineers.

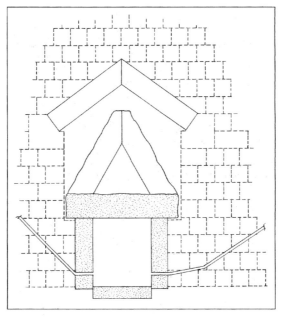

Indeed, a precedent for this design is found in the pented roof of the Queen's Chamber, which relieved its limestone walls from an even greater superincumbent weight (this chamber having being built lower down the monument). If this design worked for the Queen's Chamber, then why not for the King's Chamber?

Why, then, did the builders decide to construct four additional raised roofs in this particular part of the Pyramid?

In an attempt to answer this question, Rudolf Gantenbrink has recently suggested that the gabled roof was raised to a great height in order that the deflected forces should not push against the south end of the Grand Gallery. It is an ingenious suggestion, but, unfortunately, it is far from convincing. After all, the architect could simply have turned the gabled roof through 90°, thereby deflecting the superincumbent load to the east and the west. The presence of the Gallery to the north was simply not a problem.

We are faced, then, with a real puzzle. Why did the builders go to the trouble of positioning 1,200 tons of granite beams above the flat roof of the King's Chamber for no ostensible constructional purpose? And why, indeed, use granite for these beams, only to surmount them with a gable made of limestone?

One possibility, advocated by Elkington and Reid (and others before them),[34] is that the series of raised roofs formed the shape of the *Djed* pillar, an important symbol in Egyptian religious ritual. (The *Djed* pillar

Figure 99.
THE DJED PILLAR.
For comparison to the King's Chamber superstructure, figure 96.

signified the resurrection of Osiris, who was linked explicitly to the true pyramid in the Pyramid Texts;[35] to raise the *Djed* pillar was to re-enact the moment of creation when Osiris ascended as a spirit to the sky.) This theory is not without merit, and it would explain the use of granite on the basis that only granite was strong enough to reproduce the *Djed* pillar on this scale. However, it stretches credulity that the builders would have erected thirty-four additional granite beams with a combined weight of approximately 1,200 tons *solely* for this purpose. Surely there has to be an additional, more fundamental reason for this structure.

Might the answer lie in the resonant properties of the granite? Could it be that the granite beams in the superstructure were designed to resonate and interact with the granite beams in the King's Chamber ceiling, and with the other granite stones in the chamber below?

Astonishingly, there is evidence that this might indeed have been the case.

Firstly, it is important to note that the King's Chamber superstructure is a free-standing structure, separated from the surrounding masonry, as William Flinders Petrie observed:

> On the east and west are two immense limestone walls wholly outside of, and independent of, all the granite floors and supporting blocks. Between these great walls all the chambers stand, unbonded, and capable of yielding freely to settlement.[36]

The implication of this is that the granite beams could have vibrated, or resonated, freely, with minimal damping, interacting with each other and with the granite in the chamber below.

Secondly, the superstructure's gabled roof would have facilitated the resonance of the granite beams below. By deflecting vertical forces into the horizontal plane, it had the effect of minimising the load borne by the granite beams, thus maximising their ability to vibrate, with a minimum of damping.[37]

Thirdly, the unsupported length of the granite beams, around 17 feet, was unusual, and would have maximised their ability to vibrate. As Mark Lehner has pointed out: 'never before had the Egyptians spanned such a wide space in stone.'[38] Was acoustics the reason for this unique design?

Fourthly, the appearance of the granite beams supports their possible use in an acoustic design. The variations in their widths and heights, for example, are striking, and may reflect a desire to use beams with a range of resonant frequencies (the frequency being dependent on the mass of the stone). Furthermore, several beams have had deep grooves cut into their surfaces, whilst four beams in the uppermost roof have had bowls gouged into them. The latter are described by J.P. Lepre as follows:

> Of the seven huge floor stones in this chamber, four of them have odd-looking basins carved into them at their ends. These basins or bowls are roughly square, a strange phenomenon indeed.[39]

Might these peculiar features, otherwise inexplicable, be evidence for the tuning of the beams? The idea is by no means far-fetched in the opinion of Christopher Dunn, who writes:

> It would be possible for us to tune a length of granite, such as those found in the Great Pyramid, by altering its physical dimensions. We could attain a precise frequency by either altering the length of the beam – as a guitarist alters the length of a guitar string – or by removing material from the beam's mass, as in the tuning of bells. (A bell is tuned to a fundamental hum and its harmonics by removing metal from critical areas.)... The fact that the beams above the King's Chamber are all shapes and sizes would support this speculation.[40]

In addition, Dunn observed that the gouged holes in certain beams were consistent with his hypothesis. He suggested that the builders had tuned the beams by a simple process of trial and error. First, they would have struck the beam to induce oscillation (as one might strike a tuning fork). Then, having checked its frequency, probably by ear, they would have removed material, and repeated the process until the desired frequency was reached.

A similar view has been advocated by the acoustics expert John Reid. In discussing the almost identical resonances of the King's Chamber and its sarcophagus, he suggested that the latter may have been tuned to the former, and describes how it could have been done:

> The process of tuning [the sarcophagus] may not have been as difficult to do as one may imagine since granite is highly resonant and most large pieces of the stone emit a clearly audible sound when struck. The architect would have had access to expert stone masons who would be adept at hollowing out large blocks of stone; the process of grinding off material to alter its ringing tone is one which was well within the limits of their known technology.[41]

To summarise the argument thus far, the King's Chamber superstructure is a unique feature that warrants a unique explanation, but orthodox theories cannot explain why the builders went to the enormous lengths of piling up 1,200 tons of granite beams. Several clues, however, point to an acoustic purpose. In particular, it would seem that the superstructure may have been built in a way that would promote the vibration of the granite beams, which may have been tuned to certain desired frequencies.

Now, if this were the case, it would follow logically that the granite beams in the raised roofs were designed to interact acoustically with the corresponding granite beams in the lowest roof – the ceiling of the King's Chamber – and thence with the cavity of the chamber below. The entire structure would thus form a kind of giant soundbox.

But to what end?

To date, those researchers who have studied the subject of sound and acoustics in the Great Pyramid have worked on the assumption that the King's Chamber was kept open at the time of construction, either for the burial of the deceased king, or, more controversially, for the performance of initiation rituals by the priests. In line with this approach, Elkington and Reid have both proposed that the chamber was designed to resonate to the male voice at a frequency of 121-129 Hz. Accordingly they have been forced to exclude the superstructure from their analysis, on the basis that the male voice could not have excited the additional 1,200 tons of granite beams.

But what if the Pyramid's upper chambers were constructed, from the beginning, as a sealed system? Might there be an alternative source of vibrational energy that had sufficient power to excite the whole granite structure of the King's Chamber and its superstructure, plus the King's Chamber Passage and the Antechamber?

The answer, as we shall now see, is almost certainly yes.

The Earth's Voice

In 1998, the engineer and pyramid researcher Christopher Dunn put forward a bold and imaginative hypothesis. Noting that the Earth has a powerful vibrational energy, Dunn suggested that the Great Pyramid may have been designed to couple acoustically with the Earth, and resonate in harmony with it. The Pyramid would thus become a coupled oscillator:

> This object [the Great Pyramid] would need to be designed in such a way that its own resonant frequency was the same as, or a harmonic of, the Earth's... In harmony with the Earth's vibrations, this object would have the potential to become a coupled oscillator. (A coupled oscillator is an object that is in harmonic resonance with another, usually larger, vibrating object. When set into motion, the coupled oscillator will draw energy from the source and vibrate in sympathy as long as the source continues to vibrate.)[42]

Covering a large land area, the Great Pyramid is, in fact, in harmonic resonance with the vibration of the Earth – a structure that could act as an acoustical horn for collecting, channelling, and/or focusing terrestrial vibration.[43]

But to what end? At this point, unfortunately, Dunn's theory went off the rails. The Pyramid, he claimed, was a giant power plant. In the Queen's Chamber, a chemical reaction took place, fuelled by chemicals that were drip fed through the shafts. This process produced hydrogen gas, which flowed out through the passage into the Grand Gallery and thence up into the King's Chamber. Meanwhile, Helmholtz-type resonators, placed in the Gallery, transformed the Earth's vibrations into sound waves, which were channelled into the King's Chamber via an acoustic filter (housed in the Antechamber). These sound waves caused the King's Chamber and its superstructure to become 'a vibrating mass of thousands of tons of granite'. In addition, the chamber became filled by electromagnetic energy, released from the quartz in the granite through the 'piezoelectric effect'. The acoustical and electromagnetic energies were then absorbed by the hydrogen atoms, which were 'pumped' into a higher energy state. Meanwhile, a microwave signal from space passed through the northern shaft into the chamber, where its power was boosted by a crystal box amplifier contained in the sarcophagus. This microwave signal then interacted with the pumped-up hydrogen atoms, stimulating them to emit microwave energy. This process having repeated itself exponentially, the microwave energy was collected in a receiver contained in the mouth of the southern shaft, and thence through a metal-lined (!) shaft to the outside of the Pyramid. There, it was beamed up to an orbiting satellite, which in turn channelled the energy back to Earth to provide electricity for the ancient Egyptian civilisation, and perhaps also for an earlier, lost, global civilisation of Atlantis.[44]

But silliness aside, Dunn makes an interesting point about the Earth's vibrational energy and the Pyramid's ability to resonate in harmony with it. Did the Earth provide the 'voice' that moved the 1,200 tons of granite above the King's Chamber, as well as the granite ceiling, walls and floor of the room? Was the Earth the driver of the acoustic system, the player of the notes, so to speak? I decided to check out the possibility.

Firstly, with regard to the Earth's vibrational energy, David Elkington confirms the importance of this phenomenon in his book *In the Name of the Gods*:

> The Earth resonates, or vibrates, at an extremely low frequency, or
> ELF for short. This resonance is produced from a variety of sources,
> but the most influential are from space: electromagnetic radiation from

the Sun and cosmic rays, which are actually high energy particles coming in from all over the cosmos... The best way to describe Earth resonance is to picture the planet as a gigantic bell... When a church bell is struck by a hammer, it vibrates, and no matter how loud it might seem, the frequency of vibration always remains the same. There may, however, be overtones, or undertones, which are variations on the resonant frequency. These are dependent upon the shape of the bell, the material, and any cracks or other anomalies. Similarly, our Earth is struck by the incoming energies and therefore vibrates at a particular frequency along with its overtones... Our planet sings to the rhythm of the cosmos by being struck (or some would say 'played') by cosmic waves, much like a bell being struck by a hammer. In this way the Earth gives off her own vibratory rhythm...[45]

I contacted Elkington, and put it to him that the Pyramid might have been designed to resonate in harmony with the Earth's vibrations. He agreed. The Pyramid, he said, was built of stone, and was therefore an extension of the Earth; as such, it would naturally have vibrated in harmony with it. Dunn, incidentally, had muddled this point by supposing the need for a priming mechanism that would set the Pyramid resonating.[46] But, in fact, the sympathetic vibration would have occurred automatically. The very act of building the Pyramid constituted the priming mechanism.

At this point, it is worth noting an intriguing observation about the King's Chamber, which may be particularly significant in the context of Earth resonance. The observation comes from Lambert Dolphin of SRI International, who conducted a survey of the Pyramid (and various other sites) in 1977 using a variety of remote-sensing technologies.[47] In respect of the King's Chamber, he was prompted by his findings to make the following astonishing assertion:

> The foundation of the King's Chamber goes all the way to the base of the pyramid and is separate from the foundation of the rest of the pyramid.[48]

Quite how Dolphin can know this for certain is beyond my wit to fathom, since the floor of the King's Chamber lies about 140 feet above the base of the monument. But it is, nonetheless, an intriguing suggestion, and there may be something in it. If future surveys are able to corroborate this theory, then the case for acoustic intent would be strengthened, with Earth resonance being the prime contender for the driver of the system.

My next task was to determine the frequency of the Earth's vibration. Might it match the resonances found in the King's Chamber?

Here, I found Dunn and Elkington's work a little vague. They spoke of the Earth's fundamental frequency, but provided no precise definition of what that frequency was (Elkington suggested 32 Hz, but did not cite his sources).[49] Also, it was unclear whether there was a single frequency or a whole range of frequencies. I therefore decided to consult *Encyclopaedia Britannica*, but, to my amazement, drew a blank. In frustration, I turned with some reluctance to the Internet, where information can sometimes be unreliable, and found reference to a fundamental Earth resonance of 'approximately 10 Hz'.[50] The reader is advised to regard this figure with all due caution.

What did become apparent, however, on the Internet, as well as in the works of Dunn and Elkington, was the importance of something called 'the Schumann resonance', which is, apparently, a quite different kind of Earth resonance.

The Schumann resonance, named after the German physicist W.O. Schumann, who predicted its existence in the early 1950s, refers to the resonance of the Earth-ionosphere cavity, i.e. the spherical shell whose inner boundary is the Earth's surface and whose outer boundary is the ionosphere. This cavity has its strongest resonance at 7.83 Hz, but in fact consists of a series of seven frequencies: 7.83 Hz, 14 Hz, 21 Hz, 26 Hz, 32 Hz, 38 Hz and 45 Hz.[51] These vibrations are thought to be caused by electromagnetic activity in the space between the Earth's surface and the ionosphere. They are not Earth resonances in the sense of being *in* the Earth or *from* the Earth, but they are Earth resonances in the sense that they surround our planet and affect everything that lives or exists on its surface.[52] The Schumann resonances of 7.83 Hz and 32 Hz fit well with the *c.* 30 Hz resonance observed in the King's Chamber by Danley.

In summary, whilst it is possible that the King's Chamber and its superstructure were caused to resonate by the *interior* vibration of the Earth at a prime frequency of 10 Hz (if that figure is to be trusted), it is also possible that they were caused to resonate by the *exterior* vibration of the Earth, the Schumann resonance, at 7.83 Hz, 14 Hz, 21 Hz, 26 Hz, 32 Hz, 38 Hz and 45 Hz. At the present time, neither possibility should be excluded, and it might even be the case that both sources of vibration were being used in tandem.

I put these ideas to Reid and Elkington, neither of whom objected in principle. Both researchers agreed that the huge granite beams above the King's Chamber might have been tuned to vibrate to Earth resonance, in which case a low-pitched sound would have been created, centred on the granite structure of the King's Chamber.[53] The only proviso at this stage was that the frequency (or frequencies) of the sound and the amplitude of the waves were unknown.

Can this really be possible? The reader may find the scenario a little hard to grasp. How can sound be created out of thin air, so to speak? The answer, in a word, is vibration. As explained earlier, sound *is* vibration, and vibration *is* sound. So, just as the male voice, in the frequency range *c.* 95-110 Hz, can excite the King's Chamber, so too can the voice of the Earth, at the lower frequency of perhaps 8 or 10 Hz. The two sources of vibration are no different in principle. Consequently, if a granite beam has the same resonant frequency as the Earth, then that beam *will* begin to resonate in sympathy, in the same way that a tuning fork, calibrated to 440 Hz, say, will be induced to vibrate in tune with another tuning fork of the same frequency that is sounded nearby. It is not magic, though it might seem like it. It is elementary schoolbook physics.

Nevertheless, an issue arises concerning the prime frequency of the design, since 7.83 Hz (the lowest and strongest Schumann resonance) and 10 Hz (the suggested subterranean resonance) both lie beneath the limit of human hearing. What would have been the point of making the King's Chamber resonate to a subaudible frequency?

A possible solution is suggested by the striking variation in the widths and heights of the granite beams (they all share the same length), the largest beams having more than twice the mass of the smallest. From this curious and hitherto unexplained fact, two possibilities emerge.

Firstly, it is possible that the granite beams were designed to capture not only the 8 Hz Schumann resonance but also the higher resonances, perhaps at 14 Hz, 21 Hz, 26 Hz and 32 Hz, the latter three frequencies being clearly audible. As mentioned earlier, several beams have had deep grooves cut into their surfaces, whilst four beams in the uppermost roof have had bowls gouged into them, as if they were tuned individually to resonate at precise frequencies.

Secondly, it is possible that the granite beams were designed to create harmonics of the fundamental frequencies (something similar had been suggested by Dunn, but in the context of his far-fetched power plant theory).[54] A fundamental frequency of 8 Hz, say, would not only cause oscillation of a beam tuned to 8 Hz but also of a beam tuned to its second harmonic (16 Hz), and to its third harmonic (24 Hz), and so on, up the scale, albeit in diminishing intensity. Likewise, a beam vibrating at 16 Hz, say, would induce oscillation in a nearby beam tuned to its second harmonic (32 Hz), and to its third harmonic (48 Hz), et cetera. In this way, by means of harmonics, a whole range of audible sounds (above 16 Hz) could be created from a fundamental tone of 8 Hz.

In support of this theory, Danley measured the vibrational signatures of the cavities above the King's Chamber and found 'a large number of room modes, some going below 20 Hz'.[55] Unfortunately, electrical noise swamped most of his accelerometer readings, making it difficult to draw any definitive conclusions.

Both Reid and Elkington offered support in principle for these ideas, whilst stressing that no firm view could be taken in the absence of further data, i.e. the resonant frequencies of individual beams. We are all agreed, however, that these measurements should be taken as soon as possible, so that the theory might be tested and further developed.

Thus, for now, we cannot state for certain that the beams did function in one or other (or even both) of the hypothesised manners, but we can claim plausibility for the idea that subaudible frequencies were raised to audible tones. On this note, we must leave aside speculation on how the beams functioned, and direct our focus to what was happening below, in the King's Chamber itself.

The King's Chamber: an Acoustic Amplifier?

The King's Chamber is dominated by its flat roof, the nine granite beams of which have a combined weight of more than 300 tons. Crucially, these beams are replicated in the superstructure, in which another 1,200 tons of granite is to be found. The overall design gives the impression of having been engineered to maximise the vibration of the granite beams (witness the free-standing design of the superstructure, its stress-relieving pented roof, and the extraordinary length of the beams) and to transmit that vibration into the chamber below.

In the chamber, there are yet more signs of an acoustic intent. Already, we have noted the remarkable acoustic properties of this room: its long reverberation time, its strong resonance at low frequencies, and its ability to produce harmonics of intoned sounds. But there is more, particularly with regard to the floor.

The floor of the King's Chamber is known to be unusual in that it is fitted *between* the walls (see figures 96 and 97), but in 1996 Tom Danley discovered another strange thing. According to Boris Said, who worked alongside Danley in Egypt, his acoustic survey revealed that the floor did not rest upon flat masonry, as had been presumed, but upon a nodular underlay, whose many nodes kept the area of contact to a minimum (the pattern has been compared to an upturned corrugated egg carton).[56] This design would have allowed the twenty-one floor stones to vibrate freely with a minimum of damping (reminiscent of the superstructure's design), and is unmistakably suggestive of an acoustic intent. Danley's findings, it should be noted, have not yet been published, let alone independently verified. But if this discovery is published and confirmed, the case for acoustic intent becomes unanswerable.

Another peculiar feature of the King's Chamber is the diversity of the blocks used in its floor and walls; the stones, far from being of uniform size, as one might expect, follow a seemingly random and haphazard pattern (see figure 35 in chapter two). The reader's attention is drawn, in particular, to the large stones at the top of the walls, the single immense stone above the entrance, and the shafts that are formed, astonishingly, of three separate wall stones. But the floor too is made up of a bewildering range of different-sized stones. Why? To my knowledge, no explanation has ever been offered. But might acoustics be the key to it?

Earlier, I described how the King's Chamber, as a cavity, had its own prime resonant frequency, dictated by its size and shape, and I described how this prime frequency had natural harmonics and subharmonics. But could it be that, in addition, the stones in the floor resonated to audible harmonics of the frequencies that were generated in the superstructure? Was the King's Chamber in effect an amplifier of audible sound?

In support of this idea, practical experiments have demonstrated that the King's Chamber produces harmonics when certain prime notes are intoned in the room, whilst Danley in his acoustic survey found a range of resonant frequencies in the chamber, some audible, some subaudible, forming the pattern of an F-sharp chord. In his article for *Live Sound!* magazine, he wrote:

> I found some very low frequency sound – resonances which start at a few Hz and go upward to 15-20 Hz or so... This sound was present even if everyone is silent. I crunched the measurements, and they were sent on to a musicologist who was part of the staff... he identified that there was a pattern of frequencies, which roughly form an F-sharp chord. Not all the resonances fell in the right place, but many did and some repeated the pattern for many octaves. In other words, it [the chamber] was roughly tuned to F-sharp over many octaves.[57]

So far, so good. But what was the point of creating audible sound in the King's Chamber, especially if, as I have argued, that chamber was sealed off at the time of construction? Only one answer suggests itself: the audible sound was conveyed to the outside world via the two so-called 'airshafts'.

Acoustic Shafts?

If sound had been created in the King's Chamber, as harmonics of Earth resonance, would it have travelled up the shafts and been heard in the outside world? I put my scenario – let us call it the acoustic shaft theory – to Reid and Elkington to elicit their reaction. Whilst both researchers held to their view that the Pyramid's acoustics had been driven by the voice of the priests rather than the voice of the Earth, they nevertheless responded positively to my theory, and Reid, in particular, offered some useful suggestions.

The first crucial question was whether the sound would have travelled up the shafts. Reid confirmed that it would. Any sound waves produced in the chamber, he said, would have been compelled to pass through the shafts by the laws of pressure equalisation. If these sound waves had been audible in the first instance, then they would have remained audible at the top of the shafts, albeit some loss of amplitude would have occurred. If the shafts had been open to the elements at their outer ends (more on this in a moment), then the sound would, theoretically, have been heard outside the Pyramid.

Reid then made an intriguing observation, which may turn out to be of academic interest, but nevertheless requires an airing. The 8-inch-square shafts, he said, bear a remarkable similarity to organ pipes, specifically those made of wood, which are constructed in square section of about 8

Figure 100.
THE GREAT PYRAMID, VERTICAL SECTION, LOOKING WEST.
The King's Chamber shafts travel all the way to the exterior of the Pyramid.

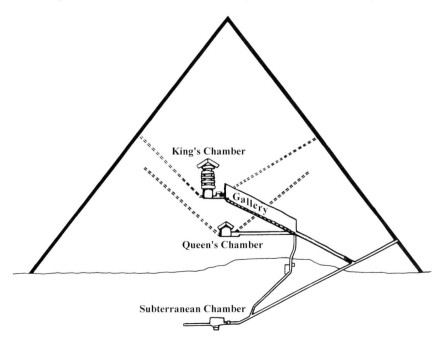

inches by 8 inches.[58] These organ pipes, he informed me, have very low frequencies, the exact tones being calculable according to a standard formula, the main variables of which are the length of the pipe and the air temperature therein.[59] Applying this formula to the King's Chamber shafts, based on lengths of 235 feet and 174 feet and a temperature of 66.2° F, the resonant frequencies come out at 2.4 Hz for the northern shaft and 3.2 Hz for the southern shaft (an additional 10° F raises these frequencies by 0.33 Hz and 0.44 Hz respectively).[60] The shafts thus have extremely low prime resonant frequencies in the infrasound range, well below the limit of human hearing. Nevertheless, in accordance with the laws of harmonics, higher frequencies would also be generated, and these would become audible at the fifth harmonic upwards, albeit at relatively low amplitudes. The following table illustrates the harmonics for the prime frequencies just quoted:

	Northern shaft	Southern shaft
Prime frequency	2.4	3.2
2nd harmonic	4.8	6.4
3rd harmonic	7.2	9.6
4th harmonic	9.6	12.8
5th harmonic	12.0	16.0*
6th harmonic	14.4	19.2*
7th harmonic	16.8*	22.4*
et cetera... *		

(Note: All figures in Hz; an asterisk indicates an audible frequency)

Now, these illustrative figures reflect the cavity resonances of the shafts, which do not come into play unless the cavities are energised by a sound source. If we exclude the possibility that wind generated a 'Coke bottle' effect across the tops of the shafts (such an effect would surely have been minimal), then the only possible sound source is the King's Chamber. In other words, the shafts would have resonated only if they had a harmonic relationship with the sounds produced in that chamber, in which case the latter, acting as carrier waves, would have conveyed the shaft resonances to the outside world. But whether or not this was the case is difficult to say, since the exact frequencies of the chamber and the shafts are not known (in the latter case, the operating temperature is uncertain). All that one can say is that *in principle* the sounds produced in the chamber *may* have generated audible harmonics in the shafts, in which case those sounds too would have been heard outside the Pyramid.

It may be the case, of course, that the shafts were never designed to act

Figure 101.
PATTERN OF THE KING'S CHAMBER SOUTHERN SHAFT, AS IT EXITS
THE CHAMBER.

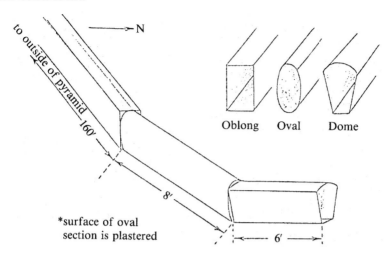

Oblong   Oval   Dome

*surface of oval
section is plastered

as organ pipes, and were built merely to convey the sound produced in
the King's Chamber to the outside world. After all, if sonic output was
the goal, then the architect had no choice but to build narrow shafts from
the chamber to the outside of the Pyramid. Shaft resonances at very low
frequencies would thus have been unavoidable, theoretically speaking,
and might even have been undesirable.

However, if the shafts were built to be conduits for sound, and nothing
more, one would expect their patterns to be virtually identical, and this is
patently not the case. On the contrary, the southern shaft differs from the
northern in having an unusual dome-shaped aperture at its lower end, and
an equally strange oval-shaped pipe above that (only then does it settle
into the rectangular shape that is shared with its northern counterpart).
Might these features reflect a desire on the architect's part to modify the
sound that was emitted via the southern shaft? Reid too was intrigued by
the dome-shaped cavity, and volunteered his impression, as an acoustic
engineer, that it resembled a tuned Helmholtz resonator.[61] He had never
explored the idea before as it seemed too speculative, but now, in the
light of my proposal, it was worth investigating.

Another puzzling design feature worth investigating is the positioning
of the shaft apertures with respect to the chamber. It was odd, Reid
observed, that the shafts had not been placed half way along the walls,
nor at the points that marked the central north-south axis of the Pyramid,
but rather upon an alternative north-south axis in the room, for no reason
that anyone had ever been able to fathom. Indeed, in deciding to build

the shaft apertures here, the builders had actually made construction of the shafts more difficult, since it had become necessary to incorporate a series of bends to redirect them towards the central north-south axis of the Pyramid (and, in the case of the northern shaft, to avoid the Grand Gallery). It was plausible, said Reid, that the unusual positioning of the shaft openings might have been dictated by acoustic considerations. Had it been necessary, perhaps, to maximise the distance between the shaft apertures and the sarcophagus in order to create, or avoid, a particular acoustic effect in the former or the latter? Further testing of the acoustic nodes and antinodes in the room might shed some light on this question.

Finally, Reid raised the question of whether the shafts had been open or sealed at their outer ends. If the latter, then the shafts could not have functioned as emitters of sound. The question is valid since the layers of masonry at the top of the shafts have been destroyed, and it is not known for certain whether they were originally open to the air. It had always been Reid's assumption that the architect had sealed off the shaft outlets with casing stones, in order to prevent the ingress of birds, bats, insects, and rainwater. The same thought had also occurred to this author, and had prompted an intriguing thought. Might each outlet have been fitted with a baffle, which would have redirected the sound wave downwards, whilst at the same time doubling as a cover for the shaft?[62] Reid agreed that this was indeed a neat solution to the problem.

Even so, a fundamental question remains. *Why* would the builders of the Pyramid have invested so much time and trouble in creating a self-sufficient sound-generator and -broadcaster?

For the final piece in the puzzle, we must return to the question of the Pyramid's creational symbolism.

The Sound of Creation

As explained in earlier chapters of this book, the true pyramid was a symbol of the creation and a simulacrum in stone of the creator-god. The very act of building the pyramid commemorated the moment when the creator-god had emerged as a spirit from the abyss, and risen up into the sky to bring about the creation of the Universe. When the capstone or pyramidion (*benbenet*) was placed on top of the pyramid, the builders re-enacted that crucial moment when the seed of the creator-god had been thrust into the womb of the sky for the conception and birth of the stars, the Sun and the Moon.

The Great Pyramid is no exception to this rule. In fact, it would appear to be the epitome of the idea. Uniquely among the pyramids of Egypt (as far as we know), it contained an elevated chamber, the King's Chamber, in which, I believe, the iron seed of the creator-god was enshrined in the granite sarcophagus. This iron, in the form of meteorites, represented an actual sample of the seed of the creator-god, raised towards the sky in celebration of the First Time. It follows from this, as day follows night, that the airshafts in the King's Chamber represented symbolic channels by means of which the iron would have been spiritualised in the sky for the formation of the celestial bodies. Thus the northern shaft would have channelled the iron into the northern sky (the region of the circumpolar, never-setting stars) whilst the southern shaft would have channelled the iron into the southern sky (the region of the rotating celestial vault, comprising the Sun, the Moon, and the rising-and-setting stars).

All of this was symbolism, of course, but it nevertheless presupposed the existence of a powerful creative energy that could have spiritualised the iron and ejected it into the sky.

How appropriate it would be, then, if the King's Chamber shafts had been conduits not only for the emission of the creator-god's iron seed, but also for the utterance of his creative voice, as shown in figure 102.

Figure 102.
THE VOICE OF THE CREATOR-GOD BLASTS THE IRON INTO THE SKY VIA THE KING'S CHAMBER SHAFTS.

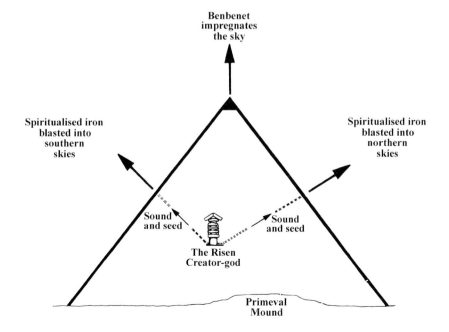

Was the King's Chamber designed to broadcast sound in re-enactment of the creation?

This idea rings true. In fact, ancient Egyptian literature testifies to the fundamental importance of sound at the time of the creation. In several versions of the creation myth, for example, the creator-god brings the Universe into being by opening his mouth and pronouncing the sacred words (his mouth being a metaphor for the mouth of the earth, which was split open dramatically in the act of creation).[63] But the idea is even more apparent in the Pyramid Texts and Coffin Texts, where the deceased king takes the role of the Great God and re-enacts the various stages of the creation. Here, a prominent theme is the creator-god's emergence from the earth and ascent into the sky, accompanied, not surprisingly, by a great noise and commotion. The earth quakes. Isis and Nephthys emit wails of lament. The gods shout. The voice of Geb, the earth, resounds. The king speaks to the sky. He comes forth as 'the Great Word' with the gods on his 'lips'. He ascends with a roar. In all of these renderings of the creation myth, the emission of sound is implicit, in keeping with the cataclysmic nature of the event. What is more, the sound in question is a low frequency sound, as evidenced by its association with the quaking and trembling of the earth. Some relevant quotations from the Pyramid Texts are cited in the panel opposite.

It would make sense, therefore, if the Pyramid emitted low frequency sound from its shafts, for such sound would have commemorated the act of creation, in keeping with the monument's creational symbolism. We should envisage the sound filling the King's Chamber, energising the iron inside the sealed sarcophagus, and travelling up the shafts towards the northern and southern skies, respectively, just as the sound, or voice, of the creator had ascended at the beginning of time. In all likelihood, the sound symbolised the soul of the Great God, which had spiritualised the iron and blasted it into the sky as a living seed.

But what of the shafts' outlets in the faces of the Pyramid? Whilst the sound, strictly speaking, should have been directed onwards and upwards *into* the northern and southern skies, it may have been expedient, for the reasons discussed earlier, to redirect it downwards by means of baffles (which would have doubled as covers for the shafts), causing the entire Giza plateau to resound to the voice of the Lord of the Universe.

I ran this latter scenario past Reid and Elkington, who both found it plausible and intriguing.

But what exactly would have been heard by inhabitants of the Giza plateau? Here, one must speculate, since the acoustic system is no longer operational, the King's Chamber having sustained serious damage from

The Cataclysmic Sound of Creation

The earth speaks: The doors of the earth-god are opened for you, the doors of Geb are thrown open for you, you come forth at the voice of Anubis...
(Pyramid Texts, Utterance 437)

The earth speaks, the gate of the earth-god is open, the doors of Geb are opened for you in your presence, and your speech goes up to Anubis...
(Pyramid Texts, Utterance 483)

My lips are the Two Enneads; I am the Great Word... O men and gods [place] your arms under me!... To the sky! To the sky! To the great throne among the gods!
(Pyramid Texts, Utterance 506)

The sky thunders, the earth quakes, the gods of Heliopolis tremble at the sound of the offering in my presence.
(Pyramid Texts, Utterance 508)

The sky thunders, the earth quakes, Geb quivers, the two domains of the god roar, the earth is hacked up, and the offering is presented before me. I ascend to the sky...
(Pyramid Texts, Utterance 509)

Geb laughs, Nut shouts for joy before me when I ascend to the sky. The sky thunders for me, the earth quakes for me, the hail storm is burst apart for me, and I roar like Seth.
(Pyramid Texts, Utterance 511)

The sky weeps for you, the earth quakes at you, the Mourning-Woman [Nephthys?] calls to you, the Great Mooring Post [Isis?] cries out to you; your feet stamp, your arms wave, and you ascend to the sky as a star, as the Morning Star.
(Pyramid Texts, Utterance 553)

The Earth is hacked up by the hoe, the offering is presented... the two nomes of the god shout before [the king] when he goes down into the earth. O Geb, open your mouth for your son Osiris...
(Pyramid Texts, Utterance 560)

The earth speaks to you, the gate of the earth-god is opened for you... that you may go forth at the voice and spiritualise yourself...
(Pyramid Texts, Utterance 610)

an earthquake (the effects of this earthquake will be discussed further in due course).

One possibility is that the Pyramid broadcast a single continuous note, perhaps 16 Hz, 30 Hz, or 32 Hz. At 16 Hz, just above the limit of human hearing (at 15 Hz), the sound would have been felt, as much as heard, as a low and mysterious hum, whilst at 30 Hz or 32 Hz it would have been clearly audible as a very deep bass note, eerie but profoundly beautiful.

Another possibility, suggested by the unusual design of the southern shaft's aperture, is that the Pyramid broadcast two separate notes, one from each shaft. A combination of two bass tones would have produced a most impressive acoustic effect. In this regard, Reid offered an intriguing thought: two dissimilar notes, separated by 7 Hz (say), would provide brain entrainment frequencies;[64] these are used today in music therapy to help destress patients by inducing alpha frequencies.

Finally, it may be possible that the Pyramid broadcast a full chord. My gut feeling is that the King's Chamber had a prime resonant frequency of 16 Hz, 30 Hz, or 32 Hz, and amplified this frequency and its harmonics, as well as producing a range of other bass notes, all of these frequencies being modulated by harmonic resonances in the shafts. The result would have been a chord that was easier on the ears than the aforementioned single note or dual notes, although it is debatable whether it would have conveyed any deeper religious meaning.

Such is the uncertainty surrounding the Pyramid's acoustic signature, or voiceprint. Not only do we not know for certain the exact frequencies involved, but also we have no way of estimating the amplitude (volume) of the sound. Would it have been heard only on the Giza plateau, or for many miles around? In Reid's view, it might well have been audible in the entire area around the plateau, since low-pitched sounds do tend to travel for long distances. In addition, there is a question of whether the sound might have varied in tone between the day and the night, or with the motions of the Moon, or at times of high tectonic activity.[65] Only a full working model of the King's Chamber will be able to resolve these unanswered questions.

What we can say, though, is that, if the Pyramid did function in this way, then it would, for a time, have been the most revered religious site in the world, offering visitors a unique and moving experience in every respect. For not only would the pilgrim have heard the sound of the creator, filling the air like an echo from the dawn of time, but also, when the Sun struck the Pyramid, he would have seen the light of the creator, ascending towards the sky as at the First Time. This was Giza's original sound and light show – a manifestation of the Great God and a testament to the enduring presence of *maat* in the land of Egypt. Without a doubt, the pilgrim would have fallen to his knees in amazement and awe. One is reminded here of the Pink Floyd rock anthem *Breathe,* and its evocative closing lyrics:

> Far away across the field,
> The tolling of the iron bell,
> Calls the faithful to their knees,
> To hear the softly spoken magic spells.[66]

The Antechamber

If the King's Chamber was acoustically self-sufficient, in accordance with my sealed system theory, then an interesting scenario results for the Antechamber, i.e. the room that is positioned in the entrance passage to the King's Chamber. Crucially, that part of the passage nearest to the King's Chamber is built entirely of granite, whilst the Antechamber itself is built predominantly of granite. Moreover, the granite floor in the passage and Antechamber is fitted *between* the walls, as in the design of the King's Chamber.[67] The use of granite stops only at the entrance to the Antechamber (at its northern end), where limestone is used instead. But why?

As discussed in chapters two and three, the Antechamber represents a real puzzle and a challenge that Egyptology has not yet risen to meet. In particular, it is not apparent how the three granite portcullis slabs could have been raised from or lowered to the floor. Rather, it would seem that the slabs just sat on the passage floor. Moreover, an intruder could have clambered over the top of these slabs, thus compromising their role as a protective device. This is a problem for orthodoxy, but also for the sealed system theory, which has not yet explained the purpose of the three slabs (unless it be accepted that they were symbolic obstacles).

The rejection of the opening-and-closing portcullis theory necessitates a major reappraisal of the Antechamber design. Already, in chapter three, I have suggested that some features were decorative/symbolic, notably the four vertical grooves in the south wall, the granite leaf, and the raised boss on the granite leaf. The vertical grooves, I observed, resembled the fluted pattern used in columns, and were an exact image of a decorative pattern found on a 1st dynasty portcullis slab, which may have signified the dwelling place of the Great God. The granite leaf, I noted, resembled the rolled-up reed-mat curtain design that was used, from Old Kingdom times, to symbolise the entrance to the 'other world'. And the raised boss, I suggested, may have symbolised the rising of the spirit of the

Figure 103.
PLAN OF THE ANTECHAMBER.

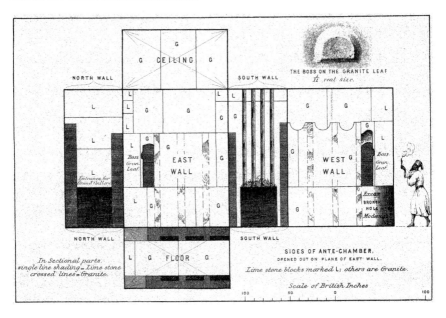

Great God. All of these ideas, it must be emphasised, are consistent with my theory that the King's Chamber was a 'chamber of creation'. But they are educated guesses and nothing more.

Meanwhile, other aspects of the Antechamber remain a mystery.

Why is there a horizontal shelf at the top of the east wainscot, but three semi-hollows at the top of the west wainscot? What, if anything, was fitted in the hollow space between these wainscots and the ceiling? The mystery has defeated the most enquiring minds. As Piazzi Smyth once wrote:

> I myself sat on a ladder, day after day, with lamps and measuring-rods, but in respectful silence and generally in absolute solitude, thinking over what it might mean.[68]

Furthermore, why do the granite walls and floor stop at the position of the granite leaf, with limestone then being used at the entrance to the Antechamber? And why are the granite walls interlaced with limestone blocks at the southern end of the room, nearest to the King's Chamber? As J.P. Lepre commented:

> The architect may well have had a rational motive in this peculiar design, but it has yet to be explained by any modern investigator.[69]

Might acoustics be the key to the mystery of the Antechamber? As noted earlier, acoustic researchers have focused on the King's Chamber to the exclusion of the Antechamber and the King's Chamber Passage, which in their view played no important role in the priestly ritual. But the fact is that the granite of the King's Chamber, which has been implicated in the acoustical studies, *does* extend into the passage and the Antechamber, implying that some kind of acoustic effect was created here also. But to what end?

A possible explanation emerges when the Pyramid's upper system of passages and chambers is viewed as a sealed repository and time capsule, as proposed in chapter six. If the reader will recall, I suggested there that the upper parts of the Pyramid were sealed at the time of construction, with the intention that a pioneering explorer from a future generation, or race, of men would break the seals and enter the secret chambers. Under this scenario, the question arises of why build the Antechamber at all? If the reader will indulge me, I would like to furnish a logical answer to this question.

Let us assume that the King's Chamber was indeed a soundbox for the Pyramid's acoustic system, and, at the same time, a sacred chamber of creation. If this was so, would the architect of this wonderful system have wanted a future explorer to break the seal and enter the room? The clear answer is "no", for any breach of the chamber would have altered its shape and acoustic balance, and perhaps exposed the intruder to a dangerous level of sound. We may thus surmise that the King's Chamber was built as a special kind of sealed room – one that was never intended to be opened.

Instead, there was the Antechamber.

Imagine, if you will, that the explorer has broken through the stone seal at the top of the Great Step, as he was meant to do, and is crawling through the first section of passage towards the King's Chamber. At this stage, the passage is made of limestone and he is well insulated from the throbbing vibrations in the King's Chamber. Then, after a distance of just 4 feet 4 inches, the explorer reaches the entrance to the Antechamber. He stands up and finds himself in a cramped space that has apparently been designed for a single standing person. Opposite his chest and head stands the granite leaf, in its slots, and staring him in the face is the raised boss, as J.P. Lepre observed:

> The boss projects at eye level into a cramped space, only 18 inches from front (where the boss is) to back. Standing quite confined in this space, the visitor contemplates the carving scant inches away from his or her face. Why should this 5 inch wide by 4 inch high object – so

Figure 104.
THE ANTECHAMBER TO THE KING'S CHAMBER, VERTICAL
SECTION, LOOKING WEST.

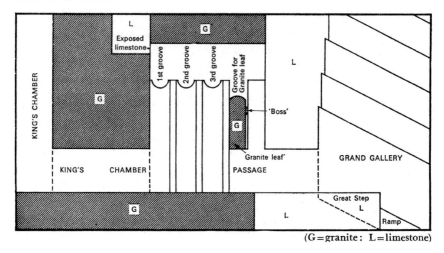

(G = granite: L = limestone)

cunningly carved – be positioned in such a closed space in such a
way?[70]

Beneath the explorer's heels is a limestone floor stone, but his toes rest
on the first granite floor stone. To his right and left, the walls are made of
limestone blocks. In front of him stands the granite leaf, surrounded by
granite on all four sides, and reinforced by granite beyond, marking a
fundamental shift in the nature of the chamber. The explorer thus stands
at a focal point and boundary in the room. If he rocks back on his heels,
he is in contact with limestone; but, if he presses forward, he can touch
granite with his head and his toes.

Now, if the acoustics theory is to be trusted, the granite stones in the
Antechamber would be resonating in tune with the granite in the King's
Chamber, probably at harmonics of the fundamental frequency. But the
amplitude of the sound would be much lower. This must have been so for
two reasons. Firstly, because the Antechamber lay just to the north of the
superstructure, not directly below it. And secondly, because the vibration
would have been damped down by the two blocks of limestone placed
strategically near the ceiling at the southern end of the room (the mystery
of these anomalous stones might thus be solved). Meanwhile, the granite
leaf, hung in its slots near the northern end of the room, may have been
tuned to a harmonic of the three huge granite slabs that stood defiantly in
their grooves behind it.[71]

The effect of this resonance on the Pyramid explorer would have been
rather interesting, to say the least. For one thing, it would probably have

Figure 105.
THE ANTECHAMBER, EAST WALL.
The damaged pilasters attest to the forcible removal of three granite slabs.

stopped him in his tracks. Although, in theory, he could have climbed up over the granite slabs and forced a passage into the King's Chamber, the strength of the resonance in the Antechamber may well have prevented him from doing so. Instead, he may have been confined to the boundary position, standing in front of the granite leaf. This, we may presume, was the architect's intention. There, the leaf, if resonating at 8 Hz or 10 Hz (the figures suggested earlier for Earth resonance), could have interacted with the explorer's brain, inducing an altered state of consciousness. To clarify, the human brain during waking hours has a normal frequency range of 13-30 Hz, the so-called Beta state. This is the wavelength of conscious thought. In certain circumstances, however, when the mind is relaxed to the point of emptiness, the brain may slip into a different mode known as the Alpha state. This state, with a frequency range of 7-13 Hz, is associated with altered states of consciousness, in which a person may experience expanded awareness, religious visions and even 'out of body' sensations.[72] The granite leaf, if it resonated at an Alpha frequency, could have induced just such an altered state. In support of this idea, the reader is informed that sound is indeed used at the Monroe Institute in America to promote altered states of consciousness and 'out of body' experiences.

There is more. According to scientific research, granite can emit radon gas, which, if it builds up in unventilated areas, can induce – you guessed it – altered states of consciousness. Reid writes:

> In unventilated areas, as was the case for the King's Chamber [note: not necessarily so, but it would certainly be true for the Antechamber] granite can produce levels of radon, a toxic gas which, in sufficient concentrations, can induce altered states of consciousness.[73]

Nor is this pure theory. Elkington, in his book, cites research that radon gas has indeed been detected inside the King's Chamber.[74] From this, we may deduce that the radon gas concentration inside the Antechamber, at the time that it was broken into by our notional Pyramid explorer, would have been unusually high, and capable, no doubt, of inducing an altered state.

So, our explorer, standing in the confined space of the Antechamber, in front of the granite leaf, might well have been subjected to forces that could have altered his state of consciousness. But to what end would the architect have designed the Antechamber thus?

The most likely possibility, suggested by ancient Egyptian texts, is that the explorer would have received 'a vision of the true God, with his divine companions'.[75] The idea here was that the veil might be lifted on the mystery of creation, allowing a man to gain knowledge of the Great God and the gods in their true, secret, mysterious forms *before* they had manifested themselves in their visible forms, namely the Sun and the stars. That such a vision might have been seen in the Antechamber is an intriguing idea in the light of the King's Chamber's role as a chamber of creation. Would the explorer have had an 'out of body' experience and witnessed the creation of all things, as was being re-enacted in the King's Chamber? Did he thus come to understand how the creator raised the iron to the sky, and how the iron-clad sky was kept from falling by the pillars or mountains of the Universe? Was he, in short, initiated into the science of levitation?[76]

In support of this intention, the Antechamber itself contains symbols that may be creational. As mentioned earlier, the granite leaf may have signified the entrance to the 'other world', which in this scenario would have been entirely appropriate. And the raised boss on the leaf may have signified the rising of the creator-god's spirit. Again appropriate. Also, in support of the altered state scenario, it may be no coincidence that the raised boss is placed an inch to the right of centre, as if to target the right brain hemisphere of the person who faced it. (The right hemisphere is the creative, spiritual and visionary side of the brain.)

In conclusion, the King's Chamber acoustics theory, in conjunction with the sealed repository theory, prompts a fundamental reappraisal of the Antechamber. Hardly a portcullis room, as Egyptologists believe, it may rather have been a chamber for human interaction with the 'voice of the Earth' in which a representative of a future generation, or race, of men was to be induced to an altered state of consciousness and granted a vision of the creation. In short, the Antechamber may have been built as an initiation room for a post-cataclysm world.

But, fortunately or unfortunately, as the case may be, this is not quite how things worked out.

When the Music Stopped

A formidable objection to my acoustic theory of the King's Chamber is that no audible sound emanates from that chamber today (if we discount the report of a faint pulse at 16 Hz discovered by Danley).[77] In addition to which, there are no ancient legends, as one might expect, of a 'singing' pyramid in Egypt. However, whilst these objections may be fuel for the sceptic, they also support an entirely different conclusion, namely that the Pyramid's sound system ceased to work a long time ago.

In support of this possibility, it is evident that the King's Chamber has suffered serious structural damage, which Egyptologists ascribe to an earthquake in ancient times. Such was the force of the shock that the roof beams were cracked or dislocated, the walls were forced outwards, and the floor stones were shaken into an uneven state.[78] Petrie described the effects thus:

> On every side the joints of the stones have separated, and the whole chamber is shaken larger... These openings or cracks are but the milder signs of the great injury that the whole chamber has sustained, probably by an earthquake, when *every* roof beam was broken across near the south side... Not only has this wreck overtaken the chamber itself, but in every one of the spaces above it are the massive roof-beams either cracked across or torn out of the wall, more or less, at the south side; and the great eastern and western walls of limestone, between, and independent of which, the whole of these construction chambers are built, have sunk bodily.[79] (original emphasis)

A diagrammatic view of this structural damage, which extended from the King's Chamber into the Antechamber, is shown in figure 106 overleaf, where the movements of the stones have been exaggerated by ten times to make the overall effect clearly visible.

Figure 106.
SUBSIDENCE AND CRACKING IN THE KING'S CHAMBER AND
ANTECHAMBER, EFFECT EXAGGERATED BY TEN TIMES.

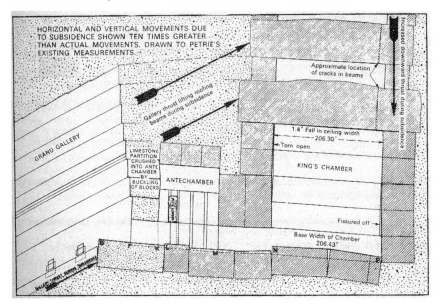

    As Petrie has affirmed, this dislocation of the chamber was extremely
serious. If the superstructure had functioned as a harmonic amplifier and
the chamber itself as a soundbox, then these functions would surely have
suffered terminal failure, brought on, in particular, by the cracking of the
roof beams. The acoustic hypothesis is thus saved; but, more than that,
the earthquake damage might well argue in favour of my hypothesis.
    The oddity is this. Of all the built chambers in the Pyramid, *only* the
King's Chamber and its Antechamber were affected by the hypothetical
earthquake.[80] No other chamber – neither the Grand Gallery, nor the
Queen's Chamber, nor the passages thereto – sustained any subsidence
damage or cracking. How could this be? Indeed, how can it be that the
Pyramid has withstood numerous earthquakes throughout the centuries,
but has suffered serious damage *only* in the area of the King's Chamber
and its Antechamber?[81]
    And here is another oddity. How can it be that the granite beams in the
superstructure were cracked and torn, and yet the limestone gables above
it were left in almost perfect order?[82]
    To Egyptologists, this merely goes to show that the flat granite roofs
were a weak spot in the design, and that the limestone gables performed
their protective task. But the structural theory, on which this presumption
is made, is, in fact, highly questionable, for the reasons outlined earlier in

this chapter.

Could the answer rather lie in the granite and its vibratory role in an acoustic system?

In this chapter, I have argued that Earth resonance may have been the driver of the Pyramid's sound system – either underground vibration or the overground Schumann resonance. This resonance, I have suggested, caused the granite beams to vibrate at the fundamental frequency and its harmonics. In this scenario, normal earthquake vibration would literally have been grist to the Pyramid mill. But what would have happened if there had been a super-earthquake, or if the Earth had been shaken by a large meteorite impact, from a comet or an asteroid? An impact close to Egypt perhaps? In such circumstances, a vibrational overload might well have wrecked the key components of the Pyramid's sound system.

Such an impact is indeed thought to have occurred c. 2350 BC, causing widespread disruption to the civilisations of Mesopotamia and Egypt.[83] A large crater, recently discovered in Iraq, may date to this period, and may have been but one of a number of impacts that triggered major climatic changes in the Near East. This impact, or series of impacts, would have injected a huge amount of energy into the Earth's crust, and triggered a sudden, massive surge in tectonic vibration.

Did this impact cause the damage to the King's Chamber? Although the Pyramid was seemingly built to survive an 'end of the world' cataclysm, we would not be doing the architect an injustice to suggest that he could not have calculated scientifically the vibrational peak that might have resulted from a meteorite impact, even if he had been able to estimate the projectile's size. It is conceivable, therefore, that a sudden injection of energy into the Earth's crust might have created a vibration wave that was beyond the capacity of the Pyramid's sound transducer, namely the granite beams in the superstructure. Thus overloaded, these beams would have overvibrated and cracked, whilst the walls and floor of the chamber below would have shaken uncontrollably. The end result would have been the cessation of the Pyramid's sound, perhaps as early as 2350 BC (only two centuries after its construction, per the orthodox chronology). A sadly premature end for an ingenious but, let's face it, experimental work of architecture.

Now, this scenario is highly congenial, for it not only explains how the Pyramid lost its voice, and lost its voice long ago (hence the absence of 'singing' pyramid legends), but it also provides a very neat explanation for two other anomalous features in the Pyramid – the rough connecting tunnel in the Well Shaft (see chapter four) and the tunnel into the cavity above the King's Chamber's roof (see figure 107).

Figure 107.
THE KING'S CHAMBER AND ANTECHAMBER, SHOWING TUNNEL
INTO SUPERSTRUCTURE FROM THE TOP OF THE GRAND GALLERY.

How does it do this?

Well, the cessation of the sound would have impelled the guardians of the Pyramid to carry out an inspection of the King's Chamber, to see whether a repair to the system was possible. And this inspection would have required the digging of two tunnels, both of which may be seen to this day in the precise locations mentioned above. Firstly, the guardians would have dug the tunnel in the Well Shaft, to extend it to the bottom of the Grand Gallery. And secondly, having removed a small section of the Gallery's lower roof (above the Great Step), they would have constructed a ladder to the upper roof, and dug a tunnel there into the lowermost cavity in the King's Chamber superstructure. In this space, they could have viewed the condition of the King's Chamber's roof beams (here the floor stones) and the beams in the first roof overhead, at which point they would have realised that the damage was irreparable. Accordingly, they would have proceeded no further, but rather retraced their steps down the Well Shaft into the Descending Passage, and reinstalled the secret door there, taking the utmost care to cover their tracks.

That this scenario, or something like it, once occurred, is evidenced by the fact that both of the tunnels head precisely to their destinations, as if dug by someone who had intimate knowledge of the Pyramid's interior design. In the lower tunnel's case, it connects directly to an obscure vertical shaft beneath the Grand Gallery, whilst in the upper tunnel's case, it connects to the lowermost cavity via a dogleg route, using the limestone east wall to circumvent the granite north wall.[84] It can therefore be stated with cast iron certainty that these were no robbers' tunnels, but were rather dug by the Pyramid's guardians.

In which case, the question must be asked: what compelling reason did the guardians have to force their way into the heart of the Pyramid? What concern could have been so great that they would have jeopardised the future security of the monument by opening up a back door route (via the Well Shaft) into its upper compartments?

In this chapter, I believe, a plausible explanation has been given.

Chapter Seven Summary

- It has long been known that the King's Chamber and its sarcophagus possess exceptional resonant properties. In recent years, this has been confirmed by scientific tests and measurements, which suggest that the room was designed deliberately towards an acoustic end.

- The prime resonant frequency of the King's Chamber would appear to be very low, possibly 16 or 30 Hz.

- The theory that the King's Chamber was built to resonate to the voices of the priests does not explain the use of granite in the superstructure and the Antechamber. It is also inconsistent with the evidence that these chambers were sealed off when they were built.

- The purpose of the King's Chamber's multi-roofed superstructure is a mystery. The orthodox theory is unsound, whilst alternative theories have as yet failed to explain why the builders used 1,200 additional tons of granite beams. But several clues combine to suggest that this structure was built for an acoustic purpose.

- It is possible that Earth resonance caused the granite beams to vibrate, and it is furthermore possible that the beams were designed to create harmonics of the fundamental frequency, or frequencies. In this way, subaudible frequencies may have been raised to audible tones, which would have been amplified in the King's Chamber below.

- Why would the builders have wanted to generate sound in the King's Chamber? Only one answer suggests itself: the sound was intended to be broadcast to the outside world via the shafts. This theory offers a potential explanation for a number of curiosities in the design of the shafts.

- The broadcasting of low frequency sound from the King's Chamber would have had a powerful religious symbolism. Such sound would have re-enacted the voice of the creator-god, i.e. the noise of the proto-earth splitting apart. This theory is supported by the Pyramid Texts, and fits perfectly with the Pyramid's creational symbolism, especially if it is accepted that the sarcophagus enshrined the iron of creation.

- If this theory is correct, the King's Chamber would not have been a repository in the conventional sense; the intention would have been that the room remained sealed. The Antechamber, however, has the hallmarks of an initiation room for a single individual who, standing before the granite leaf, would have been induced to an altered state of consciousness by the low frequency vibrations. The purpose of this initiation would have been to grant the privileged individual a vision of the true God and the act of creation.

- The King's Chamber and the Antechamber sustained major structural damage in antiquity, seemingly the result of an exceptionally powerful earthquake. It is to be theorised that this caused a vibrational overload which wrecked the key components of the sound system; hence the lack of sound today. This disaster may have occurred as early as 2350 BC, thus accounting for the absence of 'singing' pyramid legends.

- The cessation of the Pyramid's sound might well have triggered an inspection of the monument by its guardians, to see whether a repair to the system was possible. This scenario would explain the rough tunnel in the Well Shaft and another rough tunnel that connects the Grand Gallery to the lowest cavity in the King's Chamber superstructure.

- The builders' knowledge of acoustics was not necessarily an advanced science, but more likely a working knowledge, gained by observations of nature and practical experimentation.

- This theory needs to be tested scientifically, for example by building a working scale model of the King's Chamber and Antechamber (the original architecture being too badly damaged). It must be emphasised, however, that the acoustic theory is a speculative idea, which is not to be regarded as critical to the wider theory proposed in this book.

CHAPTER EIGHT

THE PYRAMID PLUNDERED

The decoding of this civilisation requires of us some of that intimate knowledge claimed for the king – of how the world and in particular the heavens move – of a very different solar system.

(Stephen Quirke, *The Cult of Ra*, 2001)

It has often been said that the first person to enter the Pyramid's upper chambers, after they had been sealed, was the Arab ruler Abdullah al-Mamun in AD 820. According to Arab tradition, the caliph had journeyed to Egypt to seek secret knowledge pertaining to astronomy, geography, and alchemy, which had allegedly been hidden inside the pyramids and temples. Arriving at Giza with his team of workmen, al-Mamun had set his mind to opening the Great Pyramid, but had been unable to locate its original entrance.[1] He had thus forced an entrance into its northern face and instructed his workers to dig a tunnel. For weeks and weeks, his men had dug through the stone masonry, but all to no avail, when suddenly one day they heard a stone fall, suggesting a cavity ahead. Redoubling their efforts, they had pushed on in the direction of the noise, and broken through into a 'hollow way' – 'exceeding dark, dreadful to look at, and difficult to pass'.[2] From this chasm, the caliph had gained access to the Descending Passage, leading to the Subterranean Chamber, but had also discovered the upper rooms – the Grand Gallery, the Queen's Chamber and the King's Chamber – all of which he found to be empty, apart from a broken granite sarcophagus which itself contained nothing.

Had someone, before al-Mamun, discovered and plundered the upper chambers?

Significantly, the Arab account, in its many similar versions, places no obstacles in al-Mamun's path as he ascends into the upper reaches of the Pyramid. There is no mention of him breaking up the bridging slab to discover the Queen's Chamber. There is no mention of him breaking out the Grand Gallery's lower roof to discover the upper roof area. There is no mention of him forcing a way through the Antechamber to the King's Chamber. And, above all, there is no plausible mention of any artefacts in the Pyramid. It is as if al-Mamun found the upper chambers empty and bare – just as they appear to this day.

Egyptologists have indeed entertained doubts as to whether al-Mamun was the first person to discover the upper chambers, although they have differed in their theories as to who beat him to it, when, and how. Whilst William Flinders Petrie has suggested a surreptitious plundering of the chambers via the Well Shaft in ancient times,[3] other scholars have argued that the chambers were robbed via the so-called al-Mamun tunnel, which had been dug originally in ancient Egyptian times, and only re-excavated and enlarged by the Arab caliph.[4] The pyramid expert Mark Lehner thus writes:

> But just when the pyramid was violated remains a puzzle, though it is possible that it was in ancient times... Saite Period priests perhaps made repairs... and presumably any repairs would have been detectable. Mamun's men may have enlarged the passage made by ancient robbers.[5]

In support of this idea, Lehner highlighted the fact that the al-Mamun tunnel headed directly for the junction of the Descending and Ascending Passages, as shown in figure 108. This was an unlikely coincidence, and

Figure 108.
THE SO-CALLED AL-MAMUN TUNNEL AND CHASM.
Note the alignment of the tunnel entrance with the uppermost granite plug.

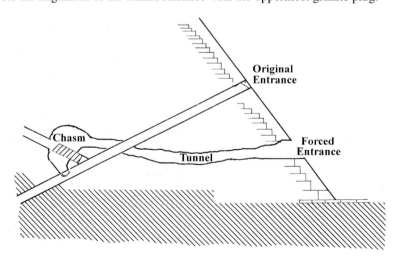

suggested that the tunnel had been dug not by al-Mamun but rather by someone with an intimate knowledge of the Pyramid's interior design.

Even so, questions remain. If the intruders had known the Pyramid's interior design, then why did they not use the original entrance and dig a much shorter tunnel to circumvent the granite plugs? By the same token, why would their tunnel have veered from south to south-east? In other words, why would they have breached the monument in the exact centre of the 6th course, rather than on the axis of the passages (offset to the east by 24 feet)? Had the tunnel been dug from the inside outwards, rather than from the outside inwards? If so, why did the tunnel bend, and was it just a coincidence that it exited in the exact centre of the 6th course? Might the tunnel constitute two tunnels, of separate origins, that had been joined together? Furthermore, if the tunnel was a means of plundering the upper chambers, why had a connecting tunnel been cut from the chasm into the Descending Passage?

These questions, unfortunately, still beg answers, largely because of the uncertainty surrounding one fundamental point. Were the Pyramid's upper chambers first discovered via the aforementioned tunnel, leading directly to the Ascending Passage? Or were they first discovered via the Well Shaft, leading up from the Descending Passage to the Grand Gallery? On this point, Egyptology has worked under the false premise that the Well Shaft tunnel was an evacuation route for workmen who had become trapped in the Gallery having sealed the Ascending Passage (see chapter four). This mistake clouds the issue considerably. But under the sealed repository theory, it becomes clear that the Well Shaft tunnel was dug upwards by someone intimately familiar with the Pyramid's design. And furthermore, it becomes clear that the same tunnellers dug above the King's Chamber in order to inspect the granite beams there that had been damaged by a powerful earthquake. The evidence would thus suggest that the tunnel in the Well Shaft was dug for inspection purposes by the guardians of the Pyramid.

In digging this inspection tunnel, however, the guardians created a back door entrance to the upper chambers, and almost certainly paved the way for the plundering of the Pyramid long before the days of Abdullah al-Mamun, probably as early as c. 2150-2000 BC (the First Intermediate Period).

In this chapter, I work up this scenario to offer a broad reconstruction of the events in which the sealed chambers were breached, before their due time, and stripped of their precious contents, which were broken up and removed via the mysterious tunnel that was described earlier – the one that al-Mamun re-excavated in AD 820.

Figure 109.
THE GREAT PYRAMID, VERTICAL SECTION, LOOKING WEST.
It is suggested that the first intruders gained access to the upper chambers via the
Well Shaft, and thereafter removed their booty via the tunnel in figure 108.

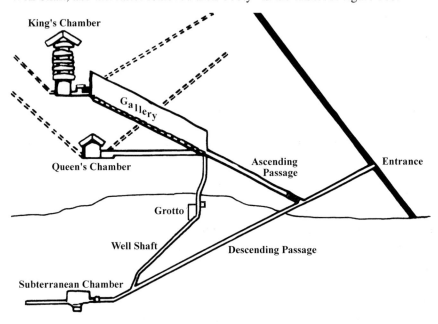

At the same time, I offer some theories as to what the intruders might
have found when they opened, for the first time, the upper passages and
chambers. Apart from the meteoritic iron in the King's Chamber, what
else was concealed behind the various false walls, floors and ceilings of
the Pyramid? Here, the reader may well form his own view, depending
on his assumption of who built the Pyramid, when, and why. My own
view, for the record, is based on the time capsule hypothesis, and on the
assumption that the Pyramid was built by an ancient Egyptian culture or
a precursor culture with religious beliefs virtually identical to those that
we know as ancient Egyptian. The student of the alternative school might
thus find my conclusions in this chapter a little trite. However, the best
revelations, more suited to their taste, are yet to come, and, if they are to
gain acceptance, require to be built on a solid and plausible foundation.

The Inspection Tunnels

Our starting point, as suggested in chapter seven, is an exceptionally
heavy earthquake which shook the Pyramid to its foundations, probably
towards the end of the Old Kingdom period, *c.* 2350 BC. This earthquake

Figure 110.
THE BEGINNING OF THE ASCENDING PASSAGE, BLOCKED BY THE
LOWERMOST GRANITE PLUG.
The undamaged plug suggests that the popular legend of al-Mamun's tunnelling
into the Pyramid is highly misleading.

inflicted serious damage upon the King's Chamber and its superstructure,
and led to the cessation (or perhaps initially distortion) of the sound that
emanated from its shafts. In response to this catastrophe, the guardians of
the Pyramid, possessing the blueprint of the monument, took the crucial
decision to enter its upper chambers, in order to inspect and, if possible,
repair the damage to the King's Chamber.

For the first time since its construction, the Grand Gallery would have
to be breached. But how would the breach be made?

As discussed in chapter four, the duty of the Pyramid's guardians was
to keep the secrets of the monument intact. It would have been with great
reluctance that they decided to breach its upper parts. Two options were
open to them. Firstly, they could have opened (or removed) the prism
stone in the Descending Passage, and dug through, or around, the three
granite plugs in the Ascending Passage (a distance of about 15 feet). This

might be termed 'the front door option'. Or, secondly, they could have
opened the secret door in the wall of the Descending Passage, climbed up
the Well Shaft, and dug a tunnel through the masonry (a distance of
about 35 feet), thus gaining access to the vertical shaft directly beneath
the Grand Gallery. This might be termed 'the back door option'.

In deciding between these two options, the guardians would have been
mindful of two concerns. Firstly, the extent to which the breach would
jeopardise the future security of the Pyramid. And, secondly, the amount
of work involved in making the breach. The first of these considerations
would undoubtedly have been paramount.

Which option did the guardians take?

Here, the archaeological evidence is clear. As regards the 'front door',
whilst the prism stone is missing, the granite plug immediately behind it
remains in place, and has not been tunnelled around (see figure 110). The
al-Mamun tunnel, contrary to the impression that is sometimes given,
connects to a point about 10 feet lower down the Descending Passage, as
shown earlier in figure 108.[6] This clumsy breach cannot be attributed to
the guardians, but must surely have another explanation, which will be
considered in due course. It can therefore be stated with confidence that
the guardians did not take the 'front door' option.

Instead, on the grounds of security, the guardians took the 'back door'
option (since it would have been easier to restore the secret door in the
passage wall than the prism stone in the passage ceiling). They climbed
up past the Grotto to the top of the old Well Shaft, dug a tunnel there for
a distance of 35 feet, and emerged in the Grand Gallery via the ramp
stone in its north-west corner. (As an aside, one wonders what happened
to the 140 cubic feet of material that they excavated; presumably it was
removed from the Pyramid, basket-load by basket-load.) The tunnel is
thus explained, and Smyth and Davidson are vindicated in their view that
the ramp stone had been blown apart from below (as evidenced by the
damage to the walls around the missing stone).

Thus did the guardians breach the Grand Gallery for the first time
since its construction. But the Gallery which they gazed upon would
have been different from the one that we see today. In particular, it had a
lower roof, fitted between the grooves that ran down the Gallery in its
east and west walls. The nature of this roof, which halved the height of
the Gallery as we know it, will be discussed in due course, but suffice to
say for now that it may have had a religious significance in addition to a
functional role.

The rest of the scenario is straightforward.

Having climbed the Gallery and reached the Great Step, the guardians

Figure 111.
THE MISSING RAMP STONE AT THE BOTTOM NORTH-WEST CORNER
OF THE GRAND GALLERY.
It is suggested that the first intruders gained access to the upper chambers via
this shaft and tunnel.

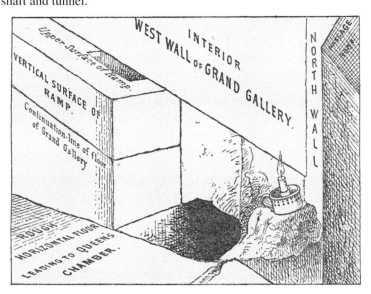

would have found the passage to the King's Chamber sealed (see chapter
six). Rather than breaking through here – causing irreparable damage to
the Antechamber and its passage – they would have inspected the King's
Chamber via its superstructure. To do this, they had no choice but to cut
a hole in the Gallery's lower roof, and climb to the heights of the upper
roof, directly above the Great Step. And the evidence that they did just
this, somewhat paradoxically, is the lack of rough chisel marks along the
two grooves above the Great Step (in contrast to the marks that span the
rest of their lengths). This is so because the guardians would have cut out
this roof panel carefully from below, whereas the rest of the roof would
have been chiselled out crudely by intruders, working from above.[7]

We may surmise that the guardians brought in wood and erected a
platform and a ladder to scale the heights of the Gallery above the Great
Step, whereupon they dug a tunnel through the wall to reach the lowest
of the cavities in the superstructure, directly above the roof of the King's
Chamber (see figure 107 in chapter seven). Again, this is consistent with
the archaeological evidence. A rough tunnel has indeed been cut through
the east wall at the top of the Gallery. It turns almost immediately and
heads south for a distance of about 24 feet, then turns back to the west,
and debouches into the hollow space that Egyptologists call Davison's

Chamber. In so doing, it avoids the granite wall on the northern side of the superstructure, and thereby testifies to an inside knowledge of the Pyramid's design.

Having surveyed the cracked and torn granite beams above the King's Chamber, the guardians would have quickly realised that the damage was irreparable. Dejected, they would have set about resealing the Pyramid and covering their tracks: they would have dismantled and removed their wooden platform and ladder; they would have restored, if they could, the panel cut out of the Gallery's lower roof; they would have repaired any damage to the Gallery's floor and walls; they would have moved the ramp stone back into position (a tricky task, working from below it); and, having descended the Well Shaft, they would have refitted the secret door (the stone slab) in the wall of the Descending Passage. This last mentioned task was of the utmost importance, for if the slab was not restored to a condition approaching the original, then the future security of the upper chambers would be jeopardised.

Another intriguing thought also occurs to this author. If it were the case that the king's body had been buried in the Grotto, as argued in chapter four, then the guardians may well have taken additional steps to secure that room and its contents. Conceivably, they might have walled over its entrance (i.e. the aperture, 28 inches square, in the vertical, built section of the Well Shaft). But it is also possible that they relocated the king's mummy. The latter question will be discussed further in chapter ten.

Thus was the Pyramid breached and resealed by the guardians, sadly to no avail. With the benefit of hindsight, it was almost certainly a fatal mistake.

The Intrusion Scenario: Phase One
The Grand Gallery

In my view, the guardians' breach of the Pyramid via the Well Shaft, possibly prompted by an earthquake *c.* 2350 BC (as discussed in chapter seven), led eventually to the discovery of that same route by an intruder, whose name and nature can only be the subject of speculation, although he might have gained his opportunity during Egypt's First Intermediate Period, *c.* 2150-2000 BC. This intrusion, it is to be surmised, led to the plundering of the treasure in the Pyramid's upper chambers, if not by this person then by others who followed. If the reader will indulge me, I shall outline a broad scenario for what happened, and venture some theories on what the intruders might have found.

The first intruder, according to my scenario, entered the Pyramid via its main door and began to explore the Descending Passage. Finding nothing of interest in the Subterranean Chamber, he began to examine the walls of the Descending Passage, inspired perhaps by rumours of a secret passage leading to upper chambers. Perhaps this person spotted a crack in the wall, or a cement repair to the secret door, or a scuff mark on the passage floor, or an indentation in the floor from an accidentally-dropped chisel. Whatever the clue, he discovered the secret entrance to the Well Shaft, made the steep climb past the Grotto, and became the first outsider to reach the heart of the Pyramid.

What we would give to see with our own eyes what the intruder saw with his, when he emerged into the Grand Gallery via that loosened and damaged ramp stone!

The first thing to be said is that this was not the Gallery as we know it, but rather, as mentioned earlier, a truncated version, roofed at a height of 14 feet. Figure 112 sets the scene, but otherwise reflects the present day Gallery, which is empty and bare.

Did the original Gallery contain any time capsule artefacts?

At the top of the hallway, the Great Step stands like a vacant plinth, as if it had been designed to support a statue of some kind. The thought has never occurred to Egyptologists, since their funeral scenario requires free access from the Gallery into the King's Chamber Passage. However, the sealed repository theory would suggest that a large statue was based here, guarding and protecting the concealed entrance to the Antechamber. It

Figure 112.
THE GRAND GALLERY, SHOWN FITTED WITH ITS ORIGINAL LOWER ROOF.
Compare figure 29 in chapter two.

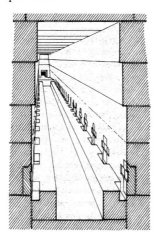

Figure 113.
THE GREAT STEP, SHOWN WITH THE GRAND GALLERY ROOFED AT
HALF HEIGHT.
The corbelling on all three walls may have influenced the shape of the statue
that once stood here.

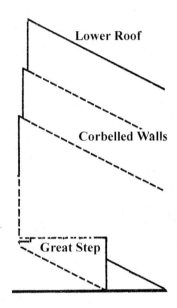

would not have been a statue of the king, but rather a statue of the Great
God, perhaps in his name of Khnum or Thoth, who were both associated
with the Pyramid.[8] It may have been anthropomorphic or theriomorphic,
or a hybrid of both. If so, we might speculate, on the basis of Egyptian
literature, that it had bones of silver, limbs of alabaster, flesh of gold or
electrum, hair of turquoise or lapis lazuli, eyes of rock crystal, the body
wrapped in a jewel-encrusted cloak, the head surmounted by a crown of
diamonds, rubies and sapphires.[9]

The size of the God's statue may be estimated from the gap between
the Great Step and the lower roof. Its maximum height would have been
about 14 feet; its maximum base size would have been 6 feet 10 inches
wide by 5 feet 2 inches deep; its shape may have been determined by the
effect of the corbelling, which narrows the width from 6 feet 10 inches to
5 feet 4 inches (at the height of the lower roof), and squeezes the depth
from 5 feet 2 inches to 4 feet 5 inches; in addition, the angle of the roof
restricts the height of the statue, at its front, to about 12 feet.

All in all, the size and position of the Great Step are very suggestive of
a statue plinth. From this vantage point, exactly on the Pyramid's central
east-west axis and fiftieth course, the Great God could have commanded

the height and gazed northwards, to survey the majestic architecture of the hallway below. Indeed, J.P. Lepre has observed that the Great Step was seemingly built for just such a purpose.[10]

But what exactly did the God's statue survey? And what exactly did the intruder perceive as he rested at the foot of this sacred artefact?

One key question pertains to the roof. Surprisingly, Egyptologists have given little thought to the composition or significance of this lower roof, but, as Lepre has pointed out, it was sufficiently valuable that thieves went to the trouble of chiselling it out. Lepre suggested that it consisted of 'cedar panels inlaid with gold', but he did not explain the significance of the panelled roof, nor why it had been fitted.[11]

According to the sealed repository theory, the lower roof was designed to seal off the upper part of the Gallery, for reasons that will be discussed shortly. But did it also have a religious significance? Perhaps so. In view of the likely presence of the divine statue upon the Great Step, it strikes me that the underside of the roof (let us assume it was made of wood) might well have been painted with stars, commemorating the creation of the sky (in the same way that the starry sky was painted on the underside of coffin lids and tomb chamber ceilings). In Egyptian religion, the stars were 'the gods', the followers of the Great God, who in the myth of creation had issued from his body and then been reunited with it for a joint spiritualisation in the sky. It would be fitting indeed if the Great God, seated upon the Great Step, surveyed his children, the starry gods,

Figure 114.
A SUGGESTED DESIGN FOR A LOWER ROOF PANEL IN THE GRAND GALLERY.

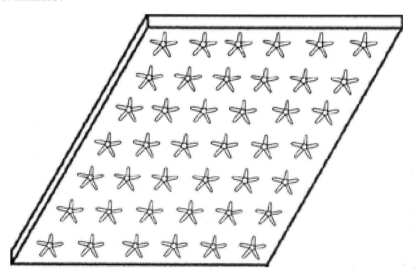

stretching up towards him like a ladder of the sky.

There is more. According to ancient Egyptian beliefs, the starry sky did not mark the outer limit of the Universe, but rather an aqueous veil *upon which the Great God rested*. This idea is exemplified by Spells 78 and 79 of the Coffin Texts, which recall the creation by Shu and the eight chaos-gods:

> I am the soul of Shu, for whom Nut was placed above and Geb under his feet... O you eight chaos-gods, whom Shu conceived, fashioned, created, knit together, begot from his efflux... (O you eight chaos-gods) whom Nun begot, whom Atum made, *whom Nut raised up under Atum, who guard the path of Nut which is under Atum...* Give me your hands, put together the ladder of Shu.[12]

> O you eight chaos-gods who went forth from Shu, whose names the flesh of Atum created, in accordance with the word of Nun in chaos, in the abyss, in darkness and gloom... we will make you according to the pattern of the word of Nun and Atum, for it was Re by means of whom Atum was on high within his realm; and I did not (yet) see Geb under my feet, for Shu was in his realm, Shu was in the abyss, when the earth-gods had not yet been knit together, when the celestial kine [the stars] of Atum had not yet come into being *so that he might come to rest upon them.*[13]

Could it be that the Gallery's lower roof symbolised the creation of the stars – forming, in effect, a kind of lower sky – and that its hidden upper area symbolised the realm of the Great God, who rested above the starry sky? It is an intriguing possibility, and would go some way to explaining the magnificent corbelled design of the Gallery, which in the opinion of Lepre may well have possessed 'a high spiritual symbolism'.[14]

What else might the intruder have seen in the original Gallery?

One of the greatest puzzles of the Gallery is the fifty-four rectangular niches, cut down into the side ramps next to the walls (see figure 112). In fifty out of fifty-four cases, these niches are adjacent to an inset stone, inserted into the wall, and fixed in place by inverted L-shaped grooves, filled with cement (the four exceptions are the two lowest niches on each ramp). Even more mysteriously, these inset stones, in forty-eight out of fifty cases, are marked by transverse, rectangular, shallow incisions.

What was the purpose of this peculiar design? Might the niches, now empty, have once held time capsule artefacts?

Egyptology has offered a number of theories for this arrangement of niches and inset stones, all of which involve, in one way or another, the granite plugs which were lowered from the Gallery into the Ascending

Passage.

Ludwig Borchardt suggested that the Gallery's lower roof was, in fact, a wooden platform upon which the granite plugs were stored (in order that they did not impede the funeral cortege). In his scheme, the fifty-four rectangular niches were used as anchor points for upright wooden posts that supported this platform. But Borchardt's theory has attracted widespread and justified criticism; in particular, it is not clear how the plugs could have been lowered from the platform to the floor.[15] And as for the idea that the niches contained upright wooden posts to support the platform, this theory too looks highly suspect. For one thing, the niches are overhung by corbelled walls, and thus lie off the perpendicular of the platform. And for another thing, the platform would have been supported quite adequately in its grooves, without any need of further support from below.

J-P. Lauer proposed a modified version of Borchardt's theory. In his scheme, the niches again contained upright wooden poles, but these were used, in conjunction with ropes, to haul surplus plugs to the top of the Gallery for use in constructing the chambers there.[16] But this theory too is highly unlikely, for if the builders had wanted to move granite blocks to the higher level, there would have been other, less complicated ways of doing it.

At this point, the orthodox camp runs out of ideas for the niches. There is a general presumption that they housed wooden poles, but no-one has been able to explain why the poles were needed.

What about the inset stones? Here, there is more of a consensus. The popular idea is that the walls once contained sockets, designed to receive the ends of wooden beams that were laid across the Gallery to hold the plugs in place, i.e. to prevent them from slipping prematurely down the Gallery's smooth floor. Both I.E.S. Edwards and Mark Lehner have lent their support to this theory, which was originally proposed by Georges Goyon in the 1940s.[17] The suggested arrangement is shown in figure 115 overleaf.

At first sight, this theory seems plausible, the positioning of the filled-in wall sockets being consistent with an average plug length of just under 6 feet. A major problem, however, arises from the fact that the sockets run the entire length of the Gallery. Was its floor once filled with plugs? Unfortunately, there is no evidence for the existence of more than three plugs (those which remain trapped in the Ascending Passage to this day), nor is there any trace of the supposed wooden beams. For these reasons, some Egyptologists are sceptical about this theory.[18]

Has alternative Egyptology come up with any better ideas? Of all the

Figure 115.
GOYON'S THEORY FOR THE SOCKETS IN THE WALLS OF THE
GRAND GALLERY.
The sockets were afterwards filled in by the 'inset stones'.

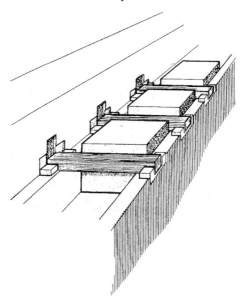

proposals, which generally verge from the sublime to the ridiculous, the most plausible is that the Gallery was once used to observe the transit of stars across the meridian, and that the ramp niches and wall sockets were used in some way or other to facilitate these observations of the skies (Proctor, 1883).[19] It is an intriguing theory, but it must be pointed out that such observation would have been curtailed early on by the fitting of the lower roof. Why, if the builders had intended to use the Gallery as an observatory, would they have fitted this roof? Advocates of this theory are no doubt capable of responding to this challenge, but, even so, their presumptions about the ramp niches and wall sockets must be regarded as highly speculative.

A number of further possibilities have occurred to this author.

As regards the ramp niches, I wondered whether they may have been been used as anchor points for a step ladder, which was slotted into four niches at a time as it was moved up the Gallery, from bottom to top. The most likely purpose for such a movable step ladder would have been to create a temporary working platform for artists who had been tasked with painting the underside of the lower roof, perhaps with stars as suggested earlier (an argument may be mounted that this task had to be performed inside the Pyramid to ritually re-enact the creation). Unfortunately, this theory is weakened by the fact that the ramp niches are overhung by the corbelled walls, as explained earlier. This would tend to suggest that the niches have no connection with the lower roof.

As regards the wall sockets, it occurs to me that these may have been cut to receive protrusions from the ramp stones, the builder having made a mistake or changed his mind about a further layer of stones on top of the ramps. (A precedent for this idea is found in the sockets cut for the bridging slab at the bottom of the Gallery.) This mistake having been realised, the builder may well have decided to retain the miscut stones, but fill in the sockets and restore the wall to its intended condition. This would explain the inset stones as well as the extraordinary effort taken to fix those stones into the wall by means of inverted L-shaped grooves filled with cement (according to Lepre, this cement was of the same type as that used to join the Pyramid's casing stones).[20] I am not yet able to explain why the faces of the inset stones were marked with incisions. But this theory nevertheless, cannot be disregarded, the potential implication being that the inset stones have nothing to do with the niches.

A crucial question in this regard, which has largely been ignored by Egyptology, is why the builders went to such lengths to fill in the wall sockets, whilst leaving the ramp niches empty.[21] If both sets of holes had fulfilled a practical purpose, then surely both would have been plugged, making the walls and ramps equally smooth. And yet, this is not the case. Why? One possible explanation is that the builders were working to strict deadlines and simply ran out of time, or forgot to complete the task. However, this scenario seems unlikely in view of the probable religious significance of the Gallery. This leaves us, I think, with only one other explanation: that the niches in the ramps were a finished element of the Pyramid's design.

So, might the fifty-four rectangular niches have been designed to hold time capsule artefacts?

At first, I resisted this idea. Intuitively, it seemed to me that the niches were just humble holes, which had some mundane but elusive practical purpose. But was I falling into the trap of interpreting the niches from a modern, materialistic point of view?

Earlier, I suggested that the Great Step had been a plinth for the statue of the Great God; we might well call it his 'Great Seat'.[22] Furthermore, I suggested that the Gallery had once been traversed, at half of its present height, by a wooden roof, its underside painted with stars – the images of the gods. In this context, then, why not suppose that the ramp niches held religious relics, or cult objects, of the gods – the followers of the Great God?

The number of niches is consistent with this hypothesis. In Egyptian religion, the oldest tradition identifies the collectivity of the gods with the number nine, the origin of the so-called ennead (*psdt*, or *pesdjet*).[23] In keeping with this, each ramp is fitted with twenty-seven niches, i.e. three times nine (the situation is confused, unfortunately, by two further niches upon the Great Step, making fifty-six niches in total).[24]

But, assuming that this was indeed the intention, what kind of relics would the niches have held?

A possible answer to this question is provided by the creation myth of Ptah, inscribed on the Shabaka Stone *c.* 700 BC, but undoubtedly drawing upon an Old Kingdom original. In the text, which scholars have entitled *The Theology of Memphis*, Ptah appears as 'the father of the gods', who in his name of Ta-tanen, 'risen earth', 'brought forth the gods'.[25] These gods, born as spirits, were then made to enter into every kind of material on the earth, prior to reuniting with their father:

> So the gods entered into their bodies of every kind of wood, of every kind of stone, of every kind of clay, or anything that might grow upon him, in which they had taken form. So all the gods, as well as their *kau*, gathered themselves to him, content and associated with the Lord of the Two Lands.[26]

Could it be possible that the gods, in these forms, were gathered together in the Gallery's niches, beneath the statue of their father, the Great God? In other words, were they present in twenty-seven, or fifty-four, varieties of wood and minerals?

At first, I was inclined to reject this proposition, since the Pyramid is not a symbol of the earth, to which this text seemingly relates. However, in the Egyptian creation myth, everything has a spiritual double, and the rising earth is, in effect, spiritualised in the sky – hence the idea of the spiritualised iron (see chapter five). It is therefore quite conceivable that the niches might have contained twenty-seven, or fifty-four, varieties of spiritualised wood and minerals. By this term, I mean terrestrial materials that have been spiritualised by ritual magic. In support of this hypothesis, in the passage cited above, the gods assemble in the presence of God, their father, not just in their physical forms but in their *kau*, or spiritual forms (*ka*, singular, meant 'spiritual energy' or 'spiritual double').

I therefore conclude, against my initial judgement, that the fifty-four rectangular niches might well have contained relics of the gods in the forms of sanctified woods and minerals, representing the materials of the creation.[27] (The status of the additional two niches on the Great Step remains unclear.) On the sizes of the niches, and hence the base sizes of the hypothesised artefacts, the reader is referred back to chapter two.

In summary, I believe that the Grand Gallery was a simulacrum of the creation, with the Great God, risen on the height, surveying the panoply of his children, the gods or stars, who are captured in their ascent to the sky. The unusual corbelled structure, it is to be surmised, signified to the builders the spiritual power of God, perhaps viewed from a mathematical or geometrical perspective. The anomaly of the lower roof, dividing this corbelled space, may have reflected the builders' belief that the true realm of God lay above and beyond the visible starry sky – an idea that is attested in ancient Egyptian literature of all periods.

Furthermore, I conclude that several artefacts have been removed from the Gallery: a statue of the Great God, a wooden, star-spangled roof, and, more speculatively, a set of fifty-four divine relics, possibly representing diverse materials of the natural world. This plundering scenario will be examined in due course, when we return to the subject of the al-Mamun tunnel. Suffice to say for now, though, that the great statue was too large to have been removed intact, and would have had to be broken up, or cut into pieces, by the robbers.[28]

The Intrusion Scenario: Phase Two
The Upper Gallery and the Queen's Chamber

The first intruder to see the Grand Gallery may not necessarily have been the one who removed the artefacts. But he may well have been the one who made the initial important discoveries. To this end, he was assisted almost certainly by the guardians of the Pyramid, who had exposed the presence of two further chambers. One of these was the upper Gallery, exposed by the removal of the lower roof panel, directly above the Great Step; it is to be surmised that this wooden panel could not be restored well, and thus drew the attention of the intruder, who climbed up above the Great Step and pushed it aside. The other chamber was the Queen's Chamber, or rather its entrance passage, which lay beneath the bridging slab at the bottom of the Gallery. This slab would have been exposed at its bottom, north-western edge when the guardians broke out the ramp stone, and it would thus have been apparent to the intruder that the slab spanned a horizontal floor (this is seen clearly in figure 111); moreover, an inspection of its joints would have revealed its unusual length. Having already discovered the 'false roof' of the Gallery, he might well have guessed that the slab was a 'false floor'. And so we have a scenario in which the intruder would have been led by the guardians' trail to two further discoveries.

As regards the upper part of the Grand Gallery, what did the intruder see when he pushed aside the panel in the lower roof?

Unaccustomed as we are to view the Gallery's upper area as a separate chamber, we must attempt to visualise it thus. What was its shape and size? Well, it was a sloping, corbelled vault about 153 feet long, with a height (from lower roof to upper roof) of about 14 feet, and a width of 6 feet, narrowing to 3 feet 6 inches. This is an unusual space, to say the least, and presents us with a puzzle. What, if anything, could this cavity have contained?

One possibility that occurred to this author was a boat – the barque of the Great God – perhaps a fully assembled version of the wooden boat that was buried on the south side of the Pyramid.[29] However, whilst the length and height of the buried boat are consistent with the dimensions of the cavity, its width, unfortunately, is three times too great. Therefore, unless we are to hypothesise an extremely narrow longboat, this idea must be rejected.

In the absence of any other ideas (suggestions please), I am inclined to think that nothing at all was hidden in this space, for the reason that the

Figure 116.
THE WOODEN BOAT (RECONSTRUCTED) THAT WAS BURIED ON THE SOUTH SIDE OF THE GREAT PYRAMID.

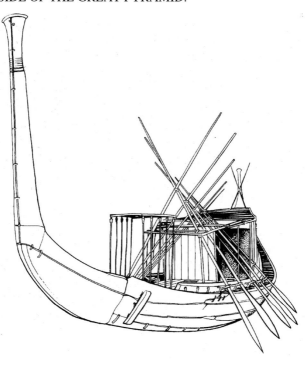

upper area was designed as a buffer zone. The meaning of this term, in the context of the sealed repository theory, will be explained in chapter ten.

Turning to the Queen's Chamber Passage, what did the intruder find when he broke up the bridging slab? For an initial distance of 109 feet, probably nothing. But at this point, 18 feet short of the Queen's Chamber entrance, the floor of the passage drops by 23 inches, for no reason that has ever been explained. Now, as discussed in chapter six, the entrance to the Queen's Chamber was probably sealed off by a camouflaging plate of stone; thus the intruder would have found himself in a blind passage, culminating in a rectangular hallway, 5 feet 8 inches high, 3 feet 5 inches wide, and 18 feet long.

Figure 117.
THE QUEEN'S CHAMBER PASSAGE, SHOWN PRIOR TO THE DISCOVERY OF THE QUEEN'S CHAMBER.

What, if anything, was contained by this rectangular space? Perhaps a granite plug that held out the promise of a chamber beyond. Or perhaps some kind of artefact, placed here as a decoy to counter the thought that a chamber might lie beyond.

Undeterred, the intruder cleared the Passage of its obstruction, broke through the pilaster of stone, and became the first person to enter the Queen's Chamber.

What did he see there? One possibility is that the chamber contained a sarcophagus. The Arab writer Edrisi in his *History of the Pyramids* (*c.* AD 1236) describes the Queen's Chamber Passage and states: 'By this door, or opening, a square room is entered with an empty vessel in it'. Later in his account, he describes the King's Chamber and states: 'An empty vessel is seen here similar to the former.'[30] This report is mentioned by William Flinders Petrie, who found Edrisi's account of the Pyramid to be otherwise 'accurate and observant'. In Petrie's opinion, a sarcophagus might well have been housed in the Queen's Chamber, only to be broken up and removed at some time between the 13th and 19th centuries.[31] J.P. Lepre also supports the possibility of a sarcophagus here, adding that, in his opinion, it would have been made of limestone:

As the King's Chamber, being fashioned from granite, contained a granite sarcophagus, so the Queen's Chamber, being fashioned from limestone, may have housed a limestone sarcophagus. A limestone sarcophagus, being much softer than a granite one, could easily have met with destruction at the hands of despoilers.[32]

The majority of Egyptologists would not share Lepre's view, since their serdab theory of the Queen's Chamber does not allow for the possibility of a sarcophagus. However, in the light of the sealed repository theory, a sarcophagus does become a serious possibility. As for its contents, we can only guess. If it was made of limestone rather than granite, as Lepre suggests, then symbolism might preclude the idea of the meteorite. We might instead look for something with feminine rather than masculine characteristics – perhaps a relic of the Great Goddess who personified the celestial ocean.[33]

Having said that, it is strange that Edrisi's report is not corroborated by earlier Arab writers. Perhaps he visited too many pyramids in the heat of the Sun, and got confused in writing up his notes. The idea of the Queen's Chamber sarcophagus must therefore be treated with all due caution.

Let us turn, then, to the focal point of the Queen's Chamber – the huge corbelled niche, let into the east wall. What did this huge cavity, 15 feet 4 inches high, contain?

According to Egyptologists, this niche contained the *ka*-statue of the king, i.e. the statue possessed of the king's spirit. However, as discussed in chapter three, there are serious problems with this idea. In particular, the concept of the *ka*-statue belonged to the realm of the body – the tomb and the underworld – whereas the Pyramid signified the exact opposite idea – the realm of the ascended spirit. The *ka*-statue theory thus depends on the view that the Pyramid *in its entirety* was a tomb – a view that this author, for one, does not share.

What else might the niche have contained? Here, we run up against a problem, namely the fact that its corbelled design is unique. Nothing like it is found in any other pyramid, tomb, nor temple of ancient Egypt, the closest parallel to it being the corbelled architecture in the Grand Gallery of the Great Pyramid itself. We therefore have little to go on, and must inevitably speculate, albeit with more circumspection than Egyptologists have displayed to date.

The most obvious solution is, ironically, a statue, although not of the kind that Egyptologists have envisaged. Instead, the likelihood is that the niche contained a statue of the Great God, or perhaps, more plausibly, a statue of the Great Goddess (for we must not forget that ancient Egyptian religion was ostensibly a duotheism).[34]

But what form would this statue of the Great Goddess have taken?

Figure 118.
THE NICHE IN THE EAST WALL OF THE QUEEN'S CHAMBER.

Although we are accustomed to think of a statue in anthropomorphic, theriomorphic, or hybrid form, the unusual corbelled shape of the niche impels us to consider another possibility.

In ancient Egypt, all popular representations of the gods and goddesses used symbols to provide insights into the mystery of the creation, without ever revealing the true essence of that mystery. Thus a statue or depiction of the Great God might emphasise one or more of his vital attributes: his fertility, his high flight, his speed, his authority, his immortality, his gift of craftsmanship to man; and thus it would celebrate the splendour of his creative act. But these 'outer truths' were but signposts to an 'inner truth' which the representation did not reveal. Who was the Great God? How did he create the Universe? Behind the outward symbolism, there lay a great secret that was known only to the initiated – probably the king and the high priest. The secret was this: the Great God personified the idea of a spiritual metamorphosis and a global cataclysm, which had occurred at the beginning of time. The Great Goddess likewise. The true form of the

God and the Goddess was thus spiritual, intangible, profound, ineffable, and mysterious. Whilst it is not incorrect to say that the God's true form personified the creation of the Universe, this would be misleading, for the deity was, in fact, not a person but an abstract idea.

Egyptologists do have some grasp of this principle, even if they do not understand the consequences of it. The eminent scholar Erik Hornung, for example, in commenting on the outward forms of the Great God and the Great Goddess, emphasised that their true nature was unknowable:

> But none of these animals, plants, and objects that are related to the manifestation of deities gives any information about the true form of a deity. According to the texts, the true form is 'hidden' and 'mysterious'; the Coffin Texts tell us that only the deceased may know the true form of a god. No thinking Egyptian would have imagined that the true form of Amun was a man with a ram's head...[35]

Indeed. Amun was the creator-god, and the ram a symbol of his fertility.

So, might the corbelled niche in the Queen's Chamber have housed a unique type of statue, not the usual anthropomorphic, theriomorphic, or hybrid image, but rather a geometric form, symbolising the abstract idea of creation? Might the corbelled cavity have contained a solid, five-tiered sacred stone, representing the Great Goddess, the feminine principle of the creation? Perhaps a sculpted piece of lapis lazuli, its deep blue colour signifying the unfathomable ocean of the sky?

This idea might strike the reader as far-fetched. However, there is a precedent for it, of sorts, in the fact that the Great God was symbolised by the pyramidal form (hence the identity between the god, the king, and the pyramid). As explained in the companion volume to this book, the true pyramids of Egypt were not built to a single pattern, but utilised various angles of slope, each embodying a mathematical principle. Now, these variations were almost certainly complementary, for the Egyptians took a multifaceted approach to their basic truths, as Henri Frankfort has argued so well.[36] It is therefore possible that the true pyramids, one and all, conveyed a single, consistent, and extraordinary idea: that God, in essence, was pure geometry and mathematics.

It follows, by the same principle, that a five-tiered stone could have symbolised the Great Goddess, and encoded in its geometry the mystery of her essence.

Is this the key to the mystery of the Queen's Chamber? Was a sacred stone hidden in this room to save it from the prophesied cataclysm? Was it designed to test the mettle of its discoverer, prompting him to study its geometrical and mathematical properties, and thereby rediscover the sacred science of the creation?

Whilst the idea is admittedly speculative, it is nevertheless consistent with my earlier suggestion (after Lepre) that the corbelled design of the Grand Gallery had a 'high spiritual symbolism'. Furthermore, one cannot help but wonder whether a similar tiered, geometrical stone might have stood upon the Great Step as a representation of the Great God. In other words, the Pyramid may have contained a pair of these strange artefacts, one representing the Great God, facing due north, and the other the Great Goddess, facing due west. (Incidentally, it is worth noting that these two statues would have overlapped each other on the same vertical axis, since the Great Step lies roughly above the Queen's Chamber niche.)[37] It would be well worthwhile investigating the corbelled designs of the Gallery and the Queen's Chamber niche to test whether they contain a mathematical basis that might yield insights into the spiritual wisdom of the builders. The approximate dimensions of the corbelled cavities are provided in chapter two, although the reader would be well advised to obtain more accurate measurements.

Finally, in the Queen's Chamber, it is likely that the discoverer walked upon a marvellous floor that was destined to be torn up and removed by later intruders; hence the rough appearance of the floor today. Lepre is of the view that the original floor slabs were 'finely cut limestone blocks', similar to those which made up the walls.[38] However, if this were so, it is curious that the intruders would have gone to the trouble of removing the slabs. Rather, it seems likely that the floor consisted of a more precious material, perhaps marble or alabaster. If there was a sarcophagus in the Queen's Chamber (see earlier comments), then it too would have been made of this more precious material, rather than limestone.

Incidentally, if Edrisi's account of the sarcophagus is to be believed, then both the sarcophagus *and the floor slabs* would have remained in the Queen's Chamber until as late as the 13th century. The niche artefact, however, would have been stolen by intruders during ancient Egyptian times. In its case, its size required that it be cut into pieces, in order that it be removed through the narrow passage.

The Intrusion Scenario: Phase Three
The King's Chamber

The discovery of the Queen's Chamber led, in time, to the discovery of the King's Chamber. Logic dictated that if a chamber was concealed behind a plate of stone at the southern extremity of the Queen's Chamber Passage, then a similar chamber might exist at the southern extremity of

Figure 119.
THE GREAT STEP AND ENTRANCE TO THE KING'S CHAMBER
PASSAGE.
The damage to the Great Step may have been caused by the removal of a statue.

the Grand Gallery, i.e. on the Great Step, behind the statue of the Great God.[39] Whether this thought occurred to the first intruder or a subsequent person cannot be known. The only thing that can be said with certainty is that the object on the Great Step must first have been forcibly removed in order that the plate of stone behind it be examined (although it is possible that a small gap at the statue's rear permitted a visible inspection). The damage inflicted upon both the Great Step and the mouth of the King's Chamber Passage can be seen clearly in figure 119. (Incidentally, I am not aware of any other theory, be it orthodox or alternative, that offers an explanation for this damage.)

Having smashed through the plate of stone, the intruder entered the passage and emerged in the Antechamber, where he stood upright before the granite leaf. Here, trapped radon gas may have had an affect on him, but the days of the low frequency resonance had long gone. The intruder

Figure 120.
THE SOUTH WALL OF THE ANTECHAMBER, SHOWING DAMAGE TO
THE CONTINUATION OF THE KING'S CHAMBER PASSAGE.

was thus able to climb up over the granite leaf and crawl across the tops
of the granite slabs as far as the wall with the unusual grooves. From this
vantage point, he was able to force his way past the third granite slab and
enter the continuation of the King's Chamber Passage (hence the damage
to the mouth of the passage in figure 120).

Moments later, the intruder became the first person to enter the King's
Chamber. A sacrilege perhaps. But what did he see there?

Probably nothing but the granite sarcophagus, which was at that time
sealed by its lid. Although Egyptologists have visualised the chamber as
being full of funerary furniture, this seems unlikely, even if the orthodox
theory is accepted, for the shafts would have conveyed air into the room,
ensuring the corrosion of any unprotected contents. But in any case, the
chamber was not a burial place for a king; rather, it was a shrine to the
creator-god – to his spirit and his seed.

The same intruder, having come this far, would have forced the lid off the granite sarcophagus (no easy task), in the process breaking the box at one of its top corners, and feasted his eyes on the Pyramid's most sacred relics – the iron meteorites that signified the seed of creation. This would not necessarily have been a disappointment, for there was a ready market for meteorites in ancient times, either for religious or secular purposes (in the latter case, the iron could have been smelted and used to manufacture weapons or tools). The King's Chamber meteorites would have fetched a tidy sum.

There is little more to be said about the King's Chamber at this stage. The only curiosity is an excavation in the north-west corner of the floor (repaired in 1999), which is attributed to al-Mamun but may have been dug by an earlier intruder. Was the sarcophagus originally placed here? It is certainly conceivable that someone moved the coffer in order to search for a secret passage beneath it;[40] otherwise, it is difficult to imagine why an intruder would have excavated in this spot.

As a result of the successful exploration behind the statue on the Great Step, the intruder would have been minded to return to the statue niche in the Queen's Chamber. Did it, too, guard a camouflaged passage? Such may have been the reasoning that led to the excavation of a rough tunnel at the back of the niche, which today extends to a depth of about 38 feet and culminates in a bulb-shaped cavern. Did the intruder find a secret passage, as some alternative theorists have suggested?[41] Perhaps so. But we will never know for sure.

The Removal of the Artefacts

Such is my scenario for the discovery of the Pyramid's upper chambers, and such are my theories for their contents. But how exactly was the monument plundered? In other words, how did the intruders remove their booty from the Pyramid? The list of artefacts is a long one:

- Statue of the Great God
  - Position: Great Step, Grand Gallery.
  - Size: 12-14 feet high; up to 6 feet 10 inches wide at the bottom, narrowing to 5 feet 4 inches at the top; up to 5 feet 2 inches thick.

- Painted wooden roof panels (quantity: 25?)
  - Position: Grand Gallery lower roof.
  - Size: 6 feet long (est.); 5 feet 4 inches wide; 7 inches thick.

- Relics of the gods (quantity: 54)
  – Position: Grand Gallery niches.
  – Size: height unknown; 20-23 inches long; 6 inches wide.

- Statue of the Great Goddess
  – Position: Queen's Chamber niche.
  – Size: 15 feet 4 inches high; 5 feet 2 inches wide at the bottom, narrowing to 20 inches at the top; at least 3 feet 5 inches thick.

- Floor slabs (quantity unknown)
  – Position: Queen's Chamber floor.
  – Size: unknown.

- Iron meteorites (quantity unknown)
  – Position: inside King's Chamber sarcophagus.
  – Size: unknown, but limited by the dimensions of the box.

- Granite sarcophagus lid
  – Position: King's Chamber sarcophagus.
  – Size: 7 feet 6 inches long; 3 feet 3 inches wide; 10-12 inches thick.

Missing from this list of removed artefacts is the granite sarcophagus of the King's Chamber, the dimensions of which exceeded the width of the Ascending Passage at its bottom (hence the fact that it has remained in the chamber to this day); a sarcophagus of the Queen's Chamber, which may, or may not, have existed; and the granite slabs of the Antechamber, which may have been removed as obstacles rather than booty.

Now, in order to remove these artefacts from the Pyramid, the intruder had to cope with the narrowness of the passages, which required that the two divine statues be cut into manageable pieces. (Egyptologists would agree that this was the fate of the niche statue.) The size of the pieces is a matter of conjecture.

How did the intruder remove these whole and dismembered artefacts from the Pyramid. The obvious route was back the way he came, down the Well Shaft and up the Descending Passage. However, this was a long path, a steep path, and a narrow path (the size of the Well Shaft is only 28 inches square) – not at all suitable for the removal of large and heavy objects. The sarcophagus lid, in particular, could not have been removed by this route, whilst the roof panels would have had to be cut down in size.

Instead, the intruder would have contemplated the Ascending Passage, which was still, at this stage, sealed by the granite plugs. This passage was much larger than the Well Shaft, with an average size of 4 feet by 3 feet 6 inches, and it evidently ran in the right direction, downwards and

northwards, towards the main entrance. Was it feasible to connect the
Ascending Passage to the Descending Passage and remove the booty this
way? If so, both the sarcophagus lid and the roof panels could be turned
diagonally and removed intact, whilst the statue material could be freed
in much larger and more valuable chunks.

In view of the obvious benefits of removing the booty in this way, it is
logical to surmise that the intruder took an axe to the uppermost granite
plug in an attempt to clear the passage. This would explain the damage to
the top of this plug, which is visible in figure 121. Now, according to
Egyptologists, it was al-Mamun, working inwards, who broke this plug.
But this makes no sense, for why would the caliph have turned towards
the hard granite as opposed to continuing his tunnel (i.e. the one that is
attributed to him) through the softer limestone? Rather, it seems more
likely that the uppermost plug was excavated from above.

Figure 121.
THE GRANITE PLUGS, SEEN FROM THE CHASM OF THE ROBBER'S
TUNNEL.
Why would the uppermost granite plug be broken?

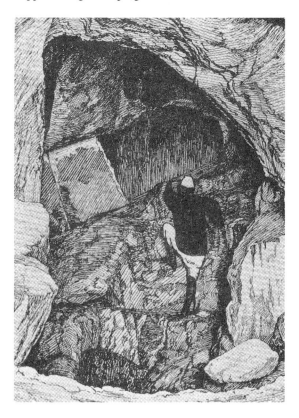

And yet, if the granite plug was assaulted from above, the workman responsible abandoned his arduous task after just a few feet. Why?

A likely explanation is that the work took too long, since only one man at a time could work on the face of the granite. The intruder would thus have grown impatient and anxious, lest the guardians of the Pyramid alert the Egyptian army to the terrible desecration of their country's most prestigious monument.

What happened next? In my view, the intruder would have pressurised the guardians, under threat of death, to reveal the length of the granite plugs and the position of the junction with the Descending Passage (i.e. the location of the prism stone). The guardians, however, realising that the plundering was now unavoidable and mindful of the Pyramid's future security, would have offered instead to dig a horizontal tunnel into the north face of the monument to intersect directly with the uppermost plug. By co-operating thus, they would have avoided any serious damage to the Descending Passage, so that the upper parts of the monument could be resealed afterwards in the most effective way. To the intruder, such a suggestion would have been a godsend.

Thus the guardians, possessing the blueprint of the Pyramid, drove a tunnel into the 6th course of masonry at the exact level of the uppermost plug, as shown in figure 108 (note: it was easier to work from the outside inward rather than from the inside outward, owing to the constant supply of fresh air, and the ease of removing the excavated debris). Crucially, the guardians began this tunnel in the exact centre of the monument's northern face, so as not to give away the true axis of its main entrance and passage system (which was offset to the east by 24 feet). The tunnel thus heads due south for about 100 feet before veering south-eastwards for the last 20 feet. But, curiously, it drifts downwards, missing its target by about six feet, perhaps because the digging was hurried. This resulted in the tall chasm, shown in figure 121, in which a series of steps lead up from the tunnel to the gap above the plugs in the Ascending Passage.

Thus did the intruder acquire a highly convenient exit route from the Pyramid. He could lower the plundered artefacts down the Ascending Passage, manoeuvre them into the tunnel, carry them 120 feet to the face of the monument, and then drop them to the ground, about 20 feet below (see figure 108). In this way, even the heaviest objects could be removed with ease, even the lid of the sarcophagus which weighed around 2.25 tons.

In summary, I believe that the mystery of the al-Mamun tunnel can be solved by supposing an intrusion into the upper chambers via the Well Shaft and the plundering of the Pyramid via the Ascending Passage and horizontal tunnel, crucially with the co-operation of the local guardians, whose interests were best served ultimately by directing the tunnelling. The al-Mamun tunnel was thus dug not to gain access into the Pyramid, but rather to remove artefacts from the Pyramid, and was dug not by al-Mamun in AD 820, but rather by an ancient intruder, perhaps as early as *c.* 2000 BC.

After the plunderers had departed, the guardians would have attempted to restore the damage. Working from the top, they would have removed all the debris from the King's Chamber, Antechamber, Grand Gallery, and Queen's Chamber; they would have refitted the ramp stone at the bottom of the Gallery; and they would have reinserted the camouflaging stone in the wall of the Descending Passage. Finally, they would have packed the 120-feet-long tunnel with masonry and refurbished the casing stone at its entrance, to remove all evidence of the tunnel's existence. In future, the Pyramid would be entered via its main door and Descending Passage, in which, significantly, the prism stone still remained intact.

Once more, then, the upper chambers were secure. Did they still have a secret to hide?

For the next two thousand years, the Pyramid would have remained unviolated, with the exception of occasional sorties into the Subterranean Chamber. There is evidence that Greek and Roman travellers descended into the depths of the monument, apparently in blissful ignorance of its upper chambers.[42] At this point in history, the prism stone remained fitted in the roof of the Descending Passage.

Then, in the 9th century AD, al-Mamun arrived in Egypt, and, failing to locate the Pyramid's main entrance, *re-excavated* the plunderer's tunnel that had been filled in thousands of years earlier. What happened next can be reconstructed. Contrary to the popular legend, al-Mamun did not hear *the prism stone* fall. But perhaps he heard *a stone* fall. He broke through to the ancient chasm opposite the uppermost plug, climbed up the hole into the Ascending Passage, and thereupon *rediscovered* the upper chambers, which had long ago been emptied of their most precious contents. Next, it may be surmised, al-Mamun discovered the loose ramp stone and sent one of his men down the Well Shaft. This man promptly broke open the camouflaging stone in the wall, and thus, by a roundabout route, located the Descending Passage and the original entrance to the Pyramid.

And so we come to the final mysteries of the al-Mamun tunnel. Who dug the short passage into the west wall of the Descending Passage, just beneath the plugs? (This rough passage can be seen in the bottom, left-hand corner of figure 121.) Why was this passage dug? And how did the prism stone come to fall from its place?

The answer, surely, lies in al-Mamun's curiosity. Having surveyed the Pyramid and calculated the proximity of the Ascending and Descending Passages, he wondered about the granite plug (singular, since he could see only the uppermost one). Did it conceal a secret cavity? In order to find out, he had one team of men cut downwards along its length, whilst another team went round to the Descending Passage and searched for the lower entrance to the plug cavity. The first team revealed a second plug; then a third plug. Meanwhile, the second team dislodged the prism stone and discovered the end of the lowest plug. At this point, a rethink was required, lest the lowest plug slip into the passage below. Accordingly, the first team changed tack, and dug a short tunnel underneath the plugs into the Descending Passage, thus to gauge the length of the plug(s) that remained. This tunnel having been dug, it became evident that the third plug was the lowest one, and that no cavity existed except for the one that had been found immediately above the prism stone. All work on the plugs was thus stopped.[43]

On that day, the Pyramid as we know it was opened for tourists.

But a thousand years would elapse before the next important discovery was made.

Chapter Eight Summary

- The rough tunnel in the Well Shaft was dug upwards by the guardians of the Pyramid in order to carry out an inspection of the King's Chamber's roof following an exceptionally heavy earthquake. Even though the guardians sealed up the secret passage afterwards, they had created, in effect, a back door route to the Pyramid's upper chambers, and thus compromised the security of the monument.

- It is proposed that an intruder discovered the extended Well Shaft and used it to reach the Grand Gallery as early as the First Intermediate Period, nearly three thousand years before the Caliph al-Mamun.

- It is further proposed that the intruder discovered the 'false roof' and 'false floor' in the Gallery as a direct consequence of the damage that had been caused by the guardians.

- The Great Step in the Gallery was probably a platform for a statue of the Great God, carved in a geometric style.

- The lower roof of the Gallery may have been painted with the stars, i.e. the gods, the children of the Great God. This prompts the thought that the Gallery was a simulacrum of the creation, its corbelled walls signifying the rising of the spirit of the Great God.

- The fifty-four rectangular niches in the Gallery's side ramps may have been filled by relics of the gods, perhaps representing the materials of creation.

- The Queen's Chamber Passage may have contained a plug or artefact, placed strategically before the sealed entrance to the chamber.

- The Queen's Chamber may have contained a sarcophagus, carved in a material that matched the room's floor. The niche would have been filled by a five-tiered geometric statue of the Great Goddess, carved in precious stone.

- The King's Chamber contained only the granite sarcophagus, fitted with its lid and enshrining the meteoritic iron of creation.

- The al-Mamun tunnel was dug not to gain access into the Pyramid, but rather to remove artefacts from the Pyramid, and was dug not by al-Mamun, but rather by an earlier intruder perhaps three thousand years earlier. The largest artefacts were cut into pieces to facilitate their removal.

- Caliph al-Mamun re-excavated the ancient robber's tunnel; he was also responsible for the excavation along the western side of the granite plugs, the removal of the prism stone, and the digging of the short connecting tunnel between the chasm and the Descending Passage.

- It is implied by the foregoing interpretation that the Pyramid, in its upper parts, was not simply a repository of physical artefacts, but rather a repository of *a religious idea* – in effect, a memorial to the creation.

CHAPTER NINE

THE SACRED BOOK

I am more profound as a scribe than the heavens, the earth, or the underworld!... The House of Books is concealed and invisible.

(An ancient Egyptian scribe)

In 1872, a new chapter was opened in the history of the exploration of the Pyramid when Waynman Dixon, a British engineer, discovered the hidden shafts in the Queen's Chamber. The story of the find was told by Piazzi Smyth in 1880 as follows:

> Perceiving a crack (first, I am told, pointed out by Dr Grant) in the south wall of the Queen's Chamber, which allowed him at one place to push in a wire to a most unconscionable length, Mr W. Dixon set his carpenter man-of-all-work, by name Bill Grundy, to jump a hole with hammer and steel chisel at that place. So to work the faithful fellow went, and with a will which soon began to make a way into the soft stone, when lo! after a comparatively very few strokes, flop went the chisel right through into somewhere or other... Next, measuring off a similar position on the north wall, Mr Dixon set the invaluable Bill Grundy to work there again with his hammer and steel chisel; and again, after a very little labour, flop went the said chisel through, into somewhere.[1]

These 'somewheres' were the horizontal cavities of the south and north shafts, which ran into the respective walls for a distance of over six feet, before turning upwards at a steep angle. But the odd thing was that these shafts did not exit in the Pyramid's faces like the King's Chamber shafts did. Rather, they terminated in the monument's masonry.

During the late-19th and early-20th centuries, a number of attempts were made to probe the Queen's Chamber shafts with iron and wooden

Figure 122.
THE METAL-HANDLED SLAB, 8 INCHES SQUARE, DISCOVERED
INSIDE THE QUEEN'S CHAMBER SOUTHERN SHAFT.

rods, but to no avail. The significance of the shafts remained a mystery.

In 1993, this mystery deepened when Rudolf Gantenbrink, a German engineer, sent a remote-controlled robot up the shafts, fitted with a video camera and a live feed. In the northern shaft, the robot was thwarted by a broken rod lying across the floor, but in the southern shaft it proceeded unhindered for a distance of 213 feet, where it revealed a limestone slab, or 'door', fitted with two metal latches or handles (figure 122).

It took nine years for this 'door' to be investigated further. In 2002, a new robot, sponsored by the National Geographic Channel, drilled a hole through the limestone slab and revealed another 'door', or rather a stone plug. The robot also succeeded in climbing the northern shaft, where it revealed another limestone slab with metal handles, matching the one that had been found in 1993 in the southern shaft. Behind this, no doubt, another stone plug lies, although confirmation, at the time of writing, is still awaited.

What is the significance of these shafts?

As discussed in chapter three, there is compelling evidence for a secret chamber above the southern shaft (this evidence was summarised there and need not be repeated here). The most significant champion of this theory is Rudolf Gantenbrink, who, from an engineering perspective, has satisfied himself of the chamber's existence. But several Egyptologists have also pronounced in favour of this theory, notably I.E.S. Edwards, Mark Lehner and Zahi Hawass, all of whom are experts on the pyramids and the Great Pyramid in particular. All agree that the secret chamber would be small, for it lies close to the face of the Pyramid where there is insufficient room for a major structure; and all agree that this chamber

Figure 123.
THE GREAT PYRAMID, SHOWING THEORISED LOCATION OF SECRET
CHAMBERS ABOVE THE QUEEN'S CHAMBER SHAFTS.

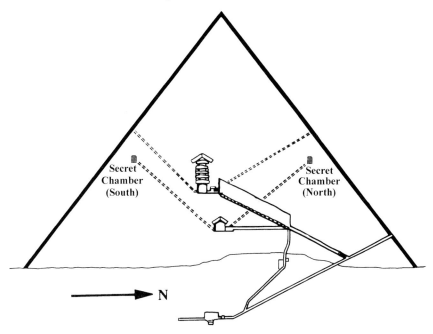

would be intact, since there is seemingly no way by which anyone could
have plundered it.

Such is the confidence of Gantenbrink, Edwards, Lehner, and Hawass
in the existence of this secret chamber that they have offered their ideas
as to what it might contain.

Gantenbrink believes that the secret chamber contains the mummified
body of Hetepheres, the mother of Khufu, although it is not yet totally
clear why he would think this, nor even whether he is fully serious in his
suggestion.[2]

Edwards proposed that the chamber would be a serdab, containing 'a
statue of the king gazing towards the constellation of Orion'.[3] However,
having advanced this idea, he immediately issued a disclaimer, stating:
'It's a wild guess; we have no precedents.'

Lehner basically agreed with Edwards. A small ka-statue of the king
might be found, he said, mirroring the larger statue that had once stood in
the Queen's Chamber niche.[4]

Hawass, however, suggested a different possibility; in his view, the
chamber might contain the religious writings of the builders, perhaps the
'Sacred Book' that had allegedly been written by Khufu.[5]

Meanwhile, in alternative Egyptology, Robert Bauval has led the way in debating the likely contents of the hypothesised secret chamber. In *The Orion Mystery* (1994), he offered the following profound comment:

> If the pyramid builders took so much trouble to conceal it [the object in the chamber], it must have been very important; more important perhaps than the mummy of a dead pharaoh. This suggests that it was something they regarded as central to their religion and perhaps connected with their motivation for building the pyramids in the first place.[6]

What could this important something be? Initially, Bauval suggested two possibilities: either the Benben Stone of Heliopolis (an iron meteorite, weighing between 6 and 15 tons), or a shrine containing 'the lost books of Thoth'.[7] Later, however, he gravitated towards the second of these possibilities. In *Secret Chamber* (1999), he wrote:

> My recent investigations into the ancient texts, however, has now made me lean more towards the idea that there could be a sort of 'sacred library' with books and 'instruction manuals' associated with the astral rebirth rituals of the pyramid builders. This is, of course, pure speculation.[8]

Bauval then made a profound observation which seemed to anticipate the sealed repository theory. He wrote:

> But why build a shaft at all? Why not just place the 'books' in a small chamber within the core of the Pyramid, then build solid masonry around it? This would surely make those 'books' totally inaccessible to intruders – indeed no-one would even suspect the existence of such a chamber. Whereas by linking such a possible chamber with a shaft that, in turn, connects with the Queen's Chamber further down the Pyramid, then should the entrance of the shaft be discovered (which it has) and should the shaft be probed (which it has) and finally should a 'door' be seen at its end (which it has), surely all this would act not as a deterrent but rather as an *invitation to find out what is behind it* (which it has). This implies to me that the ancient builders *actually wanted the 'door' to be found and, ultimately, what might be concealed behind it.*[9] (original emphasis)

This author could not agree more.

Unfortunately, Bauval made nothing of this idea, since it conflicted with his preconceived view that the shafts were soul- and star-shafts for the deceased king. Indeed, in recent years, Bauval has even dropped the 'sacred library' theory, suggesting instead that the chamber will contain a *ka*-statue of the king.[10] Repositories and sacred books are thus eschewed in favour of the serdab theory of Edwards and Lehner.

Now, the common thread linking all of the above predictions (with the exception of Bauval's time capsule ruminations) is the assumption that the Pyramid is a tomb, and nothing but a tomb, designed for a single king (or in the case of Gantenbrink, with the king's dead mother thrown in for good measure), and that the Queen's Chamber shafts have a religious significance (although Gantenbrink may be agnostic on this point). Here, however, we have a fundamental problem, for, if truth be told, not one of the predictions makes any sense at all according to the 'tomb and tomb only' theory.

Consider.

Re Gantenbrink's proposal that Hetepheres was buried in the secret chamber, this would appal the majority of Egyptologists. In their view, the Pyramid belonged to Khufu, and if he had wanted to bury his mother Hetepheres in a pyramid, then he would have built her a pyramid of her own. In any case, they would argue, why would Khufu have buried her in a secret chamber, whilst providing an 8-inch-square shaft leading to it? It is an unprecedented idea, and it makes no sense.

Similarly, most Egyptologists would be aghast at the idea that sacred books were deposited in the secret chamber. In their considered view, the Pyramid was built as a tomb, not as a library or repository. Why would the builders construct an 8-inch-square shaft leading to a library? Perish the thought, for it makes no sense.

Finally, what about the serdab/*ka*-statue idea? Here, major problems stem from the presumption that the Queen's Chamber itself was a serdab for a *ka*-statue. Firstly, there is no precedent for one *ka*-chamber being built above another, nor indeed for two *ka*-chambers being built above the one (on the logical assumption that an identical chamber lies at the top of the northern shaft). Secondly, even if we allow this to be so, for the sake of argument, why would the shafts connecting these serdabs be sealed at the top and the bottom? It makes no sense. Furthermore, serious objections may be mounted against the theory that the Queen's Chamber was itself a serdab. These objections, which were raised in chapter three of this book, are as follows. Firstly, the niche in the chamber faces to the west, whereas a *ka*-statue ought to face to the north for eternal life in the circumpolar stars, or to the east for eternal rebirth with the rising Sun. Secondly, the Queen's Chamber was a totally sealed room, whereas in serdabs the *ka*-statue was usually provided with open peepholes or a slit, through which the *ka* could establish contact with the sky. And thirdly, the *ka*-statue concept belonged to the tomb and the underworld, whereas the Queen's Chamber lies inside a pyramid at a height of 70 feet. All of this serves to undermine the theory that the shafts were *ka*-shafts and the secret chamber a serdab for a second *ka*-statue. The entire theory is but supposition upon supposition.

In summary, the very concept of a secret chamber makes no sense in the context of the orthodox 'tomb only' theory. And it is for this reason that the majority of Egyptologists, *pace* Gantenbrink, Edwards, Lehner, Hawass and Bauval, reject out of hand the architectural evidence for a secret chamber, and insist that the shafts lead nowhere other than into solid masonry. The popular view indeed is that the shafts are abandoned prototypes of those in the King's Chamber, i.e. unfinished ventilation shafts or unfinished soul-shafts, with the Queen's Chamber itself being regarded as an abandoned tomb. Now, this argument has its superficial attractions, not least in offering a rationale for the shafts being sealed at both ends, but it does contain fatal flaws, which have been highlighted in earlier chapters of this book. Egyptologists, however, have little choice but to stick to this abandonment theory, because if it is accepted that the shafts do lead somewhere then the 'tomb only' theory is in deep trouble (as we have seen).

We thus have a situation where the least bad theory prevails.

But why does it prevail?

Well, the reason is that the abandonment hypothesis has a theoretical foundation (the long-established theory that the Pyramid is 'a tomb and nothing but a tomb'), whereas the secret chamber theory, being a recent development, lacks a theoretical foundation. Consequently, Gantenbrink, Edwards, Lehner, Hawass and Bauval have all been forced to justify the secret chamber in the context of orthodoxy, when it surely deserves to have a theoretical foundation of its own. What has happened, in effect, is that the secret chamber theorists have taken a piggyback ride on a most ill-equipped horse. If the reader tries to visualise a fish catching a ride on the back of a camel, he will get the picture. A fish makes no sense on the back of a camel; it shrivels and dies, whilst the camel lives. However, if the fish is returned to its natural element, then it thrives and lives, and what is more, it swims in happy proximity to the camel. Should we not, then, return the fish to its natural element? Should we not distance the secret chamber from the 'tomb and tomb only' theory, and evaluate it in its proper surroundings?

In this book, I have proffered a complete theoretical basis for secret chambers in the Great Pyramid, namely the sealed repository and time capsule hypothesis. In brief, my argument is as follows: that the king was buried at ground level or below, probably in the cave-like Grotto; that the upper passages and chambers were sealed off as they were built; that sacred artefacts were concealed in the secret chambers, including iron meteorites in the King's Chamber sarcophagus; that these objects were, for the most part, intended for a future generation, or race, of men, who would unseal the hidden passages to access the secret vaults; and that the Grand Gallery, Queen's Chamber and King's Chamber were robbed of their contents in antiquity.

The evidence for the sealed repository theory consists of both religious and architectural elements, some of which refer to the Pyramid itself, and others of which refer to the culture that built it. Of particular importance are: the religious axiom 'the body to earth, the spirit to the sky'; the creational symbolism of the true pyramid; the position of the Grotto and the design of the Well Shaft; the importance of meteoritic iron and the precedents for it being raised towards the sky; the pattern of concealment that is evident in the Pyramid's upper chambers; the sign that marked the hidden entrance to the upper chambers; the importance of cataclysm in Egyptian religion; and the tradition recorded in the Westcar Papyrus that Khufu sought to learn the number of secret chambers in the sanctuary of Thoth in order to copy the same in the design of his own *Akhet*, the Great Pyramid. In addition, Hermetic and Arab legends offer strong support for the theory that the Pyramid was built as a sealed repository and time capsule.

We thus have a complete theoretical basis for distancing the Queen's Chamber and its shafts from the tomb theory, and reassessing it/them in the context of the sealed repository theory. Or, to use my earlier analogy, the fish can be removed from the back of the camel and returned to its natural element.

And how the fish thrives in its proper surroundings!

Fact. The passage to the Queen's Chamber was concealed beneath the bridging slab in the Grand Gallery (the architecture suggests that it was sealed off at the time of construction).

Fact. A rough pilaster exists at the entrance to the Queen's Chamber. This seems to indicate that the chamber itself was sealed off beyond the passage.

Fact. The two shafts in the Queen's Chamber were both sealed at their lower ends by a 5-inch 'left', i.e. an uncut plate of stone.

Fact. The two shafts were both sealed at their upper ends. Leaving to one side the significance of the copper-handled slabs, the stone plug in the southern shaft (which is probably duplicated in the northern shaft) resembles the granite plugs which once sealed the Ascending Passage – a gateway to the entire upper chamber system.

Fact. Despite the protestations of Egyptologists, several archaeological clues combine to make the presence of a small chamber beyond the plug in the southern shaft a virtual certainty (implying the likely existence of a similar chamber above the northern shaft).

In summary, all of these facts, which are so anomalous in the context of the 'tomb and tomb only' theory, fit perfectly with the idea of a sealed repository.

Of course, no theory is ever immune from criticism, and in this case two objections might be heard.

Firstly, is it plausible that the Queen's Chamber shafts can be conduits to secret chambers when the King's Chamber shafts evidently performed a different function (in that they were open channels from the chamber to the face of the Pyramid)? The answer, I believe, is "yes". Why should it be assumed that these two pairs of shafts were built for correspondent purposes? In my view, it is this very assumption, so unimaginative and unnecessary, that has held us back from understanding the two pairs of shafts. If their forms differed, then so too, surely, did their function.

Secondly, is it legitimate to compare the Queen's Chamber shafts, just eight inches square, with other secret passages in the Pyramid? How could a person be expected to crawl through these shafts? The answer, I suggest, is that the future explorer was not supposed to crawl through the shafts, obviously, but rather was supposed to dig a tunnel around them, i.e. to use them as guides for excavation. This may strike the reader as a little odd initially, but it is consistent with the intention that the explorer break the seals of passages and chambers elsewhere in the Pyramid, a prime example being the granite plugs in the Ascending Passage. Such an intrusive approach is at odds with modern archaeological principles, a point to which we will return at the end of this chapter, but the Egyptian way of doing things was fundamentally different, and there is no reason for us to suppose that they would have anticipated modern archaeology, nor, for that matter, the invention of remote-controlled robots.

Actually, far from being an odd idea, the excavation of these shafts to their full distance of 213 feet (plus whatever distance remains beyond the 'doors' and plugs) would have presented an explorer with his ultimate challenge, both physically and psychologically. After all, the half-hearted person would have given up such a task on the assumption that the shafts debouched on the faces of the Pyramid, perhaps via linkages to the shafts of the King's Chamber. Only someone who had insight into the nature of the Pyramid would have passed this ultimate test and excavated tunnels as far as the secret chambers.

The ultimate test for the ultimate prize?

So, to the sixty-four million dollar question: what is concealed inside the secret chamber, or chambers?

Earlier, I asked this question, and furnished in response the opinions of various commentators: the mummy of Hetepheres (Gantenbrink); a *ka*-statue of the king (Edwards/Lehner/Bauval); the Benben Stone (Bauval); or sacred books (Bauval/Hawass). However, whilst these opinions are all very interesting, they are mere speculations, as the authors concerned are the first to acknowledge (with the possible exception of Gantenbrink).[11] But, worse than that, they are speculations without a theoretical basis, for they draw upon an orthodoxy, the tomb theory, which actually precludes the existence of a secret chamber! Therefore, with all due respect to these experts, it must be stated that their predictions are worthless, since there can be no meaningful outcome from putting them to the test.

But now we have the sealed repository and time capsule theory, which does have a solid theoretical basis. The fish is in its own element, and the idea of a secret chamber begins to make sense. We are now in a position to make an informed appraisal of the secret chamber's contents, and thus generate a prediction that can be put meaningfully to the test.

And that prediction, ironically enough, is in line with the thoughts of Hawass and (for a short while in 1999/2000) of Bauval. My prediction, predicated on the likely small size of the chamber or chambers (which are less than 50 feet from the outer faces of the Pyramid), and on the kind of objects that would have been most important to the builders of a time capsule, is sacred books, which would doubtless have been stored inside a hermetically-sealed coffer of stone.

The reader may snort at this suggestion; he might well complain that the idea is lacking in originality. However, it is not my aim to be original for the mere sake of it, even if it were possible to be innovative after two centuries of unbridled speculation on this subject. Rather, it is my aim to be original in providing a theoretical basis for the secret chamber (which no other researcher has done) and, beyond that, to make a correct call on the chamber's (or chambers') contents. In this way, future explorations of the Queen's Chamber shafts can produce a meaningful result, either proving or disproving my hypothesis.

To this end, I wish to make my prediction as detailed as possible. To leave it at 'sacred books' is far too vague, whilst 'the Sacred Book of Khufu' might sound specific but does not really address the question of what that book actually was. Therefore, in the remainder of this chapter, I intend to summarise what is known about sacred books in ancient Egypt, and work up a prediction of what exactly is written in the books that I believe to be hidden inside the Pyramid. As the reader will soon realise, the reason why modern authors have so often speculated about ancient writings hidden at Giza is not wishful thinking (though in some cases it might be), but rather a long-standing tradition of sacred books in Egypt, which is particularly evident in the writings of the Arabs and the Hermeticists.

Finally, at the end of this chapter, I will offer some original solutions to the practical problems of retrieving the contents of the secret chamber, or chambers, and to the moral dilemma that faces 21st century society in deciding whether to retrieve those contents at all.

The Sacred Book

In ancient Egypt, writing was a divine science, which had been invented and taught to man by Thoth, the god of writing, science and magic. The Egyptians thus called their writing *medu-neter*, 'divine words', just as we, via the Greeks, call it hieroglyphics, 'sacred signs'. Such was the great magic behind the sacred signs that images of living creatures, when placed in the tombs, could manifest those beings in the 'other world'; for this reason, the scorpion hieroglyph was deprived of its tail, lest it cause injury or 'death' to the deceased.

The sacred book was a powerful and profound idea in ancient Egypt, from the beginning to the end of its civilisation. The earliest mention of the motif is found in the Pyramid Texts, where the king exclaims:

> I take possession of the sky, its pillars and its stars... I am the scribe of the God's book, who says what is and brings about what is not.[12]

In order to understand the significance of this claim, it is necessary to realise that the king is here emulating the creator-god, who rose up to the sky at the beginning of time. For this reason, the king identifies himself not only with the scribe, but also with 'the Great Wild Bull... the flowing fluid... Neheb-kau... the Eye of Horus'.[13] There can be no more powerful context. The implication is that the creator himself penned the first book – the story of 'what would be and what would not be' – during the so-called First Time. Thus the concept of the sacred book sprang from the myth of creation.

In keeping with this idea, the actual sacred books, written on papyrus or parchment, were held to have been inspired by the Great God, or even written by him in his identity of Thoth. Thoth, as mentioned earlier, was the god of writing, science and magic; his titles included 'scribe of the gods', 'scribe of truth', 'master of the words of power', 'great one of spells', 'master of magic', and 'knower of the mysteries'.[14] According to

Figure 124.
THOTH, THE EGYPTIAN GOD OF WRITING, SCIENCE AND MAGIC.

tradition, Thoth had authored forty-two books which contained all of the knowledge of the heavens, the earth and the underworld (the number is probably symbolic and not to be taken literally).[15]

An original book of Thoth (as opposed to a copy made by man) was attributed a hallowed status in ancient Egypt. As early as the Coffin Texts, a book of Thoth is described as being carried in procession like a holy relic:

> Hathor, who is pre-eminent in *Itnws*... she travels to Heliopolis bearing the script of the divine words, the book of Thoth.[16]

The significance of the book of Thoth is made clear in Spell 231 of the Coffin Texts, where it is used to spiritualise the king in the 'opening of the mouth' ritual:

> Ho king!... May your mouth be split open by Thoth with this wondrous book of his wherewith he split open the mouths of the gods.[17]

Here, the book of Thoth is a metaphor for the adze of meteoritic iron that was used in the ancient Egyptian ritual. But, more than that, it represents the archetype for that ritual. The book itself *is* the magic word that was pronounced by Thoth at the time of creation – the very word with which the Great God had spiritualised himself and his gods.

An intriguing theme in Egyptian literature is the concealment of the sacred book, or a chapter thereof, and the finding of this text by the king or his representative, sometimes via an act of heroism, or otherwise via the will of the gods. In some cases, it is the original, mythical book that has been hidden and is found; in other cases, it is a copy of the original that has been transcribed by the hand of man.

An example of the former appears in the Khaemwase cycle of stories from the late period. Khaemwase, the heir to Ramesses II, was a prince and magician, who was revered for his wisdom. In one tale, an elderly priest tells Khaemwase where to discover the sacred book 'which Thoth wrote with his own hand'. In this book, he would find two great spells which would grant him extraordinary powers:

> Two spells are written there. By recitation of the first you will charm the sky, the earth, the underworld, the mountains and the waters. It will allow you understanding of all that is spoken by the creatures of the air and those of the land... By recitation of the second you will be granted a vision of the true form of Re himself with his divine companions, wherever you may be...[18]

Thoth had deposited this book inside a nest of boxes, sealed inside an iron chest, which he had hidden at the bottom of a river. In days of yore, it had been stolen by the hero Nefer-Ka-Ptah, who had thus forfeited his life and taken the book with him to his tomb. The tale relates how prince Khaemwase descended into the tomb of Nefer-Ka-Ptah and, after an epic search, rediscovered the book of Thoth, which illuminated the vault with its brilliant light.[19] The story is unlikely to be historically true, but rather seems to reflect the mythical book of Thoth, which had been dictated, transcribed and hidden at the time of the creation.

Other traditions refer to man-made copies of the sacred book, and may have a historical basis. Again, however, they utilise the same theme of the book having been hidden and discovered.

The Book of Two Ways was said to have been found 'under the flank of Thoth'.[20] The book, which forms part of the Coffin Texts, comprises a detailed guide to the underworld of Rostau.

Chapter 30B of the Book of the Dead was allegedly discovered hidden beneath the statue of Thoth in Hermopolis. It had been inscribed upon a metal slab 'in the writing of the god himself'.[21] The chapter relates to the judgement of the heart of the deceased by Thoth.

Chapter 64 of the Book of the Dead was reputedly found beneath the temple of Sokar.[22] It attempts to summarise the entire Book of the Dead in one single spell.

Chapter 137A of the Book of the Dead was reportedly found 'inside a secret chest in the temple of Wenut' at Hermopolis.[23] It too was 'written in the god's own hand', i.e. the hand of Thoth. The chapter comprises the spell of the Four Blazing Flames, which was to be recited at the time of the 'opening of the mouth'. It is described as 'a great secret of the West, a secret image of the *Duat*... belonging to the mysteries of the *Duat*, a secret image in the realm of the dead.'[24]

Many of these lost-and-found books are credited with great antiquity. According to one legend, recorded in the Ebers Papyrus and the Berlin Medical Papyrus, an anatomical treatise was found hidden beneath the statue of Anubis in Letopolis and was brought to Usaphais, a king of the 1st dynasty.[25] It was during his reign too that Chapter 64 of the Book of the Dead was reputedly found by a supervisor of wall-builders beneath the temple of Sokar.[26] In both cases, it would appear that the books were old, predating the 1st dynasty. The suggestion is remarkable. But it is vouched by an 18th dynasty inscription which describes how a temple was built according to a 'great plan' that had been found in Dendera 'in old delineations written upon leather of animal skin of the time of the Followers of Horus'.[27] The Followers of Horus were mythical rulers of Egypt during an age that preceded the establishment of human kingship.[28]

All of these sacred books, once found and retrieved from the places where Thoth had hidden them, were deposited in temple archives, in a building called *Per Medjat*, 'the House of Books', which was attached to an institution known as *Per Ankh*, 'the House of Life'. There were many of these institutions in Egypt, the best known being those of Hermopolis, Abydos, Memphis and Heliopolis. The first of these receives repeated mention in Egyptian texts, since it was the city of Hermes, or Thoth. But Thoth, as the god of writing, was prominent in every *Per Ankh*, as indeed was Seshat, the goddess of writing, who was known as 'the foremost one of the House of Books'.[29]

The *Per Ankh* was the place of writing *par excellence*. But, more than that, it was a University in the truest sense of the word, for here a student could study books on every conceivable subject: agriculture, geography, astronomy, astrology, mathematics, geometry, surveying, engineering, building, medicine, justice and law, art, history, all under the overarching theme of religion, or *maat*, 'right order'. The *Per Ankh* might well have been dominated by religious books: books of the gods, their forms and names, books of temple and funerary rituals, books of mystery plays, and so on and so forth. In these books were recorded the ultimate secrets of Egyptian civilisation, which were taught only to a small élite, such as the high priest designate and the heir to the throne. For all other people, the

Figure 125.
THE EGYPTIAN GODDESS SESHAT, 'THE FOREMOST ONE OF THE
HOUSE OF BOOKS'.

House of Books was 'concealed and invisible – the council of its gods
hidden and distant.'[30]

Undoubtedly, the *Per Ankh* was the source of the magical spells and
prayers which were recited at the king's funeral and, in certain cases,
inscribed or painted inside the tomb chamber. The primary example of
the latter practice is the Pyramid Texts, which were not a book per se, but
rather a collection of spells, which varied from one tomb to another, as if
selected from a wider corpus of writings.[31] Another example is the Coffin
Texts, which bear many similarities to the Pyramid Texts. And then there
are the many illustrated books that were painted inside the tomb, on the
walls or on the sarcophagus: the Book of the Hidden Chamber (otherwise
known as the Amduat), the Book of Gates, the Book of Caverns, the
Book of the Earth, the Book of Nut, the Book of the Day, the Book of the
Night, the Litany of Re, and the Book of the Heavenly Cow.[32] All of
these illustrated books would have been drawn from library material that
was stored in the *Per Ankh*, in its archive building the *Per Medjat*. In this
sense, the figure of Thoth, the god of writing, would have stood behind
all of the compositions, even if they were edited or selected by the hand
of the priests.[33]

In addition to having their funeral arrangements directed from the *Per
Ankh*, the kings could also use the institution as a resource centre during

their lifetimes, as little or as much as they wished. For some kings, the books were essential reading. Ramesses IV, for example, claimed to have studied all the writings of Thoth in the House of Life, thereby learning all about 'the essence of Osiris',[34] whilst Khasekhemre-Neferhotep claimed to have studied the writings of Atum at Heliopolis, thereby learning how he had been created, and how the gods had been fashioned, and how their forms for worship had been designated by the council of the gods.[35] But other kings, it would seem, consulted the sacred books only in times of crisis. Thus, in the 3rd dynasty, when the Nile flood had failed for seven consecutive years, Djoser expressed a desperate wish 'to go to the chief of Hermopolis, to enter the House of Life, to unfold the written rolls, and to lay my hand upon them', thereby to learn about the Nile-god and his place of birth.[36] A learned king would, of course, have apprised himself of this essential knowledge many years earlier.

Remarkably, the *Per Ankh* building was designed as a microcosm of the Universe. The Egyptologist Dimitri Meeks describes the *Per Ankh* of Abydos as follows:

> The House of Life [*Per Ankh*] was conceived as a microcosm of the world... A sign of life could be found at the centre of the building, namely Osiris. The four corners were identified with Isis, Nephthys, Horus, and Thoth. The floor was Geb, and Nut was the ceiling. Superimposed on the material building was an invisible one; it coincided with the created Universe.[37]

Once a year, a mysterious ritual was performed in this *Per Ankh*. A tiny statuette of Osiris, bearing the name Life (*Ankh*), was placed in a coffin to signify the body of 'He who existed before'. Then, a special ritual was performed by Thoth which caused Osiris to come back to life.[38] We see here the very essence of the House of Life, with *ankh* signifying 'life' not in the coarse sense of the word, but rather in the sense of Osiris coming to life after death, marking the origin of life in the Universe.

Meeks was struck by the idea that Osiris was brought to life through the power of writing. He comments:

> It is significant that it unfolded in the House of Life, the place of writing *par excellence*. Writing harboured a power that assigned the ritual text its true raison d'etre: it was that secret book 'which breaks spells, which binds conjurations, which arrests conjurations, which intimidates the entire Universe. It contains life, it contains death.' By way of all the rituals they put at man's disposal, written texts, 'emanations of Re', made it possible to maintain the equilibrium of the Universe.[39]

In effect, says Meeks, Osiris was 'written back into existence' when the gods 'exchanged letters' on the 20th day of the first month of the year.[40]

Meeks also informs us of the remarkable fact that all the sacred books of the *Per Ankh* were known collectively as 'the manifestations of Re' or 'emanations of Re'.[41] This term is one that usually relates to the gods, the ennead, who had emanated from the Great God at the beginning of time. Once again, it becomes evident that books were lent a divine status in Egypt; in this case, they represented the very essence or substance of the creator.

Khufu, the Pyramid, and the Sacred Book

Were sacred books concealed inside the Great Pyramid? The idea is not so controversial. After all, what were the Pyramid Texts but a religious book hidden inside the pyramids? Admittedly, they were not well hidden, being inscribed in the tomb chamber, but the idea was that they be sealed away inside the pyramid for eternity, their contents known only to the king and the gods. The principle is thus established that sacred books were hidden inside pyramids, at least from the late-5th dynasty onwards, and this suggests that earlier pyramids too might have contained books, not necessarily inscribed on the tomb chamber walls or sarcophagus, but rather in the form of manuscripts cached in the foundations or in secret compartments, where they have not yet been discovered by Egyptology.

In regard to the Great Pyramid, several pieces of evidence suggest that it was indeed used as a cache for sacred books. Foremost among these is the Westcar Papyrus, which connects Khufu and the Great Pyramid to Thoth, the god of writing; but there are also other traditions that connect Khufu to Thoth and the motif of the sacred book. We will examine each of these clues in turn.

Firstly, the Westcar Papyrus, which was discussed at some length in chapter six. In this document there appears 'The Story of Khufu and the Magicians' in which Khufu asks Djedi about the number of the secret chambers of the sanctuary of Thoth. Crucially, the story informs us that Khufu had 'spent (much) time in searching for the secret chambers of the sanctuary of Thoth, in order to make the like thereof for his *Akhet*'. As explained in the earlier chapter, the name *Akhet* is ambiguous but almost certainly refers to the Great Pyramid, which was known to the Egyptians as *Akhet Khufu*. Therefore, it would seem that Khufu modelled the Great Pyramid upon the multi-chambered sanctuary of Thoth (a building which has not yet been located by archaeologists). Now, Thoth was the author of the original sacred book, and the chief god of the House of Life and

the House of Books. He was the god *par excellence* of writing, science
and magic. Thus it seems likely that the sanctuary of Thoth would have
been, first and foremost, a repository for sacred books. Is it really likely,
then, that Khufu intended to use the pattern of its multiple chambers for
purposes which excluded their original, divine purpose? On the contrary,
Khufu would surely have concealed sacred writings in at least some of
the secret chambers of his *Akhet*.

Secondly, the name Khufu would appear to be an abbreviation of the
name Khnum-khuf, 'Khnum Protects', which is found prominently in the
cavities above the King's Chamber of the Pyramid (in the inscriptions of
the work gang names).[42] Khnum was a creator-god, 'the father of fathers
and the mother of mothers', who had created mankind on his potter's
wheel. His cult centre was at Aswan, near the first cataract of the Nile,
where he guarded the minerals of the earth and controlled the flow of the
river. In this capacity, he furnished all the materials for the scribal art:
wood or stone for the palette, reeds and brushes for the pens, water and
ink for the hieroglyphs, and papyrus or other material for the impression.
Perhaps for this reason, Khnum was associated with writing. In Spell 577
of the Coffin Texts, it is asserted: 'This book was (found) under the flank
of Khnum,'[43] whilst in Utterance 524 of the Pyramid Texts it is suggested
that Khnum was the father of Thoth, the scribe of the gods.[44] Thus we

Figure 126.
THE CREATOR-GOD KHNUM, IN THE ACT OF FASHIONING MANKIND
FROM CLAY ON HIS POTTER'S WHEEL.

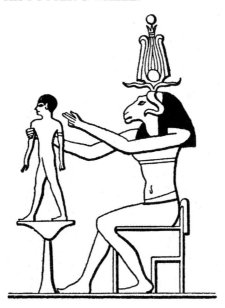

find in Khufu's full name Khnum-khuf a possible connection between the Pyramid and the concept of the sacred book. (Incidentally, it has not been possible to confirm a link between Khufu's Horus-name, *Mdjd*, and the word for book or papyrus roll, *mdjt*, despite the striking similarity.)[45]

Thirdly, according to the Egyptian priest and historian Manetho (3rd century BC), Khufu had himself written a sacred book. In his lost work *Aegyptiaca*, which is cited by Eusebius, Manetho made brief reference to Khufu (Suphis) as follows:

> Of these [4th dynasty kings] the third was Suphis, the builder of the Great Pyramid, which Herodotus says was built by Cheops. Suphis conceived a contempt for the gods, but repenting of this, he composed the Sacred Book, which the Egyptians held in high esteem.[46]

This is an intriguing assertion, for the 'Sacred Book' is not one of the titles that are known to Egyptologists. Moreover, earlier Egyptian texts make no mention of it. So, what did Manetho have in mind? How could Khufu's Sacred Book have been 'held in high esteem' by the Egyptians? A possible clue lies in his reference to '*the* Sacred Book', as if to suggest that Khufu had authored the original, archetypal book – the one that had allegedly been written by Thoth on behalf of the creator. This is plausible according to the principles of Egyptian religion in which there was an identity in spirit between the king and the creator (in this case between Khufu and Khnum or his 'son' Thoth). Nevertheless, it is an unusual and extremely bold claim that finds no precedent in any other Egyptian text.

Might the meaning be that the Pyramid was the Sacred Book, and that by building the Pyramid Khufu had authored the book? This is a definite possibility, for Egyptian texts do use the term 'book' as a metaphor, for example in the idea that the book of Thoth opened the mouths of the gods (Coffin Texts, Spell 231). In addition, Egyptian wisdom literature does draw an analogy between the book and the pyramid. For example, in the text 'In Praise of Learned Scribes' (Chester Beatty Papyrus IV), the author eulogises the scribes of ancient times whose 'books of wisdom were their pyramids'.[47] But most important of all, the Egyptians believed that the Great God and the sacred book stood for the same thing, namely the mystery of creation. As God personified the creation, so did the book delineate it; hence the divine status of the book. Therefore, just as the pyramid was a representation of the God, so it was also a representation of the book. *Q.E.D.* Khufu could have composed the Sacred Book by building the Great Pyramid. This would certainly explain the idea that Khufu's Sacred Book was held in high esteem by the people.

Of course, this interpretation of the Sacred Book goes against the idea

Figure 127.
THE GREAT PYRAMID.
Did the entire Pyramid symbolise 'the Sacred Book' of Khufu?

that Khufu composed a manuscript that he might have concealed in the Pyramid. But, on the other hand, it suggests that the Great Pyramid, more than any other pyramid, was regarded as the Sacred Book, which cannot but strengthen the case for the concealment of actual manuscripts inside it.

Finally, it is worth noting that many legends connect Khufu to the lost-and-found sacred book, either directly or via his son Hordedef, the latter being revered as a great sage, prophet, and magician in his own right.[48]

To begin with Khufu himself, his name appears twice in connection with a sacred book. In one inscription, it is said that Khufu composed a plan for the design of a temple, and buried it in a crypt at Dendera. This book, as it might be called, was then discovered eight hundred years later by Pepi, a king of the 6th dynasty, who used it to build (or enlarge) the temple of Dendera.[49] In another text, British Museum Papyrus 10059, it is said that a sacred book, pertaining to medical matters, fell from the sky and was brought to Khufu. The text reads:

> This remedy was found in the night, fallen into the court of the temple in Koptos, as a mystery of this goddess, by a lector-priest of this temple, when this land was in darkness, and it was the Moon which illuminated every side of this scroll. It was brought as a marvel to His Majesty, the King of Upper and Lower Egypt, Khufu, the triumphant.[50]

As for Hordedef, the son of Khufu, he is alleged to have discovered two sacred books: Chapters 30B and 137A of the Book of the Dead.

Of Chapter 30B, the judgement of the heart of the deceased by Thoth, it is said:

> This spell was found in Hermopolis under the feet of this god [Thoth] ... it was discovered in the time of His Majesty, the King of Upper and Lower Egypt, Menkaure. It was the king's son Hordedef who found it while he was going around making an inspection of the temples.[51]

Similarly, of Chapter 137A, the spell of the Four Blazing Flames, it is said:

> This text was copied when it was found in writing by the king's son Hordedef, being what he found in a secret chest written in the God's own hand in the temple of Wenut, Mistress of Wenut, when he was travelling upstream inspecting the temples in the fields and mounds of the gods.[52]

In summary, with so many sacred books being found, and even hidden, during the days of Khufu and his son Hordedef, it becomes increasingly plausible that Khufu sought to conceal sacred books inside the Pyramid, and that he sought to reproduce the pattern of the secret chambers of the sanctuary of Thoth for this precise purpose.

The Argument Summarised

The argument for sacred books inside the Pyramid, in the hypothesised secret chamber above the Queen's Chamber southern shaft, may now be summarised.

Firstly, the theorised size of the secret chamber is appropriate for a small artefact. A sacred book, or a library of such books, would fit the bill very neatly.

Secondly, the placement of the secret chamber in such an inaccessible location, requiring the excavation of a tunnel 213 feet long, attests to the great value of the artefact, and suggests that it was superior to the other hidden objects discussed thus far (with the exception of the meteorites in the King's Chamber, which may have been inaccessible because of other factors). A sacred book fits the bill for such an artefact, perhaps uniquely so. As we have seen, a sacred book in ancient Egypt was a magic relic, which encapsulated and enshrined the mystery of creation; hence it was regarded as an 'emanation' of the Great God, and could be conveyed in solemn procession like a statue of the divinity. And yet, unlike a mute statue, the book could proclaim the mystery of the creation in as much or as little detail as its author deigned to give. Such a book would have been a most suitable contender for the Pyramid's ultimate prize.

Thirdly, the symbolism fits. The true pyramid, as we have seen, was a simulacrum of the creation, and its rise into the sky commemorated the rise of the creator-god. But in this rise we find the very archetype for the sacred book, as attested by Utterance 510 of the Pyramid Texts, cited earlier, in which the king as creator declares:

> I take possession of the sky, its pillars and its stars... I am the scribe of the God's book, who says what is and brings about what is not.

Here, the author of the God's book is in the sky, as evidenced by the parallel myth of the *Benu*-bird, which alighted on the pyramidion, the *benben*, in Heliopolis and announced:

> I am that Great *Benu*-bird in Heliopolis, the supervisor of what exists ... *As for what exists, it means the time-cycle and the time-line.*[53]

The archetype of the sacred book thus corresponded to the heights of the pyramid, and it would have been exceptionally astute, from a symbolic perspective, if the builder of the Great Pyramid had placed in its heights

Figure 128.
THE GREAT BENU-BIRD UPON ITS PYRAMIDAL PERCH.
An analogy for the author of 'the God's book'?

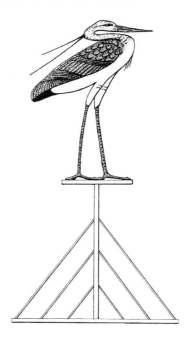

a man-made copy of the sacred book.[54]

Fourthly, symbolism again. If I am right in my belief that the Pyramid was the Sacred Book, which conveyed the story of creation in a single hieroglyph, then it would have been fitting indeed if a copy of the sacred book, in manuscript form, had been hidden inside it.

Fifthly, if the Pyramid was constructed as a time capsule for a future generation, or race, of men, as I argue, then books and manuals would have been an essential item, and to omit them would have been a glaring oversight by the builders. Unless these books were installed in one of the chambers that has already been robbed (which is possible but unlikely), then they surely remain to be found in an intact secret chamber.

Finally, as we have seen, Egyptian traditions linked Khufu to Thoth, the god of writing, science and magic, and even suggested that he had copied the secret chambers of the sanctuary of Thoth in building his own *Akhet*, i.e. the Great Pyramid. Might this legend, which has been dated to around 2050 BC, recall a genuine secret of the Pyramid's construction? If so, it is almost certain that one of its secret chambers contained the book of Thoth, or even a library of writings equivalent to the *Per Medjat* at the *Per Ankh*.

The Prediction

On the basis of my sealed repository theory, I predict that a new chamber will be discovered beyond the 'door' and plug in the Queen's Chamber southern shaft. I also predict that a corresponding chamber will be found beyond the 'door' in the northern shaft. These are critical predictions. If no such chambers are found – in other words, if both shafts abut against ordinary masonry – then I would concede failure (rather than resort to a theory of abandoned secret passages!). Future exploration of the shafts thus promises to vindicate or repudiate the main thesis of this book.

I also predict that at least one of the secret chambers will contain the sacred books of the Pyramid builders (it is conceivable that the second chamber might be an empty decoy).[55] This is a less critical prediction, since some unforeseen artefact might be found that would provide equal fulfilment of the sealed repository theory. However, two empty chambers would refute my theory, as would two serdabs containing *ka*-statues of the king.

A discovery of sacred books would provide me with the opportunity to test the wider hypothesis on which this book is predicated, namely my interpretation of ancient Egyptian religion. Here, I am able to make a unique prediction as to the contents of the hidden books. To suggest that they will contain secret images of the God and Goddess, procedures for temple building and pyramid building, and magical spells pertaining to the science of immortality – in short, to suggest that their content will be religious and magical – is to state the obvious in the light of the sacred book traditions that have been cited in this chapter. Rather, I am going to predict the revelation of a specific secret underlying all of these religious and magical ideas – a secret that, hitherto, has not been apprehended by Egyptology.

Now, when the builders of the Great Pyramid sealed their books and other sacred artefacts in its rooms (*c.* 2550 BC according to the orthodox chronology), they believed that the 'end of the world' was nigh, and that aeons might pass before a new generation, or race, of men rose up from the ashes of the past. They did not imagine that their civilisation would endure, in more or less unbroken form, for thousands of years. Nor did they envisage that the inheritors of their religion would create such an abundant legacy for posterity. In short, they did not anticipate that a modern outsider, such as this author, or a discipline, such as Egyptology, might be able to reconstruct their religion prior to studying the books in the Pyramid. But this is exactly what has happened. Today, thanks to the painstaking work of archaeologists and Egyptologists, there exists a plethora of data which can be used, in theory, to decode the religion of the pyramid builders.

But there is a catch. For such is the ambiguity of the archaeological record, such the obscurity of the writings that were made, and such the fragmentary state of the account that has survived, that ancient Egyptian religion remains an opaque, complex and controversial subject. And here is the nub of the matter. For, whilst Egyptologists believe that Egyptian religion was basically a Sun cult, framed against a mishmash of lunar, stellar, and other primitive beliefs, I have come to the view that Egyptian religion was a 'cult of creation'. And, whilst Egyptologists believe that the Egyptian myth of creation is an incomprehensible, inconsistent, and inconsequential story, I have come to the view that it is a straightforward, rational, and important account of the origin of the geocentric Universe (as the Egyptians conceived it). In consequence, there is a fundamental difference of opinion here that may be resolved in the books of the Great Pyramid. For unlike later books such as the Pyramid Texts, which were composed for the benefit of the king and the gods, and thus written in cryptic terms, the books of the Pyramid would have been aimed at a future generation of men, who would not necessarily have understood the *medu-neter*, nor the metaphors and allegories that were used to obscure the sacred secrets of the gods. In short, these books should offer us the most explicit ever account of Egyptian religion.

If I am right, the books of the Pyramid will offer a common rationale for temple building, pyramid building, and other sacred rituals pertaining to the science of the soul. All religious rituals, we will be informed, re-enacted the creation, and conjured up the magic of the First Time. The building of a temple thus re-enacted the raising of the sky from the abyss, whilst the building of a pyramid re-enacted the emergence and ascent of the creator-god in his esoteric form, i.e. as the spirit and iron seed that was ejected from the primeval earth. The king, we will be told, embodied the living spirit of the creator and personified his triumph over the forces of chaos and non-being; thus, in his lifetime, he was the source of life and *maat* in the land, whilst in 'death' he re-enacted the separation of soul from body by which the creator (the primeval earth) had first stirred and come into being; the king thus ascended as a spirit to the sky, in the process re-enacting the creation of the Universe, and becoming as one with the Sun, the Moon and the stars. The king, the creator-god, and the pyramid all represented one and the same idea. As for the act of creation, the writings will describe an archetypal cataclysm in which the primeval earth split apart and in which the primeval ocean and the terrestrial iron were spiritualised. In this newly-created sky-ocean, the molten iron came together to form the stars, the Sun, and the Moon, whilst leftover pieces of iron fell back to the earth and fertilised it. This sequence of events, we will be told, was triggered by spiritual forces, personified by the Great God and the Great Goddess, which entwined in the primeval earth. These twin powers spiritualised themselves in the creative act, and manifested themselves in the entirety of creation – the Sun, the Moon, the stars, and the celestial ocean, as well as the Earth at the centre of the Universe. And yet the true form of the creator-beings was the invisible, spiritual, all-encompassing breath of the Universe. This was the true object of worship for initiates in this cult of creation.

All of this is controversial to Egyptology at the present time, but will, I hope, be vindicated by the contents of the books that are hypothesised to remain intact in the Pyramid. If so, it will be a 'double whammy', for the books will not only vindicate my decoding of ancient Egyptian religion, but will also vindicate the creational approach that has been used in this book to decipher the architecture of the Great Pyramid. A virtuous circle indeed.

Even so, if the books tell us no more and no less than I have deduced already about Egyptian religion, then I, for one, will be disappointed. As I explain in the companion volume to this book (to be published shortly), the Egyptian creation myth does contain some notable gaps, particularly as regards the ultimate origin of the divine powers, and the true nature of their alchemical fusion in the underworld. Unfortunately, owing to the secrecy in which the myth of creation was cloaked, it is difficult to tell whether the Egyptians were unsure about these questions, or whether it was taboo to recount the full story. However, there are occasional hints in the texts that the God and the Goddess originated from elsewhere, and journeyed into the earth from another parallel realm; and there are hints that the proto-earth was affected by a cataclysm (witness the myths of the crisis of the God, and the fiery outburst of the Goddess).[56] Oddly enough, these hints appear to be amplified in the creation myths of Mesopotamia, which provide explicit accounts of the High God and the High Goddess descending into the earth following a cataclysm in the sky.[57] Here, in a collection of myths that are broadly similar to those of Egypt, the divine power is portrayed as an ultraterrestrial 'world mass' that exploded and fell from the sky, thereby sowing the seeds of life in the earth. Might this idea have filtered into Egypt, corrupting the sacred tradition there? Or might Egypt have had its own original, unspeakable doctrine along these lines? Perhaps, one day, the books of the Pyramid will shed light on this strange tradition of an antediluvian world.

Retrieving the Books – a Moral Dilemma

So much for the contents of the secret chambers, but how on earth should we go about retrieving them? Indeed, should we even retrieve them at all? As the evidence builds for the existence of the chambers, it becomes ever more important to debate the issues that will arise in the event of a confirmed discovery.

Much will depend on what exactly is found.

In the least problematic scenario, no physical artefacts will be found in the chambers, but rather the walls of the chambers will be inscribed (in like manner to the later Pyramid Texts). These inscriptions could then be examined remotely by means of a telescopic camera, and there would be no need to remove anything.

However, whilst an inscribed chamber is a possibility, the Egyptians generally kept their sacred books in chests or boxes. Earlier, for example, we heard of the sacred book of Thoth, which had been deposited inside a nest of boxes, sealed inside an iron chest. Similarly, an anatomical text, discovered during the 1st dynasty, had been found beneath the statue of Anubis in Letopolis, hidden 'among old writings in a box'.[58] And in Spell 695 of the Coffin Texts, a message is sent to Osiris in Abydos, saying: "Open the chest of writings, so that you may hear the word of this god".[59]

Here, in these examples, the chest was designed to protect and safeguard the holy books. But the chest could also have a religious significance. In the form of the sarcophagus, for example, it symbolised the realm of the underworld or, in some cases, the entire Universe (hence the image of Anubis sitting upon his chest; and the painting of stars on the underside of coffin lids).

Given the divine status of the sacred book in ancient Egypt, and given the precedent for the use of the stone sarcophagus at elevated height in the Pyramid (to enshrine the meteoritic iron in the King's Chamber), I predict that the hypothesised books will indeed have been stored inside hermetically-sealed coffers of stone. This is good in one sense, because airtight boxes will have preserved parchments or papyri in their original condition. The downside, however, is that robotic technology will be thwarted: it will not permit us to read the pages of a book that is sealed inside a box. In such circumstances, we would have no option but to take the old-fashioned approach of tunnelling our way into the chambers so as to open the boxes by hand. (I am assuming here that each sarcophagus will exceed the 8-inch dimensions of the shafts.)

Here, we encounter a potential problem, since the Supreme Council of Antiquities in Egypt is tasked with protecting the monuments under its supervision, and is reluctant to damage them. Even if the secret chambers were proven to exist, and even if sealed sarcophagi were detected within them, there is still no guarantee that the Supreme Council would sanction excavations. Indeed, given Egyptology's history of discovering *sealed but empty* sarcophagi, and given the view that prevails about the Pyramid being 'a tomb, and nothing but a tomb', there is every possibility that excavations would be ruled out as 'unnecessary and unjustified in the circumstances'.

This is where the sealed repository idea comes into play. If I am right in my decoding of the Pyramid's architecture, then the builder *intended* a future explorer to break the seals of the passages and chambers in order to retrieve the hidden artefacts. Having discovered the Queen's Chamber, the explorer was *supposed* to break the seals of the shafts, and then use those shafts as guides to tunnel through the masonry, thereby reaching the secret chambers above. In principle, then, we should not be unduly concerned about damaging the Pyramid. It was the architect's intention that this would happen, indeed *must* happen.

Fortunately, it is no longer necessary to dig upwards from the Queen's Chamber for distances of 213 feet along the northern and southern shafts. Instead, thanks to the wonders of robotic technology, we can pinpoint exactly where the secret chambers lie, and we can reach them by making short, horizontal breaches from the exterior of the Pyramid to a depth of only 50 feet or so in each case. In this regard, we are assisted by the fact (unfortunate as it may be) that the casing of the monument was destroyed in antiquity, thus exposing the layers of core masonry. It would therefore be a straightforward task to dig a couple of tunnels into the monument, provided that the locations of the secret chambers were known. All that is needed is courage, determination, and self-belief. (In this regard, it is imperative that the responsible authorities acquaint themselves with the sealed repository theory.)

The flip side of the coin, however, is that the sealed repository theory confronts us with moral considerations, as well as practical ones, for it suggests that the contents of the secret chambers were not intended for us, the denizens of the 21st century, but rather for a future generation of men, who would rebuild civilisation after the prophesied cataclysm. To discover an intact chamber now would be premature, and would present us with a potential dilemma. Should we betray the wishes of the Pyramid builders by removing the books for modern ends? Would we be justified in retrieving the scrolls merely for academic purposes, to advance our understanding of ancient Egyptian religion? Would the scrolls be of any practical use to us, say in filling the spiritual void of Western society or settling the religious divisions of the world? If the answers to these last two questions are "no", then should we not leave the books intact for the benefit of post-cataclysm man? Should we not, in fact, add to the time capsule, rather than subtract from it, to express our own concerns about future global destruction?

Perhaps this dilemma may be solved by a compromise. I suggest that we go ahead and retrieve the sacred books, produce an agreed translation of the contents, in the English language say, retranslate the contents into every world language, and then put both the originals and the translations back inside the Pyramid. Either we could return the sacred words to their original hiding place, or we could conceal them somewhere else inside the Pyramid, perhaps in a more accessible spot. For example, we could place them in the hollow behind the Queen's Chamber niche, then seal up the wall and mark it with a sign or a plaque.

In summary, I predict that an extraordinary discovery awaits us in the Pyramid – a literary treasure that will not only rewrite our understanding of ancient Egypt, but also cast light on the origin and meaning of modern religions. Somewhere out there, probably in Egypt, is an individual who, with a little courage, will become the most famous archaeologist of all time.

Chapter Nine Summary

- There is compelling evidence for a small secret chamber located above the stone plug in the Queen's Chamber southern shaft. Furthermore, it is likely that a corresponding chamber will be found above a similar plug in the northern shaft.

- The very concept of the secret chamber makes no sense according to the orthodox 'tomb and tomb only' theory. However, it makes perfect sense in the context of the sealed repository theory.

- It is proposed, in accordance with the sealed repository theory, that the shafts were to be used as guides for excavation. Here, the explorer would face his ultimate challenge, culminating perhaps in the ultimate prize.

- The existence of two secret chambers – one above the southern shaft and one above the northern shaft – is a critical prediction of the sealed repository theory. Less critically, it is proposed that at least one of the chambers will contain the sacred books of the Pyramid builders, and that these books will provide the most explicit ever account of ancient Egyptian religion, vindicating the interpretation that has been used in this book.

- The architect intended that a future explorer break the seals inside the Pyramid and dig tunnels to the secret chambers. The author therefore recommends that the authorities make short horizontal breaches from the exterior of the monument in order to gain access to the secret chambers (on the assumption that their contents are sealed inside sarcophagi).

- In view of the Pyramid's intended function as a time capsule, the author recommends that the hypothesised sacred books be copied and thereafter returned to the monument.

CHAPTER TEN

SECRET CHAMBERS

I emphasise that one of the keys to pyramid exploration is the discernment of the particular jointing patterns; for wherever stones were set into place, regardless of how precise the workmanship, the jointing pattern is there for the discriminating eye to behold.

(J.P. Lepre, *The Egyptian Pyramids*, 1990)

Despite the fact that the Great Pyramid contains more chambers than any other pyramid in Egypt, its known chambers account for only 0.06% of its interior volume; or, looked at another way, more than eight thousand additional chambers could be accommodated inside it.[1] Even if we allow for the predicted discovery of chambers above the Queen's Chamber shafts (chapter nine), sufficient space remains in the monument for many more undiscovered passages and rooms.

Mindful of such calculations, and notwithstanding their acceptance of the tomb hypothesis, many explorers across the centuries have probed the Pyramid in the firm belief that further, intact chambers must exist. In the 19th century, the preferred method of exploration was gunpowder (Howard Vyse in particular left his mark on the Pyramid thus),[2] whilst in the late-20th century explorers turned to non-invasive technologies. The results, however, have been disappointing. From the age of gunpowder, the only significant finds were the King's Chamber superstructure – not a chamber per se – and the Queen's Chamber shafts, whilst, from the age of technology, the only real find has been the 'doors' and plug(s) above the Queen's Chamber shafts. (Other investigations, whilst interesting, have proved negative, unclear or ambiguous.)[3] The bottom line, then, is that no new chambers have been discovered since al-Mamun re-opened the upper compartments in AD 820; and even he found nothing that had not already been discovered and robbed by intruders in remote antiquity.

The panel below illustrates just how sparse discoveries have been during the modern era.

It is indeed quite remarkable, when we stop to think about it, that virtually everything we know about the Pyramid has been uncovered by accident or chance.[4] If, for example, an earthquake had not damaged the King's Chamber and caused the guardians to dig the inspection tunnel in the Well Shaft, it is unlikely that the Grand Gallery would ever have been discovered; and thus none of the upper chambers would be known today. Moreover, if the guardians had not exposed the bridging slab that concealed the Queen's Chamber Passage, that passage and its chamber might have remained hidden, despite the discovery of the Gallery. And if they had not cut through the Gallery's lower roof, the upper part of the Gallery might have remained unknown. Similarly, if the guardians had not cut a second inspection tunnel into the lowest of the cavities above the King's Chamber, we would never have learned of the complex multi-roof system in its superstructure. In short, if it had not been for a severe earthquake and the damage it inflicted upon the King's Chamber, we would remain blissfully ignorant of the Pyramid's upper passages and chambers.

Chance too was surely a factor in al-Mamun's re-excavation of the old robber's tunnel. If he had not reached the intersection of the Ascending and Descending Passages, and if he had not dug a short tunnel around the granite plugs, then the upper passages and chambers, despite having been looted, would have remained unknown until the time of Howard Vyse's explorations (1836-37) or perhaps even unto the present day.

As for the Queen's Chamber shafts, which have proved so pivotal to our investigation, would Waynman Dixon have discovered them had a hairline crack not developed in the stone that covered the southern shaft? And would we have found out about the 'doors' and plug(s) in the shafts had the need not arisen for a robot that could unblock the shafts *of the King's Chamber* in order to reduce the humidity in that room?[5]

Likewise, in the environs of the Pyramid, was it not by sheer chance that the great funerary boats were discovered buried in their pits to the south side of the monument?

These contrasting fortunes between the successes arising from random occurrences and the failures resulting from deliberate explorations tend to suggest one of two things: either (a) that no further chambers remain to be found in the Pyramid (as mainstream Egyptology believes); or (b) that chambers do exist and modern era explorers have been neglectful, by and large, in their searches. Here, of course, one's preference is dictated by one's preconceptions. If the Pyramid is a tomb, and nothing but a

Great Pyramid Discoveries during the Modern Era

1837
Colonel Richard W. Howard Vyse discovers the full extent of the tiered superstructure above the King's Chamber.

1872
Waynman Dixon discovers the shafts in the north and south walls of the Queen's Chamber.

1954
Kamal el-Mallakh discovers two boat pits to the south of the Pyramid, each containing a full-size, dismantled boat.

1993
Rudolf Gantenbrink discovers a metal-handled 'door' blocking the end of the Queen's Chamber southern shaft.

1993
Zawi Hawass discovers the foundations of the Pyramid's original satellite pyramid (at its south-eastern corner).

2002
Zawi Hawass, in conjunction with National Geographic, discovers a stone plug behind the 'door' in the Queen's Chamber southern shaft, and a second metal-handled 'door' blocking the end of the northern shaft.

tomb, then further 'tomb' chambers are indeed unlikely, and modern era explorers are vindicated in their collective failure. But, if the Pyramid is a sealed repository, as I have argued, then further secret chambers must be deemed likely, implying that the explorers have been looking in all the wrong places.

Is it possible that modern exploration has so calamitously missed the mark? Indeed it is. For whilst the competence of the explorers is not to be questioned, they have generally laboured under the assumption that the Pyramid is a tomb, and nothing but a tomb, and thus have conducted their investigations half-heartedly and, in recent years, with an attitude of insouciance and scientific disinterest, brought about by an archaeological culture of caution and restraint (witness the nine-year delay in probing beyond 'the Gantenbrink door'). Whilst the style of investigation has swung dramatically from the 19th century use of gunpowder to the 20th century use of remote-sensing technology, the rationale for investigation has remained unchanged. Egyptology tolerates, rather than promotes, exploration of the Pyramid, and its philosophy precludes any systematic basis for investigation on the grounds that multiple secret chambers are incongruous in a tomb. Official policy is thus seen to be a muddle of contradictions.

The reader will not be surprised to learn that I advocate a different approach to exploration of the Pyramid, in line with the sealed repository theory outlined in chapter six of this book. It is my belief that additional undiscovered chambers do exist and can be found if we get inside the mind of the architect and examine the monument in the way that it was intended to be examined.

My approach is founded on the principle that the architect wanted the secret chambers to be discovered by someone who would make a close and careful inspection of the monument, in particular the pattern of the joints in the stones. If further secret chambers exist, then the necessary clues should be right there in the stones, allowing us to detect the sealed passages that will lead to the hypothesised chambers. All we need to do is use our eyes and our intelligence.

An approach along these lines was adopted by the Egyptologist J.P. Lepre, who, whilst supporting the orthodox theory of the Great Pyramid, believed firmly in the existence of hidden passages and chambers, which could be found by identifying anomalies in the patterns of the stones. In his 1990 book *The Egyptian Pyramids*, he wrote:

> I emphasise that one of the keys to pyramid exploration is the discernment of the particular jointing patterns; for wherever stones were set into place, regardless of how precise the workmanship, the jointing pattern is there for the discriminating eye to behold.[6]

Lepre accepted the premise made by Smyth that the anomalous joints in the floor of the Descending Passage had been a deliberate sign for the hidden entrance to the Ascending Passage, and, on this basis, he carried out a close inspection of the joints in the Queen's Chamber Passage and the King's Chamber (his observations here will be discussed in due course). Although Lepre never did explain the paradox of the architect wanting the king's tomb chambers to be found (and his untimely death has deprived us of any further thoughts that he might have had), the fact is that his philosophy anticipated to a remarkable degree that which is to be taken in this chapter on the view that the Pyramid was not only a tomb but also a repository. Lepre's work thus provides us with a wellspring of useful observations and suggestions, as well as reassuring us that our methodology is sound.

Now, in order to carry out a systematic investigation of the Pyramid's interior joints, the researcher ideally requires unfettered and undisturbed access to the monument, probably for as long as a month (Lepre's survey was much briefer than this).[7] But such a privilege would be exceptional, even for an Egyptologist; and thus the chances of this author carrying out the necessary study lie somewhere between slim and zero. Nevertheless, most (although not all) of the relevant information has been published in books and journals during the 19th and 20th centuries, and it is therefore possible, up to a point, to carry out a preliminary 'desk top' exercise to pinpoint the most likely locations in which hidden passages might be found.

In this chapter, then, I set out a number of possible locations for secret entrances to undiscovered chambers, some of them representing extant suggestions (I am particularly indebted to Lepre), others representing new ideas, and I appraise their potential significance in the context of the Pyramid's role as a sealed repository. My methodology, as the reader will see, is to identify anomalies in the jointing patterns of the stones, or in the architecture generally, and to assess the possibility of camouflaged entrances in the light of the precedents that have been theorised for the concealment of the Ascending Passage, the upper part of the Grand Gallery, the Queen's Chamber Passage, the Queen's Chamber, and the King's Chamber Passage. Only where an anomaly has first been detected in the joints or the architecture do I then consider the evidence that has arisen from the use of remote-sensing technology.

The ultimate aim of this chapter is to produce a short list of possible locations for secret passages and chambers, which the authorities can use – if they have the courage – to test the validity of the sealed repository theory.

The Descending Passage (Upper Section)

We begin in the uppermost, built part of the Descending Passage, about 40 feet down from the original entrance, where we find some anomalous joints – a pair on each of the side walls – which are not inclined with the passage, as the other joints are, but stand vertically, for no reason that has ever been fathomed. In addition, immediately below these near-vertical joints, the walls have been inscribed with an unusual pair of lines that run from top to bottom, one on each side.

Piazzi Smyth, who discovered this odd arrangement while surveying the Pyramid in 1865, was fascinated in particular by the pair of scored lines, which he theorised to be a calendrical marker (he believed that the

Figure 129.
THE ANOMALOUS JOINTS AND SCORED LINES IN THE DESCENDING
PASSAGE.

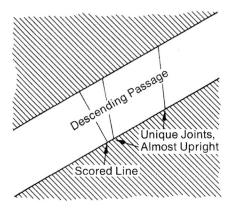

Pyramid encoded the history and destiny of mankind).[8] In his 1880 book
Our Inheritance in the Great Pyramid, Smyth described the scored lines
as follows:

> This mark was a line, nothing more, ruled on the stone, from top to
> bottom of the passage wall, at right angles to its floor. Such a line as
> might be ruled with a blunt steel instrument, but by a master-hand for
> power, evenness, straightness, and still more eminently for
> rectangularity to the passage axis.[9]

Other researchers, however, were intrigued more by the anomaly of the
vertical joints in the walls, as Smyth informs us:

> This double joint fact, in itself most easy to see, though not, I believe,
> recorded before 1865, has frequently since then been speculated on by
> various persons as possibly pointing to some still undiscovered
> chamber; and it may do so, just as the diagonal joints in the floor at a
> lower level are now clearly seen to point... to the upper ascending
> passage, and all that it leads to.[10]

Here, Smyth makes an important point. The incongruous arrangement of
the wall stones, he says, recalls a similar incongruous arrangement in *the
floor stones* further down the passage, the latter lying directly beneath the
prism stone that camouflaged the entrance to the Ascending Passage. A
clear precedent exists, therefore, for the possibility that the marks in the
walls are a 'sign for the wise' which indicate the hidden entrance to an
undiscovered passage, and perhaps chambers beyond.

Remarkably, this idea won the support of J.P. Lepre who, in his 1990 book, wrote:

> The hundreds of wall joints located in this [descending] corridor are perfectly aligned to the passage itself. This is to say, that the passage slopes downward, and the wall joints are perpendicular to its floor line. Yet, curiously, at a point 35 feet from the original entrance there are, on either wall side, two joints which rise vertically – the only such ones in the entire passage. Also, close to these two joints, on both walls, is a single chiselled line running, like the majority of joints, perpendicular to the passageway... Their exact purpose is a matter of speculation, but they could be a sign for the existence of a secret chamber, as a similar incongruent line further down the corridor and located in the floor, did in fact point to the chambers and passages in the superstructure of the monument. This particular line – a joint set opposite to the other floor joints – was discovered by Smyth in his inspection of the descending corridor. He correctly referred to it as 'a sign in the floor for the wise'. For here, at that point immediately above the unorthodox joint, lay the lower end of the pyramid's ascending passage which gave access to the upper reaches of the monument.[11]

A persuasive case can thus be made that if the joints in the Descending Passage's floor were included deliberately as an indicator for the hidden Ascending Passage (which seems reasonable under the sealed repository theory, if not under the 'tomb and tomb only' theory), then the marks in its walls, by the same token, would indicate the location of another secret passage, this one lying just 35 to 40 feet down from the main entrance. The scored lines, of course, make this location doubly significant, and add weight to the need for future investigation, using intrusive means if necessary.

But where might such a passageway lead to?

In considering the possibilities, one must first give consideration to the fact that the unusual joints and scored lines lie almost directly beneath a huge limestone double gable that is nowadays exposed in the Pyramid's northern face (actually, they lie a little way south of this gable). Might there possibly be some link between the hypothesised secret passage and this inverted V-shaped structure?

The double gable above the Pyramid's entrance constitutes a mystery in its own right, and has greatly exercised the minds of those who have bothered to study it. Normally, Egyptian builders used gables as roofs to deflect superincumbent forces and thereby relieve stresses on chambers below. In the Great Pyramid, this very constructional technique was used

Figure 130.
THE GABLE STONES IN THE PYRAMID'S NORTH FACE, JUST ABOVE
THE ENTRANCE TO THE DESCENDING PASSAGE.

for the pented roof of the Queen's Chamber and the upper, pented roof of
the King's Chamber, these gables deflecting the superincumbent forces
to the north and south. Although the roofs of these chambers are shown
diagrammatically as single gables, they might well in reality be double
gables just like the entrance stones. However, the latter have been set at
90° to the former, and would therefore have deflected superincumbent
forces to the east and west. And yet, in this position, so close to the edge
of the Pyramid, the double gable structure was totally unnecessary since,
on the one hand, the superincumbent weight was not high, whilst, on the
other hand, there was no chamber below, but only a narrow passage (the
Descending Passage).[12] Here, then, is the mystery of the entrance gable:
why was it erected for no ostensible constructional purpose in a place
that was hidden from view?

Might the gable be part of a roof of a secret chamber? For this to be
the case, the gable would have to be the northernmost end of a structure
that extends for some distance into the Pyramid. However, according to
Piazzi Smyth, who cites John Perring as his authority, 'there is ordinary
course masonry at the back of the single set of stones'.[13] The possibility
of a secret chamber beneath the gable must therefore be rejected, since
there is insufficient space between it and the Descending Passage below.

The mystery of the gable nevertheless remains. If it was not a relieving structure, then what was it? What might it convey to us about the beliefs or practices of the Pyramid builders?

Several Egyptologists have suggested symbolism in its design. Lepre, for example, imagined the gable to be 'symbolic of the grandeur which lies beyond, a sort of introduction to a high order of things',[14] whilst Paul Badham interpreted it as the hieroglyph *hepet*, meaning 'to proceed by boat, to a place'.[15] In support of this symbolism approach, the gable does contain two layers of stones, the second layer providing no significant structural benefit. Against it, however, is the fact that reconstructions of the entrance masonry make this double gable the rearmost of several sets of gable stones, which were all placed alongside each other on an incline, as shown in figure 131. Significantly, this incline, far from being parallel with the north-oriented Descending Passage, as Badham's theory would require (the king being destined to ascend by boat to the northern skies), goes upwards and southwards towards the heart of the monument.

Figure 131.
THE ORIGINAL ARRANGEMENT OF GABLE STONES ABOVE THE
DESCENDING PASSAGE (PER W.M.F. PETRIE).

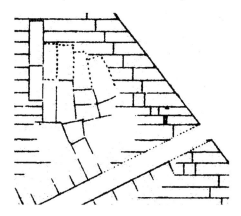

All things considered, then, neither the structural relief theory nor the symbolism theory offers a convincing explanation of the gable stones; and thus, by a process of elimination, we are left with just one plausible scenario: that the builders erected these inclined sets of gable stones as a practice run for a similar inclined roof that was to be built over the top of the Grand Gallery, to protect it from the weight of the superincumbent masonry. (To my knowledge, this idea has not been suggested before.)

We have digressed somewhat from our discussion of the mysterious joints and scored lines in the Descending Passage, but our excursion has been necessary in order to rule out any connection with the gable stones.

Now, again, I pose the question: if the joints and lines indicate a secret passage, how would that passage be oriented, and to where might it lead?

One possibility is a sloping passage running parallel to the known Ascending Passage, but above it. But, if this was the case, why would the anomalous joints not be the same as those that lie beneath the Ascending Passage? In other words, why are they placed in the walls rather than in the floor?

For this reason, I favour the possibility that the vertical joints and the scored lines mark a pair of secret passages, the entrances to which lie in the side walls. These two passages would branch out to the east and west of the Descending Passage, and, if it is not too bold a speculation, might extend for a considerable distance in those directions, before turning at right angles to head due south, thus together forming a letter U, which in Egyptian language signified the outstretched arms of the *ka*-hieroglyph, meaning 'life force' or 'vital energy'. This hypothesised passage system would skirt the northern, eastern and western faces of the Pyramid about 30 feet above ground level, and about 40 feet beneath the original casing, and would offer access either to a number of 'store rooms' at that level or, if another bold speculation may be ventured, to additional ascending passages and upper chamber systems, paralleling the single upper system that is already known.[16]

Over the years, many researchers have speculated on the possibility of such additional chamber systems, occasionally on the basis of intriguing insights, for example, geometric considerations or solstitial shadows cast onto the Pyramid by its neighbour, the Pyramid of Khafre.[17] However, beyond repeating the fact that there is plenty of room for these mooted chambers, especially to the east, west, and south of the system that is presently known, it is almost pointless to speculate on where they might be, since it is neither practical nor permissible to take the Pyramid apart, stone by stone, in the pertinent areas. Rather, priority must be given to identifying the entrances to the passages that lead to the chambers; and this is the approach that is taken in this book.

The Ascending Passage

Another strong contender for a secret passage, overlooked by Lepre, is the bottom part of the Ascending Passage, this idea being suggested by the 'model passages' that were discovered by William Flinders Petrie in 1881.

These 'model passages', or 'trial passages' as they are often called, are situated 287 feet east of the Great Pyramid, just north of its causeway,

Figure 132.
THE SO-CALLED TRIAL PASSAGES.

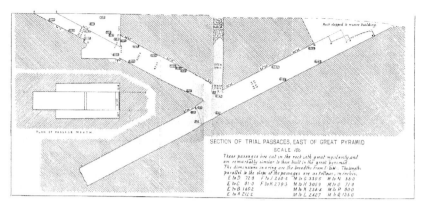

SECTION OF TRIAL PASSAGES, EAST OF GREAT PYRAMID
SCALE

where they have been cut into the bedrock to a depth of about 31 feet.[18]
Remarkably, in view of the Pyramid's uniqueness, they reproduce not
only the Descending Passage but also the Ascending Passage (tapered to
hold plugs), the lower part of the Grand Gallery, and the beginning of the
Queen's Chamber Passage (see figure 132). In the opinion of Petrie, the
passages were nothing less than a trial or model for those of the Great
Pyramid itself. He wrote:

> The trial passages are... a model of the Great Pyramid passages,
> shortened in length, but of full size in width and height.[19]

But there was one part of this system that Petrie did not recognise in the
Pyramid:

> The vertical shaft here is... the only feature which is not an exact copy
> of the Great Pyramid passages, *as far as we know them*. The
> resemblance in all other respects is striking...[20] (original emphasis)

Might this vertical shaft represent an undiscovered secret passage in the
Pyramid? If the shaft had indeed been built there, then one might expect
it to have been uncovered when the prism stone was removed from the
roof of the Descending Passage, for such is the proximity of the trial
shaft's entrance to the mouth of the ascending passage. But no such shaft
has been revealed. However, it is just possible that it remains undetected
above the roofs of the Descending and Ascending Passages, where its
lower part might be filled by a plug – this being suggested by the slight
tapering of the 'trial' shaft.

Regardless of whether these passages truly were a model for the Great
Pyramid, as Petrie believed (others have argued that they rather represent

a preparatory substructure for a queen's pyramid that was never built),[21] their astonishing similarity to the Pyramid's architecture demands that the secret passage theory be taken seriously.

Another possibility, suggested by some researchers, is that the vertical shaft has been incorporated further up the Ascending Passage, above the granite plugs.

In this regard, it must be emphasised that the area around the plugs has not been well explored. The first person to examine this area, I believe, was Caliph al-Mamun, who in AD 820 excavated along the western sides of the upper plugs and uncovered the end of the lowermost plug, but then abandoned his work, having found nothing to further pique his curiosity (see end of chapter eight). Since then, it would seem, the plugs have lain undisturbed, exactly where the builders installed them thousands of years ago.

It is also worth noting that the hypothesised vertical shaft would have a width of about 28 inches (as suggested by the 'trial' shaft), which would be significantly narrower than the width of the Ascending Passage (40 inches). It is therefore quite conceivable that such a shaft could have remained undetected, despite the excavation to the western side of the plugs.

Finally, in support of the idea of a shaft above the plugs, the purpose of the plugs is a real mystery, since the Ascending Passage was already safeguarded by the camouflaging stone at its entrance. Why, then, use plugs? And why plugs of granite? Whilst I personally detect a religious symbolism here, it is also possible that the architect used that symbolism to reward the worthy explorer. In other words, it may have been intended that the deserving individual recognise the granite plugs as a symbolic seal that was to be broken, whilst the undeserving individual see only an obstacle that was to be circumvented (i.e. by cutting a path through the limestone side walls). The architect might thus have reserved a discovery above the plugs for the genuine truth-seeker.[22]

If there is a vertical shaft above the Ascending Passage, either here or in the position described earlier, then to where might it lead? The likely answer, in my view, would be a chamber located directly above the shaft, perhaps at the level of the Queen's Chamber Passage.

In summary, it would be well worthwhile to check for cavities in both of the aforementioned areas of the Ascending Passage.

Queen's Chamber Passage

Moving up the Pyramid, our next stop is the Queen's Chamber Passage, where an anomalous arrangement of stones and joints could indicate the presence of a hidden passage. The first person to highlight this possibility was Lepre, who conducted a thorough investigation of this area in 1978 (remarkably, no-one prior to Lepre had mapped the stones in this part of the Pyramid). Writing in 1990, Lepre reported the results of his study as follows:

> As no thorough investigation of that corridor had ever been conducted, I attempted to map out the entirety of walls, floor and ceiling of that corridor, marking each and every joint of masonry. I found a total of 130 blocks of stone comprising this passageway, with the majority of them (122) being of the same relative size or oriented in the same direction. Yet eight of the 130 stones did not obey this basic rule. Two of them, although of the same general dimensions as the majority of other blocks in the corridor, were floor stones which represented the area of a single block, with a joint separating them which ran in the opposite direction of the joints of the other floor stones. This is the very same situation which exists in the Descending Passage floor and which pointed to the fact that the secret Ascending Passage system rose above that area of the Descending Passage. The reader may recall that P. Smyth termed this idiosyncracy 'a sign in the floor for the wise'. Immediately beyond these two stones lie six other blocks which are different from the others in the passageway in that they are much larger in size, being double the length of the average stone. Not only this, four of the six are exactly parallel to one another, two situated on the east wall and two on the west wall.[23]

What is to be made of this? The precedent of the anomalous floor joints in the Descending Passage would seem to suggest that a hidden passage exists here *above* the comparable floor joints. However, such a passage here would lead into an especially cluttered part of the Pyramid, where the Queen's Chamber, Grand Gallery, and King's Chamber have all been built. Since it is difficult to imagine a further chamber being squeezed into this tight space,[24] a more likely scenario is an ascending passage that turns at a right angle to head to the east or the west, where there is plenty of room for a further chamber, or indeed a whole series of passages and chambers.

There is, however, another possibility: that the secret passage is here located *below* the anomalous floor joints. In this case, the passage would lead downwards at an angle, either to the north or to the south, and might conceivably provide access to some old sacred structure on the plateau outcrop below, perhaps a 'tomb of the gods' that was ancient even before the Pyramid was built.[25] Such a structure would be located to the north of the Grotto, perhaps on the central east-west axis of the Pyramid, directly beneath the Queen's Chamber.

If the unusual floor joints are indeed a sign for a hidden entrance to a descending passage, then this might well explain the use of larger than average blocks immediately beyond this location, such blocks lending protection to the roof of the secret passage. This would be consistent, of course, with a passage descending to the south.[26]

Before moving on, it is worthwhile to note that the Queen's Chamber Passage has been the subject of several archaeological investigations during the 1980s. In the first, two Frenchmen Gilles Dormion and Jean-Patrice Goidin, prompted by the unusual arrangement of stones (which they seem to have spotted independently of Lepre), scanned the walls of the passage using a microgravimeter (a sonar-like device), and detected a possible cavity behind the west wall; permission was then granted for three holes to be bored into the wall, but all that they found was a cavity filled with sand.[27] In the second investigation, a Japanese team from Waseda University, headed by Sakuji Yoshimura, surveyed the passage using ground-penetrating radar and confirmed the presence of a cavity behind the west wall, running parallel to it for most of its length.[28] But they also detected a possible cavity beneath the floor of the passage.[29]

In the opinion of this author, the signals for cavities behind the west wall, whilst certainly of interest, probably do not reflect a secret passage system,[30] whereas the signal for a cavity beneath the floor might well be evidence of the secret descending passage that was hypothesised earlier.

The Queen's Chamber

In the Queen's Chamber itself, two secret passages have already been found, namely the 8-inch-square shafts in the north and south walls, the significance of which has been discussed in chapter nine. (The miniature size of these shafts reminds us that hidden passageways come in a variety of sizes.) In addition, it has been speculated that a secret passage once existed in the east wall, at the back of the niche;[31] hence the fact that a 38-feet-long tunnel has been excavated at this spot. In view of these observations, the chances of finding any further secret passages in this chamber might be regarded as slim.

In 1987, the Waseda University team (mentioned earlier) probed the Queen's Chamber using ground-penetrating radar, but with disappointing results. The only possible cavity lay behind the north wall, paralleling the cavities found running along the western side of the Queen's Chamber

Passage.[32] In the opinion of this author, these cavities are unlikely to form part of a secret passage system.

If a secret passage does remain to be found in this chamber (a big 'if' in view of the disappointing GPR results), it is most likely to be found in the west wall, at the height of the entrance at which the shafts were found in the north and south walls. Right now, it must be taken on trust that the Waseda University team did make a thorough examination of this west wall.

Grand Gallery

Turning to the Grand Gallery, there has been speculation that a secret chamber might lie to the west of it, at the level of the Great Step. This idea is suggested by the strange detour that is made by the northern shaft as it exits the King's Chamber, as if it were avoiding a structure in that vicinity.[33] However, I am not aware of any unusual joints or marks in the upper west wall of the Gallery, and it is therefore difficult to see how the implied room could be accessed (as is required by the sealed repository theory). It is likely, therefore, that the northern shaft's detour has another explanation, perhaps the need to avoid a large working area that had been assigned to the Gallery construction team, or, less likely, a planning error by the shaft construction team.

Another theory, suggested by two French researchers Jacques Bardot and Francine Darmon, holds that many of the inset stones in the east and west walls of the Gallery are 'false joints', which indicate the presence of passages and chambers beyond.[34] In all, thirty-one of the fifty inset stones were deemed to be 'false' by these researchers. In my view, this scenario is very unlikely in view of the sheer number of suggested leads, it being the architect's normal practice to mark a secret entrance with a singular anomaly. As discussed in chapter eight, the inset stones are probably the result of a planning error. However, lest I be wrong about this, it is worth observing that the twenty-sixth set of inset stones in the east wall and the thirteenth set of inset stones in the west wall are both anomalous, for the reasons set out in chapter two.

Elsewhere in the Gallery, no other anomalous joints or stones exist to the best of my knowledge, but it may be that a secret passage has already been uncovered in the form of the dogleg shaft which nowadays forms part of the Well Shaft but which was originally built as a sealed hollow beneath the lower western ramp stone. One possible way to shed light on this matter is to probe the corresponding area beneath the lower eastern ramp stone, on the basis that the dogleg shaft may have been one of a pair.

It is also important to realise that the Gallery was originally fitted with a 'false roof', which was slotted into its side walls, and hence its upper corbelled area represents an uncovered secret chamber of a kind. Quite what was hidden in this upper space, if anything, is hard to say, and its significance is hard to fathom. However, the architect's concealment of this area impels us to look closely at the upper parts of the walls and the roof, and when we do so a remarkable thought springs to mind which, to the best of my knowledge, has never been entertained before. In figure 133 below, I contrast the Grand Gallery of the Great Pyramid with a corbelled chamber from the Red Pyramid at Dahshur. In the latter, it may be seen that the corbels are stepped in repeatedly until the roof is formed by the standard width of one double corbel. In the former, however, the corbels are stepped in by about 3 inches on each side, but are halted at a point when they are no less than 3 feet 6 inches apart; here, instead of further corbels, a set of forty roof slabs bring the majestic structure to a somewhat inglorious end.

Now, there is some harmony in the Gallery's design in that the width

Figure 133.
ON THE LEFT, THE CORBELLING OF THE GRAND GALLERY, ON THE RIGHT THE CORBELLING IN THE RED PYRAMID AT DAHSHUR.
The comparison suggests that the Gallery's present roof conceals a secret upper roof area.

of the roof slabs matches the width of the floor between the ramps, i.e. 3 feet 6 inches. Nevertheless, it is evident from what we know of corbelled chambers in the Red Pyramid and the nearby Bent Pyramid of Dahshur (six such chambers in total) that the usual design of this period (the 4th dynasty) had the corbels support a roof that was one double corbel in width. In comparison, the roof of the Gallery in the Great Pyramid stands out as a striking exception to the rule.

The more one studies these corbelled chambers, the more one gets the impression that the Gallery's roof terminates the chamber prematurely, truncating it before its full height is reached. Indeed, one feels compelled to break out the roof slabs in order to raise the height of the roof. Perhaps this was what the architect intended.

Figure 134. CLOSE-UP OF THE GRAND GALLERY'S ROOF SLABS.

Might there be a concealed area lying above the Gallery's present roof, just as there was once a concealed area (now visible) lying above its lower roof?

In considering this question, it is pertinent to note two points: (a) that the roof slabs have a particularly interesting design, which allows each stone to be removed (in theory) independently of the others; and (b) that the roof slabs have been examined only rarely. Both of these points were made by William Flinders Petrie, who reported upon his inspection of the roof as follows:

> The roof of the Gallery and its [upper] walls are not well known, owing to the difficulty in reaching them. By means of ladders, that I made jointing together, I was able to thoroughly examine both ends and parts of the sides of the Gallery. The roof stones are set each at a steeper slope than the passage, in order that the lower edge of each stone should hitch like a paul into a ratchet-cut in the top of the walls; hence no stone can press on the one below it, so as to cause a cumulative pressure all down the roof; and each stone is separately upheld by the side walls across which it lies.[35]

Few, if any, Egyptologists have examined the roof as closely as Petrie did in 1883. However, during 1988-89, when the Pyramid was closed for repairs and restoration, Zawi Hawass inspected sixteen of the forty roof slabs and found them to be 'in critical condition'. These slabs were given stainless steel bar implants and were regrouted, but, owing to their poor condition, the opportunity was not taken to move them, nor to look above them.[36]

If this is a 'false roof' – as is suggested by: the corbelled chambers at Dahshur; the broken-out lower roof (evidenced by the chisel marks along the grooves in the walls); and the independently removable roof slabs – then what would be the height of the space overhead? Well, in order to reduce the roof width of 42 inches to about 6 inches, the walls would have to be stepped in another six times, which would equate to a further height of about 14 feet 8 inches (in total, the Gallery would then have thirteen corbels and a height of about 42 feet 8 inches).

But what on earth would be the significance of such a long, tall, and narrow space? What could possibly have been kept in a corbelled vault with a length of about 153 feet, a height of 14 feet 8 inches, and a width of 3 feet 6 inches, narrowing to just 6 inches at the top?

Earlier, in chapter eight, I asked this same question about the Gallery space that had been sealed off by the lower 'false roof', and found myself stumped for an answer. I therefore theorised that the space had contained nothing, but had instead functioned as a 'buffer zone'. In other words, it may have been left empty deliberately in order to discourage an intruder from exploring the Gallery's height, which would, of course, imply that something important was hidden there – a something that was concealed by yet another 'false roof'.

This strategy evidently worked, for there is no sign of vandalism to the upper roof, and its immense height has ensured its survival to the present day. But what would the 'something' have been? If my removable roof theory is correct, then the architect went to considerable lengths to throw an intruder off the scent. And yet, it is difficult to visualise the contents of this unusually-shaped space.

But perhaps it was not contents per se that were hidden.

As discussed in chapter eight, the Grand Gallery is no ordinary secret chamber, but rather seems to reflect a high spiritual symbolism. In the view of this author, the entire Gallery is to be read as a simulacrum of the creation, the overlapping corbels signifying the rising of the spirit of the Great God. Under this view, the roofs that divide the corbelled space take on a particular significance, as I explained in the earlier chapter, for the ancient Egyptians believed that the Great God in his true form (pure spirit) rested *above* the starry sky. Hence my proposal that the Gallery's lower roof had been painted with images of the stars, and that the space above it represented the secret realm of the God. However, in the light of the evidence that the Gallery's upper roof is surmounted by a yet higher realm, this theory must now be amended. In particular, it may now be theorised that the lower roof portrayed the stars *in the act of rising* at the

First Time, and that the upper roof, not the lower, signified the boundary of the Universe (in other words, the rising stars were *destined* for the upper roof). Under this scenario, the secret space above the upper roof would contain the God's pure and enduring form, which was symbolised in ancient Egypt, as elsewhere, by gold, which uniquely among metals is untarnished by the passing of time. But this is not to say that the supreme heavenly metal would be enclosed by this secret space. Rather, it is to suggest that gold formed the 6-inch-wide roof where the corbels were finally brought together. In other words, this most grandiose of structures might well have been sealed by bricks of gold, spanning its entire length of 153 feet, like a path of eternity across the sky.

This theory would certainly explain the need for the upper 'false roof', for, without it, the intruder who penetrated the lower 'false roof' would immediately have noticed the gleam of the golden bricks and proceeded to remove them for personal gain.

This golden roof theory does not exclude the possibility that the upper roof space might also provide access to a secret passage, which would in turn provide access to a chamber (or sequence of chambers). If such a passage existed, it would probably head to the east or the west, since the path due north would run into the superstructure of the King's Chamber (unless it doglegged around it). However, personally, I do not favour the secret passage theory in this case, since the Gallery, to my mind, was no ordinary secret chamber but primarily a religious symbol. In other words, the Gallery concealed nothing but itself, which in its full, extended form encoded the mystery of the creation.

King's Chamber

Turning to the King's Chamber, we are indebted once again to Lepre, who carried out a thorough examination of the joints in the stones with the specific aim of identifying possible secret passages. In his 1990 book, Lepre highlighted one stone that he felt was particularly suggestive – the lower left-hand corner stone in the west wall, where three open joints had been filled with plaster:

> Most of the nearly 300 joints in the King's Chamber are so tight as not to admit the breadth of a hair. Only four are in any way open, and three of those represent three sides of a square, four-sided wall block. That is to say, that one of the wall blocks located on the west wall of the chamber, at its lowest course, has three open joints surrounding it... It is worth noting that whenever a passageway enters or exits from a chamber in any of the pyramids, the aperture is usually situated at a

Figure 135.
LEPRE'S DIAGRAM OF THE THREE OPEN JOINTS IN THE KING'S
CHAMBER, WEST WALL.

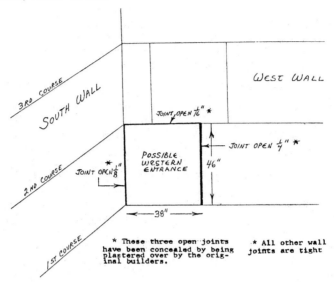

lower right-hand or left-hand corner of the chamber. The block in this
particular instance is in just such a position, occupying the lower left-
hand corner of the west wall of the King's Chamber... It appears very
significant indeed that the only stone in the entire chamber with three
open joints should occupy the unique position of that of a lower course
corner stone. Is it possible that this stone could be moved if enough
pressure were applied to it from the interior of the King's Chamber?
Again, it is the only stone in the entire chamber with open joints on
three sides, and one which is located in the exact spot where another
entrance or passage is likely to be set.[37]

In addition, Lepre highlighted the upper course corner stone at the north-
eastern end of the chamber, where a joint had opened up to the extent of
a full inch.[38] In his opinion, this stone too should be probed for a possible
secret passage.

These are interesting observations, and should definitely be followed
up (no investigation having yet been carried out in response to Lepre's
recommendation in 1990). It should be noted, however, that the King's
Chamber theory presented in these pages is to a large degree inconsistent
with a secret passage in this location, it having been suggested that the
chamber was to remain sealed, with the Pyramid explorer proceeding no
further than the Antechamber (see chapter seven). Thus any discovery of
a secret passage, whilst favouring the sealed repository theory, would be

antagonistic to the acoustic interpretation of the King's Chamber and the Antechamber. In this regard, the reader might wish to ponder on the fact that the King's Chamber is connected to the Antechamber by a section of the King's Chamber Passage. Was this connection required to convey sound frequencies to the Antechamber, for the purposes of initiation, as the acoustic theory suggests? Or was it intended to allow access to the King's Chamber for recovery of artefacts? Only future exploration, along the lines proposed by Lepre, will resolve this question.

Prioritising the Leads

In the course of this chapter, we have examined several potential leads for secret passages and chambers, some of which are highly suggestive, others less so. Below, I set out a summary of the most likely candidates, to which emphasis should be given in future explorations. The star-rating is out of five, and indicates the probability of a discovery at that location, as suggested by the sealed repository theory.

Location (clue)	Potential Significance	Rating
Descending Passage (anomalous floor joints and scored lines).	A pair of passages might branch out to the east and west, and then turn south to form a U shape. These passages might provide access to 'store rooms' at that level or to additional ascending passages and upper chamber systems.	5*
Ascending Passage (vertical shaft in 'trial passages').	A vertical shaft might lead to a chamber directly above, perhaps at the level of the Queen's Chamber Passage.	3*
Queen's Chamber Passage (anomalous floor joints and blocks).	A downward sloping passage might lead to some old sacred site on the plateau beneath the Pyramid, e.g. a 'tomb of the gods', perhaps located on the Pyramid's central east-west axis.	5*
Grand Gallery roof (precedent of 'false roof'; comparison to corbelled chambers at Dahshur; removable roof slabs).	Removable roof slabs might conceal a corbelled upper roof space, crowned by bricks of gold, symbolising the eternal durability of the Great God and his Universe.	5*
King's Chamber (three loose joints in lower left-hand corner stone in the west wall).	A horizontal passage might lead to a secret chamber to the west of the King's Chamber.	3*

If the authorities or their agents were to probe these five locations, then it should be possible to judge the validity of the theories that are presented in this book.

If all five predictions fail, then the sealed repository theory will be in serious trouble, and may have to be abandoned.

If the fifth prediction (that of Lepre) succeeds, then, depending on what is found, it may be good news for the sealed repository theory but bad news for my acoustic theory of the King's Chamber.

If the fourth prediction fails, either in part or in whole, then my theory of the Grand Gallery's religious symbolism will be weakened, although not critically so.

Overall, one or two failures in the 5* predictions would diminish my confidence in the sealed repository theory. Against this, however, if only one prediction turns out to be broadly correct, then, depending on what is found, the sealed repository theory may be clinched.

Finally, we must not forget the secret chamber hypothesis pertaining to the Queen's Chamber shafts (chapter nine). If ongoing explorations of the 'doors' and plug(s) in these shafts confirm the existence of one or more secret chambers beyond, then the sealed repository theory will be strengthened, and the case will be made for accelerated exploration of at least four of the five locations suggested above.

Addendum: the Search for Khufu's Mummy

On the subject of secret passages and chambers, the greatest discovery of all would arguably be the mummy of Khufu, hidden in a room *at ground level or below*, for such a find would negate the orthodox assumption of a burial in the King's Chamber, and would vindicate the approach that has been taken in this book, namely 'the body to earth, the spirit to the sky'. If Khufu's mummy were to be discovered thus, it would be greatly to the advantage of the sealed repository theory. Accordingly, to round off this chapter, we shall look at a number of possibilities for hidden passages and burial rooms in the basement of the Pyramid.

We must begin with the Grotto, which I theorised in chapter four was the original burial place of the king. Could it be that the king's body is still hidden in this room?

An anomalous feature of the Grotto, which I highlighted in the earlier chapter, is the composition of the low ceiling. Lepre reported that it was made of small stones that had been packed together, and that it crumbled when touched; he also observed that it was covered by a light frost, as if it were close to a water source (which he thought odd in this location). In his view, this ceiling ought to be subjected to a closer examination:

> A probing of the ceiling of the Grotto would appear to be in order, but it might prove to be a hazardous venture, due to its loose condition and to the immense weight of the core of the pyramid bearing down on it from above. Oddly enough, Pliny, the Roman scholar, writing about the Great Pyramid in AD 79, makes mention of a 'water-well' being located in the monument. Could there once have been a supply of water running through this section, with the remnants of some underground reservoir still trickling in to dampen the ceiling of the Grotto?[39]

Could the king's mummy have been hidden above an artificial ceiling in the Grotto? Such was the ingenuity of the Egyptian pyramid builders that the hypothesis must be given serious consideration. In addition, there is a remarkable correlation between Lepre's theory of a nearby water source and the report by the Greek historian Herodotus that Cheops (Khufu) had been buried under the Pyramid in subterranean chambers 'built on a sort of island, surrounded by water introduced from the Nile by a canal.'[40] If we substitute a natural spring for the water of the Nile, then the Grotto might well fit Herodotus' description of the king's tomb.

In addition to examining the Grotto's ceiling, we should also check its floor and walls. Here, the best bet is the western end of the room, since it was Egyptian practice to bury the king just to the west of a pyramid's central north-south axis.[41] In this respect, it is interesting to note that the western end of the Grotto lies exactly on the Great Pyramid's north-south axis.[42] In addition to which, it is quite remarkable that the distance to the west wall from the main entrance, via the Descending Passage and the Well Shaft, is almost exactly equal to the height of the monument (481 feet).[43] The west wall of the Grotto should therefore be probed, as should the floor in that part of the room.

Ominously, a deep hole has been dug in the floor at the western end of the Grotto, apparently in ancient times (see figure 136). With dimensions of 5 feet by 5 feet 5 inches by 5 feet 5 inches, and a maximum extension at the bottom of 6 feet 6 inches, this great hole could well have contained the mummy of the king, and in the absence of any other explanation it is tempting to believe that it once did. The implication, of course, is that the hole was dug to exhume the mummy, which was subsequently removed from the room. Tests of the soil in the hole might well be able to confirm or negate this hypothesis.

There is, however, another explanation, namely that the builders dug the hole as a decoy tomb, to protect the real tomb which lay elsewhere in

Figure 136.
THE GROTTO, GROUND PLAN.
Compare figure 61 (vertical section) in chapter four.

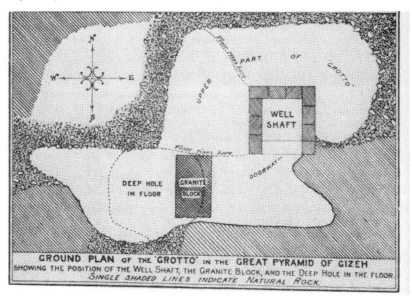

GROUND PLAN of the 'GROTTO' in the GREAT PYRAMID of GIZEH
SHOWING THE POSITION OF THE WELL SHAFT, THE GRANITE BLOCK, AND THE DEEP HOLE IN THE FLOOR
SINGLE SHADED LINES INDICATE NATURAL ROCK.

the vicinity. Thus any tomb robber who had the good fortune to discover the Grotto (via the secret door in the Well Shaft) would have been lulled into thinking that the room had been discovered and ransacked in earlier times. The real tomb might thus lie intact above the ceiling or behind a wall, as suggested earlier.

Another possibility is that the entire Grotto was a decoy tomb, the real tomb being a second cave that is hidden elsewhere in this vicinity. In this regard, it is curious that the vertical section of the Well Shaft where the Grotto is located is lined with roughly-squared limestone blocks, whereas the rest of the shaft is formed from the bedrock. Why is this? Could it be that the blocks were fitted into the shaft specifically for the purpose of concealing a second grotto – a grotto that remains undiscovered to this day? If so, the hidden entrance would be located at the top of the 10-feet-high built section in its south side (compare figure 136 to figure 61 in chapter four), and would probably dogleg to the west to run directly over the hole in the Grotto below. The real tomb might thus lie close to the water source that seemingly affects the ceiling of the Grotto.[44] The size of the limestone blocks in the Well Shaft (ten courses span the height of 10 feet) is such that the priests would have had no trouble in sealing up the door to the upper grotto after the king's burial whilst leaving the entrance to the lower grotto open to act as a decoy.

Yet another possibility is that the king was buried in the great hole in the Grotto, but that the guardians exhumed and relocated the body after the secret door to the Well Shaft had been compromised (see scenario in chapter eight). The possibility thus exists that the mummy was reburied in a more secure place.

But where?

Inside the Pyramid, the only other suitable below-ground location is the Subterranean Chamber (note: although a cavity has been detected to the west of the passage to this chamber, there is no known entrance to it, and it may just be a natural defect in the bedrock).[45] Here, the possibility of a false ceiling, wall, or floor seems utterly remote (the ingenuity of the pyramid builders did have its limitations).[46] But there is the Pit, some 50 to 60 feet deep, in which the king's mummy could have been buried. For as Lepre has noted, the Egyptians often used vertical shafts to bury their dead:

> This shaft [the Pit] is probably the least likely place within the entire pyramid where one would think to look for the secret chamber of the pharaoh Khufu. The Subterranean Chamber is so utterly crude in its design, that this pit – as it has been so ignominiously referred to – by its lowly position within this chamber, would seem to be representative of all that is insignificant or unworthy of attention. Yet

Figure 137.
THE PIT IN THE SUBTERRANEAN CHAMBER.

in this respect, it is beneficial to note that the tomb of Khufu's mother, queen Hetepheres, was found, quite by accident, at the bottom of a similar, inconspicuous shaft near to the north-east corner of the Great Pyramid. Even though her chamber may have represented nothing more than a cenotaph... a lesson might be drawn from this discovery.[47]

Lepre pointed out that exploration of the Pit during the 19th century had been abandoned because of breathing difficulties, and that the last person to explore it had been Piazzi Smyth in 1865.

Might the king's body have been buried in the Pit? Interestingly, the depth of the Pit takes it close to the water table at the time of the high Nile, reminding us once again of the report of Herodotus that the body of Khufu had been buried in subterranean chambers 'built on a sort of island, surrounded by water introduced from the Nile by a canal.' Arab legends too speak of subterranean chambers beneath the pyramids, fed by the waters of the Nile,[48] whilst one report seems to allege that the Pit in the Subterranean Chamber leads to a door, which in turn 'leads to a large room in which corpses are laid out, the sons of Adam'.[49] Modern theorists have also continued this tradition, citing geometrical arguments to support their theories of an undiscovered chamber in this location.[50] And, in fairness, it must be said that a burial close to subterranean waters would make a lot of sense in the context of the Egyptian creation myth and its fundamental link to the royal burial.[51]

In the opinion of this author, it is questionable whether the guardians of the Pyramid would have relocated the king's mummy from the Grotto to the Pit.[52] However, it must be remembered that the Grotto burial theory has not been proven (access to the Grotto via the Well Shaft may have been required for the performance of other rituals, as noted in chapter four), and it is therefore perfectly possible that *the original burial* took place in a chamber beneath the Pit. For this reason alone, it is important that a more thorough investigation of the Pit be undertaken, with the benefits of modern breathing apparatus.

If further subterranean chambers do exist, however, it is equally likely that they were accessed not from within the Pyramid itself but rather via independent tunnel systems, the entrances to which were hidden outside on the Giza plateau. This brings us to the final stage of our investigation, in which Lepre has again illuminated the way.

In his 1990 book, the indefatigable Lepre, far from being satisfied with identifying the anomalous joints inside the Pyramid, extended his survey to the plateau outside. There, in the immediate vicinity of the Pyramid, he found three unusual features that were suggestive of secret chambers or passages beneath.

The first enigmatic feature, a precision-jointed foundation stone, is located to the north of the Pyramid. Lepre writes:

> In December of 1977, while scrutinising the rock foundation on the north side of the Great Pyramid, I happened upon the most curious configuration. Precisely 70 feet west of the pyramid's north-east corner marker (a modern brass pinion pounded into the solid rock at that point), and traversing the imaginary line of the face of the once-existing casing stones of that section, was a thin, almost imperceptible, continuous rectangular joint, marking the perimeter of a 4-feet-wide by 10-feet-long stone sunk into the foundation at that point. This jointing did not represent a haphazard or crooked natural fracture in the rock foundation, but was straight and true throughout, the obvious result of fine, precision workmanship on the scale of a surgeon's incision. Why would the ancient builders sink a stone of this size into an otherwise seamless rock foundation unless to conceal something of value?... The author is certain that if the Egyptian government were to investigate this phenomenon, they would authorise an exploratory probe of this site.[53]

Lepre wondered whether this precision-jointed stone might indicate the entrance to a royal shaft tomb, although not the tomb of Khufu since the stone was almost fully covered by the lower course of the Pyramid.[54] In this respect, it is worth noting that the stone is sunk at an oblique angle to the Pyramid's base, reminiscent of the Pit in the Subterranean Chamber. Perhaps this is significant. Personally, however, I suspect that the stone protects a niche containing 'foundation deposits'. Such deposits, which were buried beneath the foundations of Egyptian buildings as a matter of ritual, would include objects that bear the name of the Pyramid's owner, and might even contain a copy of the architect's drawings that were to be used by the builders.[55]

The second strange feature, a kind of chasm, is found on the east side of the Pyramid on the site of the now-destroyed mortuary temple. Lepre writes:

> There exists at the point where its inner sanctuary once stood a huge cavity cut into the rock foundation. It could not have been a natural chasm, present at the time of the construction of the Great Pyramid, or it would have been filled with squared blocks of stone throughout by the builders. It has been cemented over with a roof or cover of a sort in modern times and has an iron grating at its entrance which is rusted shut and obviously has not been opened for quite a long period of time... It is not unreasonable to assume that this cavity, because of its

unique location beneath what was once the tabernacle of the mortuary temple, where the offering table and 'false door' were positioned, may have represented an access route into the subterranean sections of the pyramid. The site should be opened and thoroughly examined.[56]

This is a remarkably bold idea, coming from an Egyptologist, but before we discuss it, there is a third unusual feature to be considered, namely a smaller cavity, located on the north side of the Pyramid. Lepre writes:

On the north side of the Great Pyramid, at its midpoint (which is in line with its only entrance), is a like cavity, although much smaller. This is situated precisely where the north offering shrine would have been built. Here, however, the cavity has been completely filled in and is now totally inaccessible. The only indication of its presence is from photographs taken of that site over 75 years ago by the brothers John and Morton Edgar. It is incomprehensible that this cavity should have been filled in and left in its sealed condition up to this day. For the entrances to many of the subsequent 5th dynasty pyramids were located under the floor stones of the north offering shrines. Could the Great Pyramid have had a similar pattern which actually set the stage for the consistency of such entrances in those later pyramids? Indeed, the other giant pyramid at Giza, that of the pharaoh Khafre, was equipped with two northern entrances, the lower of which was situated in the immediate area of its north offering shrine. If at all possible, this filled-in cavity on the north side of the Great Pyramid should be re-excavated and left open for any investigator who wishes to try his hand at locating a second entrance that may well give rise to a subterranean crypt or storage chambers which may exist therein.[57]

Lepre thus provides us with two bold ideas for possible tunnel entrances, one to the east and one to the north, either one of which might lead to a subterranean crypt containing the body of Khufu, or perhaps indeed an entire cache of mummies dating to the beginning of pharaonic history.[58]

In addition, there may be a tunnel to the south side of the Pyramid. In 1987, a Japanese team from Waseda University used ground-penetrating radar in that location, and detected a possible passage about 10 to 15 feet underground, heading in the direction of the Pyramid.[59] No exploration is likely to take place, however, unless the entrance to this tunnel can be found.[60] (It is somewhat ironic, in this regard, that neither the Japanese nor any other team has used GPR on the bedrock to the east and north of the Pyramid, where Lepre has detected possible tunnel entrances. It is to be hoped that future exploration will be less random and more driven by the kind of intelligence that Lepre has provided, both outside and inside the Pyramid.)

Of course, it may well be that Khufu's mummy was plundered aeons ago, or that it was buried in an entirely different geographical location, as has occasionally been suggested.[61] But if we have not the courage to look for his tomb – either in the Grotto, or in a second grotto, or in the Pit of the Subterranean Chamber, or in an underground chamber accessed via a separate passage system – then how will we ever know for certain? As Lepre put it so well:

> King Tut is famous for being the only Egyptian pharaoh whose tomb was ever found intact, but Tut did not have a great pyramid. A greater find awaits mankind. Only future investigation will discern whether the world will ever have the opportunity to witness it.[62]

Chapter Ten Summary

- Virtually everything that is known about the Great Pyramid has been discovered by accident or chance. Egyptology tolerates rather than promotes exploration of the Pyramid on the grounds that multiple secret chambers are incongruous in a tomb. The sealed repository theory, on the other hand, suggests that further chambers are likely to exist, their locations being marked by anomalies in the patterns of the stones.

- The author recommends that the authorities undertake a systematic investigation of the Pyramid's interior to identify all anomalies in the joints of the stones. A number of anomalies are already known, and these are prioritised for future explorations. Negative results would falsify the sealed repository theory, whilst positive results would prove it correct. Thus the theory is scientifically testable.

- The author believes that the king's body may still be hidden beneath the Pyramid, either in the Grotto, or in a second grotto (the first being a decoy), or in another subterranean room. A number of possible entrance points to a subterranean complex are suggested.

CHAPTER ELEVEN

NEW HORIZONS

**That something was lost from the time of the pyramid
building age up to this present era is certain; otherwise,
why is it that not a single modern scholar – whether
associated with the field of physics, engineering,
archaeology, Egyptology, mathematics, geometry or
scores of others – can conclusively state exactly how
the mighty pyramids were built?**
(J.P. Lepre, *The Egyptian Pyramids*, 1990)

In this book, I have focused exclusively on the question of why the Great
Pyramid was built, or in other words *what was the Great Pyramid*? Over
the centuries, there have been countless theories and speculations on this
subject, all of them reflecting contemporary points of view on the ancient
past, and therefore destined to be swept aside by yet newer contemporary
points of view. The Pyramid has thus functioned – and will continue to
function – as a mirror to the progression of human technology and belief,
reflecting a myriad of preconceptions that are projected on to it. At one
point in history, it is interpreted as the Granary of Joseph; at another, it is
seen as a biblical prophecy in stone, or a repository of divinely-inspired
weights and measures. Then, as we enter the 20th century, it is viewed as
a giant water pump or power plant, a sundial or almanac, an astronomical
observatory, a repository of wisdom from a lost civilisation, a temple of
initiation, a navigation beacon for alien spacecraft, or an air raid shelter
against meteorite impacts.

Against this moving kaleidoscope of modern opinion, one theory has
held firm and even gained strength from the diversity of the speculation
that has been arrayed against it, namely the idea that the Pyramid is 'a
tomb, and nothing but a tomb'. And yet, as I pointed out in the Preface to
this book, Egyptology too has been compromised by every imaginable

preconception of modern times, and has thus generated a perverted view of ancient Egyptian religion, with an inevitable knock-on effect for its understanding of the pyramids and the Great Pyramid in particular. It is perhaps for this reason that Egyptology has never achieved closure in its seemingly endless battle against the massed ranks of 'pyramidiots'.

In this book, I have attempted to break the mould by allowing the true voice of ancient Egypt to be heard. My argument, summarised here and advocated in detail in the companion volume (to be published in due course), is that ancient Egyptian religion was neither a cult of the Sun as Egyptologists call it, nor a cult of the stars as others would have it, but rather a 'cult of creation' in which all myth and ritual commemorated the creation of the Universe. Accordingly, the Great Pyramid, like every true pyramid, symbolised the creation, and the very building of the monument re-enacted the moment when the creator-soul had ascended into the sky for the creation of the stars, the Sun, and the Moon. If I am right (and it is for the reader to judge for himself or herself), then the Pyramid is here being studied in its proper context for the first time.

The result is a theory that, unlike other offerings from the alternative genre, finds much in common with Egyptology. The Great Pyramid, like other pyramids, was a religious structure, designed as a memorial to a deceased king. The Pyramid symbolised, among other things, the Sun, the stars, and the primeval mound. It was a resurrection device for the king; and, in its lower parts at least, it was his tomb.

Beyond these points, however, my theory diverges from orthodoxy, with two specific conclusions arising from the creational interpretation: firstly, that the body of the king was buried in the Grotto, at ground level, in accordance with the fundamental axiom 'the body to earth, the spirit to the sky'; and secondly, that the King's Chamber sarcophagus contained meteoritic iron, representing the spiritualised seed of the creator.

These two conclusions demand a radical reappraisal of the Pyramid's interior architecture, since it now becomes clear that, with the king being buried below, the upper passages and chambers were not necessarily kept open.

Why, then, were the upper passageways and chambers built, if not for the burial of the king? Here, I have allowed my thoughts to be guided by archaeological evidence that the passages and chambers were sealed off at the time of construction, and that the architect intended these passages and chambers to be found. I have therefore drawn what I believe to be the only reasonable conclusion in the circumstances: that the Pyramid was built, in part at least, as a repository and time capsule for the benefit of a future generation of men. But it was not just a repository of physical relics and artefacts. Rather, it was a repository of *a religious idea*, which was expressed in a variety of ways. Thus in the Grand Gallery, the Queen's Chamber, and the King's Chamber, the architect utilised statues, symbols, geometry, meteoritic iron, and even sound, to recall the myth of creation, whilst in the chambers above the Queen's Chamber shafts, it may be hypothesised, the same story was enshrined in the form of the sacred book. Thus the interior architecture of the Pyramid reflected its exterior symbolism – the creation in microcosm and macrocosm.

This theory will no doubt throw Egyptologists into apoplexy, at least one scholar having gone on record to declare that 'treasure chests of lost knowledge' is a 'fantastic' pyramid theory.[1] However, in its defence, I have noted the importance of cataclysm in Egyptian religion, not just in the myth of creation, but also in the prophecy of the 'end of the world'; and I have highlighted the effect that cosmic turbulence might have had on the founding of the ancient Egyptian state and its religion; witness the concept of *maat*, 'right cosmic order'. It is entirely plausible, therefore, that the Pyramid included a repository of artefacts and knowledge, just in case the sky should fall and the present world come to an end.

Thus have I attempted to view the Pyramid from an ancient Egyptian perspective, as indeed has Egyptology in its own imprecise way. But just as Egyptology is not immune from modern preconceptions, neither am I. It is all too likely that I, too, have erred, to a greater or lesser degree, by forcing a modern interpretation upon ancient Egyptian religion. And such is the Pyramid's mute ambiguity and cunning complexity that any such error tends to get amplified to an embarrassing degree. Accordingly, it is necessary for me to express the utmost caution about my hypothesis. My decoding of the Pyramid is no more than a theory; and, like every theory, it must be put to the test.

On this note, it is appropriate, in the first instance, to pitch my theory against the orthodox theory that the Pyramid is 'a tomb and nothing but a tomb', since only by winning the status of 'preferred theory' will it be accorded the respect that is necessary for the required scientific testing to be undertaken. (Note: a full critique of alternative theories is beyond the scope of this book, as there are so many; however, I do intend to address the more serious contenders on my website.)[2] Which of the two theories provides the most complete explanation of the Pyramid's manifold features? Since so much ground has been covered in this book, I set out below a summary of my ideas compared to the orthodoxy – chamber by chamber, and feature by feature.

THE SYMBOLISM OF THE PYRAMID

Orthodoxy

The true pyramid was a solar symbol, its shape signifying the rays of the Sun falling to the earth. An identity existed between the pyramid and the king, the latter being regarded as a 'Sun-king'. In keeping with this, the pyramid's capstone, *benbenet*, is held to have been a solar icon or 'Sun-stone'. In the Pyramid's name *Akhet Khufu*, *akhet* is thought to refer to the horizon over which the Sun rose every day.

Alternatively, the Pyramid may have symbolised the primeval mound, i.e. the risen earth, but in a static, post-creation sense.

Or the Pyramid may have symbolised both the Sun and the primeval mound.

(The existence of these diverse theories underlines the uncertainty and confusion of Egyptologists on this vital question.)

Alford

The true pyramid was a creational symbol. Its shape encoded the mystery of the creation, and told the entire story in a single hieroglyph. It was a simulacrum in stone of the creator-god in his act of rising from the abyss into the sky for the creation of the Universe. Or, otherwise said, it was a representation of the primeval earth being spiritualised for the creation of the Universe. The capstone, benbenet, *signified the seed of the creator, which he thrust into the womb of the sky-goddess for the conception and birth of the stars, the Sun and the Moon. In the Pyramid's name* Akhet Khufu, akhet *refers to the spiritualisation of all things from the earth, and thus signifies the place where, and the time when, all celestial bodies (not just the Sun) experienced their first rising. Though it is beyond the scope of this book, it is possible that the dimensions of the Pyramid were chosen deliberately to encode the dimensions of the Earth, reduced to a scale of 1:43,200.*[3]

THE PURPOSE OF THE PYRAMID

Orthodoxy

The Pyramid was a tomb and nothing but a tomb, built for a single king, with the aim of protecting his mummified body and translating his soul to the sky. Its multiple chambers comprised a real tomb, a decoy tomb, and other rooms that were intended for funerary rituals or the welfare of the king's soul. However, a minority of Egyptologists concede that the Pyramid may have been built as a cenotaph and nothing but a cenotaph (i.e. an empty tomb). In addition, the monument was built as a religious symbol – of the Sun or the primeval mound.

Alford

In its lower part – at ground level and below – the Pyramid was a tomb for a king, incorporating a decoy arrangement. But in its upper part, with one notable exception, it was a sealed repository and time capsule, built to protect sacred relics, books and knowledge from a prophesied 'end of the world' cataclysm, for the benefit of a future generation, or race, of men. The exception was the King's Chamber, which functioned as an amplifier and transmitter of sound, for the purpose of re-enacting the sound of creation and inspiring awe in the minds of men. In addition, the Pyramid was built as a memorial to the creation; to build it was to re-enact the creation and renew the powerful magic by which order had triumphed over chaos.

THE SIZE OF THE PYRAMID

Orthodoxy

The huge size of the Pyramid is unexplained. No king needed a tomb this big. Nor does solar symbolism explain it. Some Egyptologists therefore regard the Pyramid as a colossal waste of time and energy,[4] whilst others suspect that it, and the other giant pyramids, functioned as job creation schemes and mechanisms for the creation of the state.[5]

Alford

The Pyramid was more than a tomb; it was a sealed repository or time capsule. Huge size was therefore important, firstly because it allowed the architect to incorporate multiple secret chambers (the total number of which remains unknown), and secondly because it enabled the Pyramid to withstand the prophesied cataclysm and endure for millennia, until a new generation, or race, of men would arise from the ashes of the past. In addition, the Pyramid was a representation of the Great God, who was conceived as a being of immense size. In this sense, the huge scale of the construction may be understood as a labour of religious devotion.

THE PRECISION OF THE PYRAMID

Orthodoxy

The unprecedented precision of the Pyramid remains a baffling mystery that has not yet been solved. The pyramid expert Mark Lehner concedes the limitations of orthodoxy, writing: 'Why such phenomenal precision? For the royal designers such exactitude may have been imbued with symbolic and cultic significance that now eludes us.'[6]

Alford

The extraordinary precision of the Pyramid has both a functional and a religious explanation. The former stems from the Pyramid's role as a time capsule, aimed at a post-cataclysm world. The precision of its build ensured that the monument would withstand the prophesied cataclysm and survive for millennia thereafter. The latter stems from the Pyramid's creational symbolism. As an image of the Great God, engaged in the act of creating the Universe, it signified a being, and an idea, that was held to be perfect in every respect. Whilst every pyramid attained to this noble goal, the Great Pyramid clearly was the ultimate expression of the idea: the first pyramid, the original pyramid, the one that broke the mould, the one built by the gods themselves at the beginning of time – the pyramid par excellence.

THE DESCENDING PASSAGE

Orthodoxy

The Descending Passage provided the sole entrance and means of access to the Pyramid. It was designed primarily for the royal funeral. The gable stones above the entrance are a puzzle; they may have been structural or they may have been symbolic.

Alford

The Descending Passage might not be the sole entrance to the Pyramid; Lepre has suggested two possible additional entrances, one positioned to the east beneath the site of the mortuary temple, the other positioned to the north beneath the site of the offering shrine. As well as providing access to the known chambers, the Descending Passage may still conceal a secret passage, or pair of such passages, located in its side walls about 35 to 40 feet down from the original entrance. The gable stones above the main entrance were probably erected as a practice run for a similar inclined roof that was to be built over the top of the Grand Gallery, to protect it from the weight of the superincumbent masonry.

THE SUBTERRANEAN CHAMBER AND PASSAGE

Orthodoxy

The Subterranean Chamber was either an abandoned tomb chamber (the king having changed his mind as to his place of burial) or a decoy tomb chamber (to persuade thieves that the burial treasures had already been plundered). Possibly symbolic of the underworld, it may have had some ritualistic significance for the departed king. But the king was not buried here.

Figure 138.
THE GREAT PYRAMID, VERTICAL SECTION, LOOKING WEST.

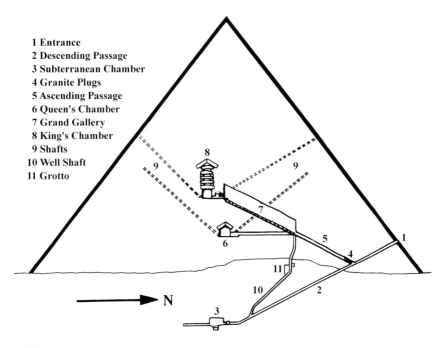

1 Entrance
2 Descending Passage
3 Subterranean Chamber
4 Granite Plugs
5 Ascending Passage
6 Queen's Chamber
7 Grand Gallery
8 King's Chamber
9 Shafts
10 Well Shaft
11 Grotto

Alford

This chamber symbolised the abyss and the underworld, and would thus have made a most suitable tomb chamber, following the old Egyptian maxim 'the body to earth'. Whilst it is possible that the king's body was buried here – in the Pit – the vulnerability of such a burial suggests that the Subterranean Chamber was a decoy tomb chamber.

THE GROTTO

Orthodoxy

The cave-like Grotto, accessed via the Well Shaft, probably dates back to the centuries before the Pyramid was built. Rarely visited, it is thought to be of little or no consequence for our understanding of the Pyramid.

Alford

The Grotto was either the true burial chamber of the king or a second decoy tomb (hence the deep hole at the western end of the room). In the former case, the king's body might still be hidden here, perhaps behind the western wall or above an artificial ceiling. In the latter case, the real burial chamber would be a second grotto, directly overhead, sealed off to this day by the masonry in the Well Shaft.

THE WELL SHAFT

Orthodoxy

The Well Shaft was cut as an escape route for the workmen who became trapped in the Grand Gallery when they released the granite plugs into the Ascending Passage, immediately after the king's burial in the King's Chamber.

Alford

The orthodox scenario is unacceptable, for it involves a flawed plan and a forgetful architect, or else a sacrilegious act of vandalism and a reckless disregard for the security of the tomb, or else, in the last resort, a deliberate burial of workmen alive, in conflict with our understanding of Egyptian culture. Rather, the lower sections of the Well Shaft were cut to provide access from the Descending Passage to the Grotto, probably for the secret burial of the king there. Later, after an earthquake, the Well Shaft was connected to the Grand Gallery by a tunnel, in order that the guardians might inspect the damage to the King's Chamber. It may be significant that the total distance from the main entrance to the Grotto, via the Descending Passage and Well Shaft is almost exactly equal to the height of the Pyramid.

THE ASCENDING PASSAGE AND THE GRANITE PLUGS

Orthodoxy

The Ascending Passage was a secret passage that provided access to the upper chambers for the burial of the king. The granite plugs were slipped down the passage immediately after the funeral to provide an additional barrier against tomb robbers. It is not certain why the plugs were made of granite, nor why there were three of them.

Alford

The Ascending Passage was a secret passage that provided access to the sealed chambers of a repository and time capsule. The granite plugs were slipped down the passage during the construction of the Pyramid, when the roof of the Grand Gallery was still open. Strictly speaking, the use of the plugs was unnecessary, given the fact that the mouth of the passage was camouflaged by the prism stone. Therefore, the inclusion of the plugs bears the hallmarks of a ritual, both as regards the sealing and the envisaged unsealing of the passage. The use of three plugs, made of granite, probably had a religious significance.

THE AL-MAMUN TUNNEL AND CHASM

Orthodoxy

The rough entrance tunnel and the excavation around the granite plugs is ascribed to the Arab ruler Abdullah al-Mamun, primarily on the basis of Arab legends. However, the fact that the tunnel leads almost exactly to the junction of the Ascending and Descending Passages tends to suggest that the tunneller had inside knowledge of the Pyramid's design. No-one has yet provided a plausible solution to this conundrum.

Alford

Al-Mamun re-excavated an old robber's tunnel. Said robbers had gained access to the upper chambers via the main entrance and the Well Shaft, after the latter had been joined to the Grand Gallery by the guardians' inspection tunnel. But the Well Shaft was too narrow for the removal of the booty. Having decided to remove these objects through the Ascending Passage, and having failed to break through the top granite plug, the robbers persuaded the guardians to dig a new tunnel from the outside of the Pyramid to the junction of the Ascending and Descending Passages. The so-called al-Mamun tunnel was thus dug not to gain entry to the monument but to remove artefacts from it. As for al-Mamun, he may be credited with a further excavation along the western side of the plugs, the short tunnel around the plugs into the Descending Passage, and the removal of the prism stone.

THE QUEEN'S CHAMBER AND PASSAGE

Orthodoxy

It used to be thought that the Queen's Chamber was an abandoned tomb chamber (the king having changed his mind as to his place of burial). But most experts now believe that the room was designed from the outset as a serdab, its corbelled niche containing a *ka*-statue of the king. Whilst it is recognised that the Queen's Chamber Passage was sealed off by the bridging slab in the Gallery, it is generally presumed that the room could be accessed at the time of the funeral.

Alford

The Queen's Chamber was a secret chamber in a sealed repository. As such, it was sealed at the time of construction, and could not be accessed except by breaking the bridging slab. The corbelled niche contained a time capsule artefact, namely a statue of the Great Goddess in geometric form, symbolising the mystery of creation. Anomalous joints and stones in the Queen's Chamber Passage may indicate a secret passage beneath the floor, perhaps providing access to some old sacred structure on the plateau outcrop below.

THE QUEEN'S CHAMBER SHAFTS

Orthodoxy

The Queen's Chamber shafts are a real puzzle on account of the fact that they were sealed at their lower ends and blocked at their upper ends. It is generally believed that they are abandoned features – prototypes perhaps of the shafts in the King's Chamber. Accordingly, it is held that they are unfinished ventilation shafts or unfinished soul-shafts. However, other Egyptologists believe that they are completed features (*ka*-shafts), and a minority even support the view that the southern shaft leads up to a small chamber, or serdab. All of these theories run into serious difficulties in explaining the sealed nature of the shafts.

Alford

The Queen's Chamber shafts were secret passages to secret chambers, differing from the Pyramid's other passages only in their miniature size. The idea was that the explorer use the shafts as guides to dig tunnels to the chambers above. The distance (213 feet in each case) made this the ultimate challenge, and tends to suggest that the chambers contain the ultimate prize, probably the sacred books and records of the Pyramid builders. The metal-handled 'doors' at the top of the shafts are probably the aperture covers that were used during construction to prevent ingress of tools, detritus, and living organisms. The plugs beyond these 'doors' suggest a ritual sealing and future unsealing, reminiscent of the granite plugs in the Ascending Passage.

THE GRAND GALLERY

Orthodoxy

The Grand Gallery was a glorious passageway to the tomb chamber, but functioned also as a slipway for the granite plugs that would block the mouth of the passage below. The Great Step is not thought to have had any particular significance. The long grooves in the side walls are a real puzzle, as they seem to suggest a lower roof that has been removed by intruders. No satisfactory explanation has ever been offered for the fifty-four niches in the side ramps, nor for the inset stones in the side walls. The corbelled architecture remains a mystery, though according to Lepre it may have had 'a high spiritual symbolism'.

Alford

The Grand Gallery was the heart of the secret chamber system, but was also a simulacrum of the creation. The Great Step was a platform for a statue of the Great God in geometric form, symbolising the mystery of creation. Dilapidation of the Great Step was caused by the forceful removal of the statue when the Pyramid was plundered in antiquity. The long grooves in the side walls contained a lower roof that spanned the Gallery at half its present height. This roof, probably made of wood, had its underside painted with stars – the images of the gods – in the act of rising at the First Time. Below, the fifty-four niches in the side ramps may have contained relics of the gods, perhaps in the form of sanctified (spiritualised) woods and minerals. Above, the upper roof demands to be removed so that the full extent of the corbelling may be seen. The final roof, thus exposed, will be a narrow strip, perhaps comprising bricks of gold to symbolise the eternality of God and the Universe. The corbelled architecture would signify the rising of the spirit of the creator-god and might encode the mystery of the creation, viewed from a mathematical or geometrical perspective. Finally, on a more mundane note, the floor of the Gallery did indeed function as a slipway for the granite plugs, whilst the inset stones in the side walls were probably the result of a planning error.

THE KING'S CHAMBER

Orthodoxy

The King's Chamber was the king's final resting place – the raison d'etre of the monument. His mummy was sealed inside the granite sarcophagus, but was stolen by tomb robbers in antiquity. The two 'airshafts' may have provided fresh air for the benefit of the funeral cortege, but most Egyptologists nowadays call them soul-shafts on the assumption that the king's soul used them for a direct ascent into the northern and southern skies. The huge granite beams in the King's Chamber superstructure are thought to have had a structural purpose – to protect the flat roof of the chamber from the superincumbent weight of masonry. The special use of granite in this chamber and its superstructure is thought to reflect that material's protective strength, but religious symbolism might also have been a factor.

Alford

The concept of burial at such a height inside the Pyramid goes against a fundamental principle of Egyptian religion which required the burial of the king's body at ground level or below ('the body to earth, the spirit to

*the sky'). It is more likely that the sarcophagus contained meteoritic
iron, representing the spiritualised seed of the creator-god. As for the
soul-shaft theory, it fails to explain why the king's soul could not have
used the Descending Passage for its ascent to the sky. The superstructure
theory is unacceptable too, since the raised roofs provided no additional
weight relief. The King's Chamber was not a burial chamber, but rather
a 'chamber of creation' in which the creation of the Universe was re-
enacted perpetually. A major component of this re-enactment was sound.
The granite beams in the superstructure were designed to vibrate in
harmony with Earth resonance and transmit low frequency vibrations to
the chamber below. The chamber, built of highly resonant granite, then
amplified these vibrations and their harmonics, and transmitted audible
sound via its so-called 'airshafts'. This sound re-enacted the sound of
creation, and in all likelihood signified the soul of the Great God. In a
symbolic sense, the sound spiritualised the iron (a sample of which was
sealed in the sarcophagus) and ejected it into the northern and southern
skies, via the shafts, to re-enact the formation of the celestial bodies: the
circumpolar stars in the northern sky, and the Sun, the Moon, and the
rising-and-setting stars in the southern sky. But the shafts also had a
practical function in broadcasting the sound of creation to the residents
of the Giza plateau, thus inspiring awe in the minds of men. Access to the
King's Chamber was not intended by the architect, but became possible
after the acoustic system was damaged irreparably by an earthquake of
exceptional force.*

THE KING'S CHAMBER ANTECHAMBER AND PASSAGE

Orthodoxy
The Antechamber was a portcullis room for the protection of the burial
chamber. It was fitted with three granite slabs (now missing) which were
lowered to the floor by means of wooden rollers and ropes. The vertical
grooves in the south wall were guides for the ropes, whilst the granite
leaf functioned as a counterweight. The use of granite, interlaced with
limestone blocks, is a puzzling and unexplained feature.

Alford
*It is not apparent how a portcullis could have functioned in this room,
and several facts argue strongly against the idea. Certain features are
better understood as decorative and symbolic. The grooves in the south
wall resemble the pattern of a fluted column, and are an exact image of a
decorative pattern found on a 1st dynasty portcullis slab, whilst the
granite leaf resembles the rolled-up reed-mat curtain design which was*

used from Old Kingdom times to symbolise the entrance to the 'other world'. In addition, there is evidence that this room was not kept open for a funeral, but was sealed by a plate, or plug, of stone, at the mouth of the King's Chamber Passage. In keeping with the acoustic theory of the King's Chamber, the Antechamber, built predominantly of granite, must have produced acoustic effects. It is theorised that the 'portcullis slabs' and the granite leaf were tuned to resonate at certain low frequencies, and that a man was intended to stand in the gap before the granite leaf, at the threshold of the room, where the granite began. The sound effect might then have induced an altered state of consciousness in the subject, causing him to see a vision of the true God and the creation. In short, it is proposed that the Antechamber was an initiation room in which a representative of a future generation, or race, of men would experience a mystical insight into the physics and metaphysics of the Universe, as conceived by the builders of the Pyramid.

Testing the Theory

Ultimately, if a new theory is to dislodge the orthodox theory, then it must offer a better interpretation of the Pyramid's architecture. It must be more complete; it must be more detailed; it must have greater internal consistency; and it must be more harmonious with everything that is known about ancient Egypt. If it can satisfy these minimum conditions, then the new theory should be raised to the status of the preferred theory – a new orthodoxy.

Unfortunately, orthodoxies are not dislodged that easily. Subjectivity tends to obscure the relative merits of a new theory, whilst an in-built bias acts to protect the prevailing wisdom. For a new theory to become accepted, it must not only prove itself via ex-post rationalisation but also via ex-ante prediction. And this latter demand can be difficult to satisfy in a discipline where controlled scientific tests are generally out of the question. Such a discipline is Egyptology.

Nevertheless, the beauty of the theory presented in this book is that it can be either proved or falsified in the architecture of the Pyramid itself. Specific ex-ante predictions, arguably unique to the theory in question, can be either confirmed or refuted by explorations inside the monument. These predictions have been outlined in the earlier chapters of this book, but may be summarised again here as follows:

- Further acoustic tests of the King's Chamber (perhaps using a full working model) will confirm that it was designed to amplify Earth resonances and transmit sound to the outside world via its shafts (see chapter seven).

- Secret chambers will be found above the Queen's Chamber shafts. At least one of these chambers will contain sacred books, stored in a chest. The books will provide the most explicit ever account of Egyptian religion, vindicating the creational approach that has been taken in this book (see chapter nine).

- In the Descending Passage, anomalous floor joints and scored lines mark the entrance to a secret passage, or a pair of passages, that leads to additional chambers. The hidden entrances are probably in the side walls (see chapter ten).

- In the Queen's Chamber Passage, anomalous floor joints and blocks mark the entrance to a secret passage. The hidden entrance is probably in the floor, such that the passage slopes downwards to an old sacred site on the plateau beneath the Pyramid (see chapter ten).

- In the Grand Gallery, the upper roof slabs may be removed to reveal a continuation of the corbelling above. This secret space will probably contain nothing, but may be topped by bricks of gold (see chapter ten).

- The mummy of Khufu will be found in a subterranean tomb, the most likely contenders being the Grotto (the burial being hidden behind the west wall or above the ceiling) or a second grotto that may be located directly overhead (its door being sealed off by the masonry in the Well Shaft, at the upper south side). Alternatively, tests of the soil in the Grotto's great hole will confirm that a mummy was once buried there prior to being exhumed.

These are critical predictions. If they succeed, then the 'repository and tomb' theory is upheld. If they fail, then the theory is negated.

But will the Supreme Council of Antiquities in Egypt be prepared to undertake or permit the necessary investigations? Here, a catch-22 acts as a brake on progress. Unless Egyptologists believe in the repository theory, they will not test it; whilst, unless they test it, they will not come to believe in it. For this impasse to be broken, courage is needed.

Fortunately, as regards the Queen's Chamber shafts, explorations have recently been reinstigated after an inexplicable nine-year delay. Despite widespread apathy among Egyptologists in general, Zawi Hawass, to his credit, has pushed ahead with the investigation, which is still ongoing. But even so, problems may arise. Firstly, if secret chambers are found, will credit be given to the sealed repository theory? Unfortunately, some Egyptologists have made their own speculations about a secret chamber, thus sowing seeds of confusion. These speculations, in an ideal world, would be regarded as irrelevant, since they lack a theoretical basis and do not put a theory at risk of falsification. But Egyptology has never really functioned as a true science (it is more of a political science), and would be unlikely to play by the rules if a secret chamber were found. Rather, it would adapt its arguments and pretend that the discovery was consistent with orthodoxy, the shafts having been sealed for some inexplicable cultic or symbolic purpose. Thus orthodoxy could survive the discovery of a secret chamber. But what if a chest (of books) was seen inside it? This brings us to the second problem: another catch-22. For in order that Egyptologists open this chest, to realise the error of their ways, they would have to dig a tunnel through the Pyramid masonry to the chamber; however, in order for them to have the resolve to damage the monument thus, they would first need to realise the error of their ways. Or, to put it another way, the repository theory uniquely instils the confidence that the architect intended the Pyramid to be breached in this way.

If these problems are to be overcome (in the event of a chamber being found), then the sponsors of orthodoxy will have to demonstrate honesty, humility, integrity and courage to a degree that has largely been missing from late-20th century academia. Only then, perhaps, will we see a full testing of the repository theory via explorations of all the areas that are listed in the summary above.

At the end of the day, Egyptologists have got nothing to lose but their egos and an incorrect orthodoxy.

Outstanding Questions

I would like to close this book on a modest note by emphasising what I have *not* achieved. Firstly, I have not identified *who* built the Pyramid, nor *when* it was built; these are fascinating questions, but they are not my primary concern in this volume. Secondly, I have not identified *how* the Pyramid was built; this, too, is an interesting question, but it lies outside my field of expertise. And thirdly, even though my focus has been on the "why" question, I do not claim to have explained every single feature of the Pyramid. Rather, I believe that loose ends remain, which may well be indicative of something more to go for.

Why was the Queen's Chamber niche placed deliberately off the axis of that room? Is there a pattern here, involving the offset main entrance and passage system, and the offset raised boss on the granite leaf in the Antechamber?

What is the precise meaning of the strange geometry of the Queen's

Chamber niche?

Similarly, what is the precise meaning of the strange geometry of the Grand Gallery?

Why do the Grand Gallery's roof slabs vary in their length? Why did the builder not use a standard length?

Why, in the Gallery, is the twenty-sixth inset stone in the east wall on the vertical, rather than slightly slanted, and why is the thirteenth stone in the west wall slightly slanted rather than vertical?

Why is the King's Chamber Antechamber fitted with wainscots to the east and the west? Why does the east wainscot have a flat upper ledge, whilst the west wainscot is surmounted by three semi-hollows? Was it done, as Piazzi Smyth believed, to encode the dimensions of the King's Chamber?[7] And, if so, why?

Why is pi (π) emphasised in the design of the King's Chamber?[8] What is its significance there, given its use in the dimensions of the Pyramid itself?

Similarly, why is phi (ϕ) incorporated in the dimensions of the King's Chamber, and in the design of the upper passage system?[9]

To these questions, I have no satisfactory answers at present. But I am inclined to think that the architect may have encoded into the architecture (the interior as well as the exterior) a message for the future, using the eternal, ever-unchanging language of mathematics, such that even if the secret chambers were robbed, the Pyramid would still guard its ultimate 'truth' for the benefit of future mankind. In which case, it may be that a mind superior to mine, suitably motivated, could yet unravel the riddle of the Pyramid using existing published data, without the need for further intrusive archaeological investigations.

What might this message be? If a little speculation might be permitted, I would hazard a guess that it refers to the physics and metaphysics of the creation, the laws of the Universe, the force that keeps the sky suspended above the earth, the nature of life, spirit, sound, and light, as these things were conceived by the builder civilisation; in short, a message pertaining to everything that was encapsulated in the image of the Pyramid itself. Indeed, the Pyramid might well be the key to it, for in Egyptian religion it signified the Great God who had brought about the creation – a being who was equated with life, spirit, sound, and light, and the raising of the sky above the earth – and this God had created himself according to the monodramatic version of the myth. The suggestion, therefore, is that the Pyramid built itself; that, as a representation of God, it was the architect of its own great architecture. Might the message therefore shed light on how *it*, like the Universe, had been built?

In conclusion, I do not regard this book as the last word on the Great Pyramid; far from it. If the Pyramid was indeed a repository, as well as a tomb, then this is not an end, but rather a beginning. It is a foundation for future research, a framework for future exploration, and a signpost for future investigation. In short, a potential key to a *real* discovery. If I may be forgiven for drawing upon ancient Egyptian myth for an analogy, the investigation in these pages may be compared to the Sun-god's journey through the hours of darkness, and his arrival in the cavern of the eastern horizon, where preparations are made for Sunrise. In reaching this cavern, the Sun-god sets the scene for the breaking of the light; but for the light to emerge, he must be joined by his followers – the stars – who will navigate his barque into the sky.

Will you, the reader, follow my lead and bring light to the cave of this archaic, archetypal, and architectural mystery?

Will you be a star in the rebirth of the Pyramid?

Addendum

In reconsidering the Pyramid in the light of creational mythology, have I, too, fallen into the trap of allowing modern preconceptions to colour my interpretation of ancient Egyptian religion? For a complete and detailed presentation of my cult of creation hypothesis, the reader is directed to the forthcoming companion volume, provisionally entitled *The Midnight Sun: The Death and Rebirth of God in Ancient Egypt*, to be published by Eridu Books in early-2004 (order via any UK bookshop, or direct from the publisher at http://www.eridu.co.uk).

ACKNOWLEDGEMENTS

Much credit for this book is due to my wife Sumu, who has endured yet more years of personal sacrifice while I have researched, cogitated, and written to an ambitious and accelerated time-scale. Without her at my side, the perilous path to truth would have been impossible to walk and the rugged road to enlightenment too difficult to even contemplate.

Much credit is also due to my mother and father, who brought me up free of religious programming, and instilled in me a curiosity and awe of the world. How might things have turned out differently, one wonders, if they had not sent me to the pyramids of Giza when I was just fourteen years of age? Thank heavens too for school educational cruises.

I would also like to thank Neil Gould for the cover design; Andrew Whitting for technical support; John Reid for his comments and ideas as documented in chapter seven of this book; David Elkington likewise; Robert Bauval for sharing his thoughts on exploration of the Queen's Chamber shafts; Graham Birdsall for offering me a platform to present my Pyramid theory for the first time, just four days after the discovery by National Geographic; and Jim Lewandowski for his technical advice and enthusiastic support in hunting down various information.

In addition, I must express my appreciation to certain people who have influenced my ideas about the Great Pyramid over the years: firstly, Erich von Daniken, whose books first alerted me to the anomaly of the Pyramid; secondly, Zecharia Sitchin who provided me an instrumental lesson in how modern preconceptions may be brought to bear upon this mighty monument; and thirdly, the late J.P. Lepre who provided a level of observational detail that was noticeably absent in the more commonly cited Pyramid text books.

Finally, I acknowledge all the Egyptologists and pyramid researchers whose painstaking studies, often at great personal cost, have made this book possible.

Illustration Credits

The author owns copyright in figures 2a, 2b, 4, 5, 10, 12, 15, 19, 21, 23, 28, 31, 34, 37, 42, 49, 50, 53, 54, 56, 57, 62, 64, 65, 72, 77, 78, 83, 84, 85, 87, 89, 90, 91, 92, 94, 102, 105, 108, 113, 114, 118, 127, 130, 133, 134, 137. In addition, the author has adapted the illustrations of others as follows: 25 (after Gantenbrink), 112 (after Edwards), 9, 11, 41, 43, 52, 58, 59, 100, 109, 117, 123, 138 (after uncertain provenance).

Copyright in the remaining illustrations is as follows: Barratt 71; Bauval/Cook 3, 74, 75; Borchardt 46; Budge 73, 79, 81, 82b, 125, 126; Davidson 38, 39, 45, 96, 97, 106; DigitalGlobe (www.digitalglobe.com) 7; Edgar 14, 17, 18, 47a, 51, 60, 61, 70, 86, 88, 93, 110, 119, 120, 121, 136; Edwards 29; Emery 47b; Gantenbrink 24, 122; Goyon 115; Lawton 40; Lepre 30, 36, 44b, 48, 101, 135; Napoleon *Description de l'Egypte* 6; National Geographic 26, 27; Petrie 44a, 131, 132; Reid 98; Rutherford 16, 32, 104; Smyth 13, 22, 33, 35, 55, 103; Uncertain provenance 1, 8, 20, 63, 66, 67, 68, 69, 76, 80, 82a, 95, 99, 111, 116, 124, 128, 129.

NOTES

PREFACE

1 See M. Lehner, 1997, p. 42; L. Cottrell, 1956, p. 92; E. Hornung, *The Secret Lore of Egypt*, Cornell University Press, 2001, pp. 83, 93, 155.

2 See the works of Piazzi Smyth, Robert Menzies, Morton Edgar, David Davidson, Havre Spencer Lewis, Adam Rutherford, and Peter Lemesurier, as cited in the Bibliography.

3 On the water pump theory, see E.J. Kunkel, 1962, or the summary of his theory in R.W. Noone, 1982. On the power plant theory, see C. Dunn, 1998.

4 On the biblical prophecy theory, see the works of Piazzi Smyth, Jean Baptiste Biot, and Moses B. Cotsworth, as cited in the Bibliography. A good summary of their ideas appears in P. Tompkins, 1971, chapter XI. On the repository of weights and measures theory, see the works of Edme-Francois Jomard, John Taylor, Piazzi Smyth, and Livio Catullo Stecchini, as cited in the Bibliography. A good summary of their ideas appears in P. Tompkins, 1971, chapters VI, VII and XVI.

5 The astronomical observatory theory was advocated by the Greek philosopher Proclus in the 5th century AD. In modern times, its main advocate has been the English writer R.A. Proctor; see R.A. Proctor, 1883; P. Tompkins, 1971, pp. 147-58, 253; I. Lawton & C. Ogilvie-Herald, 2000, pp. 159-60; and R. Bauval & A. Gilbert, 1994, p. 43. The theory was supported by P. Tompkins, 1971, p. xiv, and M. Chatelain, 1979, p. 73.

6 See R.W. Noone, 1982; A. Collins, 1998; R. Ellis, 2000.

7 This view is promoted particularly by groups such as the Rosicrucians and Theosophists; see P. Tompkins, 1971, chapter XX; I. Lawton & C. Ogilvie-Herald, 2000, pp. 144-48.

8 See M. Chatelain, 1979, pp. 73-74; Z. Sitchin, 1980, chapters XII to XIV; Z. Sitchin, 1985.

9 C. Wickramasinghe, *Cosmic Dragons*, Souvenir Press, 2001 (see also his article in *The Daily Mail*, London, 15th May 2001).

10 D. Meeks & C. Favard-Meeks, *Daily Life of the Egyptian Gods*, John Murray, London, 1997, pp. 3-4. Cf E. Hornung, *Conceptions of God in Ancient Egypt*, Cornell University Press, Ithaca, New York, 1982, pp. 30, 237-43.

11 Pyramid Texts, Utterance 305, para 474. See also the panel in chapter one of this book.

CHAPTER ONE: THE PYRAMID DECODED

1 E.A. Wallis Budge, *Egyptian Religion*, 1899, p. 39.

2 E.A. Wallis Budge, *From Fetish to God in Ancient Egypt*, Oxford University Press, 1934, pp. 4-5 (see also p. 139).

3 On the monotheism versus polytheism debate, see the companion volume to this book, provisionally entitled *The Midnight Sun: The Death and Rebirth of God in Ancient Egypt*, to be published by Eridu Books in early-2004.

4 See, for example, I.E.S. Edwards, 1993, p. 286. The title first appears with Djedefre.

5 See, for example, S. Quirke, *The Cult of Ra*, Thames & Hudson, London, 2001, pp. 122-23. The earliest known cartouche belongs to Huni, the predecessor of Sneferu.

6 I.E.S. Edwards, 1993, pp. 96, 280-86.

7 J.H. Breasted, *Development of Religion and Thought in Ancient Egypt*, University of Pennsylvania Press, 1972 (first published by Charles Scribner's Sons, 1912), pp. 70-72.

8 Ibid., p. 73. Cf M. Lehner, 1997, p. 34; S. Quirke, *The Cult of Ra*, op. cit., p. 25; R. Bauval, 1999, pp. 81, 361-62.

9 This theory clearly begs the question of why the true pyramid design had to wait until the 4th dynasty. Did the Sun not shine upon Egypt until then?

10 A. Moret, *Le Nil et la Civilisation Egyptienne*, 1926, p. 203, cited by I.E.S. Edwards, 1993, p. 282.

11 I.E.S. Edwards, 1993, p. 282. See also K. Mendelssohn, 1974, p. 46, who provides a photographic illustration of the phenomenon (plate 24).

12 I.E.S. Edwards, 1993, p. 283. Edwards might have added that in the Pyramid Texts the gods do lend the king a hand to pull him up to the sky; therefore, it might be supposed that Re was sending down his rays to the king who stood upon the primeval mound, and that the king was then lifted up to the sky upon these rays.

13 A. Siliotti, 1997, pp. 13, 34 (cf p. 156 'a purer form that materialised the protecting rays of the Sun-god Re, with whom the soul of the pharaoh would be reunited').

14 M. Lehner, 1997, p. 35 (cf p. 105 'the Sun and its rays, of which the pyramid is a symbol').

15 Ibid., p. 6.

16 S. Quirke, *The Cult of Ra*, op. cit., p. 115. But the majority of scholars have thrown caution to the wind, hence J.H. Breasted referred to the true pyramid as 'the greatest of the solar symbols' (*Development of Religion and Thought in Ancient Egypt*, op. cit., p. 74), George Hart, 1991, p. 93, referred to 'the overwhelming solar concept of the pyramid's architecture', and even Quirke himself wrote 'most solar of all symbols is the pyramid, its tip named *benbenet* 'the (stone) of the *benben*' (*The Cult of Ra*, p. 115).

17 Hence S. Quirke in *The Cult of Ra*, op. cit., p. 23, writes: 'All these disparate sources [of over 3,000 years] provide substantially consistent evidence for a single, coherent picture of creation as an act of the Sun.'

18 J.H. Breasted, *Development of Religion and Thought in Ancient Egypt*, op. cit., p. 46.

19 It has long been a mystery to Egyptologists how the Egyptian king could simultaneously be Re, son of Re, and Horus the son of Osiris and Isis. The key to it is the fundamental body-soul duality that lay behind the concepts of the creator-god and the king. This idea is discussed fully in the companion volume to this book.

20 Pyramid Texts, Utterance 600, para 1652-53; see the citation towards the end of this chapter.

21 Pyramid Texts, Utterance 527, para 1248-49.

22 H. Frankfort, *Kingship and the Gods*, University of Chicago Press, 1978 edition, pp. 380-81; E.A. Wallis Budge, *An Egyptian Hieroglyphic Dictionary*, Volume 2, p. 217; J. Baines, '*Bnbn* – Mythological and Linguistic Notes', in *Orientalia*, 39:2 (1970), pp. 389-404; M. Lehner, 1997, p. 35; R. Bauval & A. Gilbert, 1994, pp. 17, 199-200; R. Bauval, 1999, p. 358.

23 H. Frankfort, *Kingship and the Gods*, op. cit., pp. 153, 380-81; G. Hart, *Egyptian Myths*, British Museum Press, London, 1990, p. 11.

24 H. Frankfort, *Kingship and the Gods*, op. cit., p. 381.

25 The symbolism of the eyes is not well understood by Egyptologists, even though it is explicit in the ancient Egyptian texts. Several examples of eyes symbolism appear in this book (see Index), but for a full explanation and justification, see the companion volume.

26 S. Quirke, *The Cult of Ra*, op. cit., p. 116; R. Bauval & A. Gilbert, 1994, pp. 88, 106; R. Bauval, 1999, pp. 361-62.

27 S. Quirke, *The Cult of Ra*, op. cit., p. 25; R. Bauval, 1999, pp. 361-62.

28 S. Quirke, *The Cult of Ra*, op. cit., p. 116; M. Lehner, 1997, p. 17.

29 Both Budge and Breasted played down the stellar aspects of the Pyramid Texts, regarding them as a hangover and intrusion from a more ancient and primitive sky cult. My view is, of course, subjective, as is theirs. The reader is advised to peruse a copy of the Pyramid Texts, and form his own opinion.

30 I.E.S. Edwards, 1993, pp. 284-85; G. Hart, 1991, p. 93; M. Lehner, 1997, pp. 112-13; S. Quirke, *The Cult of Ra*, op. cit., pp. 115-16. My scepticism is shared by Rudolf Gantenbrink. Our doubts are prompted by the various bends in the shafts and the builder's obsession with making them exit on the central north-south axis of the Pyramid.

31 I.E.S. Edwards, 1993, p. 284; M. Lurker, *The Gods and Symbols of Ancient Egypt*, Thames & Hudson, London, 1980, pp. 92, 98; M. Lehner, 1997, p. 29.

32 J.P. Lepre, 1990, p. 156, observes that the stars on the tomb ceilings were 'symbolic of the pharaoh's association with the astral [after-] life.'

33 See S. Quirke, *The Cult of Ra*, op. cit., pp. 115-17. In September 2001, Spence announced that she would be embarking on a new study 'looking at the Pyramid Texts as an entire corpus of spells as opposed to focusing on one aspect of them, specifically how they combine both stellar and solar beliefs, often even in a single spell.' At the time of writing, her study is ongoing and has not yet been published.

34 R. Bauval, 'Investigation on the Origin of the Benben Stone: Was It an Iron Meteorite?, in *Discussions in Egyptology*, 14 (1989), pp. 5-17 (reprinted in Bauval, 1999, pp. 356-65). T. Wilkinson expressed his ideas to a Bloomsbury archaeological summer school at University College London in 2001; see 'Pyramids seen as Stairways to Heaven', in *The Guardian*, London, 14th May 2001. On the conical shape of the Benben Stone, see the panel in chapter five, which contains quotes from Bauval and Wilkinson.

35 R. Bauval, 1999, p. 359.

36 R. Bauval & A. Gilbert, 1994, pp. 273-75; R. Bauval, 1999, p. 357. The Bent Pyramid of Dahshur has an unusual shape which indeed seems to resemble an inverted conical meteorite.

37 H. Frankfort, *Ancient Egyptian Religion: An Interpretation*, Dover edition 2000 (first published by Columbia University Press, New York, 1948), p. 131.

38 See, for example, I.E.S. Edwards, 1993, p. 7; M. Lehner, 1997, p. 35; R. T. Rundle Clark, *Myth and Symbol in Ancient Egypt*, Thames and Hudson, 1993 edition (first published 1959), p. 38.

39 J.H. Breasted, *Development of Religion and Thought in Ancient Egypt*, op. cit., p. 46; M. Lurker, *The Gods and Symbols of Ancient Egypt*, op. cit., p. 42; B. Watterson, *Gods of Ancient Egypt*, Sutton Publishing, 1996 edition, p. 19; H. Wilson, *People of the Pharaohs*, Brockhampton Press, London, 1997, p. 97.

40 H. Frankfort, *Ancient Egyptian Religion: An Interpretation*, op. cit. (first published 1948); H. Frankfort, *Kingship and the Gods*, op. cit. (first published 1948); R.T. Rundle Clark, *Myth and Symbol in Ancient Egypt*, op. cit. (first published 1959).

41 H. Frankfort, *Ancient Egyptian Religion: An Interpretation*, op. cit., pp. 4, 19.

42 Ibid., pp. 50-51.

43 I.E.S. Edwards, 1993, p. 69. For a complete list of references, see the companion volume. It was similarly believed in Mesopotamia that the city was a microcosm of the place of creation, which rose up like the mountain of creation, or 'raised its head to the sky like a bull'.

44 I. Shaw & P. Nicholson, *British Museum Dictionary of Ancient Egypt*, British Museum Press, 1996, pp. 285-86. See also the panel later in this chapter.

45 G.A. Wainwright, *The Sky-Religion in Egypt*, University Press, Cambridge, 1938, pp. 16-17, 86; E. Hornung, *Conceptions of God in Ancient Egypt*, op. cit., pp. 138-42, 209, 234.

46 The king's earliest identity was Horus the sky-god; there is much confusion as to how the king as Horus could later become Re, or the son of Re, but all becomes clear in a creational and dualistic framework (see note 19 earlier).

47 For full details and references of these creation myths, see the companion volume.

48 H. Frankfort, *Kingship and the Gods*, op. cit., p. 181 (cf The Theology of Memphis). On the Two Lands as a metaphor for the entire earth, see the companion volume.

49 E.A. Wallis Budge, *From Fetish to God in Ancient Egypt*, op. cit., p. 259 (cf p. 414 where of Amun it is said 'having fashioned yourself, you moulded your members'). These two paragraphs address two distinct phases of the primeval mound's creation. In the first, the creator is seen constructing his body, the proto-earth, in the world ocean; in the second, he is seen sitting on his assembled body which has emerged in the form of the earth, known idiomatically as the God's 'seat' and 'the Two Lands'. The idea of the God embracing his own body represents a monodramatisation of the myth whereby the Goddess embraced the body of the God. Elsewhere in Egyptian myth, the primeval mound is personified by Atum or Geb.

50 A 'first person' account of Nun's spiritualisation to the sky appears in the Coffin Texts, Spell 714.

51 For the earliest references to the separation of the heavens from the earth in Egypt, see Pyramid Texts, Utterances 433, 434, 506, 519, 570, 627, 689. The idea was also fundamental in other ancient Near Eastern religions.

52 On the rape of the mother motif, see chapter five of this book.

53 H. Frankfort, *Kingship and the Gods*, op. cit., pp. 152, 354.

54 See A.F. Alford, *When The Gods Came Down*, Hodder & Stoughton, London, 2000, pp. 106-8. The disappearance of Sirius and its reappearance after 70 days had profound links to the ritual of mummification and the myth of Isis and Osiris. It is a classic example of the re-enactment of creation.

55 Of course, such insight would have been reserved for the educated – or even initiated – élite among the Egyptians.

56 H. Frankfort, *Kingship and the Gods*, op. cit., p. 161; J.B. Pritchard ed., *ANET (Ancient Near Eastern Texts Relating to the Old Testament),* Princeton University Press, 3rd edition, 1969, p. 368.

57 This idea of the specialisation of the creator-god's functions is explored fully in the companion volume.

58 H. Frankfort, *Ancient Egyptian Religion: An Interpretation*, op. cit., p. 19.

59 This idea was touched on by R.T. Rundle Clark in *Myth and Symbol in Ancient Egypt*, op. cit., pp. 31, 39, but he made little of it.

60 Pyramid Texts, Utterance 21, para 13-14; see quotation in chapter five of this book.

61 Pyramid Texts, Utterance 600, para 1654.

62 On the orthodox pyramid/earth theory, see I.E.S. Edwards, 1993, pp. 69, 279-80; M. Lehner, 1997, pp. 35, 74, 235, 240; G. Hart, 1991, p. 87; H. Frankfort, *Ancient Egyptian Religion: An Interpretation*, op. cit., p. 156; H. Frankfort, *Kingship and the Gods*, op. cit., p. 153; M. Lurker, *The Gods and Symbols of Ancient Egypt*, op. cit., p. 98; F. Turkkan in foreword to P. Smyth, 1880, p. vii. On the alternative Pyramid/Earth theory, see E-F. Jomard, 1829; J. Taylor, 1864; P. Smyth, 1880, pp. 49-50; P. Tompkins, 1971, pp. xiv, 21-22, 31, 48, 70-76, 176, 189, 201-2, 209, 285; P. Lemesurier, 1993, pp. 8, 11, 19, 30, 33, 43, 146, 309-10, 336; C. Dunn, 1998, pp. 130-33. It is interesting to note that one of the earliest investigators of the Earth-commensurate Pyramid was Isaac Newton.

63 The rising of the mound and the seeding of the sky were intimately related in that they were apparently coterminous events; see Pyramid Texts, Utterance 600, quoted later in this chapter. Hence the confusion among Egyptologists (for whom the idea of cataclysm is anathema). This is an intricate subject, which is explained and justified more fully in the companion volume to this book.

64 Pyramid Texts, Utterance 600, para 1657-58.

65 J.H. Breasted, *Development of Religion and Thought in Ancient Egypt*, op. cit., p. 73 note 3. Breasted believed that Osirian references in the Pyramid Texts were an intrusion into the solar religion (see pp. 163, 275-77). Egyptologists have followed Breasted unquestioningly in this regard. A big mistake.

66 For Osiris as the primeval ocean, see Pyramid Texts, Utterances 366, 454. These passages have not been well understood by Egyptologists, with the exception of R.T. Rundle Clark, *Myth and Symbol in Ancient Egypt*, op. cit., p. 117.

67 For example, in Utterance 303, it is stated that the gods set down reed-floats 'for Osiris when he ascended to the sky, when he ferried over the firmament with his son Horus beside him... causing him to appear as a great god in the firmament'. For further examples, see the companion volume to this book.

68 Pyramid Texts, Utterance 600, para 1652-53.

69 Shu and Tefnut were described as 'twins' (Pyramid Texts, Utterance 527), which is obviously evocative of the Sun and the Moon. For explicit references to Shu and Tefnut as the Sun and the Moon (the 'eyes' of the creator-god), see Coffin Texts, Spells 80, 607, also E.A. Wallis Budge, *Legends of the Egyptian Gods*, Dover edition, 1994, p. 177, and E.A. Wallis Budge, *From Fetish to God in Ancient Egypt*, op. cit., p. 419. Additionally, many texts seem to suggest that Shu was an ancient Sun-god (perhaps older than Re). One of the few Egyptologists to give proper recognition to Shu and Tefnut as the Sun and the Moon (as opposed to them being mere air and moisture!), is M. Lurker, *The Gods and Symbols of Ancient Egypt*, op. cit., p. 112.

70 See, for example, H. Frankfort, *Kingship and the Gods*, op. cit., pp. 152, 380.

71 There is persuasive evidence that some pyramids did not contain burials, for example where a king built more than one pyramid, or where there is no practical means of entering into or beneath the pyramid. In the latter respect, it may be that the pyramid was not a tomb but a

memorial to the creation, and nothing but a memorial to the creation. The creational theory thus provides a potential framework for understanding *all* Egyptian pyramids.

72 See J.P. Lepre, 1990, p. 20; M. Lehner, 1997, p. 18; I.E.S. Edwards, 1993, p. 288; J.H. Breasted, *Development of Religion and Thought in Ancient Egypt*, op. cit., pp. 72, 77, 80.

73 R. Stadelmann, 1998, p. 56. Cf S. Quirke, *The Cult of Ra*, op. cit., p. 127: 'There is no group of kings more solar than the 4th dynasty.' Similarly, I.E.S. Edwards, 1993, p. 286: 'The process of solarization continued under Cheops'.

74 See, for example, S. Quirke, *The Cult of Ra*, op. cit., p. 117; M. Lehner, 1997, p. 29; Z. Hawass in update to W.M.F. Petrie, 1990, p. 99.

75 I refer here to the original theory for the existence of the multiple chambers. Today, most scholars have reconsidered this view, and believe that the chambers were built to a single unified design. A full discussion of this subject will follow in chapter three.

76 I.E.S. Edwards, 1993, pp. xxii, 287, 291.

77 Z. Hawass in update to W.M.F. Petrie, 1990, pp. 99-100. He suggested that the revolution had been supported by Khafre (Khufu's son), but abandoned thereafter.

78 The name Khufu is said to be an abbreviated form of Khnum-khuf; see note 42 to chapter nine.

79 Significantly, the Pyramid Texts describe *akhet* as 'the birth-place of the gods', and numerous passages refer to this place being 'split apart' at the time of the creator-god's emergence from the abyss; and the hieroglyph for *akhet* indeed shows a split-apart 'mountain of the east'.

80 'Great Pyramid' is a modern term. However, the Pyramid of Khafre at Giza was known as 'The Pyramid, Khafre is Great', or in other words 'the Great Pyramid'.

81 The reference appears on the so-called Dream Stele, erected in honour of king Thutmosis IV of the 18th dynasty. See J.H. Breasted, *Ancient Records of Egypt*, Part II, Histories & Mysteries of Man Ltd, London, 1988, p. 323.

CHAPTER TWO: A TOUR OF THE PYRAMID

1 It ranks among man-made structures such as the Great Wall of China and the largest pyramid in Mexico. It was not rivalled in the modern era until the construction of Boulder Dam.

2 A.P. Sakovich, 'Counting the Stones', in *KMT*, 13:3 (Fall 2002), pp. 53-57. It is impossible to make an exact calculation, not least because the Pyramid is built around a nucleus of protruding bedrock.

3 M. Lehner, 1997, pp. 108-9, 206, cites an average weight per block of 2.5 tons, but p. 225 suggests that this figure requires further study (he hints at a downward adjustment).

4 I.E.S. Edwards, 1993, p. 98, citing E. Baldwin Smith, *Egyptian Architecture as a Cultural Expression*, p. 96.

5 I.E.S. Edwards, 1993, p. 99. The figures are from J.H. Cole, *Survey of Egypt*, Paper No. 39: 'The Determination of the Exact Size and Orientation of the Great Pyramid of Giza', Cairo, 1925.

6 J.P. Lepre, 1990, p. 71.

7 The figures are from the J.H. Cole survey of 1925.

8 See K. Spence, 'Ancient Egyptian chronology and the astronomical orientation of pyramids', in *Nature*, 408 (November 2000), p. 320.

9 J.P. Lepre, 1990, p. 165, cites 144,000 casing stones. However, A.P. Sakovich (see note 2), on my request, generated a revised estimate of 152,350 blocks (email correspondence 10th November 2002). The number of courses varies from publication to publication (the accepted number is 210, of which only 203 remain intact); here I split the range of 215 to 217 suggested by A.P. Sakovich in 'Counting the Stones', op. cit., p. 57. The figure 216 will, of course, be of considerable interest to students of numerical/astronomical symbolism in the Pyramid. The question of the Pyramid's capstone is a moot point, as many writers would like to think that such a stone was never fitted. My personal view, bearing in mind the symbolism of the capstone as discussed in this book, is that the Pyramid most certainly would have been fitted with an apex stone.

10 W.M.F. Petrie, 1990, p. 13.

11 Egyptologists differ slightly in the angle of slope that they quote, on account of the difficulty of precise measurement. The problem is that the Pyramid was robbed in antiquity of so much stone on all four sides and at its apex.

12 See J.P. Lepre, 1990, pp. 126-27; P. Tompkins, 1971, chapter XV.

13 In the view of many alternative writers, the sphere in question is the planet Earth; see note 62 to chapter one.

14 I have used figures from I. Lawton & C. Ogilvie-Herald, 2000, chapter three, figure 12.

15 I. Lawton & C. Ogilvie-Herald, 2000, chapter three, pp. 151-53.

16 Ibid., pp. 151, 529 (note 133). Cf J.P. Lepre, 1990, p. 126.

17 M. Lehner, 1997, p. 109.

18 S. Quirke, *The Cult of Ra*, op. cit., p. 123. He calls the Giza plateau 'an earthquake-proof platform for colossal architecture.'

19 J.P. Lepre, 1990, p. 70.

20 Ibid., pp. 65-67: 'This concavity divides each of the apparent four sides in half, creating a very special and unusual eight-sided pyramid'. See also K. Mendelssohn, 1974, pp. 122-23.

21 Al-Mamun was the son of Harun al-Rashid of Arabian Nights fame. His adventures in Egypt are related in the works of al-Hokm, al-Kaisi, al-Maqrisi, and others. For a good summary, see P. Tompkins, 1971, or I. Lawton & C. Ogilvie-Herald, 2000. There are reasons to doubt the official version of his digging of the entrance tunnel – see chapter eight.

22 Different writers cite different course numbers for the main entrance (and indeed for the rough tunnel). I follow W.M.F. Petrie, 1990, p. 17.

23 The limestone gable blocks each weigh in the region of 15 tons. The angle formed at the gable's bottom is said to equal the slope of the Pyramid, about 52 degrees (see P. Smyth, 1880, pp. 436-7). Their purpose is a mystery – see discussion in chapter ten.

24 W.M.F. Petrie, 1990, p. 72. The idea that the pyramids of Giza had doors is also supported by a statement in an Arab manuscript, *c.* AD 850, which is referenced by Vyse.

25 M. Lehner, 1997, p. 114, seems to suggest this.

26 See W.M.F. Petrie, 1990, figure VII; J.P. Lepre, 1990, Appendix B. Their suggested door designs are reproduced in chapter three, figure 44.

27 I.E.S. Edwards, 1993, pp. 111-12; M. Lehner, 1997, p. 39.

28 Again, different writers quote different figures for the Descending Passage, some of which are clearly wrong, e.g. Lehner, 1990, p. 113. Lepre gives 50 + 300 feet. Petrie gives 150 + 200 feet. I have attempted to derive a more likely set of figures.

29 W.M.F. Petrie, 1990, p. 19.

30 The idea that the Descending Passage was blocked by plugs was suggested by Vyse, and is followed by I. Lawton & C. Ogilvie-Herald, 2000, pp. 56, 135, 503-5. But the suggestion was disputed by Petrie and Maragioglio and Rinaldi; see P. Tompkins, 1971, p. 242.

31 This false bottom may have been constructed like this from the beginning, to reinforce the impression that the Pyramid had already been robbed. In other words, it may have formed part of a decoy tomb arrangement.

32 Such portcullises were provided in the Second and Third Pyramids of Giza, i.e. those of Khafre and Menkaure.

33 J.P. Lepre, 1990, p. 114, writes: 'it is as if a mad-man, rather than a master architect, had his hand at fashioning it.'

34 On the high level of the water table, see P. Smyth, 1880, Plate VI; A. Siliotti, 1997, pp. 24-25; I. Lawton & C. Ogilvie-Herald, 2000, p. 262. If carved by the hand of man, might it have been designed to reproduce the features of a pre-existing cave elsewhere which was sacred to the builders? On the latter suggestion, see note 44 to chapter ten.

35 Again, different writers quote different figures for the depth of the Pit. I follow J.P. Lepre, 1990, p. 114. Note that in the 19th century Vyse and Perring had the Pit excavated to a depth of about 38 feet.

36 J.P. Lepre, 1990, pp. 89-92, suggests that the granite block in the Subterranean Chamber may have come originally from the portcullis in the Antechamber to the King's Chamber. I have my doubts about this idea. Might it rather have come from a portcullis in the horizontal passage to the Subterranean Chamber?

37 A possible precedent for the Ascending Passage, albeit on a smaller scale and in a different context, is the ascending passage in the small satellite pyramid of the Bent Pyramid at Dahshur; see J.P. Lepre, 1990, p. 57.

38 J.P. Lepre, 1990, p. 78. He also calls it 'a very unique architectural innovation'. On the subject of the girdle stones, see also W.M.F. Petrie, 1990, p. 21.

39 W.M.F. Petrie, 1990, p. 88.
40 It was the Arab tradition to bury women in tombs with gabled ceilings and men in tombs with flat ceilings.
41 On the Dixon relics, see R. Bauval & A. Gilbert, 1994, Epilogue; R. Bauval & G. Hancock, 1996, pp. 110-16, 307; I. Lawton & C. Ogilvie-Herald, 2000, pp. 68-71. Gantenbrink has suggested that the relics were trapped in the upper part of the northern shaft and that the Dixon brothers dislocated them with their probing rods. In 1993, Gantenbrink's robot revealed further such relics, still trapped in the shafts (see note 52 below). It is not yet known whether these relics were retrieved by the iRobot/National Geographic team in 2002. If not, why not?
42 W.M.F. Petrie, 1990, p. 24.
43 The size of the gap beneath the slab was determined by means of a laser beam.
44 See Gantenbrink's website, www.cheops.org.
45 Gantenbrink, on the advice of an English metallurgist Hugh Tyrer, theorises that the fittings are made of copper or bronze (on the basis of their metallic texture and corrosion colouring). See www.cheops.org. It is believed that corrosion caused one of the two fittings to snap, perhaps along a hairline crack in the cold-forged metal. Mark Lehner has suggested the possibility of meteoritic iron coated in copper.
46 R. Gantenbrink, www.cheops.org.
47 Ibid.
48 If this theory is correct, then we would expect to see small cut marks in the shaft side walls, at the appropriate height at the end of each wall-ceiling U-block. Video footage of the shafts needs to be carefully re-examined in order to validate or invalidate this hypothesis.
49 R. Gantenbrink, www.cheops.org. In the southern shaft, from block 19 onward to 26, there are curious scratch marks on both walls, consistently about an inch above the floor. These scratch marks are not very deep – they just scratch off the patina from the stones – and they extend over the block joints, causing Gantenbrink to speculate that 'something was dragged up through the shaft subsequent to its completion'. Also curious is a piece of light-coloured mortar adhering to the west wall near block 21, as if to suggest that something was once fixed here. There is a similar imperfection at block 26, beyond which the floor of block 26 falls away, causing a downward step in the floor of the shaft. Beyond this feature, the floor of the shaft bears a long 'cutting groove' running straight along its centre (similar to that which is seen behind the 'door'). Gantenbrink believes that the drop in floor level may be an indicator for 'an as yet undiscovered structure below or above this shaft section'. But to me, it simply looks like an extremely shoddy piece of workmanship. As for the scratch marks and mortar remnants, these have not yet been satisfactorily explained. However, it occurs to me that all of these features may be explained by the assumption that the builders were recycling blocks from some earlier application, e.g. a test pyramid that had been built earlier on the site (see chapter seven). According to my theory of the purpose of these shafts (see chapter six), the quality of their finish would not have been an important factor.
50 R. Gantenbrink, www.cheops.org. The angles are based on 14 measurements taken over a distance of about 55 feet.
51 The wooden rod is accurately machined and squared, but has a fractured end. It lies beneath the hexagonal iron rod, and extends for some distance beyond the bend, lying against the left hand (west) wall. The iron rod consists of segments that are nearly 9 feet long, and is jammed up against the right hand (east) wall beyond the bend. According to some writers, the broken rods are the result of an exploration by Morton Edgar in the 1920s. The consensus, however, is that they were introduced to the shaft by Waynman Dixon in 1872, the wooden rod representing his first attempt, and the iron rod his second. An interesting twist is provided by Gantenbrink who wonders whether there might be a connection between the broken wooden rod and the bronze hook and broken wooden handle that were found in the shaft in 1872 (and indeed the similar fittings that still remain in the shaft – see note 52 below). If he is correct in his theory that Dixon broke the fittings off the wooden pole when he probed the shaft with his iron pole, then the entire wooden pole may be an original builder's artefact. But his theory is disputed by Lawton and Ogilvie-Herald. For more on this subject, see www.cheops.org; R. Bauval & A. Gilbert, 1994, Epilogue; R. Bauval & G. Hancock, 1996, pp. 111-12, 307, 321 (notes 43-44); I. Lawton & C. Ogilvie-Herald, 2000, pp. 68-69, 327-28, and plates 35-38.
52 I. Lawton & C. Ogilvie-Herald, 2000, pp. 71, 329, and plates 35-36; also R. Gantenbrink,

www.cheops.org. The drilled holes in the wooden handle appear to match up with the rivets in the bronze hook found in 1872. Gantenbrink writes that: 'It seems most probable that the hook was originally attached to a long, square wooden rod, the remains of which still lie in the shaft.'

53 R. Gantenbrink, www.cheops.org. The angles are based on 24 measurements taken over a distance of about 90 feet.

54 This prediction was made in a public lecture in Leeds, which was recorded on video, and also faxed to *The Daily Mail* in London. It was also discussed informally with a number of people.

55 J.P. Lepre, 1990, pp. 79, 81, 85-86.

56 Ibid., 79, 84-85.

57 W.M.F. Petrie, 1990, p. 25.

58 J.P. Lepre, 1990, pp. 82-83: 'Hundreds of rough chisel marks are staggered along the top edges of these grooves.' However, chisel marks are absent from the area directly above the Great Step – see further comments in chapter eight.

59 Ibid., p. 83.

60 W.M.F. Petrie, 1990, p. 25.

61 J.P. Lepre, 1990, p. 85; P. Smyth, 1880, p. 453. These inset stones have been described by some writers as 'flag stones' or 'mile stones'.

62 J.P. Lepre, 1990, p. 83.

63 Ibid., p. 85.

64 W.M.F. Petrie, 1990, p. 93.

65 See the diagram in P. Smyth, 1880, Plate XV, reproduced in figure 33 of this book.

66 W.M.F. Petrie, 1990, p. 26. Symbolically, granite represented the male principle and limestone the feminine principle; see D. Elkington, 2001, p. 389.

67 W.M.F. Petrie, 1990, p. 94; P. Tompkins, 1971, pp. 101-3; J.P. Lepre, 1990, pp. 101-3; R. Temple, *The Crystal Sun*, Century, London, 2000, pp. 370-72. Pythagorean dimensions are seen not only in the chamber as a whole, but also in the exceptionally large stone above the entrance passage.

68 J.P. Lepre, 1990, pp. 92, 98, 102. According to Lepre, Smyth's plan (figure 35) understates the number of wall stones by one.

69 W.M.F. Petrie, 1990, p. 28; I. Lawton & C. Ogilvie-Herald, 2000, p. 134 (the authors state that two different types of plaster have been used). H.Wilson in *People of the Pharaohs*, op. cit., p. 159, states: 'the chemical composition of ancient Egyptian plaster was similar to that of limestone and it was not so useful for repairing faults in granite or quartzite'.

70 This report comes from Boris Said, who accompanied Tom Danley during his acoustical survey of the Great Pyramid; see C. Dunn, 1998, pp. 158-59.

71 J.P. Lepre, 1990, p. 280. Cf M. Lehner, 1997, p. 114.

72 M. Lehner, 1997, p. 114; P. Lemesurier, 1993, p. 114. However, although the box is aligned with the floor stones in the King's Chamber today, it was in fact skewed from this position when Smyth surveyed the chamber in 1880 (see figure 35; my thanks to J. Reid, 2001, p. 21, for pointing this out). The original position of the box is thus a matter of conjecture, but it may be significant that treasure-hunters made a deep excavation in the floor in the north-west corner of the room. Was this the original position of the box?

73 P. Tompkins, 1971, pp. 266-67; L.C. Stecchini, 1971, p. 324; A. Collins, 1998, p. 15.

74 J.P. Lepre, 1990, pp. 92-93, 280-81.

75 M. Lehner, 1997, p. 114. Further damage to the box has been caused by hordes of visitors seeking souvenirs. P. Smyth, 1880, p. 153, states that in 1865 the damage was 8-10 inches worse than in 1837.

76 It is not known for certain whether the shafts penetrated the outer casing stones, since these stones were stripped off in Arab times. Some writers have indeed wondered if the shafts were originally sealed at their outer ends (M. Lehner, 1997, p. 112; J. Reid, 2001, p. 23). Around AD 1220, the Arab writer Abd al-Latif described 'openings and windows' in the King's Chamber, 'which appear to have been made to admit air and light'. This would seem to indicate that *at that time* the shafts were open to the outside world (I. Lawton & C. Ogilvie-Herald, 2000, pp. 26, 321). But as to the original design, a great deal of uncertainty remains.

77 R. Gantenbrink, www.cheops.org; J.P. Lepre, 1990, p. 95; R. Ellis, 2000, p. 27. The lower part of the shaft is well known, access to it being possible via the excavation that was made by Giovanni Battista Caviglia (early-19th century) in the west wall of the Antechamber.

78 R. Gantenbrink, www.cheops.org; I. Lawton & C. Ogilvie-Herald, 2000, pp. 52, 323. As usual, different writers report different 'facts'. In particular, Gantenbrink accuses Maragioglio and Rinaldi of having calculated incorrect data: 'As we verified in 1992, the upper southern shaft emerges on the exterior at the 101st layer, the upper northern shaft at the 102nd layer. In this regard, Maragioglio and Rinaldi report incorrect values.'

79 Again, different writers quote different figures. I follow J.P. Lepre, 1990, pp. 95, 97, and I. Lawton & C. Ogilvie-Herald, 2000, p. 323.

80 The mouth of the shaft was forced open by Caviglia. The humidity was caused by the hordes of tourists.

81 See diagram in P. Lemesurier, 1977, p. 100. Cf J.P. Lepre, 1990, p. 95.

82 R. Gantenbrink, www.cheops.org; J.P. Lepre, 1990, pp. 95, 97-98; R. Ellis, 2000, p. 22. W.M.F. Petrie, 1990, p. 29, states that the angle in the outer 70 feet of the shaft varies from 44° 26′ to 45° 30′.

83 R. Gantenbrink, www.cheops.org; J.P. Lepre, 1990, p. 95. (Cf W.M.F. Petrie, 1990, p. 17, who claimed an exit of the shaft in the 104th course, and P. Lemesurier, 1993, pp. 41, 112, 335, who claimed an exit in the 102nd course.)

84 J.P. Lepre, 1990, pp. 97-98; I. Lawton & C. Ogilvie-Herald, 2000, p. 323.

85 The iron plate was found by Vyse's assistant, Mr J.R. Hill, who sent it to the British Museum with the following certification: 'This is to certify that the piece of iron found by me near the mouth of the air-passage, in the southern side of the Great Pyramid at Gizeh, on Friday, May 26th [1837], was taken out by me from an inner joint, after having been removed by blasting the two outer tiers of the stones of the present surface of the Pyramid; and that no joint or opening of any sort was connected with the above mentioned joint, by which the iron could have been placed in it after the original building of the Pyramid. I also shewed the exact spot to Mr Perring, on Saturday, June 24th.'

86 R. Bauval & A. Gilbert, 1994, p. 236; R. Bauval & G. Hancock, 1996, pp. 102, 104-8.

87 W.M.F. Petrie, 1990, p. 85, was convinced that the iron plate was an authentic ancient Egyptian artefact: 'though some doubt has been thrown on the piece, merely from its rarity, yet the vouchers for it are very precise; and it has a cast of a nummulite on the rust of it, proving it to have been buried for ages beside a block of nummulitic limestone, and therefore to be certainly ancient. No reasonable doubt can therefore exist about its being really a genuine piece used by the Pyramid masons.' J.P. Lepre, 1990, p. 245, states that this discovery amounts to 'conclusive proof that the pyramid builders were using iron at a very early date'. I. Lawton & C. Ogilvie-Herald, 2000, pp. 52-53, 211, urge scholars to embrace the significance of this find.

88 M. Lehner, 1997, p. 45; I. Lawton & C. Ogilvie-Herald, 2000, p. 33.

89 I choose my words carefully; I am not suggesting that the superstructure protected the chamber from superincumbent weight (as Egyptologists maintain); rather, I am suggesting that the gabled roof protected *the superstructure* from superincumbent weight. A plausible purpose for such a design is advanced in chapter seven of this book.

90 W.M.F. Petrie, 1990, p. 31.

91 J.P. Lepre, 1990, p. 109; M. Lehner, 1997, p. 109; I. Lawton & C. Ogilvie-Herald, 2000, pp. 32-33, 193. The 70-ton stone is the high central floor-stone in Arbuthnot's Chamber, which measures roughly 27 by 7 by 5 feet. Other stones weigh considerably less. Lehner p. 114 suggests 25-40 tons for the roof beams in the chamber.

92 An interesting suggestion, put to me by J. Reid and J. Lewandowski, is that the rough upper sides are 'the business end' of the beams, the flat undersides having been necessary to facilitate the transportation of the stones to the site.

93 J.P. Lepre, 1990, p. 109. For photographs of these unusual grooves and bowls, see Lepre pp. 107, 250.

94 M. Lehner, 1997, p. 111.

CHAPTER THREE: NOTHING BUT A TOMB?

1 E.A. Wallis Budge, *The Mummy*, 2nd edition, 1925 (first published in 1893), p. 406.

2 J.P. Lepre, 1990, pp. 280, 265-70. A Great Pyramid cenotaph theory was also suggested by N. Wheeler, 1935.

3 J.P. Lepre, 1990, p. 280.

4 Ibid.

5 Ibid.

6 Ibid., p. 281.

7 Ibid., p. 282. Lepre here suggests that the plundering of the tomb occurred 'at the time of the ninth century Arab penetration'. However, most Egyptologists assume that the body and treasure were stolen in ancient Egyptian times.

8 Ibid., p. 278.

9 Tomb robbery was already a major problem in Old Kingdom times. See the quote by Michael Hoffman in chapter four, note 3.

10 W.M.F. Petrie, 1990, pp. 20, 23, 86-87; L. Cottrell, 1956, pp. 227-28; I.E.S. Edwards, 1993, pp. 101-4; J.P. Lepre, 1990, pp. 78, 110-11, 114-16.

11 W.M.F. Petrie, 1990, p. 21; I.E.S. Edwards, 1993, p. 103; J.P. Lepre, 1990, pp. 76-78. Ludwig Borchardt argued that the girdle stones were in fact parts of internal buttress walls through which the passage had been cut, but this view has been countered by Somers Clarke and Rex Engelbach (see L. Cottrell, 1956, p. 230; K. Mendelssohn, 1974, p. 122).

12 I.E.S. Edwards, 1993, p. 103.

13 V. Maragioglio & C.A. Rinaldi, 1965; P. Tompkins, 1971, p. 240. A big clue is the fact that the blocks at the bottom of the Ascending Passage are of exceptional size and quality and have been fitted together with particular care.

14 I.E.S. Edwards, 1993, pp. 104-5, 110-11, 289.

15 On the trial passages, see chapter ten of this book.

16 W.M.F. Petrie, 1990, p. 93. Basically, the angle of the Ascending Passage and Grand Gallery were fixed such that the Gallery terminated at its southern end at the exact height (that of the King's Chamber floor) 'where the vertical section of the Pyramid was halved, where the area of the horizontal section was half that of the base, where the diagonal from corner to corner was equal to the length of the base, and where the width of the face was equal to half the diagonal of the base.', all this whilst ensuring that 'the Gallery length (horizontal) is equal to the vertical height of its end above the base'. An ingenious geometrical design.

17 Z. Hawass, in update to W.M.F. Petrie, 1990, p. 99; M. Lehner, 1997, p. 111; A. Siliotti, 1997, p. 51; R. Stadelmann, 1998, p. 61. Stadelmann notes that there was a tendency to build three chambers, or spaces, in Old Kingdom pyramids, albeit the functions of the triple rooms are 'only partially understood'.

18 I.E.S. Edwards, 1993, pp. xxii, 287, 291.

19 For example, M. Lehner, 1997, p. 114: 'The red granite sarcophagus near the western wall of the King's Chamber was the final resting place of Khufu's body'. The theory has magically become fact.

20 P. Smyth, 1880, pp. 162, 254-55; W.M.F. Petrie, 1990, p. 88; J.P. Lepre, 1990, p. 94; M. Lehner, 1997, p. 114.

21 In later times, per Diodorus Siculus, there were foot holes leading up to the entrance (W.M.F. Petrie, 1990, p. 73). But originally such a method of scaling the Pyramid would have been inconceivable, as it would have given away the location of the entrance. A temporary ladder or platform must therefore have been used.

22 The King's Chamber shafts *are* unique. I.E.S. Edwards, 1993, p. 285, was quite incorrect (embarrassingly so) when he suggested that the walls of Khafre's Pyramid contained the beginnings of ventilation shafts; see J.P. Lepre, 1990, p. 100; I. Lawton & C. Ogilvie-Herald, 2000, pp. 38-39, 60. Recently, a comparison was drawn to 'two openings' in the burial chamber of a 4th dynasty tomb (see *Ancient Egypt* magazine, July/August 2002, p. 8); at the time of writing, however, the extent of the resemblance is unclear, and it may be that the comparison has been drawn in haste.

23 J.P. Lepre, 1990, pp. 97-100.

24 A. Badawy, 'The Stellar Destiny of Pharaoh and the so-called Air-shafts in Cheops's Pyramid', in *Mitteilungen des Instituts fur Orientforschung Akademie der Wissenschaften zu Berlin*, 10 (1964), p. 190. See also R. Bauval & G. Hancock, 1996, pp. 53-55; C. Dunn, 1998, pp. 44-45, 192.

25 R. Gantenbrink, www.cheops.org.

26 J. Capart, *Etudes et Histoires*, I, Bruxelles, 1924, p. 182; G. Steindorff, *Egypt*, Baedeker, 1929, p. 140; A. Badawy, 1964, pp. 189-206; V. Trimble, 1964, pp. 183-87 (reproduced in R. Bauval

& A. Gilbert, 1994, Appendix 1).

27 I.E.S. Edwards, 1978, p. 88; I.E.S. Edwards, 1981; I.E.S. Edwards, 1993, pp. 284-85; M. Lehner, 1997, p. 114; E.C. Krupp, *Echoes of the Ancient Skies*, Oxford University Press, 1983, pp. 103-5; R. Bauval, 1989; R. Bauval, 1990 (reproduced in R. Bauval, 1999, pp. 368-73); R. Bauval, 1993; R. Bauval, 1999; R. Bauval & A. Gilbert, 1994, pp. 99-104, 131-32, 206-9, 264-71.

28 K. Mendelssohn, 1974, p. 27; M. Lehner, 1997, pp. 27, 31, 33, 77, 79-81, 92, 105, 120, 135-36, 240. See also figure 49 in this chapter.

29 I.E.S. Edwards, 1993, p. 284. This idea is well attested, sloping passages being found, almost without exception, in the north faces of the pyramids.

30 I.E.S. Edwards, 1978, p. 88. Cf I.E.S. Edwards, 1993, pp. 284-85.

31 I.E.S. Edwards, 1993, p. 285: 'the southern ventilation shaft had no recognizable antecedent'.

32 J.P. Lepre, 1990, p. 100.

33 R. Stadelmann, 1998, p. 61: 'They [the shafts] provide a direct route up to Heaven for the deceased king's soul.' He likes to quote Pyramid Texts, Utterance 258. See also A. Siliotti, 1997, p. 51.

34 J.H. Breasted, *Development of Religion and Thought in Ancient Egypt*, op. cit., Lecture V, pp. 142-64. I disagree profoundly with Breasted's perception of Osiris in the Pyramid Texts.

35 For evidence of the granite slabs' removal, see figure 105 in chapter seven of this book. It is presumed that the slabs were removed in order to facilitate the removal of what was hidden in the King's Chamber sarcophagus, along with the lid of that box. J.P. Lepre, 1990, p. 87, estimates that the slabs weighed around half a ton each (but on the height of the slabs, see note 71 to chapter seven of this book). Lepre pp. 86-87, 90-92, 114, devotes considerable attention to the fate of the granite fragments (his scenario is not convincing in my opinion).

36 P. Smyth, 1880, pp. 200-1; J.P. Lepre, 1990, pp. 87-88 (see quotation later in this chapter).

37 J.P. Lepre, 1990, pp. 87-88. See also P. Smyth, 1880, pp. 174-76: 'The granite leaf is, therefore, even by the few data already given, a something which needs a vast deal more than a simple portcullis notion to explain it. And so do likewise the three broader empty pairs of grooves to the south of it, remarkable with their semi-cylindrical hollows on the west side of the chamber. Various ideas as to their uses have been given out from time to time, but none commended themselves to my mind at the place...' Smyth suspected that the arrangement was symbolic, pertaining perhaps to geodesy and geophysics.

38 J.P. Lepre, 1990, p. 89. Contrast this with the view in W.M.F. Petrie, 1990, pp. 26-27. Lepre nevertheless went on, despite his concerns, to assume that the Antechamber housed an operable portcullis. How can one challenge an orthodoxy when one has no better theory to put in its place?

39 Tomb 3035, belonging to Hemaka, possibly the chancellor of the 1st dynasty king Den (Udimu). See W. Emery, *Archaic Egypt*, Penguin Books, 1991 edition, pp. 77, 78, 91.

40 W. Emery, *Archaic Egypt*, op. cit., pp. 142-43 and plates 11, 16.

41 On the rolled-up reed-mat curtain motif, see M. Lehner, 1997, p. 135, and illustrations in R. Schulz & M. Seidel eds., *Egypt: The World of the Pharaohs*, Konemann, 1998, pp. 80-83. On the false door, see note 28 earlier.

42 P. Lemesurier, 1993, p. 107 note 50, makes a plausible comparison between the raised boss and the hieroglyph *kha*, denoting 'the Sunrise of creation'. If this interpretation is valid, then there is a good possibility that the granite leaf's two parts conceal the secret name of the king or god to whom the Pyramid was dedicated, this name having been inscribed in the faces of the two stones that are now cemented together. It is curious that Egyptologists have never sought to break this seal and separate the two blocks.

43 Other writers have made this observation: P. Smyth, 1880, p. 175; I.E.S. Edwards, 1993, p. 106; G. Hancock, *Fingerprints of the Gods*, Mandarin paperback edition, 1996, chapter 38, p. 349.

44 J.P. Lepre, 1990, pp. 79-81. On the uniqueness of the Grand Gallery, see my comment in chapter two, which is echoed by Lepre p. 79.

45 J. Greaves, quoted in L. Cottrell, 1956, p. 89. See also P. Tompkins, 1971, p. 25.

46 W.M.F. Petrie, 1990, p. 88. Petrie's measurements proved that the plugs could not have been stored in the Queen's Chamber or Queen's Chamber Passage (Petrie pp. 87-88; I.E.S. Edwards, 1993, p. 108).

47 L. Borchardt, 1922; L. Borchardt, 1926; L. Borchardt, 1932. Borchardt was to German Egyptology what Petrie was to British. He was one of the founders of the 'change of mind' theory for the multiple chambers of the Great Pyramid. See L. Cottrell, 1956, pp. 182, 227-30; P. Tompkins, 1971, pp. 240-41.

48 I.E.S. Edwards, 1993, p. 110.

49 J.P. Lepre, 1990, p. 82.

50 Ibid.

51 Ibid., p. 83.

52 Ibid., p. 81.

53 I.E.S. Edwards, 1993, p. 111.

54 J.P. Lepre, 1990, p. 77.

55 D. Davidson, 1927; D. Davidson, 1932; J. Bruchet, 1965; P. Tompkins, 1971, pp. 245-53; R.W. Noone, 1982, p. 181; P. Lemesurier, 1993, p. 176; G. Hancock, *Fingerprints of the Gods*, op. cit., chapter 37, p. 337; C. Dunn, 1998, pp. 21-22, 26.

56 J.P. Lepre, 1990, pp. 75-77: 'This funnel shape is good evidence that the corridor was tapered to better receive the plug stones, which were not built *in situ*, but were slid down the passageway from above.' Incidentally, the so-called 'trial passages' at Giza show the same tapering pattern in the ascending passage. Another possible piece of evidence is a pair of slots, 3 inches long, on the underside of the lowermost granite plug, as if designed for wedges or levers to control the lowering of the plug; see G. Goyon, 1963; P. Tompkins, 1971, pp. 252-53.

57 W.M.F. Petrie, 1990, p. 88. See also V. Maragioglio & C.A. Rinaldi, 1965, p. 144; P. Tompkins, 1971, p. 243; I.E.S. Edwards, 1993, p. 290. Possibly the liquid cement lubricant was used only at the bottom of the passage, where the fit of the plugs was most tight.

58 I.E.S. Edwards, 1993, pp. 108, 290.

59 Ibid., p. 107.

60 Ibid., p. 111.

61 W.M.F. Petrie, 1990, p. 87; I.E.S. Edwards, 1993, p. 291.

62 The vertical section of the Well Shaft immediately beneath the Grand Gallery may have some other explanation; see discussion in chapter four of this book.

63 I.E.S. Edwards, 1993, p. 111. Cf I. Lawton & C. Ogilvie-Herald, 2000, p. 138.

64 J.P. Lepre, 1990, p. 74 (cf p. 279). Note the word 'removable'. I.E.S. Edwards, 1993, p.111, likewise assumes that the prism stone was inserted in the passage ceiling after the funeral. The exact position of the protrusions, illustrated in figure 53, is unclear and subject to confirmation.

65 A similar problem is implied by the theory of a pivoting main entrance door. Hence J.P. Lepre in his suggested design (see figure 44 in this chapter) provides a recess in the floor to facilitate the manoeuvre. However, in the mouth of the Ascending Passage, such a recess would not have been feasible.

66 P. Smyth, 1880, p. 422. The scenario of the prism stone falling out at the onset of al-Mamun's exploration is surely incorrect; see comments in chapter eight of this book.

67 J.P. Lepre, 1990, p. 74.

68 I.E.S. Edwards, 1993, p. 104.

69 J.P. Lepre, 1990, pp. 110-11.

70 W.M.F. Petrie, 1990, pp. 23, 87; I.E.S. Edwards, 1993, p. 104.

71 I.E.S. Edwards, 1993, p. 104. According to orthodoxy, this is not a sign of an unfinished chamber per se, but rather a sign that the chamber would no longer be the primary tomb; see J.P. Lepre, 1990, pp. 111-12.

72 L. Borchardt, 1922; L. Borchardt, 1926; L. Borchardt, 1932; I.E.S. Edwards, 1993, p. 104; J.P. Lepre, 1990, pp. 111-12. This theory originally supposed that the shafts had been stopped at *the floor level* of the King's Chamber – a presumption that was contradicted by Gantenbrink's discovery in 1993. It seems to me a mere coincidence that the shafts are plugged at the approximate level of the King's Chamber's uppermost roof, for such is the angle and trajectory of the shafts that they could not be built any higher than this (see figure 58 in this chapter).

73 J.P. Lepre, 1990, p. 114.

74 See figures 54, 55. For a very clear photograph of this pattern, see A.C. Carpiceci, *Art and History of Egypt*, Bonechi, Florence, 1994, p. 58.

75 The alternative is to believe that some lazy or incompetent fool skived or neglected his task of cutting open the mouths.

76 *Collins English Dictionary*, 1979, p. 1330; I. Shaw & P. Nicholson, *British Museum Dictionary of Ancient Egypt*, p. 261. W.M.F. Petrie, 1990, p. 89, informs us that 'serdab' is 'the Arabic name for the secret hollow in tombs in which the statue was placed.'

77 The earliest references to the Queen's Chamber statue theory appear in Arab accounts of al-Mamun's exploration of the Pyramid. Subsequently, it was repeated by the English explorer John Greaves in 1638 (see W.M.F. Petrie, 1990, pp. 52, 89). Today, it is a widely-held and popular theory among Egyptologists: see I.E.S. Edwards, 1993, p. 104; J.P. Lepre, 1990, pp. 110, 112; G. Hart, 1991, p. 92; M. Lehner, 1997, pp. 111-12; R. Stadelmann, 1998, pp. 61, 64.

78 M. Lehner, 1997, p. 112 (cf p. 111).

79 A classic example is the statue of Djoser in the serdab of the Step Pyramid at Saqqara. The serdab is placed to the north of the pyramid, and the statue gazes to the north.

80 On the subject of the serdab and the *ka*-statue, see A.M. Blackman, 'The *ka*-house and the serdab', in *Journal of Egyptian Archaeology*, 3 (1916), pp. 250-54.

81 Pyramid Texts, Utterance 600, para 1653.

82 M. Lehner, reported in *The Sunday Telegraph, Review*, 15th September 2002, p. 4. The article, by journalist Anna Murphy, is entitled 'Inside the Chamber of Secrets'.

83 M. Lehner, in *Pyramids Live: Secret Chambers Revealed*, screened by the National Geographic Channel, 16th-17th September 2002.

84 R. Stadelmann, in *Pyramids Live: Secret Chambers Revealed*, screened by the National Geographic Channel, 16th-17th September 2002. The term 'magical instrument' was coined by Jean Kerisel on the BBC2 documentary *The Great Pyramid*, 6th February 1994.

85 R. Gantenbrink, www.cheops.org; R. Bauval & A. Gilbert, 1994, p. 173; R. Bauval & G. Hancock, 1996, p. 123; R. Bauval, 1999, p. 246; I. Lawton & C. Ogilvie-Herald, 2000, p. 331.

86 R. Gantenbrink, www.cheops.org.

87 In its outermost 80 feet, the Queen's Chamber southern shaft runs almost parallel to the track of the King's Chamber southern shaft. See R. Bauval & A. Gilbert, 1994, p. 99; *Archeologia*, Vol. 293 (September 1993), p. 6; *Stern* magazine, No. 28 (July 1993), pp. 24-25.

88 R. Gantenbrink, www.cheops.org. This relationship between the upper and lower shaft was highlighted, albeit somewhat confusingly, by R. Bauval in R. Bauval & A. Gilbert, 1994, pp. 224, 265, 303 (note 34). Gantenbrink also cites as evidence a long cutting groove in the floor, at block 26 and beyond, running straight up the middle of the shaft. He argues that these floor blocks were used as bases for making precise cutting joints prior to being placed in the shaft. However, since the casing stones were cut in their final position, and since all known chambers had already been completed at this height, the need for precise cutting joints in this location is a puzzle. Gantenbrink writes: 'This gives rise to a crucial question: exactly which precision joints were cut here?... Taken together, these findings constitute a compelling case for a possible, as yet undiscovered structure – for which precision joints were made – in this upper region of the southern, Queen's Chamber shaft.'

89 J.P. Lepre, 1990, p. 113, states that the shafts terminate 20 feet from the exterior of the Pyramid, as does M. Verner, 2002. However, I. Lawton & C. Ogilvie-Herald, 2000, pp. 323, 330, argue for a distance of 50 feet. It must be remembered that several outer layers of stone have been removed from the southern face of the Pyramid without revealing signs of any unusual interior structure.

90 My first reaction upon seeing the rough, wavy underside of the plug was that it might be made of granite. However, R. Gantenbrink believes that the plug is made of a similar limestone to that of the metal-handled slab below it.

91 J.P. Lepre, 1990, p. 274. On the Dixon brothers' experiment, see P. Smyth, 1880, p. 428; R. Bauval & A. Gilbert, 1994, pp. 227, 287.

92 I.E.S. Edwards, on Channel 4, *News at Seven*, 16th April 1993. See R. Bauval & A. Gilbert, 1994, pp. 6, 176; R. Bauval & G. Hancock, 1996, p. 125; R. Bauval, 1999, p. 293.

93 Z. Hawass, in an interview with Jochen Breitenstein in Los Angeles, April 1993, broadcast on Sat. I, Spiegel Reportage, 15th August 1995. See R. Bauval & G. Hancock, 1996, p. 101; R. Bauval, 1999, p. 293.

94 Z. Hawass, interview published in *The Daily Mail*, London, *Weekend* supplement, 14th September 2002, p. 23. On the Sacred Book of Khufu, see chapter nine of this book.

95 Z. Hawass, in *Pyramids Live: Secret Chambers Revealed*, screened by the National Geographic

Channel, 16th-17th September 2002.

96 M. Lehner, interview published in *The Daily Mail*, London, *Weekend* supplement, 14th September 2002, p. 23. One wonders whether privately he holds other ideas. He told the James Whale radio show in September 2002 that there might be 'a small niche' containing 'something of great interest', whilst he told the *Sunday Telegraph*, London, 15th September 2002, that 'It would be just like the ancient Egyptians if the most inaccessible place proved to be the raison d'etre of the whole site.'

97 R. Bauval, 1999, pp. 293-94.

98 On the initial wave of official denials, see R. Bauval & G. Hancock, 1996, p. 125.

99 A. Dodson, University of Bristol, interview published in *The Daily Telegraph*, London, 18th September 2002.

CHAPTER FOUR: THE BODY TO EARTH

1 W.M.F. Petrie, 1990, pp. 19-20; L. Borchardt, 1922; L. Borchardt, 1926; L. Borchardt, 1932; I.E.S. Edwards, 1993, pp. 101-2; J.P. Lepre, 1990, pp. 111, 114; G. Hart, 1991, p. 92; M. Lehner, 1997, p. 111.

2 M. Lehner, 1997, p. 114; R. Stadelmann, 1998, p. 58.

3 M.A. Hoffman, *Egypt Before The Pharaohs*, Barnes & Noble, 1993 edition (first published 1979), pp. 111-13 (see also p. 143).

4 J.P. Lepre, 1990, p. 279.

5 I. Lawton & C. Ogilvie-Herald, 2000, p. 505, write: 'if it [the Subterranean Chamber] were built as a decoy they would surely have finished it so it looked like a proper chamber.' Is this a case perhaps of imposing modern, materialistic preconceptions upon ancient Egypt?

6 Herodotus, *History*, Book II, p. 124.

7 J.P. Lepre, 1990, p. 114. During the 19th century, the Pit was excavated by Caviglia, then by Vyse and Perring, and later by Smyth.

8 J.P. Lepre, 1990, p. 118.

9 The rocky outcrop rises about 22-25 feet above the Pyramid's exterior base, whilst the Grotto is buried about 10 feet deep in the outcrop. See J.P. Lepre, 1990, p. 116; I. Lawton & C. Ogilvie-Herald, 2000, p. 30.

10 J.P. Lepre, 1990, p. 117.

11 Ibid., p. 118.

12 Ibid., though Lepre seems to understate the block's size in view of the drawings in figures 60 and 61 (the Well Shaft being 28 inches square). Lepre suggested that the block of granite in the Grotto originated from the vandalised portcullis in the King's Chamber Antechamber (pp. 89-92), but I believe that it was inserted by the builders prior to construction of the Pyramid.

13 J.P. Lepre, 1990, p. 117.

14 Ibid.

15 P. Jordan, *Riddles of the Sphinx*, Sutton Publishing, 1998, p. 77: 'When Khufu determined to build his pyramid at Giza, he found a fairly flattish site on the edge of the desert plateau, with knolls of limestone rising here and there out of it and probably some visible natural fissures in the rock. There were also one or two mastaba tombs from the earlier dynasties and he may have decided to incorporate an existing tomb, as evidently Djoser did before him at Saqqara, or a natural fissure into the underground part of his pyramid. The so-called 'grotto'... may be the remains of such a pre-existing feature.'

16 On the dead gods idea, see the companion volume to this book.

17 J.P. Lepre, 1990, p. 118.

18 W.M.F. Petrie, 1990, pp. 89, 92; J.P. Lepre, 1990, p. 117.

19 J.P. Lepre, 1990, p. 117.

20 Ibid.

21 W.M.F. Petrie, 1990, p. 87: 'it has been cut through the masonry after the courses were completed'; I. Lawton & C. Ogilvie-Herald, 2000, p. 33: 'it is clear that the tunnel was cut through *after* the blocks had been put in place'.

22 J.P. Lepre, 1990, p. 117. Of the same opinion was J. Bruchet, 1965 (see P. Tompkins, 1971, p. 251). I. Lawton & C. Ogilvie-Herald, 2000, p. 135, write: 'there is incontrovertible evidence that the Well Shaft is an original feature which was dug from the top down' (see also p. 511).

The giveaway feature may be seen in figures 67 and 68 of this chapter.

23   V. Maragioglio & C.A. Rinaldi, 1965.

24   I.E.S. Edwards, 1993, pp. 290-91.

25   M. Lehner, 1997, p. 114.

26   P. Tompkins, 1971, p. 242.

27   N.F. Wheeler, 1935, pp. 179-80; V. Maragioglio & C.A. Rinaldi, 1965. See P. Tompkins, 1971, p. 243; I. Lawton & C. Ogilvie-Herald, 2000, pp. 137, 511.

28   I. Lawton & C. Ogilvie-Herald, 2000, p. 137.

29   P. Smyth, 1880, pp. 455-56 and plate xii. I.E.S. Edwards, 1993, p. 111, similarly envisaged the workmen dropping the ramp stone into place above their heads as they descended.

30   D. Davidson, 1927; D. Davidson, 1932. See P. Tompkins, 1971, p. 247.

31   For a classic example of writers falling into this trap, see I. Lawton & C. Ogilvie-Herald, 2000, pp. 137-38, 511-12. Their bias is obvious; they wish to vindicate the 'tomb and tomb only' theory at any cost.

32   The lower entrance to the Well Shaft does tend slightly northwards, making a convenient angle for insertion of the mummy. See, for example, P. Lemesurier, 1993, p. 81 (note 25), and see figure 66 in this chapter.

33   M. Lehner, in *Venture Inward*, November/December 1985, p. 45.

34   J.P. Lepre, 1990, pp. 116-17.

35   A. Hillier, *Egypt News*, August 1998. See I. Lawton & C. Ogilvie-Herald, 2000, p. 433.

36   The existence of this vertical hollow has come to our attention only by sheer chance (see general comments in chapter ten). For all we know, there may be many more such hollows scattered through the Pyramid's superstructure.

37   The idea of sand is suggested by explorations of radar-detected cavities alongside the Queen's Chamber Passage, which revealed the presence of a special sand, perhaps included in the structure for an arcane religious purpose; see chapter ten of this book.

38   However, the dogleg shape of the hollow makes it difficult to visualise what kind of object(s) might have been hidden here.

39   My diagrams follow J.P. Lepre, 1990, p. 64.

40   One of the hieroglyphs that has been identified with the primeval mound bears a striking resemblance to a step pyramid; see R.T. Rundle Clark, *Myth and Symbol in Ancient Egypt*, op. cit., p. 39; H. Frankfort, *Kingship and the Gods*, op. cit., p. 153.

41   On the temple as simulacrum of creation, see the panel in chapter one, the references for which are as follows: R.T. Rundle Clark, *Myth and Symbol in Ancient Egypt*, op. cit., p. 27; B.E. Shafer, 'Temples, Priests and Rituals: An Overview', in B.E. Shafer, ed., *Temples of Ancient Egypt*, Cornell University Press, 1997, p. 8; L. Bell, 'The New Kingdom Divine Temple', in B.E. Shafer, ed., *Temples of Ancient Egypt*, op. cit., pp. 132-33; G. Burkard, 'Conceptions of the Cosmos – The Universe', in R. Schulz & M. Seidel eds., *Egypt: The World of the Pharaohs*, Konemann, 1998, p. 449. Egyptologists sometimes confuse the temple as a whole with the primeval mound; however, as H. Frankfort, *Kingship and the Gods*, op. cit., p. 152, has pointed out: 'in fact, each and every temple was supposed to stand on it [the primeval hill].'

42   H. Frankfort, *Ancient Egyptian Religion: An Interpretation*, op. cit., p. 153. See also H. Frankfort, *Kingship and the Gods*, op. cit., p. 152; M. Lurker, *The Gods and Symbols of Ancient Egypt*, pp. 42-43. Lurker writes: 'The basic element of the primeval mound is reflected in the architecture and planning of some temples where there is a gradual rise in the floor level from the entrance towards the naos in the sanctuary, which on its elevation represents the primeval mound. It is a feature readily apparent in sectional drawings of temples, especially in the temple of Horus at Edfu.'

43   H. Frankfort, *The Intellectual Adventure of Ancient Man*, University of Chicago Press, 1946, p. 22. Cf I.E.S. Edwards, 1993, p. 279. Edwards highlighted the importance of the mound above graves in pre-dynastic times, and suggested that 'it had acquired some magico-religious significance'. He wrote: 'Only one explanation suggests itself, namely that it [the mound] had already come to be regarded as a symbol of the primeval mound which emerged from the waters of chaos... the symbol of existence'.

44   The thought has occurred to a few Egyptologists. For example, I.E.S. Edwards, in a private letter to R. Bauval in 1993, wrote: 'I believe it [the outcrop of rock underneath the Great Pyramid] represented the primeval mound on which life first appeared.' See R. Bauval & G.

Hancock, 1996, pp. 200, 333 (note 11). However, nothing has been made of this idea, which has not featured in the mainstream literature.

CHAPTER FIVE: THE IRON OF CREATION

1 Pyramid Texts, Utterance 723, para 2244.
2 Pyramid Texts, Utterance 413, para 735-36. Cf Utterance 536.
3 Pyramid Texts, Utterance 461, para 873. Cf Utterance 459.
4 Pyramid Texts, Utterance 667A, para 1945. At the end of this spell, the king is urged to raise himself as Min and fly up to the sky. Min was a god of fertility, seed, and meteoritic iron.
5 Pyramid Texts, Utterance 669, para 1961, 1965-70.
6 Pyramid Texts, Utterance 483, para 1015-16.
7 Pyramid Texts, Utterance 582, para 1560-62.
8 Pyramid Texts, Utterance 509, para 1121, 1123-25.
9 Pyramid Texts, Utterance 257, para 304-5.
10 Pyramid Texts, Utterance 469, para 907-8. Cf Utterance 584. *Ba-ka* is a mysterious part of the sky, the location of which is unknown.
11 Pyramid Texts, Utterance 214, para 138-39.
12 Cf Coffin Texts, Spells 474, 475, 479. These 'fisherman texts' envisage a great net in the sky, the floats of which are made of iron – 'the iron which is on the hands of Re'.
13 Coffin Texts, Spell 159. Cf Book of the Dead, Spells 109, 149.
14 Coffin Texts, Spell 479. It is from this great plain in the sky that the fisherman's nets are lowered (see note 12).
15 Coffin Texts, Spell 62.
16 Coffin Texts, Spells 223, 816 (quoted later in this chapter), 989.
17 E.A. Wallis Budge, *The Gods of the Egyptians, or Studies in Egyptian Mythology,* 2 vols, London, 1904, Vol. I, pp. 156-57, Vol. II, p. 241; R. Bauval & A. Gilbert, 1994, p. 203; G. Hancock, *Fingerprints of the Gods,* op. cit., chapter 42, p. 390; R. Bauval, 1999, p. 361; R. Temple, *The Crystal Sun,* op. cit., pp. 294, 320.
18 Pyramid Texts, Utterance 684, para 2051-52.
19 Coffin Texts, Spells 358, 464, 870; D. Meeks & C. Favard-Meeks, *Daily Life of the Egyptian Gods,* op. cit., p. 78.
20 Coffin Texts, Spell 227. This was 'that day when the rivals fought, when the Eye was injured', 'that day of slaying the Oldest Ones', 'that day of cutting off the heads of the mottled snakes', 'that night of making war and felling the rebel', 'that day of breaking up the earth', 'that day of reckoning with the robbers in the presence of the Lord of All', etc, etc.
21 Coffin Texts, Spell 335, Part I.
22 Coffin Texts, Spell 280. Generally, the blame was placed on Seth; in the 'Songs of Isis and Nephthys', we read: 'Seth is all the evil which he has done. He has disturbed the order of the sky.'
23 See, for example, Coffin Texts, Spell 75, where Shu states: 'I am he who calmed the sky for himself, I am he who reduced the Two Lands to order for himself'. On the Two Lands as metaphor for the whole earth, see H. Frankfort, *Kingship and the Gods,* op. cit., p. 19, and my own comments on the Horus and Seth myth in the companion volume to this book.
24 Pyramid Texts, Utterances 320, 341, 437, 525, 573, 667A; Coffin Texts, Spells 50, 75, 80, 129, 464, 469, 631, 993, 1099. Egyptologists believe that the clearing of the sky is a mundane idea, as in the clouds giving way to sunlight. But this is to take the references out of their creational context.
25 Pyramid Texts, Utterances 260, 356. Thoth was the peacemaker of the gods *par excellence.* One of his epithets was 'Judge of the Fighting Gods'. According to one myth, he was the offspring of Horus and Seth, hence perhaps his unique role in reconciling the warring duo.
26 Coffin Texts, Spell 7.
27 In Pyramid Texts, Utterance 670, Osiris-the-king's mouth is split open by the iron fingers of the Four Sons of Horus. Elsewhere, the same task is performed by the finger of Horus (Utterance 540). The finger of Seth splits open the king's eyes (Utterances 69, 70), whilst his sacrificed foreleg or thigh – in the shape of the iron adze – opens the mouth (Utterance 21). On

the fingers of Thoth, see Coffin Texts, Spell 335. Coffin Texts, Spell 334, contains a revealing insight into this myth, the Lord of the gods using his fingers to break into the body of Isis, caused the goddess to faint. On the connection between the fingers, the foreleg/thigh, and meteoritic iron, see G.A. Wainwright, 'Letopolis', in *Journal of Egyptian Archaeology*, 18 (1932), pp. 160, 163, 171.

28 Pyramid Texts, Utterance 233, para 237.

29 Coffin Texts, Spell 80, lines 30-31.

30 M. Lurker, *The Gods and Symbols of Ancient Egypt*, op. cit., p. 64.

31 Book of the Dead; see R. T. Rundle Clark, *Myth and Symbol in Ancient Egypt*, op. cit., p. 137.

32 K. Freeman, *The Pre-Socratic Philosophers*, 2nd edition, Basil Blackwell, Oxford, 1966, p. 270, cited by R. Temple, *The Crystal Sun*, op. cit., p. 288. On the basis of this knowledge, Anaxagoras predicted the fall of a meteorite at Aegospotami *c*. 468-7 BC.

33 K. Freeman, *The Pre-Socratic Philosophers*, op. cit., pp. 268-69, cited by R. Temple, *The Crystal Sun*, op. cit., p. 288.

34 Ammianus Marcellinus, *Roman History*, Book XXII, chapter 22; see R. Temple, *The Crystal Sun*, op. cit., p. 287.

35 E. A. Wallis Budge, *Legends of the Egyptian Gods*, op. cit., p. 206.

36 R. Schoch, *Voices of the Rocks,* Thorsons edition, 2000, p. 179. Meteoritic iron can be distinguished from terrestrial iron by its high nickel content and unusual mineral structure.

37 A.M. Roth, 'Fingers, Stars and the "Opening of the Mouth": the Nature and Function of the *ntrwj*-blades', in *Journal of Egyptian Archaeology*, 79 (1993), pp. 57-79, cited by R. Temple, *The Crystal Sun*, op. cit., p. 293. See quotation in the panel later in this chapter.

38 K. Sethe, *Amun und die acht Urgotter,* Leipzig, 1929, p. 118, cited by H. Frankfort, *Kingship and the Gods*, op. cit., p. 380 (note 26).

39 H. Frankfort, *Kingship and the Gods*, op. cit., pp. 153, 380-81; G. Hart, *Egyptian Myths,* op. cit., p. 11.

40 On the conical shape of the Benben Stone, see: H. Frankfort, *Kingship and the Gods*, op. cit., p. 153; I.E.S. Edwards, 1993, pp. 6, 282; R.T. Rundle Clark, *Legend of the Phoenix*, University of Birmingham Press, 1949, pp. 15, 17; R. Bauval & A. Gilbert, 1994, p. 200. See quotations in the panel later in this chapter.

41 E.A. Wallis Budge, *Cleopatra's Needles*, London, 1926, chapter 1; J-P. Lauer in J. Leclant & J-P. Lauer eds., *Le Temps des Pyramides*, Editions Gallimard, Paris, 1978, pp. 79, 336; R. Bauval, 'Investigations on the Origins of the Benben Stone: Was it an Iron Meteorite?, in *Discussions in Egyptology*, 14 (1989), pp. 5-17 (reproduced in R. Bauval, 1999, pp. 356-65); R. Bauval & A. Gilbert, 1994, pp. 204, 300 (note 30); T. Wilkinson, Bloomsbury lecture, reported in T. Radford, 'Pyramids seen as stairways to heaven', *The Guardian*, London, 14th May 2001.

42 R. Bauval, 'Investigations on the Origins of the Benben Stone: Was it an Iron Meteorite?, op. cit., pp. 15-16; R. Bauval & A. Gilbert, 1994, p. 204.

43 G.A. Wainwright, 'Letopolis', op. cit., p. 159. See also G.A. Wainwright article in *Annales du Service des Antiquites de l'Egypte*, xxviii, p. 177; G. A. Wainwright, 'Amun's Meteorite and Omphali', in *Zeitschrift fur agyptische Sprache und Altertumskunde*, 1935, pp. 41-44; G.A. Wainwright, 'Some Aspects of Amun', in *Journal of Egyptian Archaeology*, p. 147. All three gods – Amun, Min and Horus – are parallel forms of the One Great God.

44 H. Grapow, *Die bildlichen Ausdruke des Agyptischen*, Leipzig, 1924, p. 78, cited by H. Frankfort, *Kingship and the Gods*, op. cit., p. 180.

45 H. Frankfort, *Kingship and the Gods*, op. cit., p. 188. D. Meeks & C. Favard-Meeks, *Daily Life of the Egyptian Gods*, op. cit., p. 67, notes that Min's liaison with his mother led to the birth of the Sun.

46 H. Frankfort, *Kingship and the Gods*, op. cit., pp. 179, 189.

47 Ibid., pp. 177, 180, 387 (note 81).

48 The mother-son paradox is explained further in the companion volume to this book.

49 G.A. Wainwright, 'Letopolis', op. cit., p. 159; see also pp. 161, 165.

50 Ibid., p. 169. Wainwright emphasises that to ancient man the thunderbolt and the meteorite were the same thing (pp. 159, 161, 169).

51 Ibid., p. 165.

52 Pliny, *Natural History*, Book II.

53 E.A. Wallis Budge, *Legends of the Egyptian Gods*, op. cit., p. 230.

54 E.A. Wallis Budge, *From Fetish to God in Ancient Egypt*, op. cit., p. 194; Book of the Dead, Spell 1; G.A. Wainwright, 'Letopolis', op. cit., p. 163; B. Watterson, *Gods of Ancient Egypt*, op. cit., pp. 62, 102; G. Hart, *Egyptian Myths*, op. cit., p. 32.

55 E.A. Wallis Budge, *From Fetish to God in Ancient Egypt*, pp. 273, 289; G. Hart, *Egyptian Myths*, op. cit., p. 32; Pyramid Texts, Utterance 219; Coffin Texts, Spells 773, 1079, 1080.

56 The Great *Benu* of Heliopolis had a counterpart at Herakleopolis; see E.A. Wallis Budge, *Egyptian Religion*, op. cit., p. 127; E.A. Wallis Budge, *Legends of the Egyptian Gods*, op. cit., p. xxvi. Benben stones were worshipped by Akhenaten who may have regarded them as Sun-stones (i.e. stones that had fallen from the Sun) and the material counterpart of the Sun's invisible, spiritual energy; see J.H. Breasted, *Development of Religion and Thought in Ancient Egypt*, op. cit., p. 330; E.A. Wallis Budge, *From Fetish to God in Ancient Egypt*, p. 403; A. Collins, 1998, pp. 134-36, 332.

57 Irene Seco Serra, a Spanish expert in prehistory and archaeology, writes in *Meteorite*, 6:2 (May 2000), pp. 26-7: 'It is even thought that meteorites might, after all, be the very source of baetylism, artificially-shaped stone baetyls being later substitutes of gods-sent meteoritic images. Be that as it may, it seems from our textual references that many baetyls were actually meteorites...' The mythologist Robert Graves has entertained similar thoughts: R. Graves, *The Greek Myths*, combined edition, Penguin Books, 1992, p. 628.

58 G.A. Wainwright, 'Letopolis', op. cit., pp. 159, 161 (note 4).

59 Ideally, because meteoritic iron was rare and not always available. The adze was made in the image of either Ursa Major or Ursa Minor, the northern circumpolar constellations, which represented the Two Enneads of the Great Gods Horus and Seth.

60 A.M. Roth, 'Fingers, Stars and the "Opening of the Mouth": the Nature and Function of the *ntrwj*-blades', op. cit.; E.A. Wallis Budge, *The Mummy*, op. cit., pp. 326-27; I. Shaw & P. Nicholson, *British Museum Dictionary of Ancient Egypt*, op. cit., p. 211.

61 I. Shaw & P. Nicholson, *British Museum Dictionary of Ancient Egypt*, op. cit., p. 211; G.A. Wainwright, 'Letopolis', op. cit., pp. 165, 171.

62 Pyramid Texts, Utterance 21, para 13-14.

63 Pyramid Texts, Utterances 540, 670; Coffin Texts, Spell 228; Book of the Dead, Spell 23; E.A. Wallis Budge, *The Mummy*, op. cit., p. 350; E.A. Wallis Budge, *Egyptian Religion*, op. cit., p. 98; E.A. Wallis Budge, *From Fetish to God in Ancient Egypt*, op. cit., p. 349.

64 Coffin Texts, Spell 816.

65 G.A. Wainwright, 'Letopolis', op. cit., pp. 160, 163, 170.

66 Ibid., p. 170. The doors on earth were particularly associated with Letopolis, pp. 167-68, but they could also exist elsewhere, e.g. in Rostau (Coffin Texts, Spell 48).

67 Ibid., p. 169.

68 Ibid., pp. 168-69.

69 Ibid., p. 169.

70 Coffin Texts, Spell 1080. Cf Spell 547: 'Osiris has placed his efflux in his coffin'.

71 G. Hart, *Egyptian Myths*, op. cit., pp. 30, 53. The researcher Simon Cox is adamant that Rostau was a real place, as well as a mythical place, but this idea lies beyond the scope of this book.

72 Coffin Texts, Spells 1018, 1079, 1086, 1087, 1184, 1185; Book of the Dead, Spell 1b.

73 Coffin Texts, Spell 314. This is almost certainly an allusion to the time of creation.

74 Coffin Texts, Spell 241.

75 The preceding description of the Sokarian underworld is drawn from E.A. Wallis Budge, *The Egyptian Heaven and Hell*, Dover Pubs., 1996 combined edition (first published by Kegan, Paul, Trench, Trubner & Co Ltd, London, 1905, as 3 volumes in the series *Books on Egypt and Chaldaea*), I, pp. 85-115. However, the creational slant is my own.

76 Coffin Texts, Spells 137, 217, 307, 480, 493, 553, 647; Book of the Dead, Spells 85, 162. It is thus unlikely that Osiris was the original buried god of Heliopolis.

77 S. Tower Hollis, 'Otiose Deities and the Ancient Egyptian Pantheon', in *Journal of the American Research Center in Egypt*, XXXV (1998), pp. 62, 67; B. Watterson, *Gods of Ancient Egypt*, op. cit., p. 183.

78 D. Meeks & C. Favard-Meeks, *Daily Life of the Egyptian Gods*, op. cit., p. 180. There is a parallel here to the myth of the Seven Sages of Edfu; see E.A.E. Reymond, *The Mythical Origin of the Egyptian Temple*, Manchester University Press, 1969. A similar group of dead gods was worshipped at the city of Esna.

79 G. Hart, *Egyptian Myths,* op. cit., p. 22.

80 E.A.E. Reymond, *The Mythical Origin of the Egyptian Temple*, op. cit.; A. Collins, 1998, pp. 174-75, 193-95.

81 Pyramid Texts, Utterance 600, para 1652-53.

82 Pyramid Texts, Utterance 527, para 1248-49.

83 On the obelisk as a 'sky-splitter', see the companion volume to this book.

84 In many instances, the stone pyramidion was covered in a metal which the Egyptians called *tcham* – possibly a reference to electrum or white gold.

85 J.H. Breasted, *Development of Religion and Thought in Ancient Egypt*, op. cit., p. 72 (see the panel earlier in this chapter); I.E.S. Edwards, 1993, p. 6.

86 R.H. Wilkinson, *Reading Egyptian Art*, Thames and Hudson, 1994 edition, p. 169.

87 It is said that from the nostrils of the head of Osiris, which was buried at Abydos, there came forth the scarab beetle – the symbol of the self-created creator-god (see E.A. Wallis Budge, *Egyptian Religion*, op. cit., p. 62, citing Von Nergmann, *Aeg. Zeitschrift*, 1880, p. 88 ff.). There is a remarkable parallel here to the scarab emerging from the bell-shaped chamber in the underworld of Sokar (figure 73). It is therefore tempting to view the bell-shaped chamber as 'the head of Sokar-Osiris' and as the subterranean form of the bell-shaped 'head' on the pole of the fetish of Abydos (figures 76, 82).

88 E.A. Wallis Budge, *From Fetish to God in Ancient Egypt*, op. cit., pp. 107, 273; R.H. Wilkinson, *Reading Egyptian Art*, op. cit., p. 169.

89 P. Bagnall, interviewed in *Focus* magazine, August 1999, p. 70. According to Rob Elliott, the hydration of the iron meteorite produces ferric chloride which attacks the iron from within and continually refuels itself, creating more ferric chloride, until the iron is mostly destroyed. This process is known in the trade as the 'ferric chloride cycle' or 'Lawrencite's Disease'.

90 Email correspondence with Rob Elliott, 9th December 2002. Elliott writes: 'Trying to achieve an RH of less than 30% isn't really practical for mechanically-driven dehumidification units, but I find that hitting this mark just about halts oxidisation well.' To purchase a meteorite from Rob Elliott, visit his website at www.meteorites.uk.com.

91 There is a small town in Australia called Coober Pedy (halfway between Adelaide and Alice Springs), where many of the public buildings are located underground; these buildings enjoy a constant temperature of 22° C (70° F) compared to an outside temperature that fluctuates to a maximum of about 50° C (120° F). Elsewhere in the world, certain rooms are constructed below ground level in order to achieve a constant temperature and barometric pressure, e.g. the Paris Observatory at a depth of 85 feet.

92 C. Dunn, 1998, p. 97.

93 Ibid.

94 Pyramid Texts, Utterances 246, 254, 260, 273, 304, 306, 307, 319, 365, 408, 436, 437, 467, 472, 510, 568, 610; Coffin Texts, Spells 37, 199, 212, 237, 241, 317, 573, 575, 658, 967, 1011, 1028, 1076; H. Frankfort, *Kingship and the Gods*, op. cit., pp. 156, 162, 166-71, 173-80, 380-81 (notes 26, 27); M. Rice, *The Power of the Bull*, Routledge, 1997.

95 Coffin Texts, Spell 1119.

96 Coffin Texts, Spell 1080. Granite is an igneous rock, and there is some evidence that the ancient Egyptians regarded it as a fire-stone.

97 Coffin Texts, Spell 547.

98 The efflux of Osiris could refer either to the iron or to the floodwaters that flowed out from his body. However, in this context, I feel it less likely that water would have been placed inside the god's coffin.

99 Coffin Texts, Spell 1087. This would seem to be a particularly important spell, as it was written entirely in red ink. It is an alternative version of Spell 1080.

100 D. Meeks & C. Favard-Meeks, *Daily Life of the Egyptian Gods*, op. cit., pp. 79, 103-4.

101 Ibid., p. 47.

102 G.A. Wainwright, 'Letopolis', op. cit., pp. 160-62, 165.

103 Coffin Texts, Spells 399, 546, 724, 1019; Book of the Dead, Spell 151; I. Shaw & P. Nicholson, *British Museum Dictionary of Ancient Egypt*, op. cit., pp. 34-35; B. Watterson, *Gods of Ancient Egypt*, op. cit., p. 174.

104 M.C. Betro, *Hieroglyphics*, Abbeville Press, 1996, p. 77: 'Anubis was represented... stretched out on a chest, the mysterious container from which was derived the epithet "keeper of the

secrets", also given to some priests.'

105   Coffin Texts, Spell 647.

106   See note 76. Another tradition held that Osiris was the corpse in Heliopolis.

107   E. Hornung, *The Ancient Egyptian Books of the Afterlife*, Cornell University Press, 1999, p. 79 and figure 42 (bottom).

108   E.A. Wallis Budge, *The Egyptian Heaven and Hell*, op. cit., I, p. 144. Cf E. Hornung, *The Ancient Egyptian Books of the Afterlife*, op. cit., pp. 38-39 and figure 21 (bottom).

109   On the Book of Caverns, see D. Meeks & C. Favard-Meeks, *Daily Life of the Egyptian Gods*, op. cit., pp. 151-63 and figures 18-23; E. Hornung, *The Ancient Egyptian Books of the Afterlife*, op. cit., pp. 83-95. The corpses are said to possess 'the living word'.

110   D. Meeks & C. Favard-Meeks, *Daily Life of the Egyptian Gods*, op. cit., p. 153. Cf Coffin Texts, Spell 1080, 'the sealed thing' that contains the efflux of Osiris.

111   E. Hornung, *The Ancient Egyptian Books of the Afterlife*, op. cit., p. 88.

112   Ibid., pp. 97, 196 and figure 57 (top right hand corner).

113   Ibid., pp. 99, 106 and figure 57 (bottom).

114   E.A. Wallis Budge, *From Fetish to God in Ancient Egypt*, op. cit., p. 442. Cf D. Meeks & C. Favard-Meeks, *Daily Life of the Egyptian Gods*, op. cit., p. 71.

115   For a full discussion of the Eye and the Goddess, see the companion volume to this book.

116   The creation myth at Letopolis, for example, spoke of 'two eyes of *ds*'. On the subject of eyes, in the myth of the Contendings of Horus and Seth, the mutilated eyes of Horus are each placed in a box. The boxes are then stolen and hidden by Seth, but Anubis tracks them down and recovers the eyes. See D. Meeks & C. Favard-Meeks, *Daily Life of the Egyptian Gods*, op. cit., p. 75.

117   Pyramid Texts, Utterance 506, para 1094-95, 1100-1.

118   Pyramid Texts, Utterance 528, para 1250.

119   Pyramid Texts, Utterance 483, para 1019; Utterance 511, para 1152.

120   E.A. Wallis Budge, *Legends of the Egyptian Gods*, op. cit., p. 230. The symbol was called *Ta-Wer*, meaning 'Great Land' or 'Most Ancient Land'.

121   E.A. Wallis Budge, *From Fetish to God in Ancient Egypt*, op. cit., p. 273. Cf ibid., p. 107: 'The box held the head of Osiris'. H. Frankfort, *Kingship and the Gods*, op. cit., figure 31, thus calls the *Ta-wer* fetish 'the reliquary of Abydos', whilst M. Lurker, *The Gods and Symbols of Ancient Egypt*, op. cit., p. 94, calls it 'a reliquary for the god's head'.

122   M. Eliade, *A History of Religious Ideas*, Volume 1, University of Chicago Press, 1978, p. 52; A.M. Roth, 'Fingers, Stars and the "Opening of the Mouth": the Nature and Function of the *ntrwj*-blades', op. cit.; R. Temple, *The Crystal Sun*, op. cit., pp. 285, 294. See quotations in the panel later in this chapter.

123   R. Bauval & A. Gilbert, 1994, p. 216; R. Bauval, 1999, pp. 90, 93.

124   That the King's Chamber would have benefited from a constant temperature was noted by several 19th century Pyramid theorists, who hypothesised that the chamber was a repository of weights and measures. See E-F. Jomard, 1829; P. Smyth, 1880, pp. 182-83; I. Lawton & C. Ogilvie-Herald, 2000, p. 54.

125   P. Smyth, 1880, p. 184; P. Tompkins, 1971, pp. 67, 83; Z. Sitchin, 1980, p. 288; C. Dunn, 1998, p. 43; J.P. Lepre, 1990, p. 97; I. Lawton & C. Ogilvie-Herald, 2000, p. 54. Lepre found that the temperature of the King's Chamber fluctuated in the range 70-80° F, but commented: 'Perhaps if the northern air channel were not fractured the chamber might well retain the ideal [68° F] temperature.'

126   It occurs to the author that the northern shaft bearing might reflect the duality of Horus and Seth, whilst the southern shaft bearing might reflect the duality of Osiris and Isis.

127   This is surely more plausible than the official theory that the word 'pyramid' derives from the Greek *pyramis* meaning 'wheaten cake'! See I.E.S. Edwards, 1993, p. 277.

CHAPTER SIX: CAPSULE OF ETERNITY

1   I.E.S. Edwards, 1993, p. 102.

2   J.P. Lepre, 1990, p. 74. Cf P. Smyth, 1880, p. 422.

3   I do not exclude the possibility that the plugs were built *in situ*, or slipped into position while the Ascending Passage was only partially constructed. W.M.F. Petrie, 1990, p. 86, observes

that 'over the north doorway of the gallery the stone is left roughly in excess'. Is this a sign that the top of the Ascending Passage was sealed off at the time of construction?

4 J.P. Lepre, 1990, p. 110 (cf p. 182). See also I.E.S. Edwards, 1993, p. 105; P. Tompkins, 1971, p. 12; M. Lehner, 1997, p. 111.

5 J.P. Lepre, 1990, p. 82.

6 The idea is not so outrageous. Cf the concealment of the upper chamber in the Red Pyramid (I. Lawton & C. Ogilvie-Herald, 2000, p. 131).

7 L. Cottrell, 1956, p. 98. The protrusion is just over an inch thick (W.M.F. Petrie, 1990, p. 86).

8 P. Lemesurier, 1993, p. 72 (note 20). He saw a possible connection with the sealed 'airshafts'.

9 W.M.F. Petrie, 1990, p. 86.

10 J.P. Lepre, 1990, p. 111. His figure of 20 feet is an estimate. The true figure is nearer 50 feet.

11 For example, *circa* 2350 BC. See the fully-indexed archives of the CCNet scholarly electronic network, at http://abob.libs.uga.edu/bobk/cccmenu.html. To subscribe to CCNet, contact the moderator Benny J. Peiser.

12 V. Clube & B. Napier, *The Cosmic Winter*, Basil Blackwell, 1990, p. 165.

13 C. Wickramasinghe, 'Pyramid to Paradise', in *The Daily Mail*, London, 15th May 2001, p. 11.

14 Pyramid Texts, Utterance 254, para 277-79. See also D. Meeks & C. Favard-Meeks, *Daily Life of the Egyptian Gods*, op. cit., p. 17.

15 Coffin Texts, Spell 1130. See also E. Hornung, *Conceptions of God in Ancient Egypt*, op. cit., p. 163; G. Hart, *Egyptian Myths*, op. cit., p. 11.

16 Book of the Dead, Spell 175. The translation is a composite of E. Hornung, *Conceptions of God in Ancient Egypt*, op. cit., p. 163, and R.O. Faulkner, *The Ancient Egyptian Book of the Dead*, British Museum Publications, 1985 edition, p. 175, except for 'something-else serpent' which is my own innovation.

17 J.B. Pritchard ed., *ANET*, op. cit., pp. 444-46.

18 D. Meeks & C. Favard-Meeks, *Daily Life of the Egyptian Gods*, op. cit., pp. 174-75.

19 The translation is a composite of E.A. Wallis Budge, *From Fetish to God in Ancient Egypt*, op. cit., p. 134, and E. Hornung, *Conceptions of God in Ancient Egypt*, op. cit., p. 165, but I have paraphrased at the end.

20 E.A. Wallis Budge, *From Fetish to God in Ancient Egypt*, op. cit., p. 445.

21 E. Hornung, *The Secret Lore of Egypt*, op. cit., p. 28.

22 Ibid., p. 29.

23 H. Frankfort, *Kingship and the Gods*, op. cit., pp. 21-22, 129.

24 Hesiod, *Theogony*.

25 Hesiod *Works and Days*. Cf Plato, *Timaeus*, 23; Plato, *Critias*, 109-10.

26 K. Mendelssohn, 1974, p. 196.

27 W.M.F. Petrie, 1990, on several occasions attributes sloppy workmanship inside the Pyramid to the demands of phased construction deadlines.

28 It is possible that the king expected to reincarnate into this new world, and personally take on the role of exploring the Pyramid and leading the new race up the path to civilisation.

29 Plato, *Timaeus*, 21-23; Plato, *Critias*, 108-12.

30 A. Collins, 1998, pp. 99-100.

31 R.H. Charles, *The Book of Enoch or 1 Enoch*, Oxford University Press, 1912.

32 A. Collins, 1998, pp. 199-200.

33 *The Works of Flavius Josephus*, Book 1, p. 43; *The Complete Works of Josephus*, Kregel Publications, Michigan, 1991, p. 27.

34 Giza was linked to the idea of a pillar; it was called 'Horizon of Iunu [Pillar] in the West' (Dream Stele of Thutmosis IV, Sphinx, Giza). In addition, Khufu's pyramid was linked closely with Khnum, who is referred to in Pyramid Texts, Utterance 324, para 524, as follows: 'You [Khnum] are one of the two pillars of the Great Mansion.'

35 A. Tomas, *On the Shores of Ancient Worlds*, Souvenir, 1974, chapter 15, cited by I. Lawton & C. Ogilvie-Herald, 2000, p. 232.

36 On Baalbek, see N. Jidejian, *Baalbek Heliopolis "City of the Sun"*, Dar El-Machreq, Beirut, 1975. Macrobius, *Saturnalia*, 1.23.10, reported that the cult statue of the god of Baalbek-Heliopolis had originated in Heliopolis, Egypt, and had been carried there by the priests. A. Tomas believed, as I do, that Baalbek was probably the Syriad pillar.

37 *Kore Kosmou*, section 66, cited by I. Lawton & C. Ogilvie-Herald, 2000, p. 235.

38 *Kore Kosmou,* section 8, cited by R. Bauval & G. Hancock, 1996, pp. 270, 314 (note 1); R. Bauval, 1999, pp. 11-12.

39 Ibid.

40 Coffin Texts, Spell 148. See R. Temple, *The Crystal Sun,* op. cit., pp. 286-87.

41 The ascent of a god usually coincides with a cataclysm, e.g. in 'the Legend of Shu and Geb' (see chapter five). On *herma,* see R. Graves, *The Greek Myths,* op. cit., Index; W. Burkert, *Greek Religion,* Harvard University Press, 1985, p. 156; M.L. West, *The East Face of Helicon,* Clarendon Press, 1999, p. 34.

42 A. Tomas, *On the Shores of Ancient Worlds,* Souvenir, 1974, chapter 15, cited by I. Lawton & C. Ogilvie-Herald, 2000, p. 233.

43 Ibid. See also R. Bauval & G. Hancock, 1996, p. 85; A. Collins, 1998, p. 170.

44 E. Hornung, *The Secret Lore of Egypt,* op. cit., pp. 156-57.

45 E. von Daniken, *The Return of the Gods,* Element Books, 1997, p. 52, citing al-Maqrizi, *Hitat,* chapter 33. The Arabs knew three Hermes, one antediluvian, the others post-diluvian (see E. Hornung, *The Secret Lore of Egypt,* op. cit., pp. 38-39).

46 Al-Halabi; see E. Hornung, *The Secret Lore of Egypt,* op. cit., p. 157.

47 A. Collins, 1998, p. 199; E. von Daniken, *The Return of the Gods,* op. cit., p. 52. The name Idris meant 'progenitor'.

48 L. Cottrell, 1956, p. 72; E. Hornung, *The Secret Lore of Egypt,* op. cit., pp. 53, 82.

49 E. Hornung, *The Secret Lore of Egypt,* op. cit., pp. 82, 156; L. Cottrell, 1956, p. 72.

50 P. Tompkins, 1971, p. 218. See also E. Hornung, *The Secret Lore of Egypt,* op. cit., pp. 82, 155.

51 Al-Maqrizi, *Hitat,* chapter 33, cited by E. von Daniken, *The Return of the Gods,* op. cit., p. 52.

52 For Balkhi's version, see L. Cottrell, 1956, pp. 61-62; E. Hornung, *The Secret Lore of Egypt,* op. cit., p. 157.

53 J. Greaves, 1646, pp. 80-83.

54 P. Smyth, 1880, pp. 12-13; I. Lawton & C. Ogilvie-Herald, 2000, p. 16.

55 Ibid.

56 Ibid.

57 R.H. Vyse, 1840-42, Vol. 2, appendix, p. 322. See also L. Cottrell, 1956, pp. 62-63; A. Collins, 1998, p. 31; I. Lawton & C. Ogilvie-Herald, 2000, p. 17.

58 L. Cottrell, 1956, p. 63; A. Collins, 1998, p. 32.

59 A. Collins, 1998, p. 32 (cf p. 33).

60 E. Hornung, *The Secret Lore of Egypt,* op. cit., p. 157; A. Collins, 1998, p. 32; I. Lawton & C. Ogilvie-Herald, 2000, p. 234.

61 E. Hornung, *The Secret Lore of Egypt,* op. cit., p. 53.

62 Ibid.

63 Ibid., p. 157.

64 M. Lehner, 1997, p. 40. Manetho read the cartouche as Suphis.

65 J.B. Pritchard ed., *ANET,* op. cit., pp. 444-46.

66 Ibid., p. 444.

67 G. Hart, *Egyptian Myths,* op. cit., p. 69; M. Lehner, 1997, pp. 38-39; H. Wilson, *People of the Pharaohs,* op. cit., pp. 95, 101.

68 Westcar Papyrus, 7, lines 5-8; see R. Bauval & A. Gilbert, 1994, pp. 251, 254; R. Bauval, 1999, p. 33. On the translations 'secret chambers' and 'sanctuary', see A. Gardiner, 1925.

69 A. Gardiner, 1925. See R. Bauval & A. Gilbert, 1994, p. 252; R. Bauval, 1999, p. 33. In other words, the box contains a papyrus detailing the number of (or perhaps even the plan of) the secret chambers. *Sipty* may have meant 'Inventory'.

70 H. Wilson, *People of the Pharaohs,* op. cit., p. 95.

71 G. Hart, *Egyptian Myths,* op. cit., p. 70.

72 A. Gardiner, 1925; see R. Bauval & A. Gilbert, 1994, pp. 254-55.

73 A. Gardiner, 1925; see R. Bauval & A. Gilbert, 1994, p. 251.

74 The determinative sign is the cylinder seal, used elsewhere for the verb *htm* 'to seal up' or 'close'; see R. Bauval & A. Gilbert, 1994, p. 252.

75 The story skips over the reigns of Djedefre and Shepseskaf.

CHAPTER SEVEN: ECHOES OF CREATION

1 I. Lawton & C. Ogilvie-Herald, *Giza: The Truth*, Virgin Publishing, first published by Virgin Publishing in 1999, paperback edition 2000.
2 A working knowledge of acoustics is implicit in the design of musical instruments.
3 L. Cottrell, 1956, p. 81.
4 Ibid., p. 84.
5 Ibid., p. 90.
6 Ibid., p. 96.
7 M. Lehner, 1997, p. 114.
8 J. Reid, 2001, p. 41.
9 J. Reid, 2001, p. 7. A provisional summary of Reid's work is included in D. Elkington, 2001, Appendix 6, pp. 416-28.
10 J. Reid, 2001, pp. 7-8.
11 Ibid., p. 40.
12 J. Reid, email correspondence, 5th January 2003. Alternatively, per the dictionary, resonance is defined as 'sound produced by a body vibrating in sympathy with a neighbouring source of sound'.
13 P. Horn, *Paul Horn – Inside the Great Pyramid*, Mushroom Records, Los Angeles, 1977.
14 C. Dunn, 1998, pp. 140-43.
15 J. Reid, 2001, p. 20; D. Elkington, 2001, p. 420.
16 J. Reid, 2001, p. 20 (cf p. 23); D. Elkington, 2001, pp. 420, 423, 425; I. Lawton & C. Ogilvie-Herald, 2000, pp. 209-10.
17 Tom Danley's work for NASA included research into acoustical levitation. The Schor Foundation is funded by Joseph Schor, the American millionaire. For further details on Danley and Schor, see I. Lawton & C. Ogilvie-Herald, 2000, pp. 208, 260, 364-66, 368-71, 480; C. Dunn, 1998, pp. 139, 239.
18 T. Danley, 'Early Reflections and Ancient Echoes', in *Live Sound!* magazine, 9:4 (July/August 2000), pp. 44-50. See comments in D. Elkington, 2001, pp. 395, 489.
19 T. Danley, 'Early Reflections and Ancient Echoes, op. cit., p. 47, refers to a frequency of 'precisely 16 Hz' occurring spontaneously in the King's Chamber.
20 D. Elkington, 2001, p. 426.
21 J. Reid, 2001, p. 10; D. Elkington, 2001, p. 426. See comment by D. Elkington, 2001, p. 489 (note 12).
22 J. Reid, 2001, p. 19: 'In discussions with Northumbria University, it was pointed out to me that the architect's choice of a simple 2:1 ratio for the chamber's length and width is significant, particularly at bass frequencies where distinct room modes would be expected to arise.' (cf p. 23). See also D. Elkington, 2001, p. 425: 'The architect's choice of chamber length and width are ideal for establishing powerful low frequency resonances and, again within context, could be viewed as acoustic design intent.' (see also pp. 423-24).
23 J. Reid, 2001, pp. 9, 20; D. Elkington, 2001, p. 426.
24 D. Elkington, *In The Name of the Gods*, Green Man Press, 2001. Note: this book is planned for expansion and re-release in 2004 under the title *The Vision, the Power, the Place*.
25 R. Jahn, P. Devereux & M. Ibison, 'Acoustical Resonances of assorted ancient structures', in *Journal of the Acoustical Society of America*, 99:2 (1996), pp. 649-58; P. Devereux & R. Jahn, 'Preliminary investigations and cognitive considerations of the acoustical resonances of selected archaeological sites', in *Antiquity*, 70:269 (1996), pp. 665-66; G. Lawson, C. Scarre, I. Cross & C. Hills, 'Mounds, megaliths, music and mind: some thoughts on the acoustical properties and purposes of archaeological spaces', in *ARC*, 15:1 (1998), pp. 111-34; W. Watson & D. Keating, 'Architecture and sound: an acoustic analysis of megalithic monuments in prehistoric Britain', in *Antiquity*, 73:280 (1999), pp. 325-36; P. Devereux, *Stone Age Soundtracks: The Acoustic Archaeology of Ancient Sites*, Vega, London, 2001.
26 J. Reid, 2001, p. 7.
27 I. Lawton & C. Ogilvie-Herald, 2000, pp. 209-10, 478, makes a dogmatic defence of the orthodox 'tomb and tomb only' theory, and yet lends support to the King's Chamber acoustics theory. In particular, the authors like the idea of an acoustic ritual to despatch the king to the afterlife.

28 J. Reid, 2001, p. 14; D. Elkington, 2001, p. 426.

29 J. Reid, telephone conversation, 20th November 2002.

30 J. Reid, email correspondence, 5th January 2003, notes that the prime resonant frequency of the Grand Gallery (250 Hz) is double that of the King's Chamber (125 Hz), and suggests that the architect may have sought an acoustic coupling of the Gallery and the King's Chamber via the Antechamber. He chose not to publish this idea in *Egyptian Sonics* because its scope would have become too broad, but he plans to publish it in a future book. I am sceptical of this idea, however, because the Gallery space today is higher than it used to be, making it impossible to assess its original resonance.

31 R.H. Vyse, 1840-42; I.E.S. Edwards, 1993, pp. 106-7; L. Cottrell, 1956, p. 111; J.P. Lepre, 1990, p.106; G. Hart, 1991, p. 93; M. Lehner, 1997, pp. 53, 111, 114; A. Siliotti, 1997, pp. 27-28, 51; R. Stadelmann, 1998, p. 61; I. Lawton & C. Ogilvie-Herald, 2000, p. 49. However, Edwards and Lawton & Ogilvie-Herald do express doubts as to the efficacy of the design.

32 J.P. Lepre, 1990, p. 106. It is also worth noting that the uppermost raised roof (exceptionally) has limestone (and not granite) supports. Was this designed to absorb any subsidence and protect the granite structure below, as Davidson suggested (P. Tompkins, 1971, p. 248)?

33 P. Lemesurier, 1993, p. 115; C. Dunn, 1998, pp. 15, 154-55; R. Ellis, 2000, p. 81; D. Elkington, 2001, pp. 390-91; J. Reid, 2001, pp. 9, 37. I am also grateful for the advice of Jim Lewandowski, who has challenged the orthodox theory on the Maat Internet discussion group.

34 A.C. Carpiceci, *Art and History of Egypt*, op. cit., p. 72; D. Elkington, 2001, pp. 391-92; J. Reid, 2001, pp. 9-10, 23. A criticism that has been made of this theory is that the *Djed* pillar of the Old Kingdom contained only four elements, and not five.

35 Pyramid Texts, Utterance 600, para 1657.

36 W.M.F. Petrie, 1990, p. 31.

37 C Dunn, 1998, p. 221.

38 M. Lehner, 1997, p. 114.

39 J.P. Lepre, 1990, p. 109.

40 C. Dunn, 1998, pp. 156-57.

41 J. Reid, in appendix 6 to D. Elkington, 2001, p. 421.

42 C. Dunn, 1998, p. 138 (cf p. 135). Dunn p. 147 suggested that the Earth-commensurate dimensions of the Pyramid may have benefited the harmonic resonance: 'if the dimensions of the Earth determine the wave characteristics of vibrations emanating from the core, then it would obviously be beneficial to incorporate these dimensions in a receiver of these vibrations.' (see also pp. 134, 139).

43 C. Dunn, 1998, p. 144 (see also pp. 127-8, 129, 136, 138).

44 Ibid., p. 144 and chapters nine to fifteen. For the reader who takes this theory seriously, it must be pointed out that the 'opening' of 'the Gantenbrink door' in 2002 failed to provide any evidence of the hypothesised chemical storage tanks or pipes.

45 D. Elkington, 2001, pp. 125, 206-7 (cf p. 138).

46 C. Dunn, 1998, pp. 147, 149, 177, 220. Dunn also muddled another point by supposing that Helmholtz resonators were required in the Grand Gallery, in order to convey the Earth's vibrations into the King's Chamber. But the terrestrial vibrations would have affected the King's Chamber *directly*.

47 On SRI International and their work at Giza, see I. Lawton & C. Ogilvie-Herald, 2000, pp. 271-78, 280-82.

48 Email from L. Dolphin to I. Lawton & C. Ogilvie-Herald, 1st February 1999; see I. Lawton & C. Ogilvie-Herald, 2000, p. 278.

49 C. Dunn, 1998, pp. 127-29, 136; D. Elkington, 2001, p. 125.

50 http://sidereal7.org.

51 On the Schumann resonance, see P.V. Bliokh, A.P. Nikolaenko, & Y.F. Filippov, *Schumann Resonances in the Earth-Ionosphere Cavity*, Peter Peregrinus, London, 1980; C. Dunn, 1998, pp. 128-29; D. Elkington, 2001, pp. 125, 396; or do a search on the Internet. It should be noted that the higher Schumann resonances are *not* harmonics of a prime.

52 D. Elkington, 2001, pp. 125-27.

53 In fact, Elkington had already suspected an acoustic purpose (2001, p. 391), but had regarded it as secondary to *Djed* pillar symbolism, and hence not taken it further.

54 C. Dunn, 1998, pp. 155-56, 183.

55 T. Danley, 'Early Reflections and Ancient Echoes', op. cit., p. 49. He also made an interesting comment on the chamber's lowermost roof beams, p. 44: 'a helmholtz resonator and transmission line model suggested resonances starting at 2.5 Hz or so'.

56 C. Dunn, 1998, p. 158; I. Lawton & C. Ogilvie-Herald, 2000, p. 209. Said disseminated this information on the Art Bell radio show in America.

57 T. Danley, 'Early Reflections and Ancient Echoes', op. cit., p. 49 (see also p. 47). See also *Fate* magazine, interview with Said, April 1998; C. Dunn, 1998, pp. 139-40; I. Lawton & C. Ogilvie-Herald, 2000, pp. 208-9; J. Reid, 2001, p. 10.

58 J. Reid, email correspondence, 2nd December 2002. The fact that the shafts contain bends would not be a problem (compare the design of trumpets and other wind instruments).

59 J. Reid, email correspondence, 2nd December 2002.

60 The figure of 66.2° F is an estimate, based on the rationale in chapter six of this book.

61 J. Reid, verbally and email correspondence, 5th January 2003.

62 Such a cover may have been fitted with a fine mesh to prevent ingress of airborne sand. The location of the shaft covers – at such a great height – would have ensured that they were not visible from the ground. Note: the iron plate that was blasted from the northern face in 1837 lay too deep in the masonry to have formed part of this cover.

63 On these creation myths, see the companion volume to this book.

64 J. Reid, email correspondence, 5th January 2003. The definition of brain entrainment is 'The process whereby brain wave frequencies are altered by the influence of rhythmic events, typically induced via the eyes or ears.' The dome-shaped section of the southern shaft is described in detail in chapter two; figure 101 shows a simplified form of this unusual pipe.

65 I am indebted to David Elkington for this suggestion.

66 Pink Floyd, *The Dark Side of The Moon*, EMI/Harvest, 1973, Side One, Track 2. Then, as now, sound was the soul of religion.

67 W.M.F. Petrie, 1990, p. 28.

68 P. Smyth, 1880, p. 175.

69 J.P. Lepre, 1990, p. 89: 'There does not appear to be any logical reason for the uneven distribution of the blocks of granite and limestone...'.

70 J.P. Lepre, 1990, p. 89.

71 The height of these three missing slabs might be judged by the extent of damage to the pilasters that once held them, as shown (partially) in figure 105. Did the slabs reduce in size towards the north end of the room?

72 D. Elkington, 2001, pp. 126-27, 159, 198, 367, 396.

73 J. Reid, 2001, p. 7; D. Elkington, 2001, p. 417.

74 D. Elkington, 2001, pp. 131, 229, 392, 397.

75 H. Wilson, *People of the Pharaohs*, op. cit., p. 102; E.A. Wallis Budge, *From Fetish to God in Ancient Egypt*, op. cit., p. 123.

76 Sound was associated with levitation in ancient myths. By a curious coincidence, Tom Danley worked in the experimental field of acoustic levitation prior to his investigation of the Great Pyramid for the Schor Foundation.

77 T. Danley, 'Early Reflections and Ancient Echoes', op. cit., p. 47. Danley attributed this vibration to the effect of the wind playing across the tops of the airshafts – the so-called 'Coke-bottle effect'. This explanation seems inherently unlikely.

78 On the uneven floor, W.M.F. Petrie, 1990, p. 28, attributed it to poor workmanship. Similarly, J.P. Lepre, 1990, p. 89, attributed an unevenness in the floor of the King's Chamber Passage to 'a deliberate adjustment by the architect'. Surely these observations are better explained as a consequence of the earthquake that shook the King's Chamber.

79 W.M.F. Petrie, 1990, p. 27.

80 I am not the first to question this. C. Dunn, 1998, pp. 15, 39-40, asked: 'Why would an earthquake seek out one lonely chamber in a giant complex of masonry, passages and chambers?'

81 On earthquakes at Giza, see J.P. Lepre, 1990, pp. 64, 75, 110.

82 The same question is asked by D. Elkington, 2001, p. 391.

83 See the fully-indexed archives of the CCNet scholarly electronic network, website address http://abob.libs.uga.edu/bobk/cccmenu.html.

84 I. Lawton & C. Ogilvie-Herald, 2000, p. 33, write: 'it is clear that the tunnel was cut through

after the blocks had been put in place'.

CHAPTER EIGHT: THE PYRAMID PLUNDERED

1 J.P. Lepre, 1990, p. 71, suggests that the original entrance had become unfindable 'owing to the great number of extracted casing blocks which had accumulated at that section of the north face of the monument.'

2 P. Smyth, 1880, p. 115; P. Tompkins, 1971, p. 9.

3 W.M.F. Petrie, 1990, pp. 87, 89, 91. Cf I.E.S. Edwards, 1993, p. 100.

4 G. Goyon, 1944; V. Maragioglio & C.A. Rinaldi, 1965. See also P. Tompkins, 1971, pp. 243, 252. One way or the other, it is believed that the Pyramid had already been robbed. I. Lawton & C. Ogilvie-Herald, 2000, p. 17, write: 'there are arguments to suggest that... the entire edifice had already been explored in remote antiquity.'

5 M. Lehner, 1997, p. 41.

6 According to legend, al-Mamun heard the prism stone fall, and, having located its position, dug a tunnel along the side of the plugs. This gives the impression that he breached the lowermost plug. But in fact the plug remains intact.

7 J.P. Lepre, 1990, pp. 82-83.

8 Khnum's association follows from the graffiti in the hollows of the superstructure, in which the name Khnum-khuf – a form of Khufu – features prominently. Thoth's association follows from the Westcar Papyrus (see chapter six of this book).

9 E.A. Wallis Budge, *Egyptian Religion*, 1899, p. 124; E.A. Wallis Budge, *Legends of the Egyptian Gods*, op. cit., p. 206; E.A. Wallis Budge, *From Fetish to God in Ancient Egypt*, op. cit., pp. 424, 524; E. Hornung, *Conceptions of God in Ancient Egypt*, op. cit., p. 134; B. Watterson, *Gods of Ancient Egypt*, op. cit., p. 41; D. Meeks & C. Favard-Meeks, *Daily Life of the Egyptian Gods*, op. cit., pp. 57, 121.

10 J.P. Lepre, 1990, p. 85.

11 Ibid., p. 83.

12 Coffin Texts, Spell 78 (emphasis added). Nut personifies the sky, or celestial ocean.

13 Coffin Texts, Spell 79 (emphasis added).

14 J.P. Lepre, 1990, p. 81. An independent American researcher Clesson Harvey has reached a similar conclusion; he claims that the shape of the Gallery resembles the hieroglyph in the Pyramid Texts translated 'gate of the sky'. It also resembles the double stairway hieroglyph, which was used as determinative in the terms 'ascent', 'ascend', and 'high place'.

15 See chapter three of this book.

16 See I.E.S. Edwards, 1993, p. 110.

17 G. Goyon, 1963; I.E.S. Edwards, 1993, p. 110; M. Lehner, 1997, p. 113.

18 See, for example, G. Hart, 1991, p. 93.

19 See P. Tompkins, 1971, chapter XII.

20 J.P. Lepre, 1990, p. 83.

21 I.E.S. Edwards, 1993, pp. 109-10 suggested that the wall sockets had been superseded by the ramp niches, and hence the former had been filled in.

22 On the term 'Great Seat', see the Theology of Memphis and the Edfu Building Texts.

23 G. Hart, *Egyptian Myths,* op. cit., p. 13: 'The concept of nine gods and goddesses indicates a plural of plurals'.

24 Fifty-four and fifty-six are not known numbers of the gods in ancient Egyptian literature. However, the gods are counted in groups of nine or eight.

25 J.B. Pritchard ed., *ANET*, op. cit., p. 5.

26 Ibid.

27 The Pyramid's connection with Khnum, the god of minerals at Aswan, offers tentative support for this hypothesis. In the Legend of Khnum and the Seven Years' Famine, it is stated that 'there he keeps an account of the products of the Land of the South and of the Land of the North.' (E.A. Wallis Budge, *Legends of the Egyptian Gods*, op. cit., p. 127).

28 Treasure-hunters in ancient times had a reputation for smashing statues in the hope of finding something more valuable secreted therein.

29 This boat, buried in pieces, has been rebuilt and is now exhibited in the boat museum at Giza. Khnum, the god of the Pyramid, was renowned as the builder of the celestial barque, as well as

the keeper of minerals (see, for example, Pyramid Texts, Utterance 300, para 445). He was also the maker of the ladder of the sky. Indeed, Khnum was the builder-god *par excellence*.

30 See W.M.F. Petrie, 1990, p. 89; I. Lawton & C. Ogilvie-Herald, 2000, pp. 24-25.
31 W.M.F. Petrie, 1990, p. 89.
32 J.P. Lepre, 1990, pp. 113-14.
33 The goddess' main symbol was the water-pot.
34 There is feminine symbolism in the limestone, and possibly even in the pointed roof (per later Arab tradition). On the concept of duotheism, see the companion volume to this book.
35 E. Hornung, *Conceptions of God in Ancient Egypt*, op. cit., p. 124. Cf p. 117: 'The gods may indeed inhabit these representations as they may inhabit any image, but their true form is 'hidden' and 'mysterious', as Egyptian texts emphasise continually'.
36 H. Frankfort, *Ancient Egyptian Religion: An Interpretation*, op. cit., pp. 4, 19.
37 In this respect, two points should be noted: (a) the Great Step overlaps the Queen's Chamber Passage on the east and west sides; and (b) the base of the statue may have projected beyond the niche cavity.
38 J.P. Lepre, 1990, pp. 113-14.
39 Alternatively, it is possible that the King's Chamber was discovered via the discovery and examination of the tunnel at the top of the Gallery that leads into Davison's Chamber.
40 W.M.F. Petrie, p. 89, hints at this idea, albeit in a slightly different context. The excavation was probably enlarged by subsequent treasure-seekers.
41 Edward Kunkel, cited by C. Dunn, 1998, p. 197. The tunnel has a fairly flat floor and is unusually well squared.
42 W.M.F. Petrie, pp. 89-91; P. Tompkins, 1971, pp. 2-3; J.P. Lepre, 1990, p. 74; M. Lehner, 1997, pp. 38-39.
43 My reconstruction differs significantly from the popular Arab account of how al-Mamun entered the Pyramid. However, I am not the first to question the accuracy and reliability of the Arab tradition. See K. Mendelssohn, 1974, p. 52; M. Lehner, 1997, pp. 40-41; I. Lawton & C. Ogilvie-Herald, 2000, pp. 137-38.

CHAPTER NINE: THE SACRED BOOK

1 P. Smyth, 1880, p. 428.
2 R. Gantenbrink, interviewed on German television, and widely reported on the Internet. His long-awaited book on this subject has suffered yet another delay.
3 See note 92 to chapter three. This theory is also supported by P. Jordan, *Riddles of the Sphinx*, op. cit., p. 79.
4 See note 96 to chapter three.
5 See notes 93 and 94 to chapter three.
6 R. Bauval & A. Gilbert, 1994, p. 4.
7 Ibid., pp. 224-25.
8 R. Bauval, 1999, p. 293 (cf pp. 316-17 the same prediction, but here for a chamber underneath the Sphinx).
9 Ibid., p. 294.
10 R. Bauval lecture in London, 16th November 2002, and subsequent telephone conversation. On the basis that the shaft is inclined and oriented towards the stars, he sees a connection to the serdab of Djoser at Saqqara, and thus predicts a secret chamber that is likewise tilted on an incline.
11 See R. Bauval & G. Hancock, 1996, p. 125; R. Bauval, 1999, p. 293. Gantenbrink has the air of someone who *knows* what is there.
12 Pyramid Texts, Utterance 510, para 1146-47.
13 Ibid. Neheb-kau is the great serpent; the Eye of Horus is the Great Goddess.
14 E.A. Wallis Budge, *The Mummy*, op. cit., p. 228; E.A. Wallis Budge, *From Fetish to God in Ancient Egypt*, op. cit., p. 156; H. Frankfort, *Kingship and the Gods*, op. cit., p. 145; R. Bauval, 1999, pp. 18, 38, 106.
15 R. Bauval, 1999, pp. 18, 106.
16 Coffin Texts, Spell 225, line 240.
17 Coffin Texts, Spell 231.

18 H. Wilson, *People of the Pharaohs*, op. cit., p. 102. Cf E.A. Wallis Budge, *From Fetish to God in Ancient Egypt*, op. cit., p. 123; D. Meeks & C. Favard-Meeks, *Daily Life of the Egyptian Gods*, op. cit., p. 102; R. Bauval, 1999, p. 27.

19 Ibid.

20 E. Hornung, *The Ancient Egyptian Books of the Afterlife*, op. cit., p. 9.

21 R.O. Faulkner, *The Ancient Egyptian Book of the Dead*, British Museum Publications, 1985 edition, pp. 14, 56; E.A. Wallis Budge, *From Fetish to God in Ancient Egypt*, op. cit., p. 285.

22 R.O. Faulkner, *The Ancient Egyptian Book of the Dead*, op. cit., p. 15; E. Hornung, *The Ancient Egyptian Books of the Afterlife*, op. cit., p. 19.

23 R.O. Faulkner, *The Ancient Egyptian Book of the Dead*, op. cit., pp. 15, 127-30; E.A. Wallis Budge, *From Fetish to God in Ancient Egypt*, op. cit., p. 126.

24 R.O. Faulkner, *The Ancient Egyptian Book of the Dead*, op. cit., p. 130. *Duat* is the 'other world'. On the Spell of the Four Blazing Flames, see also E.A. Wallis Budge, *The Mummy*, op. cit., pp. 352-53.

25 J.B. Pritchard ed., *ANET*, op. cit., p. 495.

26 R.O. Faulkner, *The Ancient Egyptian Book of the Dead*, op. cit., p. 15: 'the spell could scarcely claim to be more ancient'.

27 H. Frankfort, *Kingship and the Gods*, op. cit., p. 90; R. Bauval & G. Hancock, 1996, p. 202.

28 *Cambridge Ancient History*, Volume I, pp. 249-50; H. Frankfort, *Kingship and the Gods*, op. cit., pp. 90-91.

29 E.A. Wallis Budge, *From Fetish to God in Ancient Egypt*, op. cit., p. 61; M. Lurker, *The Gods and Symbols of Ancient Egypt*, op. cit., p. 109. Seshat was renowned also for her role in the 'stretching of the cord' ritual.

30 H. Frankfort, *The Intellectual Adventure of Ancient Man*, op. cit., p. 60.

31 E. Hornung, *The Ancient Egyptian Books of the Afterlife*, op. cit., pp. 4-5: 'we can suppose that the texts were selected from a larger collection...'.

32 For a good overview of all these books, see E. Hornung, *The Ancient Egyptian Books of the Afterlife*, Cornell University Press, 1999.

33 E.A. Wallis Budge, *From Fetish to God in Ancient Egypt*, op. cit., p. 321.

34 E. Hornung, *The Secret Lore of Egypt*, op. cit., p. 7.

35 A. Weigall, *A History of the Pharaohs*, Volume 2, Thornton Butterworth, London, 1927, pp. 155-56; A. Collins, 1998, p. 128.

36 E.A. Wallis Budge, *Legends of the Egyptian Gods*, op. cit., pp. lxiv, 123.

37 D. Meeks & C. Favard-Meeks, *Daily Life of the Egyptian Gods*, op. cit., pp. 173-74.

38 Ibid. The statuette simultaneously signified Re.

39 Ibid., pp. 174-75.

40 Ibid., p. 105.

41 Ibid., pp. 173, 175.

42 M. Lehner, 1997, p. 108; I. Shaw & P. Nicholson, *British Museum Dictionary of Ancient Egypt*, op. cit., p. 152.

43 Coffin Texts, Spell 577. Cf D. Meeks & C. Favard-Meeks, *Daily Life of the Egyptian Gods*, op. cit., p. 7.

44 Pyramid Texts, Utterance 524, para 1238. The king is both Thoth and 'son of Khnum'.

45 Egyptologists suggest various meanings for the name *Mdjd*: 'straight', 'true to the mark', or 'energetic'.

46 Manetho, *Aegyptiaca*, cited by Eusebius; see R. Bauval & A. Gilbert, 1994, p. 162. Manetho is himself credited with having written a book (unfortunately not extant) called *The Sacred Book*; see I. Shaw & P. Nicholson, *British Museum Dictionary of Ancient Egypt*, op. cit., p. 169.

47 J.B. Pritchard ed., *ANET*, op. cit., pp. 431-32. Per D. Elkington, 2001, p. 192, Gothic cathedrals have been called 'books in stone'.

48 On Hordedef (rendered by some as Dedef-Hor or Hertataf), see E.A. Wallis Budge, *From Fetish to God in Ancient Egypt*, op. cit., pp. 120-21, 126, 285, 321.

49 W. Marshal Adams, *The Book of the Master*, Putnam, New York, 1898, cited by R. Bauval, 1999, pp. 27-28.

50 J.B. Pritchard ed., *ANET*, op. cit., p. 495. The idea that books or temple plans fell from the sky is found also in other Egyptian texts.

51 R.O. Faulkner, *The Ancient Egyptian Book of the Dead*, op. cit., pp. 14, 56. In fact, Hordedef

was the son of Khufu, not Menkaure; see E.A. Wallis Budge, *From Fetish to God in Ancient Egypt*, op. cit., p. 126; J.B. Pritchard ed., *ANET*, op. cit., p. 419; K. Mendelssohn, 1974, p. 51.

52 R.O. Faulkner, *The Ancient Egyptian Book of the Dead*, op. cit., pp. 15, 130.

53 Coffin Texts, Spell 335, Part I (with glosses), lines 199-201, translation by S. Quirke, *The Cult of Ra*, op. cit., p. 30. Cf R.T. Rundle Clark, *Myth and Symbol in Ancient Egypt*, op. cit., pp. 84, 247-48: 'I am that great *Benu*-bird in Heliopolis, who determines what is and what is not to be'.

54 In addition, several myths refer to the idea of a sacred book or plan falling from the sky. The book thus belonged in the sky, and would be at home in the height of the Pyramid.

55 That is to say the architect wanted the books to be found not by a speculative treasure-hunter but by someone who had the courage of his convictions. On account of this possibility, it is imperative that both shafts be explored in parallel.

56 On these ideas, see the companion volume to this book.

57 A.F. Alford, *When The Gods Came Down*, op. cit., chapters 2 to 8; A.F. Alford, *The Atlantis Secret*, Eridu Books, 2001, chapters 8 to 13.

58 J.B. Pritchard ed., *ANET*, op. cit., p. 495.

59 Coffin Texts, Spell 695, para 328.

CHAPTER TEN: SECRET CHAMBERS

1 J. Perring, in R.H. Vyse, 1840-42, Volume II, appendix, p. 113 (56,000 cubic feet divided by 89 million cubic feet = 0.06%); J.P. Lepre, 1990, pp. 287-88 (94 million cubic feet divided by 11,000 cubic feet = 9,000 chambers). I have amended the figures to reflect a total Pyramid volume of 91.2 million cubic feet. The statistics are purely theoretical.

2 The large scar in the Pyramid's southern face was caused by Vyse.

3 On these other investigations, see I. Lawton & C. Ogilvie-Herald, 2000, chapter 6.

4 J.P. Lepre, 1990, p. 279: 'Historically, it was not ingenuity that enabled modern man to penetrate this far into the Great Pyramid, but sheer luck.'

5 The background to Gantenbrink's exploration is described in R. Bauval & G. Hancock, 1996, chapter 7, and R. Bauval, 1999, chapter 11.

6 J.P. Lepre, 1990, pp. 276-77.

7 Ibid., p. 104.

8 P. Smyth, 1880, pp. 465-67, claimed that the lines marked the Pyramid's construction date, 2170 BC.

9 Ibid., p. 467 (cf p. 468).

10 Ibid., p. 466. Smyth notes that these quasi-vertical joints are *not* exactly opposite one another.

11 J.P. Lepre, 1990, pp. 73-74. He commends Smyth for noticing these joints, and observes that if Greek and Roman visitors had been as attentive then 'the King's Chamber could well have been discovered 1,000 years or more before the penetration of the 9th century AD.'

12 P. Smyth, 1880, pp. 436-37.

13 Ibid.

14 J.P. Lepre, 1990, p. 71.

15 P. Badham, *Inscription*, 5, p. 38, cited by J. Reid, 2001, p. 9.

16 Against this possibility, the King's Chamber, on account of its airshafts, would appear to be the primary chamber of the Pyramid.

17 R. Cook, 1992; R. Temple, *The Crystal Sun*, op. cit., pp. 217, 371-72, 374-75, 377, 407.

18 The trial passages are located close to the tomb of Hetepheres I.

19 W.M.F. Petrie, 1990, p. 15.

20 Ibid., p. 16.

21 R.H. Vyse, 1840-42, Volume I, p. 89; M. Lehner, *The Pyramid Tomb of Hetepheres and the Satellite Pyramid of Khufu*, Mainz and Rheim, 1985, pp. 63 ff, and figures 9 and 15; Z. Hawass, in A. Siliotti, 1997, p. 56. The fact that the trial passages were cut into the bedrock puts the lie to the idea that they were intended as a trial run for the Pyramid's passages, since the latter were constructed, for the most part, above ground level.

22 Hence one reason why the guardians did not take the 'front door' option (see chapter eight).

23 J.P. Lepre, 1990, p. 105.

24 Note, however, that a possible cavity has been detected in this area; see I. Lawton & C. Ogilvie-Herald, 2000, pp. 275, 278.

25 On the 'tomb of the gods' idea, see the companion volume to this book.

26 Lepre does not reveal the exact location of the unusual joints. Might this descending passage be built in mirror image to the Ascending Passage?

27 G. Dormion & J-P. Goidin, 1987, p. 92. See J.P. Lepre, 1990, pp. 104-5; Z. Hawass, in update to W.M.F. Petrie, 1990, p. 101; I. Lawton & C. Ogilvie-Herald, 2000, pp. 285-89; M. Lehner, 1997, p. 67.

28 Z. Hawass, in update to W.M.F. Petrie, 1990, pp. 101-2; M. Lehner, 1997, p. 67; I. Lawton & C. Ogilvie-Herald, 2000, p. 287.

29 I. Lawton & C. Ogilvie- Herald, 2000, p. 287.

30 For once I agree with M. Lehner, 1997, p. 67.

31 See chapter eight, note 41.

32 Z. Hawass, in update to W.M.F. Petrie, 1990, pp. 101-2; I. Lawton & C. Ogilvie-Herald, 2000, p. 287.

33 See diagram in I. Lawton & C. Ogilvie-Herald, 2000, chapter 8, p. 325.

34 http://www.abc.net.au/science/news/scitech/SciTechRepublish_279993.htm.

35 W.M.F. Petrie, 1990, p. 25. Cf I.E.S. Edwards, 1993, p. 105; P. Tompkins, 1971, pp. 153-54.

36 Z. Hawass, in update to W.M.F. Petrie, 1990, pp. 103-4.

37 J.P. Lepre, 1990, p. 103.

38 Ibid., pp. 105-6. Could this not simply be earthquake damage?

39 Ibid., pp. 117-18.

40 Herodotus, *History*, Book II, p. 124.

41 J.P. Lepre, 1990, p. 271.

42 See diagram in P. Lemesurier, 1993, p. 141. On this axis too lies the sarcophagus in the King's Chamber.

43 The entrance to the Grotto lies approximately 466 feet from the Pyramid's main entrance (323 feet down the Descending Passage, plus 143 feet up the Well Shaft). If we add to this figure the distance from the Grotto's entrance to its western wall, 14 feet 5 inches, the total distance to the hypothetical tomb becomes 480 feet 5 inches – almost identical to the height of the Pyramid.

44 The thought occurs that if there is a second grotto then its shape might have inspired the otherwise-inexplicable pattern of the Subterranean Chamber. In other words, the latter may have been modelled upon the former.

45 Survey by Jean Kerisel in 1992. See R. Bauval & G. Hancock, 1996, pp. 50-51, 180, 331 (note 54); C. Dunn, 1998, pp. 204-5; R. Bauval, 1999, pp. 59-60; I. Lawton & C. Ogilvie-Herald, 2000, pp. 289-90.

46 I have personally inspected the walls and ceiling of the Subterranean Chamber, but to no avail; there is surely nothing here but solid rock. In 1995, J. Kerisel drilled into the floor of this chamber and found nothing (M. Lehner, 1997, p. 67).

47 J.P. Lepre, 1990, p. 114.

48 L. Cottrell, 1956, p. 63; I. Lawton & C. Ogilvie-Herald, 2000, p. 234.

49 E. von Daniken, *The Eyes of the Sphinx*, Berkley Books, New York, 1996, p. 200. Cf P. Tompkins, 1971, p. 269.

50 See R. Bauval & G. Hancock, 1996, p. 50.

51 On the other hand, the Pit may represent an attempt to penetrate the subterranean water table for ritual, magical purposes that are not directly connected to a burial. Such a practice was commonplace in Egyptian temples.

52 The security benefit from such a relocation of the king's mummy would have been marginal at best.

53 J.P. Lepre, 1990, pp. 276-77. Originally, this precision-jointed foundation stone would have been covered by the pavement and casing stones (now missing).

54 Ibid.

55 On pyramid and temple foundation deposits, see E.A. Wallis Budge, *The Mummy*, op. cit., pp. 450-52; D. Meeks & C. Favard-Meeks, *Daily Life of the Egyptian Gods*, op. cit., p. 125; H. Wilson, *People of the Pharaohs*, op. cit., pp. 44-5. Such deposits could also include sacred books.

56 J.P. Lepre, 1990, p. 275.

57 Ibid.

58 A.F. Alford, *The Phoenix Solution*, Hodder & Stoughton, 1998, pp. 411-12. J.P. Lepre, 1990,

p. 268, notes the astonishing number of mummies that are missing. K. Mendelssohn, 1974, p. 60, notes that large subterranean galleries have been found beneath the three earliest step pyramids. In addition, it should be noted that Giza was used as a burial site long before the 4th dynasty.

59 S. Yoshimura et al, *Studies in Egyptian Culture No. 5: Non-Destructive Pyramid Investigation (1) – by Electromagnetic Wave Method*, Waseda University, Tokyo, Japan, 1987. See M. Lehner, 1997, p. 67; Z. Hawass, in update to W.M.F. Petrie, 1990, pp. 101-2. Hawass notes that 'the results are 'ambiguous and somewhat speculative.' A southern entrance would be unusual from what we know of Old Kingdom pyramids; however, in the 12th dynasty, Senusert II included such an entrance in his pyramid at Illahun.

60 Might the entrance to the tunnel be hidden in one of the two southern boat pits?

61 Diodorus Siculus, *Histories*, Book I, chapter v, p. 66; P. Smyth, 1880, p. 132; N.F. Wheeler, 1935, pp. 181-82; W.M.F. Petrie, 1990, p. 88; P. Lemesurier, 1993, p. 6; J.P. Lepre, 1990, p. 269.

62 J.P. Lepre, 1990, p. 288.

CHAPTER ELEVEN: NEW HORIZONS

1 A. Siliotti, 1997, p. 8.

2 http://www.eridu.co.uk. To be a serious contender, a theory must make a detailed attempt to explain the Pyramid's interior architecture, as for example C. Dunn, 1998.

3 P. Tompkins, 1971, introduction and chapter XVI; L.C. Stecchini, 1971, p. 378; W. Fix, *Pyramid Odyssey,* Mayflower Books, New York, 1978, p. 232; G. Hancock, *Fingerprints of the Gods*, op. cit., pp. 195, 459-61, 467; R. Bauval & G. Hancock, 1996, p. 38; C. Dunn, 1998, pp. 133-34; A. Collins, 1998, pp. 13, 317-18.

4 In the 1st century AD, the Roman writer Pliny referred to the pyramids as 'that idle and foolish exhibition of royal wealth'. In the 1890s, Professor F.A.P. Barnard mocked the Egyptians for 'the stupidly idiotic task of heaping up a pile of massive rock...'. In 1971, K. Mendelssohn, p. 77, described the giant pyramids as 'magnificent madness... on the face of it, a useless expense of labour'. In 1994, R. Bauval, p. 2, suggested that on the 'tomb only' theory the pyramids seemed to be 'a colossal waste of time and energy'. The idea that the pyramid builders would have required some kind of tangible return on their investment is, of course, a reflection of modern materialistic preconceptions.

5 Cornelius de Pauw, 1773; K. Mendelssohn 1971; M. Lehner, 1997, pp. 9, 20, 228-9. There might just be a grain of truth in this theory. If a populace was living in fear of the 'end of the world', the construction of the pyramids would have kept its energy focused and prevented it from descending into a state of hopelessness or anarchy.

6 M. Lehner, 1997, p. 109.

7 P. Smyth, 1880, pp. 201-3. See also note 37 to chapter three.

8 W.M.F. Petrie, 1990, p. 94; P. Tompkins, 1971, p. 101; J.P. Lepre, 1990, pp. 98, 102.

9 R. Temple, *The Crystal Sun*, op. cit., pp. 370-72.

BIBLIOGRAPHY

I. THE PYRAMIDS, ORTHODOXY

Badawy, A., 'The Stellar Destiny of Pharaoh and the so-called Air-shafts in Cheops's Pyramid', in *Mitteilungen des Instituts fur Orientforschung Akademie der Wissenschaften zu Berlin*, 10 (1964), pp. 189-206.

Borchardt, L., *Gegen die Zahlenmystik an der grossen Pyramide bei Gise*, Berlin, 1922.

—— *Langen und Richtungen der vier Grundkanten der grossen Pyramide bei Gise*, Berlin, 1926.

—— *Einiges zur dritten Bauperiode der grossen Pyramide bei Gise*, Berlin, 1932.

Cottrell, L., *The Mountains of Pharaoh*, Robert Hale, 1956.

Edwards, I.E.S., *The Pyramids of Egypt*, Penguin Books, 1993 edition (first published in 1947 by Pelican Books).

—— 'Pyramids: Building for Eternity', in Billard, J.B., *Ancient Egypt Discovering its Splendors*, Washington DC, 1978, pp. 72-101.

—— 'The Air-Channels of Chephren's Pyramid', in Simpson, W. & Davis, W., *Studies in Ancient Egypt, the Aegean and the Sudan (essays in honor of Dows Dunham on the occasion of his 90th birthday)*, Boston, 1981, pp. 55-57.

Gardiner, A., 'The Secret Chambers of the Sanctuary of Thoth', in *Journal of Egyptian Archaeology*, 11 (1925), pp. 2-5.

Goyon, G., *Les inscriptions et graffiti des voyageurs sur la Grande Pyramide*, Cairo, 1944.

—— 'Le mechanisme de fermeture de la pyramide de Kheops', in *Revue Archeologique*, 2 (1963), pp. 1-24.

—— 'Quelques observations effectuees autour de la pyramide de Kheops', in *Bulletin de l'Institut francais d'archeologie orientale*, 67 (1969), pp. 71-86.

Greaves, J., *Pyramidographia*, London, 1646.

—— *Pyramidologia*, London, 1663.

Hart, G., *Pharaohs and Pyramids*, The Herbert Press, London, 1991.

Jackson, K. & Stamp, J., *Pyramid: Beyond Imagination*, BBC Books, 2002.

Lauer, J-P., *Le probleme des Pyramides d'Egypte*, Payot, Paris, 1948.

—— *Observations sur les pyramides*, Cairo, 1960.

Lawton, I. & Ogilvie-Herald, C., *Giza: The Truth*, Virgin Publishing, London, paperback edition 2000 (first published in 1999 by Virgin Publishing).

Lehner, M., *The Complete Pyramids*, Thames & Hudson, London, 1997.

Lepre, J.P., *The Egyptian Pyramids*, McFarland & Co, Jefferson, 1990.

Maragioglio, V. & Rinaldi, C.A., *L'Architettura delle Pyramidi Menfite, Parte IV*, Turin and Rapallo, 1965.

Mendelssohn, K., *The Riddle of the Pyramids*, Thames & Hudson, London, 1974.

Perring, J.S., *The Pyramids of Gizeh*, James Frazer, London, 1839-42.

Petrie, W.M.F., *The Pyramids and Temples of Gizeh* (with an update by Z. Hawass), Histories & Mysteries of Man Ltd, London, 1990 (first published in 1883 by Field & Tuer, London).

Siliotti, A., *The Pyramids*, Weidenfeld & Nicolson, London, 1997.

Stadelmann, R., 'Royal Tombs from the Age of the Pyramids', in R. Schulz & M. Seidel eds., *Egypt: The World of the Pharaohs*, Konemann, 1998, pp. 47-77.

Trimble, V., 'Astronomical Investigations concerning the so-called Air-shafts of Cheops's Pyramid', in *Mitteilungen des Instituts fur Orientforschung Akademie der Wissenschaften zu Berlin*, 10 (1964), pp. 183-87.

Verner, M., *The Pyramids: Their Archaeology and History*, Atlantic Books, 2002.

Vyse, R.H., *Operations Carried Out on the Pyramids of Gizeh*, 3 volumes, James Frazer, London, 1840-42.

Wheeler, N.F., 'Pyramids and Their Purpose II: The Pyramid of Khufu', in *Antiquity*, IX (1935), pp. 172-85.

II. THE PYRAMIDS, ALTERNATIVE THEORIES

Alford, A.F., *The Phoenix Solution*, Hodder & Stoughton, London, 1998.

Bauval, R., 'A Master Plan for the Three Pyramids of Giza Based on the Configuration of the Three Stars of the Belt of Orion', in *Discussions in Egyptology*, 13 (1989), pp. 7-18.

—— 'The Seeding of the Star Gods: A Fertility Ritual Inside Cheops's Pyramid', in *Discussions in Egyptology*, 16 (1990), pp. 21-29.

—— 'Cheops's Pyramid: A New Dating Using the Latest Astronomical Data', in *Discussions in Egyptology*, 26 (1993), pp. 5-7.

—— 'The Upuaut Project: New Findings in the Southern Shaft in the Queen's Chamber of Cheops's Pyramid', in *Discussions in Egyptology*, 27 (1993).

—— *Secret Chamber*, Century, London, 1999.

Bauval, R. & Gilbert, A., *The Orion Mystery*, William Heinemann Ltd, London, 1994.

Bauval, R. & Hancock, G., *Keeper of Genesis*, William Heinemann Ltd, London, 1996.

Biot, J.B., *Recherches sur plusiers points de l'astronomie egyptienne*, Didot, Paris, 1823.

Bruchet, J., *Nouvelles recherches sur la Grande Pyramide*, Aix-en-Provence, La Pensee Universitaire, 1965.

Chatelain, M., *Our Ancestors Came From Outer Space*, Dell Publishing, 1979.

Collins, A., *Gods of Eden*, Headline, London, 1998.

Cook, R., *The Pyramids of Giza*, Seven Islands, Glastonbury, 1992.

Cotsworth, M.B., *The Rational Almanac*, privately published, 1902.

Davidson, D., *The Great Pyramid*, Williams & Norgate, London, 1927.

—— *The Great Pyramid, Its Divine Message,* Williams & Norgate, London, 1932.

Dormion, G. & Goidin, J-P., *Kheops: Nouvelle Enquete*, Editions Recherche sur les Civilisations, Paris, 1986.

—— *Les Nouveaux Mysteres de la Grande Pyramide*, Albin Michel, 1987.

Dunn, C., *The Giza Power Plant*, Bear & Company, Santa Fe, 1998.

Edgar, J. & M., *The Great Pyramid – Its Scientific Features*, MacLure & MacDonald, Glasgow, 1924.

Elkington, D., *In The Name of the Gods*, Green Man Press, Sherborne, 2001.

Ellis, R., *K2 Quest of the Gods*, Edfu Books, Cheshire, 2000.

Jomard, E-F., *Description generale de Memphis et des pyramides*, Imprimerie Royale, Paris, 1829.

—— *Remarque sur les pyramides*, Imprimerie Royale, Paris, 1829.

Kingsland, W., *The Great Pyramid in Fact and in Theory*, Rider, London, 1932.

Kunkel, E.J., *Pharaoh's Pump*, privately published, 1962.

Lemesurier, P., *The Great Pyramid Decoded*, Element Books edition, 1993 (first published in 1977).

Lewis, H. Spencer, *The Symbolic Prophecy of the Great Pyramid*, Rosicrucian Press, 1936.

Muck, O.H., *Cheops und die Grosse Pyramide*, Olter Walter, Berlin, 1958.

Noone, R.W., *5/5/2000*, Three Rivers Press, New York, 1982.

Proctor, R.A., *The Great Pyramid: Observatory, Tomb and Temple*, Chatto & Windus, London, 1883.

Reid, J., *Egyptian Sonics*, Sonic Age Ltd, Ponteland, 2001.

Rutherford, A., *Pyramidology*, Institute of Pyramidology, Dunstable, 1961.

Seiss, J.A., *The Great Pyramid: Miracle in Stone*, Porter & Coates, Philadelphia, 1877.

Sitchin, Z., *The Stairway to Heaven*, Avon Books, New York, 1980.

—— *The Wars of Gods and Men,* Avon Books, New York, 1985.

Smyth, P., *Our Inheritance in the Great Pyramid*, 4th edition, 1880 (first published in 1864 by A. Straham & Co, London).

Stecchini, L.C., *Notes on the Relation of Ancient Measures to the Great Pyramid*, in appendix to Tompkins, P., *Secrets of the Great Pyramid*, 1971.

Taylor, J., *The Great Pyramid: Why Was It Built? & Who Built It?*, Longman, London, 1864 (first published in 1859).

Tompkins, P., *Secrets of the Great Pyramid*, Harper & Row, New York, 1971.

III. RELIGION AND MYTHOLOGY

For a complete reading list on ancient Egyptian religion and mythology, see the Bibliography in the companion volume to this book.

INDEX

GREAT PYRAMID INDEX

GREAT PYRAMID PHOTO & DIAGRAM INDEX

The following references are to figure numbers, with page numbers shown in brackets: